Taylorism
Transformed

———

Stephen P. Waring

Taylorism Transformed

Scientific Management

Theory since 1945

The University of North Carolina Press

Chapel Hill and London

© 1991 The University of North Carolina Press

All rights reserved

Manufactured in the United States of America

The paper in this book meets the guidelines for permanence and
durability of the Committee on Production Guidelines for Book
Longevity of the Council on Library Resources.

95 94 93 92 91   5 4 3 2 1

Library of Congress Cataloging-in-Publication Data

Waring, Stephen P.

Taylorism transformed : scientific management theory since
1945 / by Stephen P. Waring.

p. cm.

Includes bibliographical references and index.

ISBN 0-8078-1972-7 (alk. paper)

1. Industrial management—History. I. Title.

HD30.5.W37 1991

658'.001—dc20   91-11027

CIP

To Mom and Pop

and to the memory of

my grandfathers

Contents

———

Preface

ix

Introduction

Politics in Management History

1

1

Taylorism and Beyond

Bureaucracy and Its Discontents

9

2

Management by the Numbers

Operations Research and Management Science

20

3

Economics and Cybernetics

The Bureaucratic Rationality of Herbert A. Simon

49

4

Virtue as Managerial Vision

Peter F. Drucker and Management by Objectives

78

5

The Rationality of Feelings
Sensitivity Training and the Democratic Manager
104

6

Capitalism without Class?
Job Enrichment and the Baby Boomers
132

7

The American Samurai
Japanizing American Corporatism
160

Conclusion
The Management Theory of Value
187

Notes
205

Bibliography
237

Index
277

Preface

If books grow from the lives of authors, then this book stemmed from my upbringing on the Nebraska prairie. From populist roots, it voices the suspicion of centralized power, concern for social responsibility, desire for individual autonomy, and hope for democracy that can still flourish in farms and country towns.

And like any book that grew from a dissertation, this one emerged from listening to teachers and reading other books. Although I am primarily interested in the social history of ideas, this book was especially influenced by "institutional" and "new labor" historians. Institutional scholars like Robert Wiebe and my advisor Ellis Hawley taught me to look for political issues in technical debates, to study professions as power centers, and to respect the diversity and complexity of contemporary America. And labor historians like David Montgomery and my teacher Shel Stromquist offered instruction in the struggles in the American workplace. For better and for worse, however, my scholarship has partly turned from the paths of my mentors and has moved in a different direction, tracing the ideas that guide economic institutions.

Indeed this book was shaped by the philosopher Alasdair MacIntyre's *After Virtue* (Notre Dame, 1981). MacIntyre was especially convincing in refuting the scientific pretensions of managerial experts. He used game theory as his example, analyzing its very abstract concepts in a very abstract way and describing its technocratic premises as moral claims. I did not, however, accept all of MacIntyre's arguments. His Aristotelian criticism of liberalism was entirely too "liberal" (liberal readers might be happier replacing "liberal" with "conservative"). It tended to presume the morality of existing social structures, and so his notion of "virtue" could be used to integrate people into corrupt practices. And MacIntyre wrongly disregarded the radical tradition originating in the Enlightenment, slighting particularly Rousseau's conception of virtue.

Even so, MacIntyre helped inspire me to plunge into research on recent management theory. Like him, my purpose was to describe management ideas as moral philosophy. But unlike MacIntyre, I proposed to put business management ideas in a social and historical context and to select ideas more influential than game theory. In addition, I intended to show that although the management theorists were usually not aware of it, they argued like philosophers.

This approach to management history is in some ways heretical. The Introduction explains its differences from business and labor historiography, particularly from the interpretation of Alfred Chandler.

Given these differences, I hope business and labor historians, as well as scholars in other disciplines, will tolerate an intellectual historian and old-fashioned humanist. But readers expecting a comprehensive study of recent management theory and practice will be disappointed. No effort was made to survey all of recent business history or even all management ideas; instead important, representative ideas were studied. In addition, my research into application of the ideas was indirect, drawing from theorists' stories. And my stories about their stories seldom offer blow-by-blow accounts of applications but summarize theorists' conclusions about what happened. This method, I decided, best kept fundamental political ideas front and center.

Of course a history of management ideas is subject to all the normal criticisms of intellectual history. Particularly it could be interpreted as being too ivory-tower and too ideological and as slighting the productive advances, technological developments, and organizational changes of recent corporate history. But studying the ideas of educators of elites can provide important insights into how elites chose their values, defined their problems, and developed strategies. Indeed in the last century, the business elite has not been restricted to managers; it has included academics in universities and experts in consulting firms who tried to direct the thinking of managers. And their writings and ideas offer fertile pickings for intellectual history.

All thinkers, even management thinkers, need a community, and this book began in a community of friends and colleagues in Iowa City. The University of Iowa awarded the Louis Pelzer Dissertation Fellowship, and the history department gave employment. Alan Spitzer exposed me to European corporatism. Alan Megill encouraged me to read MacIntyre. Mitch Ash helped with Kurt Lewin. Steve Vlatos made suggestions on Japanese management. Steve Pyne told me to find my "voice." Dick Jankowski helped with bibliography. With good humor, Don McCloskey tolerated my politics and naive questions about economics. Shel Stromquist taught me more than he thought he did. And my mentor, Ellis Hawley, suggested the topic, saved me from error and sin, labored over my prose, abided my enthusiasms, laughed at my bad jokes, and treated me with respect even when I did not deserve it; he was my first professional colleague.

Many people, all of whom I would love to mention, sustained me with friendship; among them were Lee Anderson, Fred Bjornstad, Charlotte Fallon, Andy Federer, Marcelline Hutton, Russ Johnson, Elizabeth McCartney, Joe McMillan, Pat McNamara, Tim Mattimoe, Jeff Myers, Gary Olson, Janet Owens, Doug Parks, David Roethler, Doc Rossman, Rosanne Sizer, Tom Smith, Ken Staggs, and Mary Strottman. A few buddies will always be just like family; they include Ruth Wheeler, Brenda Child, Janusz Duzinkiewicz, Jeff and Rosemarie Ostler, the Tuckers, and Brin. And my family back in Bloomington and beyond know where my heart is.

New friends and colleagues at the University of Alabama in Huntsville read chapters and made important recommendations; they include Glenna Colclough, Andy Dunar, and Tom Wren. Dan Rochowiak helped with Herbert Simon and satisficing. Particularly I am indebted to Johanna Shields who offered kind words and sage advice on writing history.

I am also grateful to Lewis Bateman, Ron Maner, Stephanie Wenzel, and the staff at the University of North Carolina Press.

These good people strengthened my ideas and even my character. Nonetheless I am responsible for the errors and eccentricities of this book.

Taylorism
Transformed

———

Introduction

———

Politics in
Management History

The modern business corporation is a polity, managers are its princes, academicians working in business schools are its philosophers, and managerial techniques are its constitution. Such premises guide this intellectual history of the more important recent theories and techniques of American business management.

Studying management ideas as political theory makes sense for several reasons. The political scientist Herbert Kaufman argued that political theorists and management theorists were "different species of the same genus." They investigated similar problems of governance and studied how to instill obedience, reconcile individual and collective interests, and coordinate groups. They offered advice about how society should be organized and sought to find the "one best way" of organizing human affairs, thus arriving at similar judgments on indoctrination, rewards and punishments, top-down direction, and bottom-up participation.[1] Because management writers offered advice to rulers and because they inevitably made choices about ends and means, their ideas were inherently political. Although they sought to make their advice "scientific," they never worked out a unitary, positive system of management and constantly quarreled with one another. Their debates accordingly had the interminable quality characteristic of political discourse; their arguments were based on differing conceptions of human nature, social analysis, and government organization and hence were founded on moral propositions that were difficult, and sometimes impossible, to reconcile. For these reasons, their publications provide rich material for the intellectual historian.

Of course, numerous observers have long recognized the political dimensions of the modern corporation and its management. Some of the earliest commentators, including Max Weber and Thorstein Veblen, mixed economic and political metaphors in describing business bureaucracy. American progressives debated whether corporate managers were robber barons or industrial statesmen. And the depression resurrected fear of business power and led writers like Thurman Arnold and Robert A. Brady to deny that any hard and fast distinctions separated public government and private business.

Using political approaches to subjects conventionally seen as economic became particularly prominent after the late 1950s, and since then many writers have explicitly recognized the political dimensions of business.[2] Political scientists like Robert Dahl, Earl Latham, and Grant McConnell, sociologists like C. Wright Mills, economists like John K. Galbraith, and historians like William A. Williams, Gabriel Kolko, Robert Wiebe, James Weinstein, and Ellis Hawley produced pioneering studies of the integration of public and private power and the interchange of managers between business and government. Moreover, friends and foes of business have described managers as political actors. For instance, a British management writer argued that politics in corporations resembled that in medieval governments and hence derived lessons for managers from episodes of courtly intrigue and principles of royal statecraft.[3] And the consumer advocate Ralph Nader and the economist William Taylor wrote biographies of chief executive officers that were identical to profiles of politicians, examining the executives' careers, values, and methods and emphasizing their arbitrary exercise of power and its pernicious effects on their companies and communities.[4]

Very few historians, however, have consciously set out to study business as government in its own right, regardless of its relationship to other political systems. Such an approach has not been adopted by business historians, and even labor historians have not fully utilized the idea.

Contemporary business historians have generally been averse to political studies largely because they have adopted the outlook of Alfred D. Chandler. Indeed, Chandler, whose basic interpretation has been widely praised and imitated and whose magnum opus, *The Visible Hand*, won the Pulitzer, Bancroft, and Newcomen prizes, has spent his career arguing that political interpretations of business management have been unscientific. He dismissed previous historians who had investigated people in business "more in moral than in analytical terms" and who tried to identify individuals either as "exploiters (robber barons) or creators (industrial statesmen)." Worse than being subjective, Chandler said, the "moral" approach had been irrelevant because cultural determinants and individual choices have had less influence on the evolution of business than material determinants and institutional imperatives. Hence in his view the value judgments and political choices of the business community were completely distinct from technology and market structures, and only the latter needed to be studied in order to understand managerial capitalism.[5]

As avowedly apolitical as the subject that Chandler chose to study was the way he chose to study it. Denying that he had selected data "to test and validate hypotheses or general theories" and claiming that he was just "setting the record straight," he sought to show how the "invisible hand" of the marketplace gave way to the "visible hand" of management and how the evolution of the bureaucratic firm was a natural, inevitable "institutional response" to changes in technology in the nineteenth century. Technological changes, especially the use of steam power in transportation and production, spread operations over numerous locations, expanded the size of markets and firms, increased the speed and number of transactions, and swelled the amount of capital required, thereby making businesses more expensive to set up and more difficult to operate. Railroad companies were first affected by these challenges and responded by creating bureaucratic organizations characterized by separation of ownership from control, centralized decision making, specialized functional departments, financial and statistical controls, and salaried managers.[6]

In Chandler's account other industries had in the late nineteenth century tried to copy the bureaucratic model. But it could be established only in sectors where technological efficiencies permitted it, and in these its development was natural and inevitable. Proof of the influence of technology could be found in the fact that bureaucratic enterprise evolved in much the same way in the different cultural and legal environments of Britain, Germany, and Japan. The rise of the modern managerial enterprise in the last half of the 1800s had been "an economic phenomenon," not a political one, one that stemmed from the power of technology and the imperatives of market forces, not the power of business professionals to dominate government and labor or the imperatives of culture.[7]

Nor had the new business class of professional managers, Chandler insisted, been a creature of political struggles. Professional managers had been created "because they had to be," because they were necessary to maximize use of the new technology. And while the first managers frequently were West Point graduates accustomed to martial organization, their backgrounds in civil engineering had led them to "respond" to organizational problems "in much the same rational, analytical way as they solved the mechanical problems of building a bridge or laying down a railroad." They had realized, moreover, that their prosperity was tied to the success of the firm, and this dependent status had disciplined their minds, committed them to long-term growth, and led them to "perfect" techniques for controlling "information" and thus to achieve efficiencies that made their companies and their nation rich.[8]

Yet, however brilliantly Chandler has discussed the influence of technology on the transition from market capitalism to managerial capitalism, his aversion to politics has led him to ignore some important subjects. Critics have pointed out that he ignored the role government played in encouraging economic growth and in establishing the legal and financial infrastructure in which managerial capitalism evolved, the costs and externalities that oligopoly power allowed big business to impose on labor and society, the inefficiencies of administrative overhead that continued even after firms had adopted bureaucratic structures and the multidivisional form, the persistence of short-term profit seeking under managerial capitalism, the impact of class conflict on managers and business, and the social values and moral visions that led to the development of mass production technology and bureaucratic organization.[9] The common criticism was that he failed both to examine struggles for power and to study the efforts of the business community to define the goals of public life.

These failures resulted equally from Chandler's determinism and his faith that bureaucratic firms and their professional managers were legitimate and generally rational. Such beliefs he formed while a graduate student working with Talcott Parsons at Harvard. Parsons, he later explained, greatly influenced his thinking, introducing him to structural-functionalist sociology and to the organizational theories of Max Weber, Emile Durkheim, Frederick Taylor, Elton Mayo, Chester Barnard, and Herbert Simon. All these men believed in the rationality of bureaucracy, and one of his admirers has suggested that Chandler's "absorption of Weber's maxim that bureaucracy represents the institutionalization of rationalism" caused his lifelong "preoccupation with rationality."[10] Indeed, he came to assume that managers were so rational that they "perfected" their techniques (an expression used twenty-three times in *The Visible Hand*, four times on one page[11]). His notion of perfection amounted to a managerial standard of morality that evaluated techniques according to their productive efficiency and longevity; if a technique contributed to material growth and was used for a long time, it had been perfected. Presumably, he rejected standards that evaluated costs to workers or the public as being more moral than analytical and as therefore not being "scientific."

In effect Chandler threw political standards out the front door and unwittingly let them in the back. Like many intellectuals of his generation, he sought analytic theories that were value-neutral but selected ones which were value-laden. The thinkers he believed were positive scientists will be studied in the following pages as political theorists.[12] And like any political theorists, their ideas have been criticized by others with different values, particularly by those in the management community who doubted that bureaucracy was as rational as Chandler believed.

Debates within the management profession belie determinism, revealing the realm of choice. By taking sides in the debates, managers and theorists chose the ends and means of government. Such value choices can be investigated as empirically as technological changes. And such investigations can show managerial rulers adapting to specific historical-cultural environments. The method thus portrays modern business as a human agency rather than a technological force.

Not surprisingly, labor historians and sociologists with leftist sympathies have studied more of the politics of business than Chandler. They have described struggles between managers and workers for control over work and have shown how conflict spawned managerial elites and techniques.[13] Like business historians, however, their recognition of political issues has sometimes been limited, and some have claimed that managers have easily controlled workers. Harry Braverman, for instance, portrayed Frederick W. Taylor's "scientific management," which had become "the bedrock of all work design," as an oppressive system. But by presuming that the degradation of work under Taylorism had successfully controlled workers and solved managers' problems, his interpretation in effect proclaimed the end of political struggles in the firm because management had won. Thus he overlooked the degree to which managers have been dissatisfied with Taylorism and have tried to develop more effective and efficient techniques.[14]

The sociologist Richard Edwards improved on Braverman's ideas by showing that managerial "systems of control" had contradictions that spawned class conflict.[15] But Edwards did not discuss how the systems had been legitimized and criticized in management theory or explain the value choices that shaped the systems. Edwards, like many radical scholars, tended to pooh-pooh managerial discourse as mere "ideology," as rationalizations intended to justify hierarchy to people outside management. In a critique of Braverman, Edwards chided him for using managerial publications, arguing that their ideological content was misleading and that readers could easily confuse rhetoric with reality.[16]

Such views have encouraged scholars to leave management writings to managers. But their publications are, I would submit, too important to be left with them. Management writers, rather than addressing outsiders, addressed an audience of managers. Their ideological notions, rather than being reason to avoid their publications, should be reason to study them.

Changing managerial ideology from an obstacle to seeing reality into another reality under study can be useful in several ways. Studying ideology can reveal managers making history, not just responding to it, and help show how they developed and legitimized governmental methods. Moreover, examining the ideology of managerial thinkers offers unique opportunities to understand the thoughts and actions of managerial practitioners, demonstrating particularly how the range of possible ideas was narrowed by the rationality and structures of capitalism and bureaucracy. And analyzing management ideas can also show conflicts among theorists and practitioners; it can thus transcend the reductionist polarities in some radical scholarship and can show hegemonic struggles within the managerial elite.

My intellectual history therefore has not been patterned after approaches like that of the sociologist Reinhard Bendix. Based on a misunderstanding of audience and a narrow definition of ideology, he studied management literature for messages to workers and concluded that they learned of their inferiority and obligations to superiors.[17] Never pausing to consider that workers seldom read *Business Week*, let alone the *Training and Development Journal*, Bendix omitted study of discourse within the management community and of the rhetoric managers used with one another.

In my reading of management publications, I proceeded as do historians of political theory. I studied writers' conceptions of human nature, methods of social analysis, definitions of governmental problems, objections to and agreements with other writers, beliefs regarding the purposes of government, theories about decision making and power holding, and techniques for improving government. I did not accept at face value the scientific persona that management writers typically adopted. Although they claimed that they were scientists making empirical tests of the most efficient means to given ends, they became philosophers when they made existential choices about the meaning of efficiency (not to mention when they accepted the ends of business as givens). Behind their positivist pose, they were defining ends when answering such questions as "efficiency at what? efficiency for whom?" and were choosing a particular government when selecting means. Rather than scientists of positivist myth, they are better seen as new "mandarins"; they were managerial scholastics, not independent intellectuals, whose values and vision were limited by their membership in a governing class.

This study examines the debates and decisions of the management mandarinate. The first chapter provides background and an overview, and the rest follow a general pattern. In evidence, each is based on information that passed in books and journals through the marketplace of ideas. In organization, each traces the development of a single idea, analyzes its basic content, assesses its influence, and discusses the criticisms directed against it. In content, each shows that mandarins' ideas were shaped by many influences, including technological changes, labor markets, business environments, government policies, scientific conventions, intellectual climates, professional developments, and academic institutions. As important as these influences, however, each chapter shows that recent ideas were shaped by a management theory of value which presumed that the best government was a managed government.

This management theory of value was so important because the central issue addressed by mandarins in the decades after the Second World War was a series of attempts to overcome problems that Taylorism helped create but could not solve. They saw that Taylorism helped create conflicts between workers and managers, between departments, between business and the public; it engendered bureaucratic organizations whose specialized operations could not be controlled through time-and-motion study, spawned work that could not be easily managed through separation of planning from doing, and bred workers who resented being treated as factors of production. They put forward alternatives that attempted to progress beyond Taylorism and bureaucracy.

Differences in their criticisms of Taylorism and in their solutions divided the mandarins into two philosophical schools, the post-Taylorist bureaucrats and the post-Mayoist corporatists. Post-Taylorite bureaucratic thinkers believed in the basic rationality and legitimacy of centralized power and specialized tasks; but they observed that theoretical explanations of bureaucracy were inadequate and realized that specialized operations could not be integrated through the methods of scientific management alone. They therefore developed theories that validated faith in bureaucracy and invented mathematical and mechanical techniques that could help make it more efficient. In contrast, post-Mayoist corporatists questioned some aspects of the rationality and legitimacy of bureaucratic forms of managerial capitalism; they believed that Taylorism produced conflicts between managers and a new generation of professional employees and educated, affluent workers. They sought to explain the dysfunctions of bureaucracy and to develop "democratic" styles of leadership and participative methods of management that could bring harmony to the workplace or at least reduce conflict.

The bureaucrats and corporatists became involved in bitter debates and verified the observations of Harold Koontz, a mandarin who recognized that discourse in contemporary management was "a kind of confused and destructive jungle warfare," with each school trying to dominate by clobbering its competitors.[18] The bureaucrats and corporatists portrayed each other as ideologues from opposite ends of the political spectrum. And indeed they frequently seemed to propose different ways of governing. Their differences, however, were often more matters of style than substance. They found the techniques of Taylorism easier to transcend than its basic premises, and in the end they formed different schools of scientific management.

Ideas from each school are discussed in the following chapters, and each topic represents an important tendency in contemporary management. Each chapter attempts to explore one part of what Koontz called "the management theory jungle." Instead of surveying all recent management ideas, I selected subjects according to two criteria: innovativeness and influence. Chosen topics either departed from previous ideas or influenced managerial rhetoric and behavior in important ways.

Examples of postbureaucratic thought are found in chapters 2 and 3. Chapter 2 relates how mathematicians and natural scientists tried to use the quantitative methods of management science to eliminate politics from decision making. Chapter 3 shows how the Nobel Prize winner Herbert A. Simon mixed metaphors from economics and cybernetics and helped promote the use of artificial intelligence in business.

The remaining chapters examine post-Mayoist theory. Chapter 4 shows how management guru Peter F. Drucker developed management by objectives to integrate European political ideas with American management and to direct the new professional employees that he called knowledge workers. Chapter 5 discusses how Kurt Lewin and his disciples established sensitivity training as a way to replace authoritarian leadership with democratic leadership. Chapter 6 describes attempts by psychologists and engineers to replace Taylorism with job enrichment, initially in order to counter the blue-collar blues of the baby-boom generation and to increase productivity. And Chapter 7 tells how Americans in recent years became fascinated with the Japanese management system because of its corporative way of transcending Taylorism. The conclusion discusses the persistence of previous patterns and assesses the significance of management debates.

Taylorism
and Beyond

Bureaucracy and
Its Discontents

At the beginning of the twentieth century, members of America's progressive
business community were pursuing a parallel strategy. Inside firms, they began
rationalizing their organizations by adopting bureaucratic governance. On the
outside, they began developing and disseminating scientific knowledge about
management by establishing professional societies, journals, and schools. As
time passed, they guided their strategies using Frederick W. Taylor's scientific
management. Although managers repudiated parts of Taylor's prescriptions,
his fundamental premises met their philosophical and technical needs and by
mid-century had come to dominate managerial theory and practice. Even in
the second half of the century, moreover, many in the management community have continued to believe that successful management and Taylor's
scientific management were one and the same. One recent management writer
has gone so far as to claim that Taylor's ideas were as influential as those of
Marx and Freud but were more "objectively valid."[1]

Such paeans indicate continued faith in Taylorism as well as fear of heretics.
Indeed, from the beginning, heretics have understood the hegemony of Taylorism and criticized its premises. They understood that reforming business
government depended on transcending Taylorism, either by refining it or by
repudiating it altogether.

Reformers developed innovations in a social context of bureaucratic firms
and professional managers. So understanding recent ideas requires understanding the history of bureaucratization and professionalization that provided
the setting in which Taylorism became dominant. This chapter briefly de-

scribes that history, focusing especially on the dysfunctions of Taylorism and on the early expressions of its corporatist variants.

As business and labor historians have shown, bureaucratic firms run by professional managers were established in the last decades of the nineteenth century and the first decades of the twentieth.[2] This new managerial capitalism emerged from a search for ways to coordinate operations and control workers. It was the outcome of technological evolution, adjustment to market forces, value choices, and political struggle.

In the years after the Civil War, entrepreneurs faced problems that proved difficult to solve using traditional techniques. They were pressured particularly by falling prices, periodic market gluts, and a transportation revolution that increased the size and competitiveness of their markets. In some industries, moreover, changes in machinery led to output imbalances and a reorganization of work. Yet adjustments proved difficult because workers and organizations were nearly beyond executive control. Labor was expensive because of high turnover and dependence on well-paid skilled workers. Control from the top was limited because operations were typically directed by skilled workers who followed craft customs and inside contracting systems and by foremen who used the despotic "drive" mode of supervision. Such ways of organizing work, to be sure, often benefited shop floor elites. But from the perspective of owners and top managers, the methods led to ineffective planning, inadequate coordination, incomplete information about costs, irregular scheduling, and intermittent returns; these problems were compounded for leaders of newly consolidated firms with large and scattered operations. So business professionals gradually decided to wrest control by establishing and legitimizing a new constitutional system.

They began founding bureaucratic government as early as the late nineteenth century. The traditional drive system, to be sure, lasted well into the twentieth century even in large firms because shop floor managers worked to preserve their personal authority by resisting systematic methods. But top managers continued to introduce bureaucratic reforms. Reluctant reformers were prodded by federal policies designed to stabilize competition and stimulate production and especially by union efforts to escape arbitrary foremen and irregular employment. Such efforts particularly accelerated bureaucratization during the First World War and the depression. As a result, bureaucracy gradually advanced with the application of written rules to guide supervisors, the use of central personnel departments to erode foremen's power, the introduction of machines that undermined craft autonomy and its organization of work, and the construction of job ladders and compartmentalized buildings.[3] This process specialized tasks and separated planning from doing.

Building bureaucracy transferred the reins of power from subordinates to superiors. Mechanizing and specializing jobs restricted the discretion of those on the bottom of the organization and expanded the power of those on top. Both changes also reduced the costs of wages and training, since using semi-skilled workers minimized the costs of turnover even without lowering its rate. In addition, lowering and homogenizing skill levels improved the bargaining power of management. It engendered a labor surplus that made workers dependent on employers and imposed the discipline of the reserve army of the unemployed. Homogenization in skill was accompanied by stratification in status and income, a system that rewarded workers for their seniority and subservience, not to mention their sex, race, and ethnicity. Specializing tasks, moreover, made it easier to measure individual performance against organizational standards and to motivate workers through productivity-based wages. And finally, homogenized and standardized jobs helped to simplify the functions of management to the point that some managers came to believe they were scientists applying general principles to specific cases.[4]

These changes were normally not part of any comprehensive plan. But the clearest ideology for building bureaucracy came from the mechanical engineer and consultant Frederick W. Taylor (1856–1915). Some of his techniques, including time-and-motion study and skill transfer from workers to managers, were not widely practiced before the late 1920s, partly because of concern with the added costs of administrative overhead[5] and partly because business leaders and foremen feared that power would shift to college-educated engineers.[6] But many people in business seemed to accept the efficacy of bureaucracy even as they rejected Taylor's techniques for establishing it.[7] Taylor himself argued that "the mechanism" of his system should "not be mistaken for its essence, or underlying philosophy." And his philosophy of "scientific management" quickly proved very attractive to business people in and to technocratic intellectuals outside business.[8]

In his speeches and writings, Taylor proposed that managers should become scientific, study the organization of work, and invent apolitical methods for overcoming industrial waste and conflict. He thought they especially needed to overcome disputes between foremen and workers about work organization and compensation. The disputes, he claimed, could be escaped only if business and labor underwent "a complete revolution in mental attitude" and realized their shared interest in maximizing income through maximizing output. Accepting a common productive goal would eliminate political controversy and make governing the corporation purely a technical matter of discovering the "one best way." Then scientific managers could conduct experiments to find the one best way of working and allow rule by science to replace government by soldiering work gangs and whip-cracking foremen. The maximum capacity of a worker would become known and could be used to assign a "fair day's work" in exchange for a fair day's wage. And under the "intimate, friendly cooperation" of scientific management, labor and business would benefit, and the politics of the firm would be based on "harmony, not discord."[9]

Taylor's enlightened despotism, as Samuel Haber, Daniel Bell, Judith Merkle, and others have described it, was an early bureaucratic variety of what became known as "end-of-ideology" political theory.[10] It assumed the naturalness of capitalism, accepted its goals, defined the social good in monetary terms of productive growth and efficiency, presumed that corporate government could be free from disputes over values, argued that an apolitical elite should make decisions based on scientific calculations of economic rationality, and presumed that employees were subjects obliged to obey and perform specific roles. And partly because Taylorism effectively expressed and legitimized the developing attraction to centralization and specialization, America's management community quickly embraced it. They also accepted it because it helped create a professional agenda for managers in modern corporations and educators in newly formed business schools, urging them to make scientific studies to improve the management of bureaucracy.

Taylorism thus became the political philosophy of bureaucratic government. Peter F. Drucker, the management guru who knew political theory, got it right when he described Taylor's scientific management as an "all but systematic philosophy of worker and work." Its influence, he said, could well be described as "the most powerful as well as the most lasting contribution America has made to Western thought since the Federalist Papers."[11]

The popularity of Taylor's philosophy and of bureaucracy itself, however, did not mean that the management community had solved its problems. Bureaucracy helped create new problems that were particularly evident in workers' reactions at the turn of the century. Workers objected to the way Taylorism and bureaucracy accelerated the pace of work, restricted autonomy, destroyed craft skills and hierarchies, lowered product quality and standards of workmanship, reduced workers from people to machines, undermined status and identity in the community, and caused wages to lag behind productivity and profits. Consequently they denied that Taylorism and professional managers were scientific and value-neutral. Workers' disgust for the system provoked individual and collective acts of defense and defiance.

Although bureaucracy debilitated some of their traditional strategies, workers found weaknesses in the system, which they could exploit. Individually, workers took advantage of the way the diminution of skills made jobs accessible, which resulted in very high rates of turnover. Collectively, they restricted output, demanded higher wages, joined the Wobblies, went on strike over control issues, and formed unions. Workers in federal arsenals successfully secured congressional protection from Taylorism.[12] Ironically, workers' collective efforts to check managerial bureaucracy often produced more bureaucracy, particularly in the form of union contracts and personnel departments.[13]

In response, some managers tried to tighten discipline. They assumed that achieving efficiency and control required more even homogenization. So they mechanized and simplified more jobs, waged open-shop and union-busting campaigns, or introduced even closer supervision; Henry Ford even extended supervision into leisure time. But greater exercise of power and intensified homogenization, they found, often stimulated more flight or fight among workers.[14]

Some managers and progressive reformers began to see the irrationality of bribing and bullying workers and took a few tentative steps beyond centralization and specialization. During the First World War, for instance, some of Taylor's disciples acknowledged that scientific management was arousing the class conflict it had been designed to avoid. H. L. Gantt and several engineering professors blamed the problem on old-fashioned businessmen who had incorrectly used it to exploit workers rather than to expand production. To correct this, these "engineering intellectuals" concocted a volatile blend of English guild socialism and scientific management; their "scientific collectivism" called for shop councils of workers and production experts to plan production. This call was not heeded by workers, who figured the councils would only replace rule-of-thumb managers with college-educated ones. Moreover, Donald Stabile has explained that these pseudosyndicalists really did not transcend scientific management because they continued to see workers as another factor to be engineered. They sought ways to make "every worker his own Taylorite."[15]

Heretical Taylorites did not give up, however, and they tried other methods of ending class conflict. Some scientific managers tried working out agreements with unions. In these cases the authority of managers was checked by negotiated work rules and grievance procedures. But such cases were rare, and scientific managers usually cooperated with unions only when they were forced to, particularly during the labor shortages of the First World War and after the organizing drives of the 1930s.[16]

Still other methods for reconciling workers to bureaucracy came from the personnel management movement. The movement involved some of Taylor's heirs, including Henry S. Dennison, Ordway Tead, Robert B. Wolf, and Robert

G. Valentine. They supported personnel schemes that could help eliminate inefficiency and disharmony.

Personnel management took various forms depending on the background of its supporters. Some personnel managers had been social workers; they wanted to make the firm into a welfare state. Their corporate welfare programs led to health, safety, and sanitation improvements, housing assistance, pension plans, insurance packages, recreation facilities, and profit-sharing programs. Other personnel managers had been teachers; they wanted the firm to become a school, and their vocational education schemes sought to upgrade skills, inculcate a professional attitude toward manual work, and match workers with suitable jobs. Still others saw themselves as progressives who were trying to bring "industrial democracy" to the firm. Their company unions sought to make workers more loyal by giving them some voice on some matters. But none of these reforms went significantly beyond Taylorist government. By eliciting consent without reorganizing bureaucracy, personnel management hid the iron cage in chintz curtains.[17]

While the demand for more rational government came from conflict inside firms, the supply of managerial techniques often came from outside. By the 1920s, many academics had become management mandarins and were increasingly developing scholastic theories and governmental innovations for dealing with dysfunctions in bureaucracy. Psychologists, for instance, attempted to design intelligence and personality tests similar to those used by the army during World War I and thus to help managers select employees for specific jobs. And more important in the long run, they and other social scientists began conducting studies of "human relations" at work. They investigated the attitudes and behavior of workers and the rationality of managerial techniques, intending to discover information that could be used to help managers.[18]

The most famous of the human relations experiments in a factory setting was conducted by National Research Council investigators, Western Electric managers, and Harvard University researchers at the Hawthorne works near Chicago from 1924 through the early 1930s. Initially, they undertook studies of fatigue and the effects of lighting on productivity. But their investigations soon turned to examining informal relationships to learn how managers could manipulate workers and maximize output.[19] From the Hawthorne experiments, mandarins helped codify a new set of managerial postulates and prescriptions. These were most clearly expressed by Australian-born psychologist George Elton Mayo (1880–1949).[20]

Much influenced by European theories of "psycho-pathology" and especially by Emile Durkheim's social psychology, Mayo believed that industrialization and destruction of craft systems had caused "social disintegration" and norm-less, maladjusted behavior. Workers suffered from "an inadequate social inter-relation with other people," stemming especially from their misunderstanding and distrust of managers. Managers contributed to this maladjustment by being more concerned with economic efficiency than social solidarity and drove workers to seek asylum in informal work groups. Mayo denied, how-ever, that worker groups were rational means for members to maximize wages, employment, and autonomy. On the contrary, they irrationally restricted out-put, thus inhibiting economic growth and hampering members' ability to exploit incentive wages. And consequently for Mayo, the "problem of admin-istration," indeed the problem of industrial civilization itself, was workers' "anomie" rather than the centralization and specialization inherent in bureaucracy.

While Mayo's diagnosis tended to blame the victims, his solution was an intimate style of management. Nurturant supervision could adjust workers to bureaucratic life and get informal groups of workers to accept the formal goals of managers. It would convince workers that managers were their friends and that bureaucracies were communities, thus giving them "a sense of participa-tion," "a feeling of release from constraint," and a desire to cooperate. But specialized jobs and centralized power would remain. Workers would partici-pate only in social decisions, in choosing such things as the colors of restroom walls, and not in governmental decisions about personnel or organization. In addition, they would explore their personal problems by participating in nondirective counseling, which, the Hawthorne researchers found, worked to diffuse discontent and inspire trust in authority.[21] In general, as the sociologist C. Wright Mills would later put it, the prescriptions of Mayo and his followers were intended to manipulate the sentiments of workers by creating "pseudo-gemeinschaft islands" in a gesellschaft swamp.[22]

Over the last several decades, judgments like Mills's have been attacked and defended in debates about the meaning of the Hawthorne experiments.[23] What both radical and conservative scholars entangled in the controversy usually overlooked, however, was that many mandarins agreed with Mills, at least in part.

Most prominently, mandarins like Douglas McGregor and Chris Argyris criticized the human relations school for trying to eradicate the dysfunctions of bureaucracy without reforming bureaucracy itself. Mayoists, these man-darins thought, blamed inefficiency on managers as individuals, not on bu-reaucracy as an institution. Mayoists had assumed that the bureaucratic firm was benevolent and naturally harmonious, which made worker resistance pathological, and, consequently, they concluded that a paternalistic supervisory style and friendliness away from the point of production could easily make workers cooperate with managers. For mandarins like Argyris, who were willing to concede that conflict was normal and had caused managers to establish controls in the first place, the advocates of human relations could be dismissed for offering palliatives to fight a permanent pandemic.

As social scientists continued to study conflicts at work in the 1940s and 1950s, many pointed out how the unintended consequences of bureaucracy limited its rationality. In particular, they said its parts were hard to integrate, its authoritarian regime spawned rebellious behavior, its restricted jobs under-utilized workers by depriving them of discretion, and its separation of plan-ning from doing eroded entrepreneurial and engineering skills. These dys-functions led to conflicts that undercut production and profits.

Consequently, their search for harmony moved some of them toward politi-cal philosophies that appeared more like varieties of corporatism than any-thing else.[24] They can be put, in other words, with theories that students of European ideas have classified between classical liberalism and privately gov-erned firms on one side and state socialism and party government on the other.[25] This ambiguity gave corporatism appeal across the political spectrum. Its European prophets have included conservative aristocrats and clerics like Hegel and Pope Leo XIII, anarchist and utopian socialist intellectuals like Proudhon and Saint-Simon, artisanal and syndicalist labor leaders like Louis Blanc and G. D. H. Cole, neo-royalists like Charles Maurras, bourgeois so-ciologists like Durkheim, industrialists and technocrats like Walther Rathenau and Ernest Mercier, and fascists like Mussolini and Pétain.

These diverse figures shared a set of beliefs that explain corporatism's charm. They shared a hostility to liberalism, especially to competitive individ-ualism, which those on the right saw as inefficient and destructive of the traditional social order and those on the left saw as dangerous to working-class security and solidarity. They also shared a hostility to Marxian socialism, which the right saw as threatening the rights of private property and the left saw as threatening local control and self-government. In addition, they shared an attraction to harmonious economic communities and believed that harmo-ny, a value equally hostile to individualism and class struggle, could found a new social order. They envisioned new communities of producers united by collective goals and made up of members whose individual goals could be achieved through social service. And given their common goals, they thought that government could be an administrative search for the best means. Conse-quently they were drawn to avowedly apolitical forms that could mediate between conflicting classes and interests. Technocracy and councils of workers and managers were the preferred methods, while democracy, especially the notion of one-citizen, one-vote, was especially feared by the right as a threat to established power and privilege.

Another common feature of corporatism in Europe was a penchant for its philosophy to outstrip its practice. Indeed, it had a long history of achieving more harmony in word than in deed. Corporatists on the left had often lacked the resources to establish cooperative communities, and typically their ideas had attracted only handfuls of skilled workers and alienated intellectuals. Proletarians had preferred union contracts and social democratic parties over cooperatives and shop councils, and leftist schemes of labor-management cooperation had foundered because managers refused to renounce their prerogatives. In fact, corporatists on the right often refused to practice the cooperation they preached. Except for periods of war, tight labor markets, or other circumstances in which labor had some bargaining power, Europe's clerical, conservative, bourgeois, and fascist corporatists had expected workers to cooperate on terms favorable to elites and were quite willing to use coercive methods when workers refused to obey. Accordingly, the institutions that were established by the right were often ritualistic or repressive, as seen in the corporative agencies in Fascist Italy, Nazi Germany, and Vichy France. Although coercive methods belied the existence of class harmony, the right usually continued to claim that their institutions were cooperative. It was only after the Second World War, which discredited the radical right and legitimized the democratic left, that corporatist arrangements like the German practice of codetermination experienced some success.[26]

In the United States, corporatists of the right dominated the stage, acting as if they were taking cues from Saint-Simon and Durkheim and pushing a variety of leftist utopians and anarchists to the wings. Modern American exponents of the philosophy, however, owed less to European political and religious doctrines than to the ideas of the new professions. Progressive educators, political scientists, economists, social workers, psychologists, and engineers had a corporative ethic. They wanted to use scientific methods and knowledge to eliminate social conflicts and eradicate economic inefficiencies, and they tried to avoid overt exercise of power, turning instead to educational propaganda, therapy, and apolitical expertise. Their managerial mentality meant rejecting classical liberalism and Marxism and searching for a form of managerial capitalism that was efficient and harmonious.[27]

The new professions often chose Edward Bellamy as their prophet. His vision of technocratic government and social harmony in *Looking Backward*, although it contained radical ideas, was decidedly bourgeois and more professional than proletarian. Indeed, many new professionals adopted Bellamy's novel as their handbook, became leading acolytes in Nationalist clubs that publicized its ideas, and wrote dozens of elaborate sequels and imitations.[28]

The problem was that the new professions and American managers took many paths to harmony. In fact Taylorism had originated in the same social and intellectual environment as corporatism, and ironically the greatest single prophet of corporatism was Taylor himself. He wanted to engender class harmony and expected that jobs designed by experts would be healthy for individual and firm. Moreover, his plea for a "mental revolution" often drew on corporative language, especially when he called for management based on "cooperation, not individualism."[29] But his ideal of the scientific manager was vague enough to inspire disciples with conflicting interpretations. And they often took paths away from him and from one another. Their search for rationality and harmony quickly led to a schism, and partisans were divided into two philosophical schools, post-Taylorite bureaucrats and post-Mayoist corporatists.

The bureaucrats remained convinced that the most rational government came from hierarchical controls, specialized tasks, and professional managers. In these respects, they were latter-day Taylorites who remained true to the basic premises of scientific management, especially its disdain for the judgment of the unprofessional and its positivist dream of the manager as a scientist. Yet in seeking the harmony that their mentor had promised but did not deliver, they were trying to go beyond Taylorism and were searching for new theories and techniques of bureaucratic governance that could eliminate its dysfunctions. In the late 1930s and early 1940s, their positivism was leading them toward what they believed were value-free disciplines that could yield principles and tools for a more effective science of management; they turned toward methods of mathematics that could eliminate politics from decision making, models of economics that could explain the virtues of bureaucracy, and metaphors and machines of cybernetics and computer science that could facilitate communication and control.

The corporatists, in contrast, were latter-day Mayoists who wanted Mayo's corporate communities but doubted that harmony could be achieved without decentralizing power and unifying tasks. They searched for explanations of the dysfunctions of bureaucracy and for ways to flatten hierarchies, utilize individual talents, integrate firm and employee, and create industrial clans. This quest led them to the social sciences, especially psychology and sociology. In the late 1930s they conducted experiments on democratic styles of leadership, and during the war they observed trials of participative management schemes. By the 1950s they often used concepts like self-actualization to explain the conflicts caused by Taylorism and to guide them to harmony at work.

Because corporatists and bureaucrats thought they were proposing to govern capitalism in different ways, their quarrels were often vitriolic. Corporatists wrote as if bureaucrats were tyrants who treated people as instruments and thereby triggered reactions that threatened not only the success of individual firms and managers but the long-term survival of capitalism itself. Bureaucrats wrote as if corporatists were anarchists who made social harmony an end in itself and put the welfare of employees ahead of the survival of the firm.

Yet, despite the rancor in their squabbles and the reality of their disagreements, the two schools of thought overlapped in many ways. Bureaucrats sometimes turned to corporatist language and techniques when their approaches floundered and advocated participative management to convince people to cooperate with technocrats. And even while corporatists attempted to break free of bureaucratic traditions, their theories and techniques normally accepted centralized power and specialized jobs, and their efforts to adjust workers to bureaucracy became especially evident when they encountered problems. Indeed, partisans of corporatism in American management often replicated the behavior of their predecessors in the European right, preaching cooperation but practicing manipulation. Their pursuit of communal harmony was often indistinguishable from a search for managerial efficiency, and their ideal of a democratic manager was often the spitting image of a scientific one. And whatever their differences, the corporatists shared with the bureaucrats the management theory of value, which presumed that managerial rule was right and rational. Accordingly, corporative democracy and participation worked within hierarchy and were not ways to do without it.

Obviously, transcending Taylor and Mayo proved difficult. Corporatism could transform itself into bureaucracy, and bureaucrats could wrap themselves in corporatism. This could lead to the conclusion that each was a different color of the same chameleon and that corporatist philosophy was merely the ideological camouflage favored by bureaucrats. But given the determination that people in the management community have shown in pursuit of efficiency and harmony, a fuller explanation is necessary. Corporatism was an ideal state some said they were working to achieve, while bureaucracy was a real one that most would accept.

2

Management
by the Numbers

Operations Research and
Management Science

For centuries thinkers in the West have been attracted to the notion that mathematics could decipher the secrets of nature. To the Greeks nature was designed according to Euclidian geometry, which meant that eternal verities could be deduced by tracing proofs in the sand. Later thinkers like Galileo and Hume helped initiate the modern view that mathematics was a language created by the mind. By Hume's time scientists saw it as their fundamental language. And liberal social scientists, beginning with the Physiocrats and the positivists, wanted to go beyond using mathematics as a tool for interpreting nature; they wanted to use it to guide social policy.[1]

Managers have also used quantification. Some of their most important governing tools, like double-entry bookkeeping and time-and-motion studies, have been quantitative. But no managerial techniques have used so much sophisticated mathematics as the procedures of operations research (OR) and management science.

The British and American scientists and mathematicians who invented the new tools during and after the Second World War claimed that they had created the first positive management science that could overcome some of the failings of Taylorism; their methods could, they said, direct complex organizations by integrating specialized operations and formulating strategy without resort to politics. Like all post-Taylorist bureaucrats, however, only their methods, not their premises, departed from Taylor's. They shared his faith that the best government was the most technocratic one and his notion that people were factors of production. By the early 1960s their ability to mix old theories with new techniques helped their influence spread from the crooked corridors of the Pentagon to the plush executive suites of the biggest corporations.

By the late 1960s, however, management science was under attack. Critics charged that mathematical techniques contained crippling flaws that led to failures in government. Confidence was shaken more deeply in the late 1970s when critics blamed the techniques for failures in business. Criticism from without was accompanied by criticism from within as many management scientists became sensitive to how political power was exercised within businesses. Turning away from their old positivist and bureaucratic ways, some sought new directions for their profession. In America some reformers turned to corporatism; in Britain some radicals even abandoned the premises of management science and sought to develop a workers' science.

The story of operations research in business shows how technicians trained in mathematics and science tried to achieve Frederick Taylor's goal: to transform the politics of running a business into a science. It also shows how, for all their scientific sophistication and quantitative savvy, the mathematician-kings were no more successful than Taylor's time-and-motion experts.

Born in War

The use of scientists trained in mathematics to solve managerial problems began in Britain in the late 1930s. The Royal Air Force, wanting to discover how to use radar effectively, enlisted the help of an interdisciplinary team of physical scientists and mathematicians skilled in mathematical techniques. The team's assignment differed from weapons research, the sort of project the military usually gave to scientists, in that its purpose was not to develop new equipment. Rather, its members were searching for the best way to deploy existing equipment. They were involved in operations, assessing possible outcomes of proposed decisions in order to make optimal choices. Accordingly, in 1937 the RAF named the team "the operational research section." Later the British applied the label operational research to all such work, particularly to using mathematical techniques for solving managerial problems. The radar team was successful, and by the beginning of the Second World War the British military had created other teams. The Royal Navy, for instance, used a team to learn how deep to drop depth charges to sink German U-boats. To find the optimal depth for detonation, the navy assembled a scientific team that examined past records of attacks on subs, studied the capacities of the depth charges, and made specific recommendations. The Admiralty followed their advice and subsequently conducted more effective antisubmarine warfare.[2]

The American navy and air corps were impressed with British successes and early in 1942 began imitating them. Engaging in what they called "operations research," Americans used teams of scientists to evaluate and improve weapons, tactics, and organizations; to analyze countermeasures devised by the enemy; and to predict the results of possible events. Typically the scientists studied low-level, easily quantifiable problems and attempted to improve tactics and equipment deployment. They studied search procedures for planes, ships, and subs; navigation methods for bombers; and defense tactics against submarine and kamikaze attacks.[3] After the war, techniques were codified and became the models for operations researchers in business.

Later business applications were affected by the wartime image the scientists had developed. They acknowledged that they were not professional military experts. Their special skill lay in scientific training, which had taught them how to define research projects, gather information, analyze data using mathematics, and arrive at objective conclusions. Relying on such scientific methods and on steady, cumulative, quantitative research was more effective than relying on the sporadic insights of the rare military genius. Indeed they disdained individualistic notions of leadership, insisting that isolated individuals could only see limited perspectives. But teams of scientists could help a professional military leader see the whole picture. They could offer crucial, objective advice about managing modern warfare, advice about balancing conflicting subgoals to achieve the overall goal and about selecting optimal tactics to maximize the effectiveness of a strategy.[4]

After the war, most operations researchers believed their wartime contributions had been significant. But later some would look back on the war years and recognize that they had first encountered the problems that would plague them in peace. Some problems centered on their access to power. Military commanders were often suspicious of the methods and recommendations of ivory-tower scientists. Philip Morse, a physicist who directed the antisubmarine group in the navy, remembered that his superiors often objected to "a bunch of questionable characters intruding on their field and their prerogatives." In practice, operations researchers evidently did not have much influence if they allowed the facts to speak for themselves; influence depended on their skills in politics and persuasion.

The operations researchers had also experienced methodological difficulties in the war. Their expertise was really in mathematics and statistics, not in military arts. This had led some of them to seek problems that they could solve, carrying around mathematical cookbooks looking for ingredients needed in their recipes. Such problems usually were easily defined, low-level ones, for which regular military personnel had often already used trial-and-error methods to work out satisfactory solutions. Morse recalled that his group often recommended no changes or sought to prevent changes.[5]

Conservatism went beyond their conclusions to include the basic premises of operations research. The scientists were not assigned to challenge the basic premises of decision makers, to realign strategy, or to make innovations in weapons; nor did they normally seek to do so. At the bottom of the pecking order, they had to accept goals and equipment as givens and look for the best ways to achieve those goals with existing resources. In later years this approach would have dangerous side effects; in fighting the long war of attrition in Vietnam and waging never-ending campaigns against innovative competitors in business, it helped lead to a bastard sort of planned obsolescence.

Moreover, the ethical dimensions of operations research were obscured by the special circumstances of the Second World War. The American and British leaders and scientists agreed that the conflict was "a good war." Consequently, ethical criteria were simple and clear. In a negative-sum competition between good Allies and the evil Axis, a good player sought to destroy the most at least cost. Efficiency could be pursued without concern about moral complexities. But after the good war, white and black often faded into a patchwork of greys. Later, limited wars were not fought with as much consensus or against an enemy so well understood, which meant that the goals were never so easily defined and pursued. As time passed, operations researchers in the armed forces, like everybody else in the military establishment, were subjected to tighter political limits and deeper moral dilemmas. Throughout the fifties and much of the sixties, however, members of the profession acted as if life was ethically simple and as if ethics did not apply to their work.

Flourishing in Peace

After returning to civilian life, many veterans of military operations research were eager to sell their tools. They turned naturally to the business market since it had problems similar to military ones and offered rewarding opportunities. One group of operations researchers in the air force, for instance, decided to offer their services to some corporation; they became "the whiz kids" who helped reorganize Ford during the forties and fifties.[6]

Success in business, the scientists discovered, depended on selling their instruments to corporate managers. People in business did not understand sophisticated mathematics and often distrusted long-haired scientists who wanted to tell them how to run their enterprises. To overcome suspicion, get employment or consulting contracts, and be effective once they got jobs, the scientists had to prove that their skills were useful and unique.[7]

One strategy was to sell their techniques as tried-and-true military surplus. They explained what they had contributed to winning the war and argued that war heroes who had "helped to lick Hitler" could help a business lick its competition. An important step in describing their war work came when the navy declassified reports on operations research. Philip Morse and George Kimball synthesized the reports, explained the mathematical techniques, and discussed how the approach could be applied to business. Their work, *Methods of Operations Research*, was published in 1951 and became the first book devoted to the method. Later, the highly influential first textbook on operations research by C. West Churchman, Russell L. Ackoff, and E. Leonard Arnoff also emphasized how military applications could be adapted to civilian use.[8]

In another promotional strategy, the scientists pointed to "a new class of managerial problems" that only they could solve. Business, they said, was becoming ever more complex. Taylorism had helped fragment operations, which meant that top management was finding it increasingly difficult to understand all the parts and put the corporate Humpty-Dumpty together. In addition, the specialized processes of mass production and multidivisional firms often led to inconsistent, conflicting activities. The engineering department, for example, often preferred static production runs in a few widgets, while the marketing department preferred numerous widgets and a flexible production process that could be immediately adapted to changing demand. While these problems were scarcely new to the 1950s, the scientists were offering new tools for managing harmony. The first textbook even defined operation research as a new means to provide managers "with a scientific basis for solving problems involving the interaction of components of the organization in the best interest of the organization as a whole."[9]

Not surprisingly, the operations researchers advertised their scientific status in the marketplace of ideas. After decades of rhetoric about the benefits of scientific management, entrepreneurs probably expected such appeals in business journals. Nonetheless, the operations researchers could claim to be real scientists as proven by their advanced degrees. They sought to legitimize themselves by denigrating less empirical approaches to management. Managers were accused of basing decisions on mere "experience," "intuition," "trial-and-error," "opinion, vague generalities, or lore." Even those who had embraced Taylor's scientific management had failed to realize that maximizing the efficiency of the parts would not inevitably lead to efficiency for the whole. Often it led to greater problems and conflicts because each unit in the organization sought to become more efficient by competing for resources and trying to impose its goals on the others.

The operations researchers urged business to go beyond Taylorism. Their scientific training was more rigorous than the time-and-motion expert's. It had taught them to be objective, to separate fact from opinion, and thus they could help managers make decisions based on empirical research. Their mathematical tools, which had already been successfully applied in understanding and controlling nature, could also be readily applied to organizations. And their lack of expertise in any specialized function was actually an asset; it made them generalists who could adapt to new fields, learn new ideas, and see the organization as a whole. Most importantly, their experiences as scientists had taught them to see the firm as an interrelated pattern. In this respect they were unlike Taylorist managers who saw firms as a series of isolated operations. They could see the firm as a system and were, they claimed, uniquely qualified to integrate its components into a harmonious whole.[10]

Of course they did not intend to bury Taylorism so much as to build on it. They maintained faith in the fundamental premises of Taylorism by accepting as givens the specialized division of labor and separation of planning and doing. Indeed their claim to expertise in abstract techniques assumed the distance between planning and doing would be wider than before; their analytical tools would enable them to be planners for planners. This appeal was probably very attractive to clients because managers could utilize operations research without dramatically reorganizing their firms or reorienting their ideas.

In going beyond the specialized approach of scientific management to the generalized one of management science, the operations researchers developed techniques that were consistent with "systems theory." They assumed that efficiency could best be achieved, first, by clarifying the objectives of the whole firm; secondly, by insuring that the subgoals of each part were consistent with the goals of the whole; and finally, by unifying the work of each part. Otherwise, improving the efficiency of one part might lead to "sub-optimizing," which could adversely affect the performance of other parts and could hamper the whole system.[11]

Systems metaphors permeated the early literature on operations research. These originated in communications theory and cybernetics. Such disciplines interpreted organizations as communication networks and managers as regulators of information and controllers of behavior.[12] The rhetoric of information, which appeared apolitical, had a natural charm for consultants trained in the natural sciences. As sociologist Robert Lilienfeld has noted, the systems style of thinking became part of an ideology naturally suited to the aims of technocrats.

Lilienfeld explained that the scientific claim that everything was organically related and was best studied as a part of a whole was vacuous. Since the whole universe could not be studied at once, the scientist had to define arbitrarily the subsystem being examined and spend much time arguing with other scientists about these arbitrary definitions. But whatever its emptiness, systems theory was politically valuable to bureaucrats. It anthropomorphized organizations, making organizational goals appear to be givens inherent in nature rather than objectives chosen by managers. Projecting goals into the nature of things allowed operations researchers to appear as positivists far above the muck of politics. Reification also justified giving power to management scientists who claimed to understand how the system functioned and how to improve it. In Lilienfeld's view, systems theory was just "a new variant of organic" ideology like that espoused by nineteenth-century statists and conservatives.[13]

Lilienfeld's interpretation, though, assumed that systems theory was merely advertisement directed at people outside the profession. Thus he ignored how the ideas also addressed practitioners and prescribed strategies for carrying out their jobs. Indeed systems theory was part and parcel of operations research as a governing tool. It helped mathematicians, who were either employees low on the totem pole or consultants outside the normal chain of command, get their superiors to clarify objectives; and without clear objectives, quantitative tools could not be used to select the best means. Thus systems thinking was in part a technique adopted by consultants to help them adapt to their ambiguous position on the organization chart and their dependence on sponsors.

More importantly, the very emptiness of the theory, which Lilienfeld assumed made it technically useless, actually had considerable utility. This can be seen by examining the crucial initial steps of an operations research project.[14] At the beginning the consulting team met with the sponsoring manager to define the problem to be studied and solved. Especially important was establishing a set of specific objectives and appropriate quantitative criteria that could be used to evaluate effectiveness. In business of course the purpose of the system was to maximize profits, and the measure was usually either maximum return on investment or net dollar profit. Specifics about the project were often clarified after several meetings, typically after the team had studied past operations and current problems. Eventually the participants defined the system that the consultants were supposed to work in, understand, and try to improve. Since the system varied from case to case, the manager and team could adapt to the particular circumstances of each project by filling in the blanks of systems theory.

For the sponsor, the process of defining systems, problems, goals, and measures of effectiveness involved important political decisions. It was an opportunity, according to Peter Drucker, to synthesize conflicting objectives, to integrate the goals of profitability, market share, innovation, productivity, resource availability, personnel development, short-range versus long-range planning, and public responsibility. Once goals had been clarified and unified, the manager could then direct the consultants and use them to impose values and control government.[15]

For the team, system definition was also useful. It defined their authority, narrowed the focus of their research, and established a strategic framework that guided their search for the optimal tactics. It also allowed them to study past operations and construct a mathematical model of the system. A working model allowed for trial of alternative solutions so consequences could be predicted. And eventually, assuming the model was accurate, the team could find an optimal solution that could remedy defective procedures without having dysfunctional consequences disrupt other parts of the system. If the problems were not solved, the team changed the solution, reformed other parts, or even started over.

In practice, OR mandarins assumed that managers faced only a few types of quantitative problems, so they developed a set of standardized tools. Russell Ackoff and Patrick Rivett, who were American and British pioneers, argued that managerial problems existed in only eight forms: inventory, allocation, queuing, sequencing, routing, replacement, competition, and search. Hence the operations researcher only had to figure out the form of the specific problem under study.[16] Then the researcher could determine the appropriate techniques. There were the tools of statistics and probability theory, linear programming, queuing theory, sequencing theory, game theory, operational gaming and Monte Carlo simulation, integer programming, nonlinear programming, replacement theory, utility theory, and network analysis for planning and scheduling.[17] Such tools had mainly been developed during the 1940s and 1950s and apparently did not change much thereafter.

Indeed, an outstanding feature of operations research as it grew during the fifties and sixties was its lack of controversy and the absence of criticism of past performance. Scarcely any debates occurred in the professional journals, and few expressed concerns about problems inherent in the techniques. Evidently practitioners encountered operational problems they could solve, or problems they could convince sponsors that they could solve. In any event, the basic steps for research projects—formulating, modeling, solving, testing, evaluating, and implementing—were quickly formalized and accepted by virtually all practitioners; this meant that they developed standardized ways of describing systems, defining problems, and designing solutions.[18]

Formalization was accompanied by professionalization and establishment of two professional societies, each with a journal. In 1952 the Operations Research Society of America (ORSA) was formed and began publishing its journal, *Operations Research*. And in the following year, the Institute of Management Science (TIMS) was founded and began its journal, *Management Science*. The goals of these organizations and publications were essentially identical; both sought to build a professional community, expand the business clientele, and, as TIMS put it, to "identify, extend, and unify scientific knowledge that contributes to the understanding and practice of management."[19]

Meanwhile, mandarins were establishing operations research as an academic discipline in business schools. They developed a curriculum that could teach the technique. So by the 1960s, particularly after the Ford and Carnegie foundation reports had endorsed education that taught general management skills and management science techniques, they were making this curriculum, with its assumptions about the utility of applied mathematics, the core of business education. Soon business schools were mass producing number-crunchers. And academics, who assumed that theoretical advances could improve practice, were soon mass producing applied mathematics publications. One study of the literature found 139 general texts on operations research listed in the subject guide to *Books in Print* for 1977–78, not including works that dealt with the various mathematical specialties in the field. The study also revealed, however, an essential similarity in paradigmatic content with that of the first text of 1957.[20]

As operations research became a profession and an academic discipline, it became increasingly popular in business. From the technique's beginnings, people in business had been very curious about it; and in the fifties and early sixties, even though surveys revealed that they did not know much about it, they had tremendous faith in it. With faith that scientific sophistication amounted to moral progress, they accepted the claims of its advocates, believing that science could help them eliminate the use of intuition in decision making, standardize routine decisions, render the future more predictable and controllable, improve planning, and integrate complex operations.

In the immediate postwar period, operations research had been more wide-ly used in Great Britain than in the United States, probably because the British government sponsored it in newly nationalized industries. In 1951 only about fifty operations researchers were making a living in American business, and only a handful of firms were using the system. But thereafter the profession grew like July corn. By 1956 the number of operations researchers in Ameri-can business had climbed to approximately one thousand, money spent on the technique had multiplied over thirty times, and the list of American com-panies with OR departments had become "too long to publish." By 1963 major users included Boeing, Ford, GM, Dow, DuPont, AT&T, General Electric, and US Steel.

In these companies, the early applications of operations research imitated military ones. Typically the problems were short term and clearly defined. Such tasks were most prevalent in transportation firms—air, railroad, truck-ing, and marine shipping—as well as in such industries as electricity, oil, coal, steel, and mass-production manufacturing. The earliest applications of quan-titative techniques in manufacturing usually occurred in production engineer-ing and operations management. The tools were especially used in rationaliz-ing decisions in large-scale, capital-intensive, continuous process operations where there were a series of static problems and a small number of inputs, production steps, and outputs.[21]

From the beginning, though, despite frequent application in business and lack of controversy in professional journals, OR mandarins and managers encountered difficulties in using quantitative techniques. Some of these prob-lems could be dismissed as mere misunderstandings or misapplications. But others seemed to call into question its fundamental premises.

For one thing, managers and management scientists had trouble com-municating with one another. Managers complained that they could not un-derstand what the eggheads were doing or saying. They often could not make heads or tails of the mathematics, were suspicious of using formal analysis as a substitute for simple rules of thumb, and were understandably reluctant to implement recommendations they could not comprehend. On their part, management scientists complained that the managers they dealt with, espe-cially the older ones, were uneducated Neanderthals. From their point of view, the techniques were not at fault; people were. They blamed failures on politi-cal obstacles set up by backward bureaucrats.

Some managers also doubted the cost effectiveness of operations research. Too often the money spent on a project exceeded the benefits gained, or the research time exceeded the duration of the problem. Too often the research interests of scientists led them to analyze problems and develop alternatives while ignoring the nitty-gritty work of implementing solutions that could translate the research into improved practices. And too often the technique was applied to low- and middle-level tasks, like scheduling or inventory control, where room for improvement was slight and progress could have relatively little effect on the profit or loss of an entire enterprise.[22] Because greater technical sophistication did not normally lower costs through increases in output or decreases in labor, some managers doubted that it led to greater profitability.

Still another problem that existed from the beginning was the difficulty of creating an apolitical science of government. OR mandarins and managers in the fifties and sixties sublimely ignored this problem and blissfully accepted the ends and means of bureaucratic capitalism. Because of their positivism, the scientists thought mathematics could separate administration from politics, find optimal tactics for given strategies, define problems and balance goals without controversy, and make recommendations without bias. They also assumed that managers and employees would accept their analyses and that their research would not only help the firm but the public as well. Because of their faith in their techniques, they did not see decision making as an inevitably political process involving conflicts over power and values. Nor did they heed the warnings of people like Peter Drucker and B. O. Koopman. Drucker pointed out that choices about means and goals inescapably involved value judgments and that management science could become more scientific the more it systematically considered values and the difficulty of integrating conflicting goals.[23] Koopman argued that many practitioners were so devoted to bureaucracy that they did not question the goals set by managers and were so enthralled with numbers, mathematics, and computers that they fallaciously equated maximum profit with the social good.[24] Such warnings were ignored, however, and operations research continued to follow the golden rule of maximizing profits and to preach a naive scientism.

Still, the field continued to grow. Business use of operations research further increased as computers became more affordable and enhanced the power to manipulate numbers. By 1977 four of five large firms in America were using the techniques, although the popularity of OR should not be exaggerated. One survey found that many small and middle-sized firms did not use the system, and one-half of all users applied it to four tasks or less.[25]

Continued growth also changed the way practitioners were trained and employed. Before the mid-1960s, the overwhelming majority of operations researchers had been trained outside of business schools, either in the military or the sciences. Forty-five percent had been mathematicians, statisticians, or natural scientists, and over 40 percent had been trained as engineers.[26] These people worked primarily as consultants selling their services to business. After the middle years of the 1960s, however, management scientists were increasingly educated in business schools. By the mid-seventies the second largest group of degree holders in operations research, after those with degrees in mathematics and the sciences, were educated in business fields. Increasingly, moreover, managers preferred that their operations researchers be employees. Probably managers wanted people who were more familiar with business problems in general and with the problems of their company in particular. Bringing technicians inside the company was also a way to control their activities.[27]

As time passed, the organization and tasks of management scientists also changed. The mathematicians were initially conceived as troubleshooters brought in from the outside or from a staff department to wrestle with temporary difficulties. In part technological imperatives demanded centralization; maximizing use of expensive and complex mainframe computers encouraged use of staff specialists. By the mid-1960s, however, computers had become more flexible, and timesharing on mainframes enabled access via terminals in functional departments. And by the early 1970s, on-line services made computers more user-friendly, a trend that was accelerated by the development of personal computers and standardized software in the late seventies and early eighties.[28]

With these changes, OR specialist-troubleshooters became organization persons with a permanent departmental assignment to rationalize daily operations. In production management, for example, they came to occupy permanent line positions dealing with the routine problems of forecasting, scheduling, and inventory control. And much more than in the early years, they were assigned where they could study the financial, control, and planning problems of top management. By 1977, 58 percent of large companies were using operations research for capital budgeting, whereas in 1964 the figure had been only 39 percent and in 1958 only 11 percent.[29]

Several factors help to explain why mathematical tools were now used on entrepreneurial decisions. For one thing, more powerful and flexible computers and more skilled programmers could process large amounts of data and provided an opportunity to tackle the complex problems of planning for a whole firm. For another, managers had become more familiar with operations research, partly through experience with it, partly because some of the scientists had now been promoted into top ranks. Naturally such managers wanted the help of mathematics in making difficult decisions. And finally, the development was the logical culmination of an ideology that from the beginning had claimed that operations researchers were the first true scientific managers who could govern a whole business system. In moving from aligning tactics with strategy to determining strategy itself and managing corporations by the numbers, the operations researchers were trying to live up to their promises.

Floundering in War and Peace

The use of management science to guide strategic decisions, however, meant that the problems encountered were far more complex and the consequences far less predictable. Planning for the future meant meeting the challenges not just of allocating resources but also of defining rationality for entire organizations. And when the technicians became involved in these ill-structured problems of government and business, they also became more deeply immersed in political controversies and conflicts. They came under attack, in particular, for the role they played in the stalemate in Vietnam and in the stagnation of American business in the late seventies and early eighties.

Ironically, the arena in which operations research had enjoyed its first successes, the military, was also the first to experience major failures. The failures were overseen by President Kennedy's secretary of defense, Robert McNamara, who with great fanfare elevated the techniques to a higher status in the Pentagon. Even before McNamara went to Washington, his faith that mathematics was the salvation of management was already legendary. He had been an operations researcher in the air corps during the Second World War and one of the original whiz kids at Ford. At the Department of Defense, which he referred to as the third largest managed economy in the world, he decided to apply the most sophisticated methods of management science available. So in 1961 he created the Office of Systems Analysis, later known as the Office of Program Analysis and Evaluation. Staffed with more whiz kids, the office sought to help civilians better manage the military.

The economists adopted systems analysis, a method developed by the RAND Corporation. Determining policy, they believed, was an economic problem, a quest to find the optimal means to achieve a given end. Although they initially analyzed tactics, weapons, and intelligence, they soon moved into policy planning. They regarded the movement as a natural step up, since the selection of weapons and tactics depended on strategic goals and strategy depended on accurate intelligence about the enemy.[30]

The movement from shaping tactics and intelligence to determining strategy, the sociologist James W. Gibson has argued, helped to institutionalize a managerial style of thinking that led to American defeat in Vietnam. American leaders came to see military conflict through managerial terms and numbers; they sought to maximize credits and minimize debits by using resources efficiently, and they tried to increase production and concurrently decrease waste and cost. They also assumed that this method was suited to modern wars, which were essentially wars of attrition. Based on that assumption, they adopted kill-ratios as their criteria of success in the business of wearing down the enemy. They could not see that the war was a political struggle to win Vietnamese hearts and minds. They never realized that waging a war of attrition, which involved napalming villages and ruining farmland, was counterproductive and dissatisfied customers. Their measures told them that victory was inevitable and led them to overlook how the Vietnamese replaced their losses even at the peak of U.S. involvement. Hence, for Gibson, American defeat in Vietnam was inherent in the managerial thinking that was institutionalized in the Pentagon and in American society. Managerial techniques were perfectly applied, but to problems for which they were unsuited, and that was why America lost.[31]

Similarly, the results of management science in the war discredited its assumptions, particularly the notion that quantitative information allowed policymakers to distance themselves from confusing details, transcend politics, and make rational decisions. In practice, systems analysts found that information was always politically loaded. When analysts' data about enemy strength showed that the United States was losing the war, the generals and admirals rejected the data. The brass complained about "computer types" who had no expertise in military matters and did not know "their ass from a hole in the ground." Pentagon leaders soon fought science with science, quickly hiring their own mathematical mercenaries. As a result of stalemate among systems analysts, policy was made the old-fashioned way, according to who had the most power rather than who had the best data. Yet when systems analysts embraced the preconceptions of the Pentagon brass for fear of offending their bosses, they still remained stuck in political muck. By accepting optimistic intelligence estimates that showed the war going the American way, they generated figures and charts that helped justify the continuation of the war and the perpetuation of infantry tactics, defoliation projects, and bombing campaigns that were not only military failures but morally reprehensible.[32] Such numerical abstractions distanced leaders from the destruction and human suffering caused by their decisions. As a test case, Vietnam showed that quantification provided no escape from scientific error, strategic blunders, bureaucratic politics, or ethical judgment.

As an aid to weapons evaluation and procurement, systems analysis fared little better.[33] Failures to live up to positivist promises were particularly evident in the debate that occurred in the late 1960s and early 1970s over a proposed antiballistic missile (ABM) system. In that debate, operations researchers inside the Pentagon convincingly demonstrated the Soviet threat to U.S. intercontinental ballistic missiles and the need for a defensive system. Meanwhile opponents outside the defense establishment showed, equally convincingly, how the proposed defense system was impractical. Since the analysts were using identical methods but arriving at contradictory recommendations, they appeared less like scientists and more like lawyers. They were defending points of view like a lawyer making the best case for a client by interpreting evidence in the most favorable way. Some management scientists, looking back on the embarrassing spectacle after the United States had abandoned the ABM plan, described the ABM system as an emperor without clothes and the Pentagon analysts as sycophants trying to prove that he was dressed.

During the debate, leaders of ORSA became concerned that the "contradictory testimony" by analysts before congressional committees was calling into question "the validity of the entire operations research approach to the solution of important problems." It was, they said, undermining "the confidence of the public" in OR techniques and causing government leaders to "become confused rather then enlightened." To address the issue, the organization established an investigatory committee. The committee, however, knew who buttered their bread and, not surprisingly, discovered faults in the presentations of the opponents of the ABM system. Their report also established guidelines, which were supposed to direct management scientists in their work and public testimony. The guidelines called for analysts to become more "professional" by purging themselves of "prior prejudice," breathing in the "scientific spirit," and feeling out "the public interest." Yet the committee acknowledged that operations research could not settle disputes apolitically when it admitted that each analyst had responsibilities to "the sponsoring elements."[34]

Nevertheless, during this same period, management science was also being institutionalized in federal and state government. When President Johnson prescribed one technique, planning-programming-budgeting, for all agencies of the federal government in 1967, he contended that it had "proved its worth many times over in the Defense Department" and that it would bring to government "the most advanced techniques of modern business management."[35] Eventually such methods were applied extensively in nearly every federal agency and department, and especially in space exploration, macroeconomic planning, health and welfare programs, waste and resource management, and educational reform.

Performance in these areas was affected by problems resembling those in the military sector. According to Ida Hoos, the leading chronicler of the subject, management scientists had great difficulty in clarifying goals and defining systems. Particularly in social programs, finding valid, apolitical measurement criteria was difficult. Sometimes the procedures became mere "folderol" used in "*ex post facto* justification for the preferences and predilections of persons in higher places." In addition, use of the techniques led elected officials to rely on experts and thus sometimes threatened constitutional checks and balances. Yet, as Hoos noted, the problems did not prevent continued use. Proponents could claim that no better alternative existed and that the technique was easy to use. And it continued to enjoy nearly unquestioned prestige. Myths about its success in one area justified its application in others.[36]

One major justification for its application in government had been its alleged success in managing business. But in the 1970s a crisis emerged in American manufacturing, and management science seemed to lose its magic.

Challenging Orthodoxy

Indeed, by the mid-1970s, difficulties with the techniques in the military, government, and business were creating turmoil in the profession in Britain and the United States. This was most apparent in a growing debate about what was wrong with management science and what should be done to fix it. These disagreements signified that the discipline was experiencing a "Kuhnian crisis" and dividing into schools, each struggling to establish a single paradigm for the science.[37] To establish itself, each of the new schools—the scientific, practical, political, revolutionary, and entrepreneurial—criticized the official management science paradigm.

One criticism of orthodoxy was developed by a British scientific school that was excited by the discovery that operations research was unscientific. To these critics, the pioneers of the profession had taken elaborate measures after the Second World War to create a "myth" that theirs was a positive science like physics. Unfortunately, this public relations "front" ended up deceiving practitioners. Ideology had clouded vision and had prevented OR mandarins from understanding the organizations they were trying to improve, diverted their attention from becoming the scientists they claimed to be, bogged them down in impractical publications in "applied mathematics," and discouraged them from testing rival theories in order to come up with "a general problem solving approach." Lacking the understanding of scientists, they had become mere technicians; and their schools had trained more technicians, thereby creating a "self-reinforcing" process that prevented the field from becoming scientific. And lacking general scientific knowledge or skills beyond inapplicable mathematics, they had always had more success with simple, tactical problems than with complex, strategic ones.

The British scientific critics wanted to reform the profession, but their proposals were vague. They simply concluded that the profession could best achieve technical success by adopting a more accurate self-image, a more appropriate epistemology, a more general methodology, and a more realistic organization theory.[38]

The imprecision of the scientific critics prevented them from having much impact. In many respects the scientific school's lack of precision stemmed from a misunderstanding of their profession's history. They placed too much emphasis on ideology and not enough on market standing, thus distorting the reasons why they were schizophrenic, split between the personality of the abstract mathematician and that of the tactical technician. From the beginning most practitioners had known they were selling their services to bureaucracies and recognized that their scientific status was their best selling point. In business they recognized that they would be rewarded for technical potency, not for theoretical prowess. And as technicians, they had little opportunity to become scientists who tested rival theories and set forth generalizations. In the role assigned them, their working relationship with business was at least as influential as their scientific ideology in preventing them from becoming generalists. In academe, in contrast, they were pressured to publish or perish, and they published mathematics because that was what OR mandarins knew best.

In addition, the scientific critics erroneously assumed that operations research lacked a general theory of management. Actually, management scientists always had a theory: the purpose of business was to make a profit, and operations research could and should help maximize that profit. Their disappointment about periodic failure was as much a sign of excessive faith in their methods as anything else. In any event, the scientific critics were not revolutionaries; they were challenging the established paradigm so that they could fulfill its promises. They wanted to become more rational bureaucrats.

In America, critics never developed so theoretical an attack, in part because they believed that the profession already suffered from too much theory. It

had, so these practical critics charged, become an ivory-tower discipline removed from the problems of managers; management scientists had become
planners for planners of planners.

One early critic of this sort was C. Jackson Grayson, who thought that
managers and management scientists worked in "two separate cultures." The
scientists were so fascinated with their techniques that they took too long to
respond and tried to make decisions based on data that was "inaccessible,
nonexistent, or uncompiled." And often, Grayson contended, they worked on
nonexistent management problems, tackled relatively minor ones with "over-
kill tools," omitted real variables from "messy" problems, and built "elegant
models comprehensible to only their colleagues."[39]

Arguing along the same lines, Peter Drucker, once a promoter of the techniques, pronounced them "a disappointment." He blamed failures on the
pioneers' fixation with their tools and lack of understanding of managerial
goals. At one level, they looked for places to apply some "beautiful gimmick"
or wrote books entitled "155 Applications of Linear Programming." Consequently they typically worked on trivial or peripheral problems. At another
level, Drucker anticipated the entrepreneurial criticisms of the 1980s when he
condemned their "futile" quest for permanent solutions and their attempts at
"eliminating" risk. Trying to eliminate risk led to "rigidity," the "greatest risk of
all" since risk was inherent in business.[40]

Similarly, Theodore Levitt, an old school scientific manager, argued that
operations research had become a "scholasticism" that valued its processes
more than profits. Not only had it failed to live up to its promise of simplifying
decision making, but its "zeal for managerial perfection" actually made decisions more complicated. It threatened to induce "paralyzing professionalization" and "stupefying bureaucratization," particularly since its "pretensions to
utility" were exceeded only by the "awe" that managers felt toward the mathematical "shamen." They were given "increasing respect in almost direct proportion to their increased incomprehensibility and declining relevance." But
managers who realized that the techniques were "pure poppycock" were afraid
to say so for fear of being seen as "lacking in modern management sensi-
bilities."[41]

Harold J. Leavitt, a mandarin trained in psychology, believed that the profession had overemphasized some parts of problem solving. Particularly its ideal
of the "analytic manager" was not so much "wrong" as it was "limited and
incomplete." The belief that valid knowledge was measurable and numerical
and that mathematical techniques could rationalize everything had led to the
hegemony of "unidimensional" MBAs. "Number pushers" made good "staff

men" who were effective at "ordering alternatives," just like McNamara had been. But also like McNamara, they were severely limited as leaders because they lacked the experience, specialized knowledge, understanding of people, and moral vision to be effective at "problem finding" and "solution implementing."[42]

Another practical critic, by far the most influential and dramatic, was Russell Ackoff, a coauthor of the first OR textbook. In 1979 he claimed that operations research in America was "dead," or at least "catatonic." It had been struck down by professionalization, which caused practice to become technique-driven rather than problem-driven. And the profession had become dominated by academics, who taught students "the use of mathematical models and algorithms rather than the ability to formulate management problems, solve them, and implement and maintain their solutions in turbulent environments." As a result, management scientists understood management in the same abstract way that a "eunuch" understood "sex." They had become sterile, were successful only in performing simple, isolated tasks, and spent their energy searching for optimal solutions that could not be applied, looking for data that did not exist, and implementing policies that quickly became obsolete. They had, he said, become so enamored with "mathematical masturbation" that their tools were impotent when exposed to "messes," that is, to ever changing "systems of problems." "A radical transformation" would have to occur before operations research could hold its head up again and enjoy a healthy "intercourse" with management.[43]

Unlike British scientific critics, the American practical critics proposed specific reforms. They recommended that operations researchers undergo extensive, realistic training in management. For to suppose, Ackoff said, that rote learning of mathematical techniques should be the basis of managerial training was equivalent to teaching doctors surgical techniques but not anatomy. Grayson carried the medical analogy further and thought that training should include internships similar to those of medical doctors; interns could transcend mental manipulations of mathematics and gain hands-on experience with management. In addition, others recommended that university teachers mix research and practice of management science so that they could keep in touch with real business problems. Leavitt, admitting his ideas were a bit "far out," suggested that training MBAs should go beyond analytic thinking by exposing them to Zen, transcendental meditation, the right side of the brain, sensitivity training, and the teaching of Don Juan as told to Carlos Casteneda.[44]

Similarly, the critics proposed technical reforms that would be problem-oriented rather than method-oriented. Grayson advised practitioners to begin with studying the problem and searching for ways to solve it, being careful not to send "the tool in search of a problem." Drucker suggested that managers find uses for operations research that would not involve futile quests for permanent, optimum solutions. Researchers' time, he thought, was better spent testing basic assumptions, goals, and procedures; helping managers understand their organizations; and clarifying alternatives for managers to choose from. And Ackoff thought that management science should learn from its failures and abandon its attempts to predict and prepare for the future. Instead it should help managers adapt to "a turbulent environment" by helping them to "manage messes" on a continual basis; it should help them select desirable goals and discover ways to attain them.[45]

The reformers also proposed organizational changes but were of two minds about how to proceed. They were divided on whether operations research should seek out line assignments or avoid them. Grayson believed that line assignments encouraged practitioners to work on definite tasks and made them responsible for decisions. But Ackoff thought that one cause of the death of operations research had been its passage from high positions in "the head" of the organization to low places in "the bowels." In the bottom of the firm, its techniques were applied to independent problems, and practitioners lost sight of the interaction of the parts. They needed positions at the top to see and manage the entire system.[46]

Still another critique to emerge within the profession during the 1970s was the political one questioning the way in which management science had dealt with values and conflicts. Such political critics denied that practitioners could easily apply mathematics to questions of value. And unlike those writing from the scientific and practical perspectives, they directly challenged the way in which business ends and bureaucratic means had become inherent in operations research. They demanded "democratic," really corporative, reforms.

One side of the political critique insisted that the profession had political dimensions. The studies of British scholar Colin Eden, for example, showed that in practice the researcher was not simply an expert applying techniques learned from textbooks to empirical problems. The investigator was also a political actor interacting with other political actors. Sometimes the political process involved exercise of power by a superior who imposed a project and then used the researcher as a calculating instrument. On other occasions, the practitioner sought to impose definitions of problems and their solutions on the sponsor. At still other times, the sponsor and researcher negotiated, together defining problems and working out answers.[47]

Realizing that the researcher was a political actor led this group of critics to confront moral questions that were commonly ignored in orthodox literature. As early as 1970, for example, C. West Churchman, one of the most prominent pioneers who helped shape the official paradigm, had become concerned that the standard methodology had ignored the moral dilemma inherent in selecting values. As in any science, the way the practitioner collected information was influenced by his or her theoretical and moral presuppositions, which in turn were affected by how he or she identified the system in which he or she operated and the sponsor being served. If, as was usually the case, the researcher accepted the values of the manager and the system as givens and assumed that maximizing their values was good, then the research was likely to improve managerial performance and uphold managerial power. But operations research done this way denied people affected by the decision any opportunity to participate in the decision-making process. Standard operating procedure, Churchman said, thus reversed Kant's moral law by always treating people as means and never as ends.

To Churchman the standard approach, serving the manager and treating everyone else as factors of production, was morally irresponsible. But the science of operations research provided no guide for choosing values. Researchers had no mathematical technique that could make value choices objective, indicate which values should be maximized, or reconcile conflicts between the sponsoring manager and people affected by his or her choices. The moral problem had to be solved in other ways. For Churchman the answer was use of a Hegelian dialectic that would have all people affected by a decision openly debate their goals and select a synthesis of their values. Operations researchers could then use this synthetic value as a guide for their work and as a goal to be maximized. And in this way, the profession could strive to improve "the whole system," "the Whole World."[48]

Churchman's analysis and others like it gained attention and were widely discussed and elaborated as the economic crisis deepened during the 1970s and 1980s. Several theorists made his Hegelian dialectic into a full-blown system for clarifying strategy and reconciling goals in bureaucracies.[49] They envisioned a participatory process, which, as in all corporative schemes, offered a means of resolving conflicts that appealed both to democratic ideals of self-determination and to managerial ideals of group consensus. Everyone was promised access to decision making. But the form of that access was vaguely defined, and the assumption was that managers would remain managers and management scientists would be mediators. Their corporative theory promised, in other words, a technical solution to conflicts caused by bureaucracy without a revolution in existing arrangements. And this promise was attractive to practitioners who were forming strategic policy and facing political fights in their organizations. Corporatist negotiations could help them clarify goals and resolve conflicts without affecting their use of mathematical tools.

Consequently, many theorists came to see corporatist collaboration as a way to improve the performance and reputation of the profession. Gene Woolsey, for instance, who edited an operations research journal, argued that if practitioners failed to learn from the history of scientific management and did not put more emphasis on cooperation and helping nonmanagers achieve their goals, the profession would be derided as another Taylorist "theory X" that treated people as objects.[50]

Similarly, Russell Ackoff, a longtime colleague and friend of Churchman, saw corporatism as a way to "resurrect" the dying profession. He advocated what he called "interactive planning," a system in which all "stakeholders," everyone affected by a problem, would take part in studying it and determining a solution. Among the advantages was the way it could bring people from all parts of an organization to cope with "messes," that is, with interdependent problems that had to be solved as "wholes." In addition, it could help operations researchers drop their childish notions of "objectivity" and learn to accept responsibility for decisions. It also could improve "the quality of life" by bringing values other than economic growth into consideration. And by allowing stakeholders to choose ends and means, it could develop personality, release creativity, motivate effort, encourage consensus, and find a happy medium between capitalism and communism.[51]

The interactive planning and Hegelian dialectic that Ackoff and Churchman helped develop during the 1970s has been called "soft" operations research, in contrast to the "hard" techniques they had helped establish during the 1950s. Hard operations research, it was found, worked best when applied to simple, static, tactical, hard problems, where the job was well defined and all the practitioner had to do was find the best tool. It did not work well in the circumstances of the late 1960s, when practitioners began facing more complex, fluid, strategic, soft questions and had difficulty defining problems and ends. When they tried to solve soft problems with hard methods, they failed or aroused opposition. Consequently, they developed methods for achieving consensus and adapting to change before they booted their computers.[52]

While members of the profession were criticizing professional orthodoxy and developing alternatives, the economic crisis in Britain and the United States was deepening. And as the crisis deepened, orthodox operations research came under the fire of two new, very different enemies. In Britain, radical members of the profession developed a revolutionary interpretation of the technique. And in America, critics, mainly from outside the profession, formulated an entrepreneurial interpretation. Common to both perspectives were a repudiation of the legitimacy of operations research and a condemnation of the separation of planning from doing.

The revolutionary critique developed from viewing operations research through Marxist lenses. Radicals like Michael Jackson, Jonathan Rosenhead, and Colin Thunhurst now saw the science as having been created by managerial capitalism, for managerial capitalism.[53] It had grown out of the separation of managing from doing that isolated managers from the production process and limited their ability to control and exploit it. As a technology and an ideology, the radicals argued, operations research duplicated bureaucratic processes under capitalism and treated people as factors of production. As a technique, it assumed that decisions were based on scientific analysis rather than on "exercises of power," and it programmed and centralized decision making; dehumanized workers from social subjects to economic objects; treated people, machines, materials, and money in the same way; reduced human relations to quantifiable exchanges in a market; subordinated conflicts over values to monetary calculations of cost and benefit; and drove out all measures of value except the bottom line of the accountant's ledger. And even as its techniques perpetuated managerial capitalism, its ideology reified capitalism and made capitalist relations of production appear natural and inevitable. By presuming consensus on the ends of capitalism, it reduced social controversies to discussion of the best way to solve the problems of managers and thus encouraged people to entrust administration to self-proclaimed technocrats.[54]

According to the radicals, moreover, the corporatism of soft OR offered no improvement over the bureaucratism of hard OR. The participative schemes of Churchman and Ackoff assumed that individuals in rational conversations could form agreements that served the interests of everyone. But, in actuality, powerful, privileged participants with better access to financial and intellectual resources would dominate; in such a setting inequality would be reinforced rather than redressed. Because the softest things about the soft theorists were the appendages above their shoulders, they could not understand power or see that participation in a hierarchical setting only perpetuated that setting.[55]

Since management science, whatever its form, served managers, the radicals thought a "workers' science" was needed. Labor needed "a critical OR," which could demystify the operations research of managers, challenge their plans, and help the struggle against management by creating counterplans. Its methods would seek liberation rather than control, resolve conflicts through negotiation rather than power, and pursue goals beyond the bottom line. The radicals acknowledged that the beneficiaries of this new science typically lacked the resources to pay for operations research. But presumably the government would pick up the tab, because the radicals envisioned Britain as having democratic socialism and a more or less planned economy.[56]

Of course American critics seldom traced failures in operations research to permanent contradictions in capitalism. Americans believed operations research, rather than being too capitalistic, was not capitalistic enough. The approach, said the exponents of the entrepreneurial critique, had obscured entrepreneurial vision and caused economic stagnation. This view was expressed in particular by a Harvard group that included the management consultants Robert Hayes and William Abernathy and the industrial policy advocates Ira C. Magaziner and Robert B. Reich.[57]

These critics argued that entrepreneurial myopia had begun in the American way of work, especially in the Taylorist separation of managing from doing and in divisional and conglomerate organizations. Both developments had helped empower central staff analysts. The analysts differed from previous generations of business leaders by having backgrounds in law, marketing, or finance rather than in technology or production.[58] Their training, Hayes and Abernathy said, caused them to value "analytical detachment and methodological elegance" and to practice "management by the numbers."[59]

Many of these new managers, the argument continued, saw the firm as a sort of bank. Like a bank, the firm held a fixed amount of capital; and like bankers, the managers rearranged its assets to secure the highest returns on short-term, low-risk investments. So unlike classical entrepreneurs, they avoided developing new markets, pioneering innovative technology, or investing in projects that returned a profit only after a considerable time. Lacking expertise in production and technology and understanding only marketing strategy, mathematics, and the abstractions of the balance sheet, the new managers pursued policies that were purely pecuniary and catered to present consumer demand, exploited current products and processes, and imitated the successes of other companies. They sold pet rocks and uniform potato chips rather than small cars or specialty ceramics. And more significantly, they tried to generate profits through innovations in accounting, speculation, tax avoidance, or litigation, and through efforts to secure protective tariffs and governmental subsidies and to emasculate regulations.

To the entrepreneurial critics, applying fiduciary reasoning and techniques to industry was financially dangerous and morally irresponsible. It led, Robert Hayes thought, to such shortsighted practices as "discounted cash flow." This method achieved high rates of return in the present by neglecting plans for the future and by postponing necessary capital investments and putting money in safe accounts. Such a method amounted to valuing today's dollars more than tomorrow's dollars, which, Hayes reasoned, was like operating on the goose to get more eggs right away rather than nurturing its capacity to lay eggs in years to come.[60] Over the long run, businesses could not be operated like investment portfolios. For maximizing short-run returns trapped firms with archaic products and technologies, as was shown with America's smokestack industries and their declining ability to compete against innovative foreign firms.

Management science, Reich and Magaziner contended, led to practices that were undercutting American living standards and undermining national interests. Management scientists made decisions based on quantitative criteria, ignored qualitative considerations, and ended up selecting any means that maximized short-term profit. As a result, it led managers away from creating new wealth. They became engaged, so Reich and Magaziner complained, in redividing the economic pie rather than expanding it. And while this might be lucrative for the managers and firms involved, it eventually took money away from productive projects, left American markets vulnerable to competitors from abroad, and threatened American prosperity, jobs, and living standards.[61]

Worth noting, too, was how the rhetoric of such critics played on Veblenesque dichotomies. They saw business in terms of polarities between production and profit, engineering and finance, good and evil; and in terms of these opposites, quantitative techniques fell on the evil side. This came across most clearly in Reich's book *The Next American Frontier*, where he contrasted "paper entrepreneurialism" with the "real" kind. "Paper entrepreneurs," he said, could only manage "paper, not product." They earned their salary through "manipulation of symbols and the abstract scrutiny of disembodied measures of firm performance" and kept "their eyes sharply fixed on the short-term bottom line." Unlike "real" entrepreneurs, they were disengaged from "real production problems."[62]

The dichotomy was also central to the journalist David Halberstam's *The Reckoning*, a long morality tale about Ford and Nissan. At Ford, according to Halberstam, "product men" and "finance men" had struggled for control of the company, and the moral of the outcome was clear. The finance men, McNamara's whiz kids, had won, and the company floundered. Meanwhile, at Nissan, the product men generally directed the finance men, and together they made ingenious, quality cars that turned a profit and helped make their nation wealthier.[63]

The dichotomy probably made more sense as rhetorical ploy than as economic analysis, and rhetorically it did strike a responsive chord. The *Harvard*

Business Review article by Hayes and Abernathy led to more comments, mostly favorable, than any other ever published by the journal.[64] Reich's book also had considerable impact, becoming an economic *kama sutra* for Gary Hart and making Reich the business guru for Democratic presidential candidates during the eighties. And Halberstam's epic became a Book of the Month Club selection and a best-seller. Apparently, the profit-production dichotomy appealed to an older Protestant ethic that had condemned wealth acquired without community service, and this appeal could be invoked to condemn managers who fiddled with tax forms while plants closed. Just as important to its appeal, too, was the way that the Veblenesque rhetoric cloaked a Schumpeterian message; it condemned predatory managerial practices without indicting the price system and thus promised that a new cadre of engineers and entrepreneurs could save the nation from parasitic MBAs.

The idea that risk-averse techniques had caused industrial decline, however, was not necessarily sound. Industrial decline, some have persuasively argued, would probably have occurred regardless of the techniques adopted by American managers. Seymour Melman, for example, has contended that because "the permanent war economy" enabled managers to make profits without producing normal goods, directed money and talent toward nonproductive sectors, and caused managers to drop "cost-minimizing" strategies for "cost-pass-along" ones, it produced firms bloated by cost-plus contracts that were too sluggish to keep up with lean, mean foreign invaders.[65] And similarly, others have pointed out that decline was inherent in the passing of the temporary advantages in resources and technology that America enjoyed between 1945 and 1965. But after nations around the world retooled, the American economy had to pay what Veblen had called the "penalty of taking the lead."[66] It was saddled with the heavy burden of obsolete technology while foreign firms raced ahead by learning from American mistakes, purchasing the latest equipment (often from American firms), and drawing on cheaper resources.

In addition, factors besides management by the numbers could explain why business leaders chose to maximize present profits. Managers, for instance, required no sophisticated techniques to help them decide to continue product lines that were losing market standing but were still profitable, which apparently described American automakers' early response to foreign imports. Likewise the well-known turnover of American managers, their habit of circulating from job to job, firm to firm, with an eye on making a quick score and finding a better job elsewhere, no doubt contributed to a short-term outlook.[67] Furthermore, as corporate consultant Jordon D. Lewis pointed out, the unstable business environment of the seventies, manifested in unpredictable price and supply fluctuations, undermined confidence, broke the will to invest, and encouraged a focus on achieving quarterly gains. In such a setting, manufacturing firms behaved like rentiers living off past investments. And finally, entrepreneurs seeking outside capital recognized that achieving quarterly profits was necessary if they wanted to maintain the confidence of Wall Street; even temporarily weak performance on the stock market could depress share prices and drive away potential investors. Lewis concluded that economic conditions and investment structures made people in business averse to risk; but he admitted that their short-term focus encouraged using analytic techniques, which could select opportunities offering the most present value.[68] It could be that aversion to risk came first and affected quantitative techniques rather than the other way around. Risk aversion could have been a historical aberration rather than a permanent consequence of quantitative techniques.

A more radical interpretation of risk aversion by Barry Bluestone and Bennett Harrison pointed to contradictions inherent in capitalism, especially to the relentless pursuit of maximum profits that gave people in business no incentive to protect community goods. According to their view, biases in management science were not the basic cause of the problem, although the methods did make it easier for managers to "divest" from manufacturing and "deindustrialize" the American economy; the problem was inherent in capitalism itself.[69] And in this view, as in those emphasizing market instability, managerial turnover, military contracts, Third World industrialization, and capital structures, the remedy lay not in reforms of managerial techniques but in larger institutional innovations.

For their part, the entrepreneurial critics wanted to save capitalism from bad capitalists by getting rid of "pseudo-professional" managers who could only manipulate numbers. They would change corporate promotion systems and replace number-crunchers with production people who had hands-on experience with making things. In addition, Reich thought that business and government policy should encourage the "new organization of work" that was "more collaborative, participatory, and egalitarian" and associated with "flexible" as opposed to mass production. By fusing managing and doing, he said, the new organization was drawing managers closer to employees, away from stockholders, and making them more like Japanese entrepreneurs. And as they became more concerned about creating industrial clans, preserving jobs, and solving production problems, they were naturally adopting a long-term outlook. This evolution could be hastened by tax incentives that rewarded companies making productive investments, raising employee participation, and maintaining employment levels. Government could also help by setting up regional investment banks to provide long-term, low-interest loans and protect firms from the volatility of Wall Street. When firms were run by engineers with entrepreneurial vision, Reich believed, business could enjoy "economic health," and the nation could achieve "social justice."[70]

The complaints by Reich and others showed that the assets of management science in the 1950s had become liabilities by the 1980s. Their philosophical premises had committed them to modes of governance that had lost some legitimacy; positivism had committed them to abstract analysis, Taylorism to ivory-tower planning, and systems theory to a conservative outlook. Indeed the premises were decidedly conservative and attuned to adaptation and adjustment. These premises had helped operations researchers get their feet in the doorway to power. But once investigators had stepped through that door and started making strategy, an ethic of adaptation offered vague and even dangerous guidance. It led them to make their techniques and bureaucracy ends in themselves, which further led to the mathematics of cost-benefit analysis and the ethics in the profit commandment.

While profit maximization was useful to individual careers, in the long run it could also be detrimental, as Peter Drucker had been writing for decades, to the firm and free market capitalism. Profit offered no simple, unitary ethical criteria that could provide clear guidance in balancing other goals and finding a moral way to do business. Vulgar cost-benefit analysis was especially valueless for making important decisions about fulfilling social responsibilities and engineering innovation. It inspired an attraction to unproductive, beggar-thy-neighbor transactions; often led to rigidity and obsolescence; and ultimately cultivated the McNamaran illusion that managing business and people was an exercise in managing numbers.

Essentially such dysfunctions stemmed from the way that operations researchers and management scientists applied Taylorism to management. They attempted to use scientific methods and mathematics to simplify decision making and separate the planning of decisions from deciding itself. Supreme faith in their techniques had the effect of delegating power to those techniques, thus dehumanizing management and taking Taylorism to a logical but absurd conclusion. The problems that emerged made management science appear less a science and more like what C. Wright Mills ridiculed as "crackpot realism."

Recognizing some dysfunctions in Taylorism led some mandarins to corporatism. Such reformers thought that corporatism could make operations research more useful to managers, bring managers and doers closer together, consider a wider range of ideas and values, treat people more humanely, and insure organizational survival. These reformers, however, ignored how corporatism has had its own ethic of adjustment to bureaucratic capitalism and has seen harmony as a means to enhance managerial power and profit.

While no one can predict the future, the dominance of a corporatist management science in American business would appear unlikely. Federal industrial policy has not proven popular, as evidenced by the defeats of proponents like Gary Hart and Michael Dukakis. And one might expect that managers who were number-crunchers could prove reluctant to promote people-minded corporatists or production-minded engineers. This would seem particularly likely in companies that had made a profit using abstract techniques and so lacked incentive to change managerial cadres. As Reich acknowledged, whatever problems the management scientists and "paper entrepreneurs" were creating for others, they were raking in profits. Under circumstances where the techniques were a pecuniary success, appeals to "civic virtue" would most likely fall on deaf ears.[71] Each manager, moreover, would continue to face complex problems, problems that defy rationalization. And facing such problems while being watched by ambitious subordinates, suspicious boards of directors, and greedy stock traders, managers would likely wrap themselves in computer printouts, if only to cover their asses.

3

Economics
and Cybernetics

The Bureaucratic Rationality
of Herbert A. Simon

Herbert Alexander Simon (b. 1916) has been the most diversified and honored of recent management mandarins. In more than twenty books and nearly six hundred articles, he has contributed not only to organization theory and management science but also to economics, political science, statistics, cybernetics, computer science, cognitive psychology, and the philosophy of science. Joking that critics have complimented him on the range of his "dilettantism" and accused him of "wandering here and there," he has rightly replied that "scatteration" has obscured his "monomania." His whole academic career has been focused on one problem: a search for "a science of man" based on "his dual nature as a social and a rational animal."[1] And primarily for Simon's research into "the decision-making process within economic organizations," the Royal Swedish Academy of Sciences awarded him the Nobel Prize in 1978.[2]

Such achievements have made Simon the leading post-Taylorite theorist. He sought to go beyond scientific management by rejecting Taylor's mechanistic psychology and organization theory and by developing more realistic explanations of human and bureaucratic rationality. By studying how decisions were actually made in bureaucracies, Simon intended to teach managers how decisions should be made. A realistic theory of rationality, he argued, could be used to perform the task it explained in much the same sense that a scientific description of a good chess player could be used to play good chess.[3]

So intellectual an approach has proved quite remarkable, particularly when compared with the work of other mandarins. While many wrote recipes for administrative cookbooks, Simon concocted an economics and epistemology for managers. His work was so novel, indeed in some respects even revolutionary, that it helped lead not only to important theoretical advances but to progress in computer technology as well. But from the beginning his notions about rationality were challenged by economists, political scientists, philosophers, and computer scientists. They showed that for all his departures from Taylorism, he did not go beyond its basic psychology and premises.

Economics and Political Science

Looking back on his career, Simon would divide his work into two phases.[4] The first or "decision making" phase lasted from 1935 to the mid-1950s. In it, he drew on ideas from logical positivism, institutional economics, political science, and organization theory to challenge orthodox notions in economics and management. The second or "information processing" phase began in the mid-1950s and continued into the 1980s. During this phase, Simon worked out his early ideas in the new fields of cybernetics, computer science, artificial intelligence, and cognitive psychology. Central, of course, to both phases was the study of rationality.

Simon's concern with this problem developed quite early. Growing up in Milwaukee he began as a high school student to read his uncle's old college economics texts. And while still a youth, he decided that he wanted to apply mathematical techniques to social scientific problems. In 1933 these interests led him to the University of Chicago where he studied economics under the tutelage of the neoclassical "Chicago school." He decided, however, to major in political science, primarily, he recalled, to escape a dull accounting class required for an economics degree.[5]

Even as an undergraduate, Simon was dissatisfied with the theory of rationality espoused by the Chicago school. A crucial experience that shaped his thinking was an internship in municipal government in 1935. Observing a dispute between administrators, he tried to apply neoclassical price theory. But he found that neoclassical ideas were of little use in describing disputes over incommensurable values, unquantifiable production functions, and expectations about the future. Upon graduating in 1936, he determined to undertake "a single-minded search" to understand how choices were really made in bureaucracies.[6]

Simon's first steps in this quest came in graduate school in political science at Chicago and in positions at the University of California and the Illinois

Institute of Technology. His revised dissertation became his first major work, *Administrative Behavior: A Study of Decision-Making Processes in Administrative Organization.*[7]

Simon justified his study using the "logical positivism" he had learned from the writings of A. J. Ayer and the lectures of Rudolf Carnap, an Austrian émigré who had come to Chicago in the 1930s. From these philosophers, Simon learned that metaphysical statements were speculative and nonsensical; that ethical statements were imperatives incapable of scientific validation; that knowledge had to be reconstructed on scientific foundations; that the reconstruction should be based on logical precision, linguistic rigor and empirical accuracy; and that knowledge of psychology was crucial, since the mind structured experience.[8] Although the clear separation the logical positivists established between fact and value was soon blurred by philosophers and scientists of all sorts, the distinctions remained influential in Simon's thought.[9]

In *Administrative Behavior*, Simon claimed his work was scientific. He asserted that his "sociology of administration" studied what managers actually did, that it was an "organizational biology" describing "the anatomy and physiology" of the firm. It was distinct from the "practical science of administration," which told managers what they should do, and which was an organizational "medicine" prescribing cures for "ills." Prescriptions were not scientific and contained an "ethical element," an "imperative" that could not be verified as either true or false.[10]

Still Simon admitted that his work was both biology and medicine. His goal was to understand how and why bureaucrats made decisions, to know "the rationality of decisions" and how managers acted to "influence" them and achieve "efficiency." His models were Taylor's studies of metal cutting and the Hawthorne studies of fatigue, which were scientific because each separated ethical from factual elements and sought to discover the one best way. And he insisted that all managerial doctors needed to understand organizational biology before they could offer sound remedies.[11]

Simon doubted, moreover, that managers could understand bureaucratic rationality by studying classical organization theory. Theorists like Frederick Taylor, Luther Gulick, and Lyndall Urwick had developed "principles of administration" to guide management decisions. Each principle offered advice on planning, specialization, unity of command, or span of control.[12] But Simon thought the principles were hopelessly contradictory "proverbs." Each proverb contradicted others; for instance, unity of command specified that orders come from a single boss, but specialization often resulted in authority divided among experts. And since classical theory provided no objective means to choose between "equally applicable" but "mutually incompatible principles," he ridiculed it as little more than a set of "pompous inanities."[13]

Subsequently Simon would also conclude that the classical theorists did not understand psychology. They saw the employee as a passive "instrument" easily manipulated by management. In terms of Taylor's engineering psychology, for instance, people were machines, each with a limited capacity, speed, and durability, and each easily turned on by monetary reward. Likewise, Gulick and Urwick saw the employee as "an inert instrument performing the tasks assigned to him," a "given rather than a variable in the system." Failing to understand that employees had their own goals, Simon thought, had led to the assumption that bureaucracy could achieve rationality. But bureaucracy had been shown to have dysfunctional conflicts, "unanticipated consequences," and irrationality that the classical theorists could not explain.[14]

By the early 1950s, Simon had figured out why neoclassical economics was mistaken. The neoclassical theory of the firm wrongly presumed that employment was essentially a "sales contract," in which money was exchanged for a specific commodity and sellers did not care how the commodity was used by buyers. But in reality, Simon reasoned, people did not sell their labor and become "completely passive factors" deployed at the whim of the employer. On the contrary, employees were interested in how their labor was used. Both they and the employer were trying to maximize their "satisfaction functions." Therefore, understanding bureaucratic rationality required not only knowing wage rates but also knowing the values of employees and the way bosses exercised authority. Neoclassical theory was oblivious to this because it lacked conceptions of conflict and authority in bureaucracy.[15]

In addition, Simon concluded that the neoclassical theory of rationality was defective. Here he was influenced by American institutional economics, which rejected the classical rationalist psychology because it neglected culture, organizations, and politics. He was directly influenced by the institutionalism of the economist John R. Commons (1862–1945).[16]

Under Commons's influence, Simon created a new institutional economics for managers that studied bargaining inside bureaucracies. Commons, whose ideas had been much affected by jurisprudence, contended that economists should study "the transaction." They should examine how transactions in institutions were regulated by "working rules" or customs forged through bargaining. These rules regulated decisions and collectivized autonomy, while justices of the court presided over the bargaining, judging the merits of the rules and arbitrating disputes.[17] For Commons's basic terms, Simon substituted *decisions* for *transactions*, *premises* for *working rules*, and *managers* for *judges*.

Another major influence on Simon was Chester I. Barnard (1886–1961). Although largely self-taught, Barnard was one of the first American mandarins to draw on the ideas of Vilfredo Pareto and Max Weber and particularly influenced human relations theorists. Organizations, he believed, were naturally rational, "cooperative systems." And while Simon rejected this proposition, he learned from Barnard that the success of an organization depended on cooperation, that cooperation rested on consent, that consent was engineered by managers, and consequently that authority, expressed by accepting the decisions of superiors, was central to any understanding of organizational behavior.[18]

Building, then, on Commons and Barnard, Simon rejected classical rationality. In *Administrative Behavior*, this rejection was implicit; by the early 1950s it had become explicit;[19] and by the late fifties, after receiving criticism from economists, it had become vituperative. Simon charged that economists were using a purely deductive method and making assumptions that could not be sustained in a post-Freudian world. They were asserting "a preposterously omniscient rationality," in which people had consistent preferences, complete knowledge of alternatives, perfect ability to calculate consequences, and the "powers of prescience and capacities of computation resembling those we usually attribute to God." And they were moving their science toward "a state of Thomistic refinement" with "little discernible relation to the actual or possible behavior of flesh-and-blood human beings." Hence, their ideas had "little or no place in the theory of organization."[20]

A science of bureaucratic rationality, Simon argued in *Administrative Behavior* and in two essays written in 1952 and the winter of 1953–54,[21] required new conceptions of human nature and choice. It recognized that humans were not maximizers. The human was in reality "a choosing organism of limited knowledge and ability." Goals were numerous, uncertain in priority, or often contradictory. Knowledge about alternative plans of action was also fragmentary, costly to acquire, and rarely sufficient to predict consequences. Moreover, even when outcomes could be accurately predicted, definite payoffs could not be meaningfully ascribed to future events. Hence plans and results could not be ranked from least to most desirable.[22]

Because of these cognitive limitations, people adopted "simplifications." Because they could not develop a general "utility function," they formed simplified models of their preferences and sought a "minimum guaranteed pay-off" for one goal at a time. For instance, a rat, when searching for food distributed randomly in a maze, ate the food that it found and did not pass over any in hope of finding another bigger cache. Similarly, because people lacked knowledge about the costs of their search for information, they limited the search; they studied alternatives sequentially and chose the first "satisfactory" one. In searching for a needle in a haystack, they did not search for the sharpest one, but only for one that was sharp enough to sew with.

Simon also argued that because satisfaction was easier to attain if desires were satiable, people often adjusted their aspiration levels according to the difficulty of a search. Responding to a difficult problem by lowering personal aspirations made it easier to find a satisfactory alternative; and by the same token, easy problems caused aspirations to rise. For example, a family selling its home initially kept the price high, studying the offers one at a time; but if no offers met their aspirations, they accepted the one that was good enough. People, Simon concluded, were "adaptive" but not capable of "unlimited adaptation"; they could "adapt well enough to 'satisfice'" but had "neither the senses nor the wits to discover an 'optimal' path."[23]

Although satisficing seemed an alternative to Taylorist mechanism and economic maximizing, it also had some embarrassing implications for a mandarin like Simon. More than anything else, it implied moral relativism. His perfectly reasonable argument that humans were not gods meant that no human could know which conception of the good was most moral or which form of government was best. Particularly no logical positivist could know since his or her philosophy disclaimed power to verify normative claims. Ironically then, Simon's satisficing, almost certainly his most important idea, seemingly led to some sort of anarchism.

For Simon, obviously, anarchism would not do. Consequently in his mind satisficing as a psychological and epistemological idea was always connected to a political and ethical ideal; the idea that humans were not gods always meant that humans had to be bureaucrats. While the notions were logically distinct (and probably a non sequitur), Simon always connected them. He cast off omniscience but kept standardized, Eisenhooverian liberal and materialistic values. Indeed he labored hard to prove that cognitive limitation, as a philosophical premise and as a physiological fact, always led to bureaucracy.

Bureaucracies, he argued, were among the "simplifications" that satisficing people created. The "single, isolated individual" recognized that he or she could never be very rational; goals were too vague, alternatives too numerous, and information too fragmentary. Hence the individual accepted employment contracts, which provided security and the possibility of achieving at least some aims. But bureaucratic life also involved surrender of "decisional autonomy" and depression of aspiration levels. A human, being "intendedly rational, but only limitedly so," could never be a maximizing "economic man." A person must settle for being a satisficing "administrative man," and this meant that "the rational individual is, and must be, an organized and institutionalized individual."[24]

In Simon's view, then, bureaucracy facilitated rationality. An institutionalized bureaucrat did not become more intelligent or rational. But decisions were made "subject to the influences of the organization group." The bureaucrat's range of choices was narrowed by the "premises" of bureaucracy and the way bureaucracy specialized roles, restricted tasks, routinized practices, simplified information, regularized communications, standardized goals, rewarded performance, and indoctrinated members. All of these focused the attention of the decision maker and limited alternative ends and means, thus restricting decisional autonomy, helping to "channelize" choice, and causing members to "adapt their decisions to the organization's objectives." In addition, the "sunk costs" of past decisions further restricted choices, rendering a predictability that generated bureaucratic "inertia." And "consistency" of decisions provided a basis for prolonged, coordinated work, and a rationality that was impossible for an individual became possible for an organization.[25]

Simon, although believing that humans were not divine, also believed that managers were closest to heaven and were needed to attain rationality. Centralizing decision making could help create experts at making choices. In addition, centralized decision making, the "vertical" division of labor, was necessary to synthesize the horizontal division of labor. A "controlling group," a cadre of managers, was needed to "set the terms of membership for all the participants," establish organizational goals, and convert vague ethical values into definite, operational premises of decision. The managers also influenced the choices of their subordinates by "the deliberate control of the environment of decision." They supervised efforts to construct "means-ends chains" and select "appropriate means to reach designated ends." In particular, they tried to ensure that group members made decisions based on "the criterion of efficiency" and chose alternatives that maximized profit and minimized waste.[26]

Superiors could not be dictators, however, because subordinates continued to pursue personal goals. Here Simon's ideas showed the influence of Barnard's concept of "equilibrium," the notion that the survival of an organization depended on inducements to employees balancing contributions from employees. Here also he showed the influence of Mayoists and their discussions of distrust between managers and workers. People accepted employment and loss of autonomy, he said, in exchange for some satisfaction of personal goals and on the understanding that work would not violate their values. Hence, if their responsibilities fell within their "zone of acceptance," they accepted the goals of the enterprise, acknowledged its authority, and contributed to its projects. But if managers tried to operate outside the zone of acceptance, then personal goals became operative, members disobeyed, and the organization "ceases to exist."[27]

Consequently, managers sought to broaden the area of acceptance and thus elevate their authority. Again following the direction taken by Barnard, Simon contended that someone had authority when one's "premises" of decision were accepted by another and when one had "the power to make decisions which guide the actions of another." Authority, he emphasized, did not rest on agreement with the premises; it rested rather on "acquiescence," that is on "a willingness to obey," to comply "irrespective of [one's] own judgment as to the merits of that decision," to suspend one's "critical faculties for choosing between alternatives," and to adopt "a criterion of choice" that made one's "own behavior dependent on the behavior of others."[28]

Simon adopted this conception of authority because he believed that it was "non-circular," value-neutral, and empirically useful. Authority defined as agreement with the premises would have been tautological and led students of organizational behavior away from investigating the processes that encouraged or thwarted acceptance. And authority as mere acceptance of premises defined a relationship that could operate "upward" and "sidewise" as well as "downward." In some circumstances subordinates exercised authority. For instance, he thought that when a manager delegated to a secretary a decision about file cabinets and accepted the secretary's choice without examining its merits, the manager was accepting the subordinate's authority. In essence, the transmission of authority was the communication of premises; and since at any point in the transmission the receiver could choose to accept or reject the premises, each person in the organization could check the authority of others. Still, without the communication of authority, there was no bureaucratic rationality.[29]

Two types of authority existed, Simon believed, "the authority of ideas" and "the authority of sanctions." The authority of ideas existed when employees accepted goals through identification and internalization. In such cases, workers identified with their team, felt that they owned the organization, and therefore used adjectives like *my* and *mine* to describe their jobs. Individuals adopted an "organization personality" distinct from their individual personalities, and they embraced a rationality that caused them to focus on their tasks and to "narrow the range of vision" to its special goals, information, and alternatives. Bureaucrats acted to maximize the organization's utility by basing their decisions on impersonal standards of efficiency. They accepted the goals and ethical premises of the firm, their superiors, their work group, and their role as "given." Once in a role, "the organizational values and situation," not "personal motives," determined the "one and only one 'best' decision." And Simon emphasized that "two persons, given the same skills, the same objectives and values, the same knowledge and information," could "rationally decide only upon the same course of action." Bureaucratic rationality could thus be inculcated through training in technical skills, teaching vocational values, or using Mayoist participation schemes.[30]

The second type of authority was the authority of sanctions. It did not depend on a bureaucratic superego but resulted from "subjecting the subordinate to discipline and control." Superiors could use rewards and punishments to widen the "area of acceptance." Still, authority did not ultimately rest on "the power of the superior to apply sanctions in case of noncompliance." On the contrary, the use of power eventually undermined authority; coercion was less efficient than consent.[31]

For this reason, Simon believed that effective managers restrained their exercise of power. They recognized that a superior was merely "a bus driver" whose passengers left unless the bus took them in the direction they wished to go and who gave "only minor discretion as to the road to be followed." Managers had to work within the limits of their subordinates' zone of acceptance. And to Simon this meant that the goals of any organization were compromises negotiated between all of its members.[32] Accordingly the "authority relation" rested on bargains freely accepted. Within the zone of acceptance, the employee willingly became an "instrument" of the firm, turning off "the switch of his own desires from nine to five" and transforming himself from "consumer to producer and back again with every rising and setting of the sun."[33]

Scientifically, many of Simon's ideas on organization theory and economics were not original. But Simon made his contribution by combining Commons's notions of bargaining among hedonists with Barnard's conceptions of equilibrium and authority. He also added new ideas describing how cognitive limitations affected human choice and how bureaucracy structured choices by controlling premises. His theories could help managers understand conflict, consent, and control in the firm.[34]

Ideologically, Simon also provided managers with a justification for bureaucracy. In his view, people were both driven to a bureaucratic existence and chose it freely. Cognitive limitations made them unsuited to a life of autonomy. The human animal was best adapted to a routinized life in a bureaucratic habitat, occupying a standardized niche that simplified decisions and regularized satisfactions. Because they were natural bureaucrats, members of the species freely chose to limit their freedom and accept authority. And in their environment they retained sufficient freedom to restrain managerial predators who sought to exploit them. Self-seeking led to constant bargaining that civilized the bureaucratic jungle. From Simon's perspective, bureaucracy was rational and legitimate.

Politically, Simon's scientific descriptions were inherently prescriptive. He showed managers how centralized decisions and specialized tasks, when they were accepted by subordinates, could limit choice and focus attention. He was forthright in admitting that his theories were "not a description of how administrators decide so much as a description of how good administrators decide."[35] And a description of how good managers decided, by teaching managers how to manage, obliterated any meaningful distinction between organizational biology and managerial medicine. So despite adding little to Taylorism and Mayoism, his work contributed to knowledge about choices and controls, and for managers, such knowledge was power.

Had Simon published nothing more after the mid-fifties, he would have already made important contributions to post-Taylorite bureaucratism. But he had not yet weathered a storm of criticism that helped drive him to abandon traditional approaches for the study of rationality.

Challenges to Economic Simonism

As Simon drew on ideas from many disciplines to create a truly scientific management, he continually offended people in other fields who regarded him as a bad practitioner of their specialties. His early work was challenged by economists who thought that he misunderstood economics and by political scientists who thought that he misunderstood politics.

For their part, neoclassical economists were concerned that his psychology threatened their scientific paradigm. Consequently they sought to defend their assumption of maximizing and to discredit Simon's idea of satisficing, especially its epistemological and psychological aspects.

One line of attack was to argue that Simon's conception of satisficing behavior was unnecessary for understanding a market economy. Armen Alchian, for example, contended that it made no difference whether or not economists accurately understood psychology. It did not matter whether they assumed that people in business were maximizers or merely satisficers. An economist needed only to assume that, in the marketplace, different managers chose different alternatives and that some alternatives were more successful than others. Over time, the relatively higher profits that resulted from some decisions would lead to the survival of the fittest decisions, managers, and firms. Those managers who initially made bad decisions would fail or would imitate more successful rivals. So even if, in the short run, people were satisficers who lacked the knowledge to maximize, trial and error in a competitive market would in the long run select maximizing decisions. And since optimal choices were naturally selected, in the long run, individuals would appear to observers to be acting as if they were optimizing, and for this reason maximizing remained a useful working hypothesis.[36]

A similar logic was also applied to Simon's notion of aspiration levels, with the conclusion again being that his theory represented no advance over maximizing. Simon had predicted that aspirations would rise in situations of sustained success and that this would lead the decision maker to seek more information and choose different alternatives. But eventually, as returns and aspirations continued to rise, a reasonable observer would have to conclude that the decision maker was maximizing. And conversely, he had predicted that in situations of continual failure, decision makers would lower their aspirations until they were satisfied. They would do the best that they could under the circumstances. But again, to Julian Margolis and other economists, satisficing was indistinguishable from maximizing.[37]

Not surprisingly, some contended that maximizing was simpler than satisficing. George Stigler claimed that satisficing was really a form of maximizing that calculated the costs of searching for information. Choice was not limited by cognitive restrictions or by the impossibility of knowing all the variables, but by the costs of search. Choices were made when it became apparent that searching for a better option would entail extra costs without improved rewards.[38] Economists, as Stigler and Gary Becker would later argue, could better study any decision if they assumed that people had stable tastes and optimized.[39]

Even employment could be interpreted as a relationship between equally powerful maximizers. Alchian and Harold Demsetz, for example, thought that interactions in the firm involved essentially the same "revelation and exchange" of information as exchanges in the market. Just as buyers informed sellers that their prices were too high by refusing to buy, so workers informed managers that they were too dictatorial by quitting, and managers informed workers that they were irresponsible by firing them. And similarly, centralized management and corporate loyalty were selected because they reduced the costs of monitoring performance and raised pecuniary income for all.[40] Maximizing took place even in bureaucracies, at least in the long run; and maximizing assumptions could be used to describe bureaucratic rationality.

Milton Friedman and Fritz Machlup, however, were not willing to go so far. They argued that Simon had misunderstood maximizing. But if Simon had been wrong, it was also wrong to conclude that maximizing described the real behavior of specific individuals. Maximizing was an ideal type, a simplifying approximation; it simplified reality and helped economists understand aggregate behavior. By assuming that each firm acted as if it were maximizing, economists could focus on the external relationships between the market and the firm and could better predict interactions among prices and conditions. The sort of knowledge maximizing theory yielded was especially helpful in studying and directing governmental policy. It was good enough, regardless of the inaccuracy of its premises then, to yield useful predictions. And for most purposes of most economists, the maximizing hypothesis was the best simplification available.[41]

Because Simon had different purposes and problems from most economists, his ideas have not changed the premises of such thinkers. James March has lamented that Simon's theory of choice was often converted into theories of expectations or information costs.[42] Or his work, as Albert Ando has noted, was often at such a "micro level" that most economists found his ideas "remote from their everyday concerns."[43] Friedman, for instance, did not consider Simon to be an economist and was surprised when he won the Nobel Prize.[44]

What economists did not do, at least in the published literature, was to address Simon's main point. They did not explain how the individual really decided, how decisions were actually made. As Machlup admitted, Simon's theory was suited to understanding the real choices of specific individuals and was therefore helpful in answering the "normative," "advisory" questions put to economists working in business.[45]

Simon's rebuttal mainly took the form of periodically reiterating his arguments about the fallacies of maximizing. Maximizing focused on results rather than on the process or mechanism of decision making. As such, it had some usefulness as a tool for historical research; viewed retrospectively, how decisions were actually made did not matter because the economist could see that some firms profited and survived "as if" they had maximized. But Friedman's as if theory of choice was of little use in describing how decisions had been made in the first place.[46] In addition, maximizing was especially suspect in explaining how decision makers chose in the short run, or in "a complex and rapidly changing environment." In such real circumstances, business people were not ideal types. They did not make decisions in the long run; they made decisions every day.

In particular, Simon said, maximizing could not meet the needs of management scientists who used mathematical models to study problems and select alternatives. They needed obtainable data, operational goals, and observable standards of success. And because they worked in the present, they could not afford to wait for the market or trial and error to reveal perfect information, optimal standards, or the fittest choices. By waiting for certainty, they missed opportunities and risked failure. Furthermore, decision makers often found it impossible to calculate the costs of search and, in some cases, could not acquire the desired information no matter how hard they tried.

Hence, Simon remained convinced that people in organizations satisficed. They made decisions "either by finding optimum solutions for a simplified world, or by finding satisfactory solutions for a more realistic world." And he found it ironic that economists like Friedman, who insisted that people in business were maximizers, became satisficers in defending their theories. To cope with the complexities of their work and to understand economic behavior more effectively, they admitted that they lowered their aspiration levels, narrowed their focus, and adopted simplifications. In effect, Simon felt his ideas were validated by economists who "believe that businessmen maximize" but who "know that economic theorists satisfice."[47]

Simon's other early critics were political scientists interested in the old-fashioned study of political theory. They believed that he was less a positive scientist of politics than a partisan of management. Dwight Waldo, Sheldon Wolin, Herbert J. Storing, and Sherman Krupp particularly questioned Simon's ethical and political ideal of satisficing and charged that his organization theory amounted to a new "dismal science."[48] It rested on "unarticulated 'value' judgments."[49] And it naively assumed that "knowledge of how to manipulate other human beings—how to get them to do the things you want done"—was "amoral."[50]

According to these critics, Simon's effort to separate facts from values was deeply conservative. He beheld bureaucratic capitalism and saw that it was very, very good. Thus he accepted it as an unalterable part of nature stemming from cognitive limitations. And seeing bureaucracy as the one and only way had led him to deny that efficiency was a value and to ignore that, as a premise, it demanded acceptance of ends determined by elites and often designed for elites.[51] At best, he would concede only that efficiency was related to "the values and opportunity costs" of managers.[52] Simon's perspective, Storing complained, was limited by a "political myopia" that took its "bearings from the goals of top management."[53]

Wolin agreed and thought Simon's managerial bias was especially evident in his theory of rationality. Simon assumed, much like Hobbes, that people were irrational outside organizations. They were slaves to their freedom and acted erratically because they were unable to understand or choose consistent goals. But the assumption rested on managerial values. Managers feared that egoism and autonomy would frustrate their search for order and acquiescence. They wanted to domesticate autonomy because they and Simon wanted to "constitutionalize a Hobbesian society" and achieve a sort of medieval moral consensus conducive to bureaucratic rationality.[54]

A similar bias, the political scientists argued, led Simon to confuse consent with control.[55] He depicted bureaucracy as resting on the voluntary consent of employees, an "advice-acceptance" relationship between superiors and subordinates. Yet he also described how managers manipulated zones of indifference. Such "command-obedience" relationships rendered illusory any claims of autonomous consent or mutually advantageous exchange. Bureaucracy subjected employees to a standardized rationality and demanded they choose the one best way, which was to admit that bureaucratic choice was an oxymoron and that consent by a worker was merely a euphemism for repression of autonomy. When under such limits, the employee could only freely choose between quitting or accepting managerial premises. So in reality, authority was based on power, not on consent. But to describe domination using democratic language, as Simon had done, was "analogous to a description of a jungle using a theory of a farm."[56]

Finally, the political scientists denied that Simon went beyond the principles of Taylorism. He continued to see employees as passive factors of production who were continually engineered. And since he was only concerned with how superiors manipulated controls, not with how subordinates escaped them, he did not really describe the whole process of decision making in organizations. It was too narrow and too incomplete, said Sherman Krupp, to be dignified as a science and was better seen as just a "technology of organization."[57]

To such criticism, Simon made no thorough rebuttal similar to the one directed at economists. His silence seems odd, given that economists were making the criticism that Baptists make about Methodists while the political scientists were proclaiming themselves unbelievers. Indeed he regarded their claims as moral rather than scientific. In an exchange with Waldo, he belittled the ideas of political "philosophers" as being presented in a "loose, literary, metaphorical style" that was based on vague value premises, unwarranted assertions, and sloppy reasoning and exhibited a "standard of unrigor" that "would not receive a passing grade in the elementary course in logic."[58] Waldo pointed out that Simon hid behind logical positivism in order to conceal that he was "a man of deep faith" who could not tolerate "heresy and sin." In effect, he labored behind a screen labeled "Quiet! Scientist at Work."[59]

Perhaps Simon did not reply because he was undisturbed by charges that he was a mandarin. As he had indicated in his debates with economists, he intended his ideas to help managers. And since he thought that managers were necessary, he believed that his science was both expedient and ethical.[60] Feeling no guilt, he barely acknowledged the political scientists.

Still, criticism did affect both the direction and the form of Simon's work. Criticism from economists pushed him to probe deeper into psychology, seeking to understand and describe rationality in ever more detail. And as he moved in this direction, he also implicitly addressed the political scientists by attempting to show more conclusively that bureaucracy suited human nature. As he moved into new and exciting fields, however, his refusal to change any of his premises meant that his later work would remain open to the earlier criticisms.

Computers and Cybernetics

In 1949 Simon had left Illinois Tech for the newly created Graduate School of Industrial Administration at the Carnegie Institute of Technology. In short order, Simon would help lead the new school into computer simulation of human behavior, and in January 1956 he would announce to a class that "over Christmas Allen Newell and I invented a thinking machine."[61]

Simon's first steps toward that invention began in the late 1940s when he became aware of work in symbolic logic, biology, neurology, electronics, computer science, engineering design, information theory, mathematical economics, game theory, and psychology. The ideas in these fields, he later recalled, had cross-fertilized with his, and he became part of an "invisible college" researching human thought.[62]

Probably the most important scholars in the invisible college, and the ones who most influenced Simon's subsequent work, were John von Neumann and Norbert Wiener. Both were leading mathematicians, and both sought to use computers to understand rationality. Already, as John Bolter has put it, the computer was becoming "the defining technology" of the twentieth century, shaping ideas in a way comparable to the clock and the steam engine.[63] By 1947 von Neumann was attempting to use formal logic, mathematics, and analogies from computers to construct a model of the brain and of thought. During the same period, Wiener was insisting that animals and complex machines were essentially similar; both were characterized by purposive behavior and by feedback devices that measured deviations from goals and adjusted them to their environment. The activities of machines and animals, he thought, could be described using identical concepts about "communication and control" drawn from information theory and metaphors taken from engineering, servomechanisms, and electronic technology. As a name for the study of communication and control processes in mechanical, biological and social systems, Wiener chose *cybernetics*, a term he derived from the Greek word for *steersman* and for which the Latin derivative was *governor*.[64]

One project of this new science, a project that came to be called artificial intelligence, sought to develop computer programs that simulated the mind. It was based on the assumption that thought was characterized by permanent, formal patterns of information processing. The new "cognitive scientists" differentiated themselves from neurologists and sociologists by trying to study thought without reference to biology, emotion, and culture. They expected to get at the real mind stuff by isolating abstract "mental representations" through computer simulations.[65]

Simon kept up with these developments in cybernetics and the cognitive sciences. Gradually what he learned changed the way that he described his own project. It became less a study of decision making and more a study of problem solving and the communication of information. As early as 1951, he agreed with von Neumann that "suggestive analogies" between computers and organisms deserved exploration. An especially important subject to investigate, he thought, was how the rational behavior of machines and organisms occurred within a "hierarchy," or an established "frame of reference."[66]

To carry out such investigations, Simon went in 1952 to the RAND Corporation in Santa Monica, California. There, in research sponsored by the air force, he studied the planning of air defense systems through models that simulated radar networks and bomber formations. He became fascinated with how the mathematician Allen Newell used computers to go beyond number-crunching and how he saw the brain as a "logic machine." He and Newell were soon encouraging each other's efforts to use computer metaphors to describe thought. And following another trip to RAND in the summer of 1954, during which Simon learned to program computers, the two men decided to create a computer model to simulate rationality. Early in 1955 Simon arranged a position for Newell at Carnegie Tech, thus beginning a long and profitable collaboration.[67]

As a team, Simon and Newell would meet for brainstorming sessions, during which Newell did most of the talking. Concurrently, Simon began taking protocols, an exercise in which an experimental subject (often Simon or a member of his family) would be given a problem in logic and asked to verbalize the steps of his reasoning as he worked out a solution. Initially chess problems were used. But these were soon found to be too difficult, and Simon turned instead to proving mathematical theorems found in Whitehead and Russell's *Principia Mathematica*. From the protocols, Simon then performed "paper-and-pencil work," seeking to isolate the basic thinking. He hoped as well to decipher what his teacher Rudolf Carnap had called a syntax, a set of symbols and rules for using them that determined mental operations. In the beginning, the new work was characterized more by "borrowing ideas from psychology and human behavior to advance artificial intelligence" than it was by "reverse borrowing from artificial intelligence to advance psychology."[68]

Simon then turned his ideas over to Newell who converted them into a computer program. Newell was assisted by a colleague at RAND, Cliff Shaw, an actuary turned programmer who was consulted over the telephone. Together they tried to create a program that could transcend computer procedures based on rote and stereotyped directives. They hoped instead to direct a computer to use Simon's general, logical procedures to solve many different problems and thus simulate intelligent and adaptive thought. By creating such a "smart" program and having the computer record its logical steps, they expected to gain important insights into reasoning and the syntax of the mind.[69]

By December 1955 the team of Newell, Simon, and Shaw had succeeded in creating a program called Logic Theorist. The program was composed of mathematical axioms and proofs and of governing principles; these principles, called rules of thumb, or heuristics, solved complex problems by solving a series of simpler subproblems. Logic Theorist was directed to prove more theorems. Not only was it successful in proving theorems, it constructed one proof more elegant than that of Whitehead and Russell, an accomplishment that delighted Russell when Simon told him about it. At an artificial intelligence conference in September 1956, Newell and Simon delivered a paper describing Logic Theorist and were credited by their peers with having been the first to simulate intelligent behavior with a computer and the first to use an information processing language to express psychological theories.[70]

In the years that followed, Newell and Simon moved beyond the Logic

Theorist to write more sophisticated programs and enjoy other successes. In the late 1950s, they began work on a General Problem Solver that could not only prove theorems but also play chess, solve logical puzzles, and perform cryptarithmetic operations. Using it as a tool for examining human thought, they conducted investigations that eventually led to their massive work, *Human Problem Solving*, published in 1972.[71]

Initially, Simon had thought that his work only led to "suggestive analogies." But his work with smart programs caused him to argue that people and computers used identical problem solving processes. His "basic point of view" was that the "programmed computer and the human problem solver" were "both species belonging to the genus IPS [Information Processing System]." Hence it followed that people could be studied through computer simulations and described in cybernetic language.[72] By understanding the common "elementary information processes" of computers and people, Simon came to believe he could transcend the occult qualities that had for centuries obscured the mechanical operations of intelligent thought.[73]

In addition, Simon claimed that computer simulation validated once and for all his satisficing theory of rationality. Here he fell into some circular reasoning. He offered simulations as proof of his theories, but his simulations stacked the deck in his favor because the heuristic devices were based on his satisficing psychology. His simulations thus only worked to affirm and never to falsify his thesis. Nonetheless, he still claimed to have shown that all information processing systems had "puny" computational powers compared with the complex problems that they faced. Consequently, an algorithmic search for information, a search that would guarantee the best solution, was costly and slow. In a chess analogy that he was very fond of, he explained that an algorithmic search of all the alternatives 5 moves deep with 25 moves at each stage allowed for 100 million million alternatives. Not only would the search try the patience of opponents, but choosing between the alternative moves or trying to measure the marginal value of continuing the search would be difficult. Using algorithmic, maximizing methods would make it impossible to finish one chess game in a lifetime. Real life problems, of course, were even more difficult.

Maximizing, Simon concluded, was impossible, so intelligent systems adopted satisficing devices. People and smart programs sometimes thought serially and took up one problem at a time and queued the rest; in other cases they solved problems concurrently so as to address several goals simultaneously.[74] In still other cases intelligent systems used heuristics. These governing principles or rules of thumb provided guidance in dealing with unique, ill-structured problems in which clear, consistent criteria could not be ascertained or applied. A good chess player used heuristics when basing gambits on principles like "control the center of the board" or "protect the king." More generally, heuristics helped cope with conflicting goals or abundant alternatives. Heuristics directed the system to select a few alternatives for trial-and-error search and so could not guarantee optimum solutions. But rules of thumb simplified problems, limited search, and thus made choice easier and faster.

One important type of heuristic used by people and programs was "means-ends analysis" or, as he also called it, the "principle of subgoal reduction." The first step was to define a desired state, compare it with the existing situation, and identify the differences between the two. The second was to consider how these differences could be reduced by identifying a series of smaller subproblems. The third was to solve the subproblems and meet the subgoals one by one, proceeding in this fashion until the big problem was gradually overcome.[75] Simon illustrated this mechanical logic by an ordinary example: "I want to take my son to nursery school. What's the difference between what I have and what I want? One of distance. What changes distance? My automobile. My automobile won't work. What's needed to make it work? A new battery. What has new batteries? An auto repair shop. I want the repair shop to put in a new battery, but the shop doesn't know I need one. What is the difficulty? One of communication. What allows communication? A telephone. . . ."[76]

While arguing for the similarity of people and programs, Simon anticipated and tried to refute criticisms.[77] In particular, he denied that humankind alone had emotions and free will. Both humans and computers tried to be rational. Both were governed by the hierarchy of goals and commands in their programs. For both, the environment sometimes caused the command program to shift from one operation to another. In computers, an "interruption mechanism" terminated one program, selected a new one, and thus shifted goals; essentially this was the computer equivalent of human "emotion" and adaptation.[78]

In Simon's view, moreover, people were as programmed as computers and as lacking in free will as rats and ants. They did "what they are programmed to do" by environmental stimuli, much as extreme behaviorists had argued.[79] Such behaviorism was inherent in cybernetic ideas. Both natural and artificial systems were presumed to behave teleologically because they had been programmed with purposes and self-adaptive devices. Their goals and their homeostatic feedback mechanisms, as with a thermostat regulating room temperature, exchanged information between the system and its environment, signaled deviations from goals, and adjusted behavior automatically. This concept demolished distinctions between complex machines and organisms.

Such cybernetic concepts, Simon believed, verified both his notions of satisficing. Thinking of a human as an information processing system combined Simon's psychological idea (which assumed people were not gods) with his political ideal (which assumed people were bureaucrats). But his description of people as programs was hard to distinguish from Taylor's mechanistic psychology. Cybernetic Simonism saw people as passive instruments easily manipulated by programmers and thus obliterated whatever hedonism remained from Simon's economics background. He tried to escape from this conundrum by arguing that complex machines were not passive and that people welcomed programming.

To resolve the problem, Simon became interested in sociobiology and contended that programs governing humans were influenced by genetics as well as culture. He assumed that no "Master Plan" with a "comprehensive utility function" had been copied to the human data base.[80] Instead people had been genetically programmed by a centuries-long struggle for survival in which natural selection chose "selfish genes." Genes with "strong altruism," which programmed for self-sacrifice and led to defeat in the struggle for existence, had not been selected for the gene pool. Yet natural selection had also rejected predatory traits because cooperation had survival value and predation was punished by society. Human societies thus selected for "weak altruism," a genetic program of "enlightened self-interest" that caused people to accept short-term sacrifices for long-term gains and act much like "social insects."[81]

According to Simon, weak altruism helped make people easy to program. It was manifest in "docility" and a propensity to "obeying behaviors," which made people act in "socially approved ways." And as a "programmable" species, humanity could adapt to changing problems by changing its behavior and culture.[82] Furthermore, he argued, people were born as "simple things," as processors ready to be programmed or animals ready to be conditioned in a Skinner box. "The apparent complexity" of human behavior originated in "the complexity of the environment." The hesitations of a mathematician proving a Euclidean theorem were not "very different from the white rat sniffing his way through a maze," and "only human pride" caused people to believe that "the apparent intricacies of our path stem from a quite different source than the intricacy of the ant's path."[83]

For Simon, then, the mind was an information processing system that worked "according to laws and mechanisms, not some mysterious mind fluid." To him this discovery and the development of artificial intelligence were as important as the revolutions in human thought made by Copernicus, Darwin, and Freud. Man was not the center of the universe, not distinct from animals, not uniquely rational, and had "ceased to be uniquely capable of complex, intelligent manipulation of his environment."[84]

Indeed, Simon increasingly saw people and computers as interchangeable. Computers, he claimed, would "in a visible future" exhibit as much "intuition, insight, and learning" as people, and the range of problems they could handle would be "coextensive with the range to which the human mind has been applied."[85] They could "already read, think, learn, create," and within a few years they would be able to "do anything a man can do."[86] Nor did he rule out tasks that required extensive education. The tasks of doctors, managers, and college teachers could be turned over to intelligent computers almost as easily as manual tasks.[87]

Meanwhile, Simon's innovative and interdisciplinary research had been earning him an unusual assortment of positions and awards. He was honored by Carnegie-Mellon University (formerly the Carnegie Institute of Technology) when in 1966 it named him Richard King Mellon University Professor of Computer Science and Psychology. He also won, in addition to the Nobel Prize and several honorary degrees from foreign and American universities, the 1969 Distinguished Science Contribution Award from the American Psychological Association and the 1975 A. M. Turing Award from the Association for Computing Machinery.[88]

Such recognition, however, was not accompanied by much appreciation of the continuity of Simon's goals or of his ongoing contributions to management. On the contrary, by redirecting his approach and renaming his science, he inadvertently encouraged the belief that he was no longer an economist or a political scientist. While economists remained interested in him, their focus was primarily on his early ideas on satisficing. And political scientists, apparently believing that he had passed out of their specialty, ceased writing about him altogether. The artificial intelligentsia and their chroniclers, moreover, assumed that Simon had entered his new research with unformatted data disks; they did not bother to read his earlier work and only saw him as a cognitive scientist interested in psychological and epistemological matters.[89] All missed how Simon persisted in his efforts to understand management and improve it by his elaborate cybernetic metaphor.

As before, Simon accepted the naturalness of bureaucracy, insisting that it best coped with cognitive limitations. "Hierarchy," he thought, was "the adaptive form for finite intelligence to assume in the face of complexity." The modern corporation, he went so far as to claim, was rooted not merely in human nature but in nature itself. Hierarchy and specialization went "beyond the peculiarities of human organization." All complex systems, whether social, chemical, biological, mechanical, or physical, were similarly organized. Just as matter was divided into molecules, atoms, nuclei, and atoms, just as organisms were divided into tissues, organs, cells, organic compounds, genes, chromosomes, and DNA, so societies were divided into organizations, groups, and individuals.[90]

Elaborating on this point, Simon said that "the basic features of organization structure and function" were derived "from the characteristics of human problem-solving processes and rational human choice." Humans needed to cooperate efficiently and develop solutions quickly, limit alternatives and restrict attention to simple problems, routinize responses to repetitive problems, establish "a reliable and perceivable pattern of events," and identify problems that were "within the limits set by our knowledge and our computational capacities." These needs could be met through centralization and specialization. Bureaucracies were thus "factories for processing information" and as such could "magnify the computing capabilities of individual human beings."[91]

Continuing the information processing analogy, Simon also argued that both the individual and the firm were programmed. Bureaucratic roles were programs that determined particular actions for particular situations and invariably incorporated "both organizational and personal goals." Moreover, as bureaucrats tried to achieve their work goals, whether to benefit themselves, their divisions, or their firms, they encountered other people working toward their goals. The resulting conflicts imposed constraints that restricted freedom of choice and caused all goals to be "modified by managers and employees at all echelons." For this reason, top management was never able to dictate the overall goals of the organization, and power even in a bureaucracy was essentially decentralized.[92] Management was essentially a feedback mechanism. Managers, in other words, were bureaucratic thermostats that communicated information and regulated performance; they were corporate servomechanisms adjusting behavior by communicating deviations from goals.

Simon was attracted to the cybernetic meaning of control on two grounds. First, it was consistent with satisficing. Managers, when faced with uncertainty about the future and with inability to predict accurately, used a "feedback loop" that relied on knowledge of past performance to "eliminate deviations" between actual and desired results. And second, cybernetic control implied no oppression of people and conformed to his conception of authority. Rewards and punishments were just another way of communicating information about performance. What was important about feedback was not the form of its incentives but the content of its information. "Attention-directing stimuli" were just as important as affection-directing ones. By providing knowledge about performance, managers eliminated "errors" that caused deviations from goals. He thus portrayed managers as controllers of information, not controllers of people.[93]

Accordingly Simon thought his cybernetic economics was both positive and normative. It differed from traditional economics, which generally studied what he called "substantive rationality," that is, what decisions were made. His science, in contrast, studied "procedural rationality" and "normative rationality," that is, how decisions were made and how decisions should be made. Its purpose, like that of operations research and management science, was to instruct managers on how to adopt "good methods for reaching good decisions" and on how to find the one best way with least cost. It offered them a "theory of action" that could help them understand their tasks and problems. And because understanding problems was tantamount to solving them, a "theory of action" could be used to perform the task that it explained. Managers could use the "logic of action" described in cybernetics and learn to solve problems by imitating computers and heuristic programs. Descriptions of how managers decided led to prescriptions about how they should decide.[94] Practicing what he preached, Simon devoted considerable attention in the 1980s to describing how managers made decisions.[95]

Simon's scientific theories were always on a higher plane than mere technical advice. But he did inspire disciples to develop his ideas. For this reason, James March has described Simon's writings as "a collection of prolegomena."[96] Colleagues and students at Carnegie-Mellon in particular developed their master's ideas and contributed to innovations in organization theory, operations research, management education, and computer technology.

Simonized Science

One of Simon's legacies has been his influence on disciples who developed a "behavioral theory of the firm" by applying his ideas to the study of microeconomic behavior and managerial decision making. Most prominently, Richard Cyert and James March, both onetime colleagues of Simon at Carnegie-Mellon, conducted case studies of the decision-making process in business and concluded that each firm was a "coalition" of competing individuals and conflicting interest groups who were engaged in continuous bargaining. Consequently, organizational objectives were temporary, ambiguous, inconsistent, and satisficing. And managers, they said, responded to this uncertainty by "using decision rules emphasizing short-run reaction to short-run feedback rather than anticipation of long-run uncertain events." They tried to attain some stability by adopting heuristic rules, standardizing procedures, establishing bureaucracy, and coping with one problem at a time.

Cyert and March also developed a computer model of their theory, and by the 1960s, computer models of the firm had become a trademark of the Carnegie-Mellon approach. Simulations were used to study and test management decisions, and computer modeling became the managerial equivalent of wind tunnel tests of model planes.[97] The behavioral models, moreover, were more complex than those used by classical mandarins, and therefore Simonizers tended to offer heuristic prescriptions. Each business problem was assumed to have unique aspects, and every managerial strategy to have unintended, dysfunctional consequences, which made any maximizing wasteful and impossible. Hence rules of thumb were the best guides to decision making.

Ironically, Simonized rules of thumb were similar to Taylor's principles that Simon had once belittled as proverbs. Simon's disciples advised managers to analyze their assumptions; to promote playfulness, storytelling, conflict, and bargaining; and to design organizations more like "tents" instead of "palaces" so that information could flow freely. And they did not question the rationality of specialized tasks, nor did they synthesize deciders and doers.[98] Probably this conservatism resulted from their empiricism; they derived prescriptions from prevailing practice and so tended to perpetuate those practices. More than this, their failure to progress beyond Taylorist principles showed the difficulty of working out a unitary science of human behavior and management. Lyndall Urwick, one of the classicists Simon had ridiculed, argued that contradictions in management theory could not and should not be resolved; management was a "practical art," and successful managers selected a useful "principle" from many contradictory ones.[99] Thus the sophistication of the Simonists often amounted to scholasticism; they tended to make theorizing and computer modeling ends in themselves and did not consider changing Taylorist premises in the slightest. Doubtless the social relations of managers and workers would be unaffected by their knowing that bureaucracy was satisficing rather than maximizing.

Simonism did bring technical innovations in the development of heuristic programs for operations research. In the 1960s Simon's colleagues and students worked out heuristics for problems that had been difficult to standardize and solve using slow and costly algorithmic programs. Their computing techniques limited searches and helped balance assembly lines, schedule activities, plan sales routes, monitor inventory, invest capital, and locate warehouses. The utility of these heuristic techniques, however, was substantially undercut after computers became faster and cheaper.[100]

Simon's work in cybernetics and heuristic programming had its greatest influence, however, with the invention of "expert systems" during the late 1970s and 1980s. Drawing inspiration from Simon's ideas, programmers sought to develop programs that could duplicate the expertise of a human specialist and thereby assist decision making. Acting as knowledge engineers, cognitive scientists studied the methods of specialists in a field, codified their job knowledge, promulgated heuristic work rules and problem-solving strategies, and entered it all into a computer. When consulted, this intelligent or knowledge-based program could apply its knowledge to particular problems, make inferences and deductions, offer recommendations, justify its answers, and learn from its experiences. Such mechanical experts, initially used in manufacturing and financial services, were said to be capable of automating some of the skills and specialized learning of knowledge workers; they could be used to support decision making, to deskill work, or to replace humans altogether.[101] Depending on one's values, the expert program was the climax of Chaplin's nightmare of humankind caught in the cogs of a bureaucratic machine or the culmination of the Taylorist dream of a digital Schmidt. Smitten with the latter vision, Simon thought that the programs proved the utility of his theories and argued that the first, full management science had been created by merging artificial intelligence with operations research.[102]

In addition, the Simonesque approach gradually helped define business education at Carnegie-Mellon. With Simon's help, the Carnegie-Mellon faculty discarded Harvard's legalistic, case study method and instead established a curriculum that was heavily theoretical, empirical, mathematical, and cybernetic. They wanted to form a universal manager, "an industrial renaissance man," who had the tools for a whole career.

A fundamental part of the education was playing a management game. It was initiated in December 1957 and was the first computer game to be a required course in a graduate school curriculum. Based on a simulation of competing firms in a market, the game went beyond a case study by creating a more realistic "live case." The players divided into firms, abandoning collegial relationships and establishing bureaucracy. They thus acquired "simulated business experience" and applied the knowledge they had learned in their courses. Simon integrated the game into his class on administrative processes. Many of his students went on to receive doctorates and take academic posts in business schools across the country.[103]

Simon's influence on business education was enhanced by the Ford Foundation study of the late 1950s. The foundation found the Carnegie-Mellon program to be the paradigm of what a professional management education should be. Convinced by the report, business educators across the country began duplicating the Carnegie approach.[104] This became the "new look" in business education and provided a favorable environment for Simon to shape managerial consciousness. And by the 1980s, many prestigious graduate business schools, including Chicago, Wharton, and MIT, had established special centers that studied how people really made decisions, and these centers were much influenced by Simon's ideas.[105]

Challenges to Cybernetic Simonism

Even as Simon's stature and influence grew, however, he also encountered a new set of challengers. This time the attack came chiefly from philosophers, computer scientists, and corporatist mandarins. Echoing the political scientists, they argued that cybernetic metaphors made for bad psychology and bad politics.[106]

Not surprisingly, Simon's contention that people and programs were different species of the same genus, a contention that became the bedrock of his fundamentalist wing of the artificial intelligentsia, offended many. Among its opponents were Hubert Dreyfus, a phenomenological philosopher writing in the mid-1960s; Joseph Weizenbaum, a psychologist and former artificial intelligencer; and John Searle, an analytic philosopher.[107]

Building on Dreyfus's ideas,[108] Searle denied that people reasoned in the same way that computers did. A computer followed logical procedures that people supplied, which meant that it only followed formal, syntactic rules. Programmed with a syntax, it could relate signs to other signs; connect symbols into an orderly, harmonious arrangement; and follow rules of thought as if it were duplicating human thinking. But the duplication was not true because a computer lacked a semantics. It was just manipulating symbols without understanding their meaning in reference to "states of affairs in the world."

In illustration, Searle offered his famous "parable of the Chinese room." He imagined that a person isolated from the world could learn to apply syntactic rules to Chinese characters and arrange them in a grammatically correct order. But that person would neither understand Chinese nor be able to translate the symbols into referents of real things. He or she would be like a computer, equipped with a syntax but lacking a semantics and manipulating meaningless signs. A computer could metaphorically simulate some types of human reasoning but could never literally duplicate human thought.[109]

In his criticism, Weizenbaum emphasized the limits of Simon's simulations. From relatively simple logic programs, Simon had generalized about the whole range of human thought and behavior, asserted that computers could do everything that people did, and claimed that computers could replicate all aspects of human life. But in reality, Weizenbaum thought, a program was merely a language like "high-school algebra" and said no more than that about psychology. Claiming more—claiming that programs embodied the fundamental character of humanity—"dehumanized" people.[110]

Moreover, Hubert and Stuart Dreyfus argued, this meant that the notion of an expert system was an oxymoron. Attempting to codify the knowledge of a human expert "decomposed and decontextualized" it and "degraded understanding" to the level of a novice. Mechanical expertise depended on general rules, mathematical models, and "context-free facts" and could not duplicate the intuition, experience, historical knowledge, and holistic understanding of a human expert. It relied too much on "management by abstract principle" to the detriment of "management by know-how." It was just this sort of scientism, they said, that had led to "short-sighted and overly conservative" policies in American business.[111]

In addition, Weizenbaum, Dreyfus, and Searle denied that Simon's cybernetic metaphor captured the autonomy, creativity, and individuality of human rationality. Human beings could choose goals and assign meaning to their existence. They were therefore uniquely capable of learning and growth, uniquely capable of creating culture and history.[112] They were not machines with programmed utility functions. Nor were they rats trapped in a maze; humans often tried to change the maze or escape it altogether.

This meant that human rationality led to conflicts over power and values. But cybernetic metaphors, the sociologist Stanislav Andreski contended, obscured this by depicting people as computer chips, "nothing but cogs in a machine." By covering up political struggles, such analogies offered "a parable of subordination" and amounted to an ideology of "crypto-conservatism." Social cybernetics, Andreski said, was little more than a set of "platitudes, banal half-truths, or outright distortions dressed up in scientific-sounding words."[113]

Similarly, Robert Boguslaw, like Simon a programmer at RAND, said that his former colleague was under the delusion that computers could rise above "human imperfections" and convert "political problems into administrative problems." The choice of heuristic principles, Boguslaw explained, might be value-free in symbolic logic programs, but it was value-laden in management ones. Management heuristics were about "how the game is to be played rather than how to play it effectively." So when programmers chose rules of thumb, they put values in the computer and ensured that values came out. They decided political and ethical questions about the distribution and purposes of power, and they made judgments about whether the firm sought long-term or short-term profits and whether it served its owners and managers or its employees. And such judgments could not be avoided by saying that the principle was greater efficiency. Efficiency had to be defined just like any other goal, and the way managers usually defined it typically caused employees to be treated as instruments. Simon, Boguslaw concluded, had overlooked these questions and was therefore only one of many new cybernetic "utopians."[114]

Drawing out some of the implications for managers, corporative mandarins like Chris Argyris contended that Simon's approach was immoral and self-defeating. Simon, he thought, had tried to found a scientific management by "describing how the world actually exists" and accepting bureaucracies "as givens." But this led him to assume that people were easily "programmable" through bureaucratic means. He had ignored the fact that people were not machines and had needs for growth and "self-actualization." Consequently Simon did not understand that bureaucracy, by depriving people of autonomy, always triggered passivity or resistance. Simon's "rational man organization theory" was for Argyris just as unscientific and counterproductive as Taylorism had been.[115]

To these challenges, as had been the case with those from political science, Simon made only limited replies. Dreyfus's ideas, he said, were "garbage" because they came from a man with "no technical background" in artificial intelligence. He agreed with Allen Newell that making a direct, elaborate rebuttal would only publicize the charges.[116] Instead, Simon simply stuck to his argument that programmed computers were as emotional as people and people were as programmable as computers,[117] a contention that seemed to imply that no greater moral obligations were owed to one than to the other. And as for Argyris, Simon castigated him as a counterculture revolutionary. Self-actualization could not form the basis of a science of rationality because it made people so concerned with power, with the question of who controls, that they were unconcerned with economic results, with what is accomplished. Besides, business managers were "goal-oriented," not "power-oriented"; they were not bent on oppressing people but sought to meet "needs for achievement and affiliation" in order to raise performance. Nor did Simon believe that he had ever advocated oppressive controls; to him authority came from below through the voluntary acceptance of premises rather than from coercive wielding of power.[118]

Finally then, because Simon always believed bureaucracy was legitimate and rational, he perpetuated the premises of classical Taylorism. Centralized power and specialized operations were always fundamental to his theories. He was only dissatisfied with previous interpretations of bureaucratic operations and so sought new explanations of their utility, trying to show that hierarchy and simplification were natural to human existence. Although he criticized Taylor's machine psychology, he found it difficult to explain the choices of hedonistic organisms in a repressive institution and to describe their self-interest in surrendering autonomy. Consequently, he drew ever farther away from maximizing assumptions toward mechanistic conceptions; he argued that people were not rational enough to be free but were rational enough to recognize that they would be happier under restraint. By portraying human as computer and manager as programmer, Simon eventually duplicated Taylor's depiction of human as machine and manager as engineer. And because he continued to depict subordinates as passive factors of production easily deployed and controlled by superiors, Simon never sought to transcend bureaucracy.

4

Virtue as
Managerial Vision

Peter F. Drucker and
Management by Objectives

In the years following World War II, Peter Ferdinand Drucker was the most
prominent management consultant in the world. As accomplished an author
as a counselor, his books and collections of essays sold millions of copies in
several languages. Some of his books appeared on the *New York Times* best-
seller list; in 1974 the sales of *Management*, his 839-page magnum opus,
temporarily surpassed those of *The Joy of Sex*. One mandarin claimed that
Drucker's writings were "read by more managers than those of any single
author, living or dead."[1]

Despite Drucker's great reputation, mandarins have often described him as
an inconsistent thinker, an enigma, a guru. As one business journalist put it,
Drucker has been "known for many concepts" despite the absence of "a clear
and identifiable message, body of research or theory to his name." Such
perceptions may be due in part to the eclectic way in which he has illustrated
his essays and lectures, using examples drawn from history or music or art as
well as contemporary business.[2] Because of Drucker's apparently unsystematic
style, one historian has concluded that his "real contribution" to management
had been not so much in "the cash value of his ideas as in the rigorous activity
of mind" by which they were formulated and that managers could learn more
from "watching him think than from studying the content of his thought."[3]

Stylistic impressions aside, Drucker did develop a political theory of management. While describing him as the "father of the new management" at-
tributes too much to him,[4] he was as important a corporatist thinker as Simon
was a bureaucratic one. The key to his corporatism is the technique he labeled

"management by objectives and self-control," called MBO in the business vernacular. He designed it to overcome problems that Taylor and Mayo had been unable to solve. Especially he hoped to help managers stop treating people as factors of production and transcend an irrational separation of planning and performing for supervising professional employees.

The story of Drucker's method and the reaction of managers to it has never been told by a historian.[5] But the tale depicts much about the appeal of a corporatist writer. One scholar concluded that nothing in American thought has been similar to the German idea that the business corporation was a "social institution" and "the central locus of identity, loyalty, and community." But such a conclusion seems to have been reached without knowledge of what American managers have learned from Peter Drucker, an Austrian immigrant, and how they have voiced a desire for "an ethic of mutuality" and a disgust for "bourgeois egotism."[6] The story of Drucker's system also illustrates how corporatist principles often led to bureaucratic practice.

European Philosophy, American Practice

Drucker's remedy for Taylorism began in the 1940s and early 1950s when he set out to synthesize the wisdom of European political theory with that of American business practice. The synthesis became management by objectives, a technique designed to make capitalism corporative and corporatism capitalist.[7]

Capitalism and corporatism had been important parts of Drucker's youth in Vienna, Austria. There he seems to have absorbed a good deal from the conservative, Fascist, and especially Catholic versions of corporatist thinking popular in Austria after the First World War. Such ideas, developed by thinkers like Heinrich Pesch and Othmar Spann, had been disturbed by the selfishness, irresponsibility, and class conflict that accompanied industrial capitalism. They believed that these trends alienated workers, fostered socialism, endangered private property, and threatened freedom. To overcome these problems, they envisioned a harmonious polity composed of functional economic groups, or corporations.

These corporations, as corporatists defined them, had goals that took precedence over those of their members and were not merely the sum of the goals of their members. Yet because corporations were by definition organic groups, members would recognize that their needs and the needs of the group were ultimately identical and would spontaneously subordinate their desires to the demands of the group, in exchange receiving income, status, and individual fulfillment. Seeking freedom from the group amounted to self-destructive and antisocial behavior, for real freedom was in the community, especially in service to it. Because of the natural harmony corporatists envisioned between members and groups, moreover, popular sovereignty seemed at best irrelevant, at worst divisive and counterproductive. Leadership was to be exercised by a natural elite, and since this elite possessed superior wisdom and virtue and performed necessary functions by mediating conflicts and leading members toward common goals, its power was self-justifying.[8]

Given the lack of harmony in interwar Austria, however, these corporatists had from the beginning faced the problem of creating either corporate eggs or corporate chickens. In other words, they had either to convince individuals to adopt common goals so that together they could construct a corporatist system, or they had to construct a corporatist system that synthesized the goals of conflicting individuals. Above all they needed a natural elite, but they could never find one. The authority of traditional leaders of corporatist schemes, clerics and aristocrats, had been discredited in an increasingly industrial, scientific, and democratic society, and business managers were unsuitable, given workers' distrust. Eventually some of the ideologues would help establish a fascist dictatorship that used coercion to establish cooperation, a solution that contradicted the essence of corporatism but sustained the hierarchy, privilege, and private property that they had been anxious to defend.[9]

After fleeing the Nazis and beginning an academic career in America in the 1930s, Drucker described what he liked and disliked about his European heritage. In 1939 he expressed admiration for three corporatist thinkers of the Restoration Era, conservatives Joseph de Maistre and Vicomte de Bonald and right Hegelian Friedrich Stahl (about whom he had written his first book). He admired their "Christian" conception of "authority," which stressed the "duties" of property ownership, not merely its "privileges," and which called for responsible exercise of power in the interest of "its subjects."[10] Beyond this, according to his "oldest friend," Berthold Freyberg, he was trying to do for the twentieth century what Stahl had attempted for the nineteenth. He wanted to create a social and political structure adapted to the present but preserving the best of the past and offering through "responsibility" and "commitment" a "synthesis" of power and freedom. Stahl had failed because he could not find the appropriate institution to realize his goals. But Drucker came to believe that he had found the right vehicle in the properly managed business corporation.[11]

That Drucker should turn to a capitalist institution was another legacy of his central European roots. Bourgeois intellectuals in interwar Austria had been torn between desires for a corporatist and a liberal-capitalist order, reflecting a social conflict between an old professional and a new entrepreneurial middle class. Drucker had been affected by the old and the new. He had been born into a prominent family that respected public servants more than business-men. But as a young man he had worked in business, and his education, while scarcely technical, was more practical and professional than that of most of his class.[12]

Drucker had also respected another Viennese, the economist and historian Joseph Schumpeter, and had learned from him the importance of the entrepre-neur to society. For Schumpeter, the entrepreneur was the economic leader whose marketing and administrative skills converted "inventions" into "inno-vations" and thus created jobs and new wealth. But late in life Schumpeter had come to believe that entrepreneurial success was undermining capitalism; prosperity was creating cultural, institutional, and political conditions hostile to entrepreneurialism. Above all, the divorce of control from ownership had empowered a new elite of business managers who increasingly thought like employees, perpetuated current projects, and felt little incentive to innovate. These managers were motivated by an ethic of consumption rather than pro-duction and were committed to short-term personal gratification rather than long-term service to family and society. Capitalism, Schumpeter lamented, was in the process of transforming itself into socialism.[13] This prospect apparently appalled Drucker. By 1940 his search for a new social order became a quest for ways of integrating Schumpeter's innovating entrepreneur with Stahl's conser-vative, responsible ruler. He wanted business managers who could reconcile capitalist with corporative values.

It is not surprising, then, that Drucker should throughout his life claim alle-giance to the philosophy of Edmund Burke. From Burke and from his experi-ences with totalitarianism in central Europe, he had learned the folly of attempt-ing to transcend history and create a "perfect" or "infallible" society. He had become a self-professed "anti-utopian" whose goal was "an adequate, bearable society." And like Burke, he hoped to understand traditions and established institutions, to know "the new that is possible and needed," and then to use the new to make the old institutions "function effectively and perform responsibly for person and community alike." He called this "constructive conservatism" and "conservative innovation."[14] And again, the fundamental institution through which constructive conservatism could be practiced became for him the business corporation in which managers created wealth and nurtured communal harmony.[15]

In *The End of Economic Man*, published in 1939, Drucker explained what had happened when central European managers had failed to meet social responsibilities. They had, he said, valued people only for their labor and had treated them as factors of production. Treated like things, people had felt isolated and governed by irrational, "demonic forces" beyond their control. As a result, society had ceased to be a "community of individuals bound together by a common purpose" and had become a "chaotic hubbub of purposeless isolated monads." Confused and desperate, some were drawn to the nihilism of Marxism, which in turn undermined faith in traditional values and institutions and paved the way for Fascist dictatorships. Both Fascism and Marxism, as Drucker saw them, were escapist; they could establish order but never fulfill human needs. What people needed was a new "noneconomic society" that could provide freedom, "status," and "function," and it was the task of business managers to help create such a society by shaping the proletarian into the industrial citizen and the company into a community.[16]

In subsequent works, particularly in *The Future of Industrial Man* (1942), *Concept of the Corporation* (1946), and *The New Society* (1949), Drucker emphasized that only satisfying work could fulfill the needs of individuals for autonomy, security, dignity, usefulness, belonging, and peer respect. Work was needed as much to provide "status and function" as income, and only the hierarchical corporation could provide satisfying work. People were frustrated when labor was valued only as a commodity or when workers saw their jobs merely as a way to earn money. In these cases, the firm and the worker valued each other only as a means to an end. But the "apparently irresolvable conflict between the absolute claim of the group" and "the absolute claim of the individual" could be resolved if each accepted responsibility for satisfying the needs of the other. Through responsible acts of "citizenship" by manager and worker alike, the "two autonomous sets of purposes," the ends of society and of the individual, could be brought into "harmony" and thus "fulfilled in one and the same movement."[17]

Drucker found such corporative ideas both in German traditions and in American management publications of the 1930s. The German ideology of industrial leadership held that management was a calling, which was more than an avenue to status and wealth; it imposed obligations on managers to organize production in ways that served the interests of employees and the public good.[18] American mandarins like Chester Barnard claimed that the manager integrated the organizational tasks and goals of its members.[19] A manager, Drucker said, took "responsibility for the whole" by getting his subordinates to work toward a common goal. But true to his European heritage, he expressed these responsibilities in a Viennese way and compared the managerial task to that of an orchestral conductor. The conductor selected the piece, the goal. Each musician played one instrument and one part. But the conductor harmonized the efforts of all the performers in the orchestra so that the goal was achieved. "The conductor himself," Drucker explained, "does not play an instrument. He need not even know how to play an instrument. His job is to know the capacity of each instrument and to evoke optimal performance from each." "Instead of 'doing,' he leads."[20]

Drucker thus accepted management as a given and concluded that firms could no more do without managers than orchestras without conductors. The "hierarchy of command" in the business enterprise was a natural "hierarchy of skills and functions." Managers were skilled in selecting appropriate goals and in integrating the specialized tasks. And without hierarchy, organization was not possible. There was no escape from management; the choice was between management and mismanagement. For management was "grounded in the very economic and technological nature of modern industrialism."[21]

As for the goals to be implemented by managers, Drucker concluded that economic goals must come before social ones. If the firm did not perform well, it would go bankrupt and be unable to create a corporate community. Its "very survival" depended on making a profit that not only covered costs but provided insurance against the risk of failure in the future. To make such a profit, it must "create" customers by providing them with useful products and services. Profit, in Drucker's analysis, was the result of, and reward for, economic service, not the cause of it. But profit was "the ultimate test of business performance," indeed "the only possible test."[22]

The primacy of economic performance, however, should not obscure that the business corporation was "as much a social organization, a community and society" as it was "an economic organ." In the "new society," which was an employee society, the firm had a responsibility to realize social values and fulfill individual needs.

Still, as Drucker developed his theories, a central problem emerged, a problem that originated in his admission that the survival of the firm took precedence over the needs of any employee.[23] This priority could prevent the firm from acting responsibly toward its citizens. It meant that the interests of individual and firm might not be in harmony, a condition that contradicted his belief that managerial power was self-justifying because it was indispensable. Two dimensions of legitimacy were involved, one dealing with the assumed usefulness of a managerial elite to society as a whole, the other with the congruence between particular elite decisions and the needs of every organizational member. In other words, employees could condone management as an institution but condemn individual managers or specific decisions. Reconciling these two dimensions of legitimacy would continue to cause Drucker difficulty.

For Drucker legitimate power was "authority" based not on "submission to force," but on "the rule of right over might."[24] The ruled, in other words, must voluntarily grant the ruler's right to command and thereby their own obligation to obey, thus giving the ruler the capacity to govern effectively. Real legitimacy, however, would transcend passive submission to managerial authority. It would inspire active commitment by the ruled to organizational goals, the "self-discipline" that would motivate and guide their activities and produce peak performance.[25] They could work without discipline imposed by managers and would freely subordinate personal needs to those of society. Then the firm could become a harmonious corporate community.

Yet Drucker acknowledged that managerial power, because the firm could never "act primarily in the interests of those over whom the enterprise rules," would always have some illegitimacy. The firm served customers, not employees; it could not solve this problem through paternalistic forms of "enlightened despotism." When corporate interests conflicted with employee interests, those of the employee had to be sacrificed. Nor could the problem be resolved through schemes of employee ownership and democratic decision making. Even if the enterprise were a "government of the people and by the people," it could never be a "government for the people." Workers, who passively submitted to corporate authority might decide to withdraw their efficiency and refuse to "subordinate" their needs to the corporate "welfare."[26]

Legitimacy caused Drucker so much trouble because of his refusal to bring liberal ideas about government into the marketplace and replace bureaucracy with democracy. If a corporation were organized like a liberal democracy then citizens could grant legitimacy by choosing the forms of their government, its ends, its methods, and their leaders. But liberal government would threaten the management theory of value dear to Drucker. So he rejected free citizenship and would only allow employees to choose personal goals within the limits of managerial objectives. Such choices were less acts of consent by citizens than of convenience and necessity by subjects. Constrained in "voice," employees could "exit" and become entrepreneurs.

As Drucker struggled with the conflict between the need of society for managerial power and the need of the individual for satisfaction, he concluded that conflict could be minimized through methods that would lead employees to adopt "managerial attitudes" and seek fulfillment through commitment to the corporate good. Workers needed to be persuaded that employment as a social contract was both an agreement of "association" and one of "subjection." But they could experience some degree of "self-government" at work. Control over jobs, work methods, and work environments would allow workers to be participants in their "government." Participation would lead them toward the "Christian" conception of freedom, which was ethical, "responsible choice," not "license" or a right to "freedom from something." In addition, he thought that the firm should reward committed workers by promoting them.[27] But beyond this, he initially said little about the specific means for instilling a managerial attitude.

In the 1940s Drucker believed that labor unions could also help to inculcate a managerial attitude. Union leaders, although intent on protecting union members from management, were necessarily concerned with the survival of the firm; like any "loyal opposition," they could see the wisdom of working with managers to improve efficiency and help integrate corporate and employee goals.[28] After 1949, however, Drucker largely dropped this idea. With the waning of organizing drives, unions ceased to be one of his major concerns. And more importantly, by the 1950s he became attentive to a new type of nonunionized worker.

Initially Drucker labeled these new workers the "new industrial middle class," but eventually he called them "knowledge workers."[29] More recently several historical economists have named them "independent workers." Formally educated as professionals, technicians, or managers, such workers applied general knowledge and skills to unique situations. Their work was difficult to "routinize," and so they had substantial autonomy. They were expected to "internalize the formal objectives" of their organization and to accept "a kind of implicit contract," exercising initiative and solving problems while at the same time respecting "corporate authority."[30] Such workers threatened managers; Druckerism was a response to that threat in the same way that Taylorism had responded to industrial craft workers and Mayoism to restriction of output and industrial unions. Indeed, Drucker would argue that "just as the economic conflict between the needs of the manual worker and the role of an expanding economy was the social question of the nineteenth century," so "the position, function, and fulfillment of the knowledge worker is the social question of the twentieth century."[31]

Knowledge workers, as he saw it, were the new skilled workers, and their tasks and self-perceptions were different from those of manual workers. They used knowledge rather than "physical force or manual skill" and produced ideas rather than things. Each saw himself or herself as a professional, if not as an intellectual, and collectively they saw themselves "as 'part of management' without being 'managers,' and as 'workers' without . . . considering themselves 'proletarians.'" They did not command people, but their command of information influenced management.[32]

Because of their independent tasks and bourgeois self-images, these knowledge professionals caused peculiar problems for managers. Their work had to be managed because most of them were dedicated to their discipline, professional ethos, or specialized tasks rather than to the enterprise. They possessed the knowledge that the firm needed but not the "responsibility" to see that their projects were often irrelevant to "the goals of the whole," especially to the survival of the firm. Yet they could not be easily managed through the traditional forms of bureaucracy. They refused to be treated as inferiors or subordinates, and bullying tactics would likely lead them to sabotage or exit.[33]

For independent workers, Drucker doubted that Taylorism was useful because planning could not be separated from doing. Workers were hired to apply professional knowledge, to think, to innovate, and to adapt to changing circumstances. They were both planners and performers, and managers could not "take the knowledge out of the work" without destroying its usefulness. Furthermore, since knowledge workers must design their own work, a control system in which managers regulated work through formal, written rules was self-defeating. Unskilled labor and machines could seldom be adequate substitutes for professionals. Nor could the productivity of independent work be measured in quantitative terms. Other ways would have to be found that could make the necessity of autonomy a virtue and get the new workers to manage themselves.[34] Thus as early as the mid-1950s, long before "intrapreneurship" became a fad, Drucker was calling for a government consistent with entrepreneurship.[35]

In Drucker's view, moreover, Mayo's theories and the techniques of human relations had not been helpful in managing manual workers, let alone knowledge workers. Drawing on the ideas of Douglas McGregor, Drucker rejected the assumptions of Mayoism and particularly questioned the effectiveness and morality of using staff specialists and nondirective counseling to teach workers to trust managers. This approach naively assumed that managing workers required a staff specialist who could organize workers without organizing work. In addition, since resistance to corporate goals was assumed to originate in individual psychological problems, it could lead to "a new Freudian paternalism" and despotism. It also presumed that if workers trusted managers, they would become happy and productive, overlooking how irrational organization could stifle productivity. Finally, it sought merely to give workers "a sense of responsibility" and participation rather than giving them the real responsibility of helping to improve the organization. Drucker thought only genuine participation at work could legitimize corporate goals and maximize performance.[36]

This meant, Drucker believed, that corporate reorganization was needed. Knowledge work organizations would be less "pyramids" of power like those of the military or the church and more "concentric, overlapping, coordinated rings" like those of a university or a hospital. In such decentralized structures, the relationship of managers to knowledge workers would be one of mutual dependence. Although managers would still select corporate goals, they would allow their professional "juniors and colleagues" to choose their own work processes and standards. And in conjunction with their integration of corporate effort, managers would teach knowledge workers to work "under orders" and "subordinate the authority of knowledge to organizational objectives and goals." A new operational "organization ethics" would emerge, leading to a new corporate "common law" and "constitution." The knowledge worker could become a corporate "citizen" with corporate "virtue." One could help the firm, develop oneself, and "harmonize" "organizational goals and individual needs."[37]

Before Drucker, management mandarins like Chester Barnard, Henri Fayol, and especially Mary Parker Follett had emphasized that goals should be clear and legitimate. Follett had argued that managers should obey "the law of the situation" to "depersonalize" directives.[38] In the late 1940s, Drucker sought to learn more about management "as an integrating mechanism" by working inside a major corporation. He approached Westinghouse but was turned away because he talked like "a Bolshevik."[39] He turned to General Motors and in 1942 was asked to study its top management structure. Before he finished his study in 1945, he became acquainted with an organizational tool that seemed to provide at least some of what was needed. Alfred P. Sloan had used at GM something very similar to management by objectives since the 1920s. Donaldson Brown had given the method theoretical expression in a 1927 paper entitled "Decentralized Operations and Responsibilities with Coordinated Control."

Sloan developed his technique to cope with the problem of operating a large, complex agglomeration of business units that sometimes worked at cross purposes with one another. It worked through designing a central marketing strategy, creating several semiautonomous operating divisions to administer its implementation, and using a central staff to provide advice, coordinate efforts, and measure performance of the divisions. Policy was made through complex negotiations among managers that proceeded up, down, and across the organizational chart. The system combined, in Sloan's words, "the initiative, responsibility, development of personnel, decisions close to the facts, [and] flexibility" of decentralization with the "efficiencies and economies" of centralization. Drucker found such business "federalism" intriguing, and he discussed it in some detail in his 1946 book on General Motors, *Concept of the Corporation.*

In his autobiography, Drucker recalled that Charles E. Wilson of GM had told him that a generation of "Federalists" had designed the "structure" and "constitutional principles" of big business and that the subsequent generation of "Jeffersonians" would have to foster "citizenship and community."[40] Drucker would attempt to do so when he helped convert Sloan's technique for managing a multidivision firm into a technique for managing managers and knowledge workers.

Management by Objectives and Self-Control

Drucker worked out his ideas with Harold Smiddy, a vice-president at General Electric who had been impressed by Drucker's book on GM. Smiddy hired Drucker as a consultant and, with Drucker's prompting, began using participative management techniques. Superiors, the two men decided, could best get subordinates to work under self-control if goals and methods were jointly defined. Smiddy began clarifying objectives with his employees and in 1952 made the process part of company policy. Drucker labeled it "management by objectives and self-control."[41] Its purposes were to direct managerial vision into channels that would insure the survival and success of the firm, to legitimize managerial power and corporate goals, to fulfill individual needs, to guide knowledge work, and to unify ethics and entrepreneurship. By achieving these aims, it was intended to synthesize capitalism and corporatism.

Drucker first prescribed management by objectives in the sections entitled "Managing a Business" and "Managing Managers" in 1954 in *The Practice of Management.* He altered the prescriptions slightly thereafter. He quickly broadened the method from a technique for managing managers to one for managing knowledge workers. He also made it not only a strategy for directing firms but also for influencing government policy. And eventually, he would call upon government to use the system.

The technique had four parts: centralized determination of corporate goals, decentralized definition of operational targets and task organization, measurements of performance against objectives, and a system of rewards and punishments based on results.

It was important, first of all, that corporate strategy be made clear. Corporate goals comprised the "compass bearing" of the corporate ship, guiding it to its destination and preventing it from becoming "the plaything of weather, winds and accidents." Management must have a clear understanding of the "mission and purpose" of the firm. And determining this purpose required more than study of what the firm was doing, for studying present efforts might perpetuate obsolete processes and projects. It required careful market analysis of business opportunities because the customers decided "whether the efforts of a business become economic results or whether they become so much waste and scrap." Managers must learn who the customers were, who they could be, what their unsatisfied wants were, what they regarded as value, and what products would satisfy them. After such questions had been answered, entrepreneurial goals could then be set.[42]

These goals had to be clarified by converting broad aims into specific operational objectives. Managers should proceed, in other words, from learning what their business was and envisioning what it could be to marshaling the means to achieve its goals and devising a plan for utilizing these means. Operational objectives must set forth what was to be achieved in marketing, product innovation, output, resource allocation, personnel performance, corporate social responsibility, and performance measurement. The objectives must then be kept current with changing market conditions. There should be no attempt to outguess the business cycle or project the past into the future, for such attempts to escape risk were dangerous in a competitive and innovative economy. Profit making, Drucker emphasized, should not be the only objective. Overemphasis on profits would lead to shortsightedness, postponement of desirable investments, and continuation of obsolescent projects. Commitments to future actions should be used to make decisions about present means to achieve future results. When everyone in the firm knew these objectives, each could better organize his or her efforts to produce market results.[43] Obviously Drucker realized that clear goals could contribute not only to entrepreneurial effectiveness of managers but to their political effectiveness as well.

He believed that only top managers should select goals. But central control could lead to goals that subordinates did not understand or accept. Balancing despotism and legitimacy was always precarious, and initially Drucker offered only a few isolated examples of a successful balance. But by the 1960s he would point to "consensual decision-making" in Japanese corporations as the best way to set goals and would even claim that his books and seminars had taught the Japanese this system.[44] His praise of Japanese corporatism anticipated the fascination with their management that would preoccupy the American business community by the 1980s.

His view of decision making in Japanese corporations overplayed how initiatives came from the bottom and downplayed how managers used consultations to legitimize decisions from the top. He claimed that employees throughout the firm began by defining the problem to be solved. They decided what the question was before answers were solicited. Then discussions explored alternatives and their implications. The result usually was that "every decision comes up from below" and was "an expression of a general will." Finally, top management selected "the appropriate people" to make the decision, and once it had been made, their orders would be "obeyed without argument or reservation." Implementing ideas came swiftly because the decision process was seen as a means to action rather than as an end in itself. And because plans resulted from "consensus" rather than "compromises," the peculiar combination of "autocracy" and "democratic participation" insured that decisions never had to be sold to subordinates; "authority from the top down" was always matched by "responsibility from the bottom up." The system, Drucker said, could never be completely imitated by the West since it was rooted in Japanese culture and preindustrial values. But the underlying principles, he thought, might "point the way to solutions for some of our most pressing problems."[45]

After top management had established corporate strategy and made general operational objectives clear, then subordinate managers and knowledge workers were to negotiate with their superiors and draw up specific work assignments, performance goals, expected contributions, production targets, timetables, and allocations of resources. In negotiating with their superiors, subordinates were to set personal objectives that would substitute for narrow, systematic work rules and job descriptions imposed from above. The negotiation was to go beyond a Mayoist counseling interview that merely intended to give the worker a "sense of participation." Real participation, defining jobs and goals "actively and responsibly," would cause each to "commit himself" with "a positive act of assent" to "the ultimate business goals" and assume "genuine responsibility." The manager could then hold the worker to "exacting demands." This would be "upward responsibility" that would be formalized in what Smiddy had called the "manager's letter."[46]

In this [biannual] letter to his superior, each manager [or knowledge worker] first defines the objectives of his superior's job and of his own job as he sees them. He then sets down the performance standards which he believes are being applied to him. Next, he lists the things he must do to attain these goals—and the things within his own unit he considers the major obstacles. He lists the things his superior and the company do that help him and . . . that hamper him. Finally, he outlines what he proposes to do during the next year to reach his goals. If the superior accepts this statement, the "manager's letter" becomes the charter under which the manager [or knowledge worker] operates.[47]

Such goal setting was in many ways reminiscent of the nineteenth century "inside contracting" system for managing skilled workers in manufacturing firms. Under this system skilled craft workers had acted as subcontractors who bid on specific projects and organized the work themselves. Managers had found the workers hard to control and had converted the subentrepreneurs into employees.[48] But management by objectives could combine the advantages of subcontracting with those of bureaucracy. The negotiation process would atomize workers and get each to contract to individual goals, possibly encouraging heroic effort and Stakhanovite competition. Moreover, because the negotiations assumed that managerial power was legitimate, conflict would be transformed from quarrels over control to disagreements over goals. And since managers could better control their new skilled workers without directly controlling their work, they could benefit from contract and control, entrepreneurship and employeeship.

The transparency of negotiations and written contracts would help managers bridge the "communications gap." "Downward" communication, Drucker said, did not work because superiors did not understand the problems and goals of subordinates, and effective communication depended on some "prior agreement on meaning." Only after the subordinate had communicated "upward" his "values, beliefs, and aspirations" could a superior reconcile corporate and individual goals. The manager and the subordinate would understand one another and could better cooperate. A common language would help each person see what the other sees. Superior and subordinate could concentrate on their shared "objectives of performance" and unify their efforts in genuine teamwork.[49]

The third part of management by objectives was some system for measuring performance of employees relative to self-determined objectives. Drucker emphasized that measurements of results against goals must be beneficial to both the individual and the corporation. Feedback would give the individual worker information that could be used to exercise self-control over his or her work. And while measurements should not become merely tools of control from above, they should encourage rationality. With proper feedback, each employee could make independent decisions that would produce market results.[50]

Finally, management by objectives would set up rewards and punishments based on clear standards of performance. Appraising performance, Drucker concluded, was one of the most important tasks of the manager, and doing it fairly required "integrity," "the one absolute requirement of a manager." The system should develop "managerial vision"; foster "internal, self-motivation"; and encourage employees to "drive themselves." Employees should not be judged on potential or personality. Superiors should hold them "strictly accountable" for results and periodically review their contributions. And all rewards and punishments, including salaries, perks, promotions, demotions, and terminations, were to be based on performance relative to the objectives of the company. Performance was not to be judged purely on the bottom line, however, as that measured only business results, not individual ones.[51]

According to Drucker the combination of business goals, personal objectives, feedback on performance, and appropriate rewards would "harmonize the goals of the individual with the commonweal." It would substitute "management by self-control for management by domination," making management by objectives as much a "constitutional principle" as a managerial technique. Each worker would become a manager and assume responsibility not only for his or her job and work group but for the economic and social welfare of the organization. "Control from the inside" would be stricter, more exacting, and more effective than "control from the outside." As a manager, each worker would take action not because he or she was ordered to, but because "the objective needs of his task" demanded it. Hence, "by converting objective needs into personal goals," management by objectives could guarantee performance and "genuine freedom, freedom under the law."[52]

Since corporate law was determined by managers, freedom, for Drucker, was, as one commentator has suggested, a Hegelian "rationale for subordination."[53] Given this, his ideal of corporatist virtue amounted to Max Weber's concept of bureaucratic rationality. Both men assumed that functionaries would suppress goals in conflict with the corporation, accept managerial ends as givens, and methodically select means to attain them. Still Drucker realized, as Weber had before him, that rationality and harmony depended on the legitimacy of managers and on the selection of goals employees could accept.

In later years Drucker expanded his ideas by defining the social responsibilities of managers. His German corporatist ideals led him to emphasize that clear goals were as necessary in managing social responsibilities as in directing economic performance. Since the corporation was a social organization, it had obligations to its members and to society that had to be included in its corporate plan. Failure to be responsible could lead to loss of managerial autonomy if government, under pressure from unions and public interest groups, imposed controls. This danger especially concerned him after the emergence of the "new" social regulation of the late 1960s and early 1970s.[54]

Drucker's prescriptions concerning social responsibilities rejected the notion that a "hidden-hand" in the marketplace naturally converted "private vices" into "public virtues." He had never believed that competition automatically solved social problems or absolved managers of moral obligations.[55] Nor had he accepted Milton Friedman's argument that business people should stick to business and should refrain from appointing themselves guardians of the common good. They were running social organizations that could help society and realize social values. Like anyone else, they also had "a self-interest in a healthy society," so they should follow normal ethical imperatives.[56]

Moreover, for Drucker, managers were the only true leadership group in modern society. If they did not "take responsibility for the common good," then no one else could or would. Government leaders were too bogged down in politics to solve problems.

Managers, then, had to find ways of achieving economic goals and meeting social responsibilities. But they should transcend Andrew Carnegie's notions of business philanthropy. The idea of doing well in business in order to do good outside business, Drucker said, could justify using immoral methods to accumulate wealth.[57] Managers should strive to do the opposite—do good in order to do well. They should choose strategies in which profit making also solved social problems. He admired Japanese managers who "put national interest first" and pursued their private interests in ways that promoted the public interest.[58] For American examples, Drucker cited Henry Ford, who raised wages to sell more cars, and Julius Rosenwald of Sears, Roebuck, who promoted county agents and 4-H programs.[59] Similarly he argued that business managers should forgo strategies that might help their firms but hurt the commonweal. They should adopt the fundamental principle of the Hippocratic oath, "Above all, not knowingly to do harm," and find out whether a prospective strategy would be dangerous. Chemical companies should have tested the health and environmental impacts of DDT and then kept the product off the market.[60]

Drucker endorsed what he called the "Confucian approach" to ethics. In an interdependent "society of organizations," he said, everyone, from the highest manager to the lowest worker, should accept that they had responsibilities to everyone else. They should establish networks of "mutual obligation," help others achieve their goals, and nurture "harmony and trust." This "ethics of interdependence," he acknowledged, had no conception of "rights" with which members could claim "entitlements" and exemption from mutual obligations. For instance, he thought "whistle-blowers," rather than being heroic champions of the public good, were virtueless "informers" who violated their responsibilities. All organizational members should be good citizens, obey Confucian imperatives, and accept "the fundamental relationships" of society.[61]

Drucker encouraged members of the business community to be politically active. Managers should speak for "the general will" and serve as "integrators" who enhance "social cohesion" and consensus in a pluralist society. He praised the Business Round Table and the roles that Japanese business people played in their government and society. He insisted that managers who could not eliminate a socially harmful impact of business without raising costs should champion sound governmental regulation. By supporting regulation, they could insure that immoral behavior would bring no competitive advantage and that managers "who yield to temptation" would be punished without disrupting market forces. Finally, whenever possible, managers should encourage a process of "reprivatization" in government. They should get government to manage by objectives and set tasks that autonomous profit and nonprofit organizations could perform. Such reprivatization would place tasks under the control of competently managed organizations (universities and hospitals were his examples) whose success could be measured by the marketplace and whose activities could be eliminated if they failed or became obsolete.[62]

By acts of "statesmanship," by selecting goals that tried to solve social problems and avoid creating new ones, responsible business managers could help to harmonize private and public interests in ways that the market alone could not. They could also use their influence to create a government with clear goals for serving the common good, an effective administration, and a network of regulations that stopped irresponsible acts without unduly threatening business autonomy. Of course all this assumed that corporate leaders could, in Drucker's words, attain the "private virtue" that alone could define genuine social problems, achieve political consensus, mediate private and public interests, and thereby insure that government could escape from the politics of class.[63]

For and against Management by Objectives

In the quarter-century after 1954, Drucker's technique stimulated great interest among managers and mandarins, an interest measured by an extensive literature. In 1977 a fifty-five-page survey of American, British, and Canadian literature on management by objectives listed over seven hundred books, articles, monographs, dissertations, and theses. Over three hundred articles and readings appeared in foreign journals. Audio and video cassette packages, newsletters, and private corporate publications also examined the concept.[64] In England in 1971 a Management by Objectives Society began publishing *Management by Objectives*; this short-lived journal lauded the technique but also discussed difficulties encountered in applying it. Indeed, the sheer number of writers with various prescriptions is evidence of the difficulty of using the technique.

Nonetheless the technique was popular for several reasons. The formation of more multidivision and conglomerate firms isolated top managers and made governing more complicated.[65] Structural changes affected the labor market; independent workers increased from 27.8 percent of the work force in 1950 to 32.8 percent in 1970.[66] Managers complained that knowledge workers and middle managers were hard to evaluate and discipline; professional people were creative resources and resented being treated as factors of production.[67] And given a demand for alternatives to Taylorism, mandarins in addition to Drucker were supplying corporative solutions. Douglas McGregor, for instance, advised managers to abandon the Taylorist Theory X and adopt a Theory Y that organized work to satisfy workers' needs and meet organizational goals. McGregor recommended management by objectives because it evaluated workers based on performance and encouraged them to assume responsibility for improving their work. He had learned about the technique from managers at General Mills, who had been among the first to adopt Drucker's management by objectives when their company had reorganized into divisions.[68]

Empirical studies of how the system worked in practice, however, did not emerge until the late 1960s. It was adopted more because of logical appeal than because of proven usefulness.[69]

In 1974 two business educators attempted to determine how many American businesses used the system. They surveyed the Fortune 500 largest industrial firms and found that nearly one-half claimed to use the technique, but considerably fewer used it throughout the company and fewer still regarded it as a success. Additional study found that many companies that thought they were using Drucker's brand of management by objectives really were not. Many were simply setting corporate objectives and implementing them using traditional centralized authority. Subordinates were not being granted autonomy, either on the job or in setting performance goals. Goals and work rules were imposed from above. In some cases a laissez-faire method was used; managers told subordinates that results mattered but did not engage in any systematic, cooperative relations. All things considered, the authors concluded that only about 10 percent of the Fortune 500 used a management by objectives system like Drucker's. And while these companies generally regarded it as having been successful, it was not clear in what sense it had been successful, whether in terms of harmony, productivity, or control.[70]

Apparently most American business leaders continued to prefer conventional forms of bureaucracy. As Richard Edwards has argued, they probably saw advantages in written directives, narrow job descriptions, and close supervision even if it came at the cost of lower performance and less commitment. They preferred predictable performance to peak performance because it was more easily controlled and less risky; or they believed conformity to company rules was a more realistic goal than commitment to the corporate community.[71] Top managers were apparently unwilling or unable to negotiate with subordinates. Perhaps they thought it too time consuming, too threatening to their authority and power, or senseless given their own limited autonomy. In any event, the impact of management by objectives on labor management practice, while profound in certain companies, fell far short of being revolutionary.

These conclusions have been verified by most case studies. Two mandarins, Stephen J. Carroll and Henry L. Tosi, carried out the most synthetic and sophisticated study at Black and Decker in the late 1960s and early 1970s. Opinion surveys showed that management by objectives did not work quite the way Drucker had expected. Managers at all levels liked the clear goals and priorities, the easier communication between bosses and subordinates, and the way the system facilitated planning. But they did not like the red tape necessary to establish goals and measure performance or the problems encountered when trying to establish goals in fluctuating organizational, technological, and market conditions. Nor did they like the excessive attention given to quantifiable goals, the difficulty of setting nonperformance goals and measuring their achievement, the slighting of self-improvement goals, and the anxiety that resulted when they were held responsible for failures beyond their control. Upper-level managers argued that negotiations threatened their authority and committed them to "unrealistic or undesirable goals." Lower-level managers complained that they had little discretion in establishing goals and that structural factors like technology, budgets, agreements with other departments, and the limitations of job and expertise often confined them to choices of means rather than ends.[72] In practice the reconciliation of the interests of workers below top management with those of the corporation seemed problematic at best.

The fate of corporatism in practice was especially apparent in Carroll and Tosi's analysis of the essence of Drucker's management by objectives, the negotiations between superior and subordinate. They found that goals and feedback improved performance much more than participation in setting goals. Clear goals accepted by employees increased productivity. When goals were not accepted, employees became hostile, defensive, less willing to perform. While genuine participation in goal setting did not greatly increase performance, it could improve acceptance of goals and quality of decisions, and it often helped satisfy the need for self-actualization, autonomy, status, belonging, and security. But in general, after the introduction of management by objectives, managerial employees "were no more satisfied with pay or their jobs than before," and they did not experience "any more control over their work, any changes in their jobs, or any more job interest . . . than before."

Carroll and Tosi argued that management by objectives was most successful in creating harmony and improving performance when subordinates were self-confident, well informed, and high on the organizational chart and when their bosses were supportive, could reward achievements, and were willing to relinquish some power. But establishing the conditions for such success, especially redistributing power, would itself require a change in "both the philosophy and practice of management." Managers seemed to have little incentive to make such changes.[73] They could keep their power, set individual goals by executive fiat, persuade their subordinates to accept them, and get virtually as much productivity as when goals were set by corporatist negotiation and contract. And they could do so without the accompanying red tape, time-consuming negotiation, and risk.

Indeed, by the late 1960s several mandarins were arguing that Drucker's bureaucratic techniques overwhelmed his corporatist theory. A few psychologists in particular doubted that his brand of authoritarianism could instill self-motivation or corporate virtue.

Harry Levinson, a psychologist and management theorist at Harvard, contended that Drucker's system could not satisfy the needs of employees. The system, Levinson said, put corporate goals first and allowed the individual little influence over such goals and no power to pursue individual ends that conflicted with job assignments. It insured that the individual would feel like "an object," an "instrument for reaching a goal." To make matters worse, the employee was forced to set personal goals within the confines of corporate strategy so that if he failed to reach them, he would be "hoisted on his own petard." Workers under these conditions felt "like rats in a maze" who only got to choose their own "bait." Moreover, the carrots and sticks of the underlying reward-punishment psychology caused employees to act less from corporate virtue and more from selfishness. They were being bribed and bullied, not self-motivated. By treating people as "patsies to be driven, urged, and manipulated," management by objectives often intensified "the hostility, resentment and distrust" between manager and managed that it was supposed to eliminate and encouraged the withdrawal of efficiency that it was designed to overcome. Because of its contradictions, it was "self-defeating," "really just industrial engineering with a new name, applied to higher managerial levels." It could achieve self-motivation, Levinson concluded, only if it began with the needs of the individual, then proceeded to corporate goals and work assignments. Only through escape from bureaucracy could corporate virtue and the "conjunction" of individual and company requirements be secured.[74]

This implied that in an enterprise of self-directing employees managers would no longer be needed and bureaucracy would wither away. People would thus become free and governed at the same time by choosing their government and goals. No mandarin critic of Drucker, however, drew this conclusion or advocated genuine democracy. Although the term *democratic* was sometimes used, it meant that managers should undergo "sensitivity training" and become paternalist "leaders" who could understand employees and "enlist" their cooperation.[75] The traditional hierarchy of business was to remain, and harmony would come from those on top being nice to those on the bottom.

If anything, managers criticized Drucker for being too permissive rather than too authoritarian. Thomas Fitzgerald, a director of employee research and training at General Motors, argued that structural and cultural influences had caused managers to be authoritarian and workers uncooperative. Mass production required unquestioned expert leadership, so corporations selected managers who were "dominant." They could not and should not be trained to be cooperative. In contrast, workers wanted leisure, and their consumerism had undermined their "willingness to bear with the common drudgery" and sapped their desire to participate in decision making. On the contrary, if workers were called upon to negotiate with their superiors, their "persistent populism and egalitarianism" could lead them to challenge "management's present monopoly" of power. Such a redistribution of power would prove disastrous, Fitzgerald explained, because workers lacked expertise. Instead of negotiating and relinquishing power, managers should stick with Mayoism, giving up their authoritarian "style" and offering subordinates praise, recreation programs, slogans, contests, and "sets of monogrammed glasses."[76]

Other writers complained that the goal-setting part of the technique was unsuited to managerial tasks. H. E. Wrapp contended that managers could seldom establish clear goals. They had to respond to changing circumstances. Rather than managing by objectives, they managed by "wheel and deal," adapting to demands of the moment.[77] Such criticism was consistent with empirical studies that showed managerial practice to have short-term, spontaneous, and sporadic qualities.[78] All this implied that goal setting, a prerequisite for corporatist negotiation, could be difficult and inadvisable.

Ironically, another serious challenge to Drucker came from an admirer of management by objectives. Abraham Maslow had been attracted to Drucker's technique because he believed managers using the system could more efficiently produce "self-actualized," psychologically healthy people than therapists using psychoanalysis. His contribution was *Eupsychian Management*, which Drucker believed was "aimed" at him and which, he conceded, made a "real impression."[79]

Maslow exposed the assumptions about human nature and society underlying management by objectives and, in doing so, inadvertently revealed the almost utopian qualities of Drucker's corporatism. For the system to function, he argued, certain types of firms, work, managers, and workers must already exist. The system assumed that all work would be self-actualizing and therapeutic and that people would embrace work "eagerly and happily." It assumed that people had what Veblen called "the instinct of workmanship"; that all could be trusted, for if society was divided into "lambs and wolves, rapists and rapees," then cooperation was impossible; that Dostoevski's Grand Inquisitor was wrong and people actually wanted responsibility and challenges; that employees and managers could know and choose what was good for individuals and the organization; that subordinates could respect, even love, their superiors; that bosses would willingly give up power over others; and that business could help people develop in healthy ways. It also assumed a sound market standing so that "eupsychian growth and self-actualization" would be compatible with corporate performance. (In this regard Maslow proved prophetic; the firm in which he had observed the practice of management by objectives dropped the system when it went through hard times in the early 1970s.[80]) And more generally it assumed that employees and managers were healthy and homogeneous, not "psychopaths, schizophrenics, paranoids, brain injured, feeble-minded, perverts," or "addicts," among other things.[81]

Finally Maslow noted that management by objectives assumed that corporations could become "synergic" institutions in which persons pursuing selfish ends "automatically" helped others and persons acting altruistically "automatically" helped themselves. In synergy, all choices were good, no distinction existed between good and evil behavior, all acts rebounded to personal and public advantage, and "virtue" paid. Not surprisingly, the only examples he could find of this were from a nonindustrial culture, the Blackfeet Indians.[82] Although Maslow believed these prerequisites for management by objectives could be met, his optimism directly contradicted his analysis.

Drucker responded to his critics by admitting that his system had become a "fad" in the 1960s and had been "oversold and overpromoted." But he thought that when applied properly, it had worked. In *Management*, he restated his old arguments. His version of management by objectives, he acknowledged in addressing Maslow, was "a stern taskmaster" and was not "permissive." The responsibility and self-discipline that it demanded required strong and healthy people. But he denied that there were realistic alternatives. The traditional kind of bureaucratic control, with its carrot-and-stick approach, did not work in developed countries. Manual workers there resented being driven and were not appeased by gimmicks from the personnel department. Companies could not afford continually higher wage costs. Knowledge workers must be self-directed; they needed negotiation and some autonomy.

Nor did Drucker think that basing management by objectives on individual rather than corporate goals could ever be as rational as Levinson claimed. Economic survival of the firm had to take precedence over individual needs. To think otherwise, to want "organization without alienation," was the illusion of "romantics," for in a real sense, "organization is alienation." Managers could not avoid this problem by undergoing sensitivity training to become unselfish and reduce the alienation of their subordinates. These techniques threatened to create a new form of bureaucratic "control through psychological manipulation." They could lead to "enlightened psychological despotism," which was a "particularly repugnant form of tyranny" because it sought to control the mind and not just behavior. Or at least they could do so if managers could understand people in ways that would enable them to become psychological despots, which Drucker doubted was possible. Instead, managers should stick to organizing cooperation, something they could do.

Finally, Drucker argued, the firm could not become a democracy without turning decision making into "a never-ending bull session." The survival of the firm required "clear, unambiguous, designated command authority vested in one person." Production collapsed when managers were removed, as "proven," he claimed rather weakly, after the nationalization of extractive industries in Mexico in the 1930s, in Iran under Mossadegh, and more recently in Bolivia and Chile.[83] Management, he later emphasized, "will not 'wither away.'"[84]

If employees could not consent to managerial power, if they could not accept the "responsibility for contribution" that the "new individualism" demanded, then Drucker advised them to break the social contract by exercising their right to emigrate and finding employment elsewhere. To fight "old fights" of class conflict and chant "old chants" of workers' democracy were the tasks of Sisyphus.[85]

More difficult than determining the influence of Drucker's technique of labor management is assessing how, if at all, his prescriptions have affected entrepreneurial behavior. One writer claimed that Drucker's emphasis on the creation of customers had a lasting impact on marketing theory since the 1950s.[86] But by the 1980s, after a decade of stagnation in manufacturing and increased penetration of American markets by foreign firms, several economists and management theorists were arguing that Americans in business had fallen far short of Drucker's and Schumpeter's ideal of the entrepreneur. As noted previously, such advocates of industrial policy as Ira Magaziner and Robert Reich and such consultants as Robert Hayes and William Abernathy were indicting managers for having become short-term profit-seekers rather than long-term production planners, for trying to redivide the economic pie rather than expand it, for surrendering the manufacturing field to foreign invaders, and for relying on abstract techniques rather than engineering knowledge.[87]

Drucker, of course, had always held that profit was the ultimate test of business performance, a lesson that was still followed. But if the critics were right, managers had ignored his simultaneous insistence that corporate survival, indeed the survival of capitalism itself, required long-term planning and intelligent risk taking, constant technical innovation with accompanying elimination of obsolete products and processes, effective protection of market standing, and strategies that served workers and the public.[88]

Drucker has tried to define this problem out of existence by denying that any national decline in entrepreneurship occurred during the 1970s. He acknowledged a decline in mature industries like auto, steel, rubber, and petroleum, a decline that was a natural result of their evolution and technological stagnation. But fortunately, jobs lost in dying smokestack industries had been offset by new jobs created by entrepreneurs running small and mid-sized companies. By ignoring that entrepreneurs were profiting without producing new wealth, that the new jobs often paid far less than the old ones, and that foreign firms had been able to maintain high wages and profits in mature industries, he downplayed any need for dramatic, disruptive changes in management or government policy. America, he said, already had a new "entrepreneurial economy" led by "conservative innovators" who were minimizing risks by converting social problems into business opportunities and thereby making piecemeal improvements in society.[89]

Moreover, Drucker contended that the requirements of an entrepreneurial economy and the imperatives of computer technology were hastening the evolution of a new form of business organization that was reuniting planning and doing. The new environment was creating "information-based organizations," which were more like hospitals, universities, and symphony orchestras in that each employed more knowledge workers and fewer middle managers than orthodox "command-and-control organizations." Maintaining innovation and exploiting computers required knowledge workers who directed their work with feedback from colleagues and customers. Middle managers, who lacked specialized knowledge and merely relayed information up and down the newly flattened hierarchy, were therefore unproductive; nearly two-thirds of their positions could be eliminated.[90] Here also Drucker was arguing that planning and doing would soon come together again.

Still, even as he described the "low hierarchy" of the new organization, Drucker continued to emphasize that "central management" was needed; even orchestras needed conductors, and hospitals, administrators. Top managers would still have to be generalists who received professional training, and they would still maintain control by using management by objectives.[91] So whatever happened to organizational structures and the roles of knowledge worker and middle manager, the role of top management would and should continue.

Obviously Drucker was not in favor of a full fusion of planning and doing. His persistent advocacy of decentralized operations and centralized coordination through management by objectives still presumed an elite corps of top managers. And if such managers lacked operational experience and were isolated from production, the objectives they helped to set could be confined to quantitative standards and short-term profits, as they had been in the old organizations.[92] These same managers could remain primarily concerned with controlling subordinates and minimizing risk, not with allowing freedom to innovate.

Drucker, to be sure, never called for universal managers armed with advanced business degrees to replace engineers as corporate leaders. But his prescriptions presumed a distinct managerial elite; he never called for much change in the social composition of the corporate establishment. He was content with trying to teach business leaders the values of Schumpeter's ideal entrepreneur and Stahl's responsible ruler. He naively assumed that bureaucrats had the background, values, outlook, and institutional incentive to learn his ideas.

This particular problem has raised important issues not only for Drucker's management by objectives but for other managerial techniques as well. His technique presumed that managers could become what William A. Williams has described as an "industrial gentry."[93] To implement management by objectives, managers had to possess entrepreneurial talent, corporate virtue, and civic virtue and had to be able to reconcile capitalist individualism with corporatist groupism. Such managers have been rare in America, and Drucker has admitted that at best only 3 to 5 percent of American firms have been well managed.[94] And without these virtues and talents, managers probably could not or would not use his technique. Management by objectives has thus seemed self-contradictory and chimerical. To a considerable extent, it has presupposed the managers it was designed to create and has depended on prerequisites it had no way to achieve.

This helps explain the wide gap that mandarins have often seen between Drucker's prescriptions and management practice.[95] Echoing Maslow, the sociologist Rosabeth Moss Kanter has called Drucker a "management utopian" who had an excessive faith in his ideas and managers' ability to learn them. His vision of "the world-as-it-ought-to-be" obscured sight of "the world-as-it-is." His faith made him attribute failures to "ignorance" of his ideas. Faith prevented his understanding the "human limitations," managers' lust for power and money, and the "organizational limitations," those bureaucratic imperatives for centralization and specialization, that so often led to failure.[96]

In the end, Drucker's management theory of value led him to assume the existence of the corporatist leaders and organizations that needed to be created. Both the absence of social harmony and the absence of the leaders to establish it have apparently doomed his attempt to synthesize corporatism and capitalism in much the same way that it doomed the efforts of the Austrian corporatists. Drucker failed to solve the corporatist chicken-egg dilemma.

The Rationality
of Feelings

Sensitivity Training and
the Democratic Manager

Drucker and other corporative mandarins said they were trying to transcend the impersonality that Max Weber believed defined bureaucratic rationality. By its nature, Weber said, the modern, scientifically managed bureaucracy put technical efficiency ahead of personal emotions. Employees, regardless of their feelings, could only choose among ways to achieve the goals handed down by superiors. Weber lamented this but thought that efficiency developed "the more perfectly the more the bureaucracy is 'dehumanized,' the more completely it succeeds in eliminating from official business love, hatred, and all purely personal, irrational, and emotional elements which escape calculation." In the process, the individual was reduced to his or her function and became "a single cog in an ever-moving mechanism which prescribes to him an essentially fixed route of march."[1]

Weber's description of the stoic ethic demanded of bureaucrats was the central prescription in subsequent management publications. Taylor gave the idea its classic expression in his parable of Schmidt, the "first-class" pig-iron handler, and in his plea for a "mental revolution" by managers and workers. Mayo urged managers to help "irrational" workers understand the "logic" of the enterprise. Simon encouraged managers to use cybernetic metaphors to help understand behavior in bureaucracies and to think of people and computers as different species of the same genus. Typically, as sociologist Rosabeth Moss Kanter has argued, management theory has exalted a "masculine ethic" of ascetic, practical service to the corporation.[2]

Accordingly, when some psychologists and educators in the 1940s began calling for managers to adopt the values of the therapist and teacher and find ways of satisfying the needs of employees, they were seemingly repudiating the masculine ethic and its conception of bureaucratic rationality. They were challenging, so it seemed, Simon's rational man organization theory. They were substituting the idea that a combination of therapy and education—variously labeled laboratory training, executive development, group dynamics, encounter groups, managerial grid seminars, T-groups, or sensitivity training—could persuade managers and knowledge workers to become "democratic leaders" who would value individual satisfaction as much as organizational performance. Once they had been reeducated, they could become "change agents," who could then introduce "democratic" reforms in their companies. And the result would be harmony between individual and organization, making it unnecessary for employees to repress their emotions and feel reduced to vocational automatons. As Kanter and others have described it, the educators and psychologists were trying to feminize the masculine ethic of bureaucracy.[3]

Such an interpretation, however, is too simple. Corporatist mandarins thought capitalism with a human face could more efficiently instill bureaucratic rationality. Paternalistic and participative management would teach, as Drucker said, an "organization ethic" that could convert "objective needs" of the job into "personal goals."

Sensitivity training, as this chapter will show, followed a similar logic and was less a means to destroy the bureaucratic ethos than a technique to fulfill it. Designed to create a new democratic manager morally and technically superior to the scientific manager, the training was often used to prepare managers for the corporative arrangements called for in management by objectives and job enrichment. But the conservative dimensions of democratic leadership made it a means to make bureaucrats as rational as machines and so perpetuated much of Taylorism and Mayoism.

Democracy, Education, and Therapy

Sensitivity training originated in the United States during the 1940s and became another tool in what the historian William Graebner has called "democratic social engineering." By this, he meant the efforts of educators, Protestant clergymen, social workers, psychologists, and personnel managers to develop "quintessentially American" techniques of "social control," techniques that were characterized by small group discussion, a parental style of leadership, and "participation of the objects of control."[4] In particular the road to sensitivity training followed four routes: the "foremen's clubs" of personnel management, the counseling methods developed by the human relations school, the democratic practices of progressive education, and the group therapy techniques of European psychology.

Since early in the twentieth century, personnel managers had been concerned about the irrationality caused by despotic foremen. After World War I, and especially after the Wagner Act, they tried to resolve this problem through foremen's clubs. These clubs were really training forums created and controlled by managers. Upper-level managers conducted discussions, teaching the importance of legitimizing managerial ideas, treating workers decently, and improving productivity. The main goal was to make supervisors into democratic team leaders who used persuasion rather than coercion to achieve corporate goals and class harmony.[5] The subsequent sensitivity training movement shared this goal but relied on methods that were less didactic and more therapeutic.

The human relations proponents, especially Elton Mayo and Carl Rogers, had also developed an ideal of the friendly supervisor. For them a personable manager could inspire a sense of trust among workers. And counseling was one of many methods that could be used to give workers the feeling that they were part of a big, happy, corporate family. In private interviews, workers were listened to by nondirective counselors and they often experienced a cathartic feeling that made them favorably disposed toward their companies. In this form, however, counseling was conceived and used mainly to diffuse discontent among production workers. It was not used to change the values of managers. Nor was the ideal of the friendly supervisor seen as a basis for abolishing centralized power and specialized tasks. It was a way to ease anomie without eliminating bureaucracy.[6]

Progressive educators had already developed methods to make people more cooperative. Most importantly, John Dewey had developed the notions that education should be modeled after scientific inquiry; that learning should come through conversation; that conversation required egalitarian, tolerant, adaptable, inquisitive, cooperative, and open people; that "learning by doing" was more effective than the "spectator theory of knowledge" and rote memorization of symbols; that understanding was characterized by holistic insight; and that learning should be connected to the problems and experiences of the students and should nurture liberal values. These ideas and the educational systems that had developed from them were supposed to foster a democratic society that not only insured individual growth and freedom but also made sound collective decisions. Transferred to business, these methods would presumably make bureaucrats more democratic and improve their moral and technical decision making.[7]

The connections between progressive education and the beginnings of sensitivity training are clear in both institutional and individual activity. The National Education Association (NEA), a leading organization of progressive educators, became the primary sponsor of the technique in its early years. And two of its early developers, Leland P. Bradford and Kenneth D. Benne, had been in the movement. Bradford, who later served as the director of the sensitivity training group in the NEA from 1947 to 1967, had worked for the Works Progress Administration as a trainer of teachers in its adult education program. And Benne, like John Dewey, had helped to formulate educational theories that could link consensus and action, science and democracy.[8]

The connection was particularly clear in an article on democratic ethics that Benne published in *Progressive Education* in 1949. In it, he urged educators to become social engineers and change agents who worked to improve both industry and democracy. He thought that a "misfit" existed between the demands of a technologically advanced, industrial society and the traditional methods of decision making and social control. The cultural lag produced privately and poorly made decisions and "insecure, restless, 'lost'" individuals. And the remedy, Benne said, was democracy, a type of social control that could both improve decisions and secure social harmony. Democracy could be achieved by properly training people in democratic ideology and participatory decision making. Once trained, they could then check the fallibility and authoritarianism inherent in private planning, render "collective judgment" that was both rational and consistent with individual autonomy, resolve "social and interpersonal conflicts," and "construct a common interest out of . . . conflicting interests."

Benne's prescriptions had several contradictions and gaps. He called for conformity to privately managed bureaucracies and for democratic decision making. But he never clarified whether he expected managers to give up control over subordinates or merely consult with them. He also wanted an elite to teach "anti-authoritarian" values. But the elite's membership, the social engineers, was never defined. Presumably since he was writing to existing educators, Benne was assuming that they were willing and able to teach democracy. Nor did he clarify just who the student body for democratic training was to be. Blue-collar workers were never mentioned, leaving the impression that Benne's democracy would be strictly white collar.[9]

Such problems, similar to those in progressive education itself, would plague sensitivity training from its beginning. But this could be expected, given the background of its founders, a background that also helped make them receptive to two immigrant psychologists from Central Europe, Jacob L. Moreno and Kurt Lewin.

Moreno (1889–1974) was born a Rumanian, but in Vienna he developed psychological concepts that he brought to America in 1925. Psychology, he believed, should strive to develop "harmonious interpersonal relationships" so that groups could work "at the maximum efficiency and with a minimum of disruptive tendencies."[10] Hence, as the replacement for Freudian psychoanalysis, which in his view was insufficient for understanding and improving collective behavior, he offered group therapies that he called psychodrama and sociodrama. Role playing, he argued, provided more opportunities for understanding and catharsis than merely talking about personal problems. For if a "director" could create "dramatic" situations and could lead "actors" in playing out roles "on stage" in front of an audience, the actors would often reveal their real selves. Following the "play," the audience and the director could then criticize the performance with the actors, thus helping them to understand themselves and others. Particularly revealing, Moreno believed, was a drama that involved role reversal, for instance, asking a male manager to pretend he was a female worker. He also found that sociodrama often resulted in very emotional experiences, which in his view helped participants gain an aesthetic, holistic insight into relationships and become more flexible in their behavior.

Moreno's group therapy technique directly influenced the founders of sensitivity training. Leland Bradford first learned of it in the mid-1940s and used it to help veterans adjust to civilian life. Shortly thereafter, he and Ronald Lippitt, a psychologist trained at the University of Iowa, were among the first to use role playing in working with business managers. Through it, managers were supposed to become more sympathetic to their subordinates and were to learn by doing.[11]

At Iowa, Lippitt had written his dissertation under the supervision of Kurt Lewin (1890–1947), who has since been described as "the undisputed intellectual leader" of the creators of sensitivity training.[12] A German Jew, Lewin had become a prominent figure in Gestalt psychology and, in one of his first publications, an essay on "The Taylor System" appearing in 1920, had criticized scientific management for its inconsistencies with human needs, claimed that truly efficient work would be both productive and humane, and called for psychologists to integrate the goals of managers and workers. In 1933 he fled Berlin to escape Nazism and, after coming to America, won recognition for his work on group dynamics and democratic leadership.

Of particular importance to the development of sensitivity training was Lewin's "field theory," which assumed that people were naturally inclined toward life in groups. As he conceived them, groups were psychologically interdependent, organic wholes, which meant that interactions continually changed both the group and the individuals in it and that the whole and its parts could only be understood through observing its evolving processes. Groups that achieved their goals, Lewin maintained, were cohesive. Members felt a sense of belonging and were helped to achieve personal goals, and because members fulfilled themselves in group activity, they were committed to collective goals and pressured one another to conform.[13]

Given his aversion to tyranny in Central Europe and his attraction to democracy in America, Lewin was intent on understanding authoritarian groups and learning how to make them democratic. For these purposes, he helped conduct a series of famous experiments with boys' clubs in Iowa City, experiments that formed the basis of Lippitt's dissertation and a data base for devising techniques of democratic leadership. In these studies, clubs were established for ten-year-old boys to make theatrical masks, and the adult leaders then experimented with different types of social climates and leadership styles. The leaders employed authoritarian, laissez-faire, and democratic management methods while being discreetly observed by several graduate students and psychologists.

For the social scientists, authoritarianism and anarchism were proven inferior to democracy. In groups with "authoritarian leadership," the leader chose work goals and methods and tried to direct behavior through praise and criticism. This got masks produced but caused conflict. It created a repressive atmosphere in which the boys acted aggressively toward one another, used "ego-involved" language, engaged in extensive scapegoating, and worked only under compulsion. In addition, they were hostile to other groups, were inflexible and rigid, and sought status through dominating others or submitting to authority. In groups with "laissez-faire leadership," on the other hand—groups in which the adult only provided materials and answered questions, did not praise or criticize anyone, and left all decisions to the boys—permissiveness produced different dysfunctions. These "anarchist" groups were cohesive but not very productive. Members lacked a sense of accomplishment and put intense pressure on one another to conform to collective standards.

"Democratic leadership," in contrast, seemed to offer productivity, cohesion, and freedom. The democratic leaders set general goals, suggested alternatives, offered technical advice, praised or criticized the behavior of members (not their personal characteristics), and let the boys choose work methods and the division of labor. As a result the boys were productive, committed to their work, and self-supervising. They used "fact-minded" language, sought status through achievement in their tasks, and derived a sense of accomplishment from their work. They behaved these ways, Lewin and his students concluded, because democratic leadership best fulfilled the work demands of the group and the personal needs of its members. The problem-solving discussions and the participative decision making allowed members to influence the goals and activities of the group and thus broke down the distinction between the leader and the led, the group and the individual.[14]

The developers of sensitivity training concluded that lessons from the boys' clubs could be transferred to business firms. But problems would emerge from this transfer. First of all, Lewin's field theory amounted to what C. Wright Mills called psychologism, a naive attempt to explain society through interactions among individuals without taking into account the importance of institutions.[15] In reality a business corporation was not merely a group shaped by personal transactions; it was a bureaucracy defined by a hierarchical division of power. Hence an attempt to make it cooperative without eradicating hierarchy might do more to legitimize managerial power than to establish democracy. Moreover, like predecessors in industrial psychology and the human relations school,[16] the Lewinians assumed that managerial style rather than social structure was the problem. Conflicts between individuals and organizations were caused by inept managers rather than being problems inherent in bureaucracy and capitalism. Consequently, Lewinians made no attempt to understand the social and historical roots of hierarchy, authoritarianism, or the rationality Weber had described. They simply accepted bureaucracy as a given and wanted to rationalize individual bureaucrats. So their efforts to free people from authoritarianism were severely constrained by a conservative social theory. And conservatism could easily lead them to become architects of adjustment.

As conservative as their social theory was the Lewinians' notion of democratic leadership. The phrase was misleading in several ways. The adults were not leaders in a truly democratic sense because the boys could neither elect or reject them. The adults were managers who set the framework of goals within which the boys could make choices. What was being called democratic could perhaps more accurately be labeled parental or corporatist; the psychologists wanted management by wise, caring adults over unruly but precious children. Managerial power was acceptable if it led to cohesion and productivity, and the use of productivity standards to evaluate the leadership styles made the term *democratic* even less appropriate.[17] They were really applying bureaucratic standards, which meant that democratic leadership was from its beginning a contradiction in terms, more an ideal of paternal and rational management than an alternative to bureaucracy. As such, the Lewinians' ideas, ideas that were intendedly radical but implicitly conservative, fit the pattern that the historian Richard Pells found typical in American thought during the depression.[18]

Although Lewin's circle were unaware of it, conservative tendencies emerged when they tried to discover the most effective technique for persuading authoritarians and anarchists to accept their brand of democracy. In their search, they drew on Lewin's World War II research on the best method for convincing consumers to buy organ meats. He had showed that people most readily accepted facts they had discovered and were most likely to change when they learned independently that their ideas were wrong. Accordingly, autocratic methods of education, like lectures or propaganda, were less effective than individual research and group discussion, and authoritarian methods were especially counterproductive, Lewin decided, for the democratic reeducation of authoritarian leaders and followers. As he put it, "democracy cannot be imposed upon a person; it has to be learned by a process of voluntary and responsible participation." Democratic reeducation required a democratic method that could lead people to choose new values, habits, and feelings and thus establish "a new super-ego."[19]

Lewin and his disciples thought that they had accidentally invented the appropriate technique at a seminar at the New Britain State Teachers College in Connecticut during August of 1946. By that time, Lewin had left the University of Iowa and with the support of Douglas McGregor had moved his work to MIT and set up there a Research Center for Group Dynamics. After his move, Lewin had been approached by the Connecticut Inter-Racial Commission and Department of Education to direct a training session that would help teachers and social workers combat racial and religious prejudice. With additional financial backing from the Commission on Community Interrelations of the American Jewish Congress, he had, with the assistance of Lippitt, Benne, and Bradford, proceeded to set up shop in New Britain.[20]

The purpose of the seminar was to help the teachers, civil rights administrators, and social workers in it develop skills that would enable them to implement more fully the civil rights provisions of the Fair Employment Practices Act. Lewin's circle assumed that ineffective performance in groups was the problem and was the result of "inadequate group and personal action skills." Consequently they tried to help the trainees operate committees and diagnose conflicts more effectively by teaching them the "individual and group skills required for harmonious and productive living in modern society" and for attaining "democratic health." In short they used the seminar as an opportunity to train democratic leaders and to study democratic education techniques.[21]

At first the trainers used the standard repertoire of educational and therapeutic activities. They tried to show the advantages of equalizing influence and opening communication by leading group discussions and by directing sociodramas. Only "somewhat inadvertently" did they stumble upon the method that would later be called the training group.

The discovery was made in evening sessions where the trainers and observers gathered to discuss what had happened during the day and to evaluate the effectiveness of their techniques. The evening sessions soon came to include several of the trainees who, because they were bored with living on campus, asked if they could attend. Most of the trainers were reluctant to allow this, probably fearing that their scientific work would be disrupted or that the trainees might get upset. Lewin, however, overruled his colleagues and perhaps believed that in democratic education, students should be allowed access to all information. In one of the following sessions, the trainers began discussing earlier behavior of one of the attending trainees in relation to his group, attempting to determine why he had acted as he did. Eventually the trainee objected to the thrust of the conversation and tried to explain his actions. This led to an interchange between trainee and trainers that Benne remembered as having an "electric effect," and Bradford as a "tremendous electric charge." The emotional effects of discussing the immediate impact of individual behavior, without reference to any roles or relationships outside the group, created new educational opportunities. So through their discussions, the trainers and trainees had invented a new method for learning about behavior. Soon all the trainees began attending the evening sessions so as not to miss anything.[22]

With completion of research designed to test the effects of both the daytime and evening sessions, Lewin and his associates decided that they had combined therapy and education in a new way and in the process had invented an important training tool. Interviews and surveys of the graduates and their colleagues seemed to show that the graduates had become more effective in their roles, more sensitive to the feelings of others, and more adept at diagnosing conflicts and misunderstandings. These findings, to be sure, were qualified by the lack of control groups. Insufficient funding had circumscribed their follow-up research. But this deficiency was all but ignored by the educators and psychologists. Their seminar to educate democratic leaders had, in their eyes, been successful. Its popularity made them determined to try it again using the latest technologies.[23]

The Evolution of the Training

The time from 1947 to the mid-1960s was one of experimentation and con-
solidation for the partisans of democratic leadership training. Although sad-
dened by the death in 1947 of their mentor, Kurt Lewin, they continued to
pursue his quest for a harmonious and healthy society. And as part of this,
they built a network of institutional support. Beginning in 1947, they gained
the sponsorship of the NEA, a patronage that led to their group becoming in
1950 a permanent part of the NEA, at first under the aegis of its Adult
Education Division. They also established a training center in Bethel, Maine,
which they named the National Training Laboratory for Group Development.[24] By the late 1950s they had spun off many other training centers, had
inspired a variety of imitators and developed a sophisticated ideology and
methodology, and had paved the way for the astonishing popularity that their
prescriptions would enjoy among business people during the 1960s.

After the New Britain conference of 1946, the goal of the psychologists and
educators remained one of developing interpersonal skills and teaching "a
scientific and democratic methodology of group-problem solving." They
hoped to help trainees to "internalize some more or less systematic concepts"
and values of human relations and effective leadership, and they emphasized
the diagnosis of common group problems so that trainees could become aware
of how "interpersonal competition, individual needs for dominance and de-
pendency, differences in individual goals, semantic and communication difficulties, and hidden agendas" could disrupt the performance of groups. Beyond
this, trainees were also to learn how to overcome conflict and to integrate
"personal needs and purposes to group needs and purposes." Changed themselves, they were then to serve as change agents, who could become democratic reformers.[25] Training a democratic vanguard was thus expected to initiate a
sort of syndicalism from above.

To achieve these goals, the culture of the training laboratory was deliberately
designed so that trainees could learn participative management by practicing
it. Even the name itself, *training laboratory*, recalled Dewey's laboratory school.
An important part of the design was to isolate the trainees on a "cultural
island" that was remote from vocational demands and from conservative influences of the organization "back home." The first training site was in Bethel,
Maine, and the spin-offs were in similar locations. Another deliberately designed feature was informality, which was expected to encourage an open and
egalitarian spirit. No one wore neckties, and everyone, including the trainers,
called everyone else by their first names. In addition, recreational activities in

the evening, dancing and singing, were supposed to duplicate "middle class America."[26]

The heart and soul of the two weeks spent at the laboratory, however, were the two hours a day spent in the training session. First called the basic skills training group, this had become the T-group by 1949. In it the trainers practiced the technique of immediate discussion of group experiences that had been discovered at New Britain.

The early T-groups were "stranger groups," consisting of ten to twenty complete strangers coming from a variety of professions. They assembled on their first day in a room with a trainer and an observer. As they sat around a table, the trainer told them that they were there to study interpersonal behavior and to develop human relations skills and that they could do this any way that they wanted. The trainer provided them with no agenda or methodology. In effect, the trainees were left in a social and organizational vacuum where they had no status, no rank, no leader, and no rules. To one another they appeared as naked personalities, one result being that any individual's effort to "get the group organized" based on appeals to some status in the outside world or based on claims to hierarchical authority within the group was looked upon with suspicion by his or her peers. Conflicts would develop, which in theory would provide an opportunity to study group behavior, learn about oneself, and practice democratic leadership.[27]

The T-group sessions were often emotionally charged. In fact the developers of the technique believed that tension and anxiety were essential to the learning process. The anxiety created by the conflict and criticism encouraged the trainee to question his or her values and leadership style.[28] The following story written by a T-group trainer was designed to show what was supposed to happen in a typical T-group.

At the fifth meeting the group's feelings about its own progress became the initial focus of discussion. The "talkers" participated as usual, conversation shifting rapidly from one point to another. Dissatisfaction was mounting, expressed through loud, snide remarks by some and through apathy by others.

George Franklin appeared particularly disturbed. Finally pounding the table, he exclaimed, "I don't know what is going on here! I should be paid for listening to this drivel! I'm getting just a bit sick of wasting my time here. If the profs don't put out—I quit!" George was pleased; he was angry and he had said so. As he sat back in his chair, he felt he had the group behind him. He felt he had the guts to say what most of the others were thinking! Some members of the group applauded loudly, but others showed obvious disapproval. They wondered why George was excited over so insignificant an issue, why hadn't he done something constructive rather than just sounding off as usual. Why, they wondered, did he say their comments were "drivel"?

George Franklin became the focus of discussion. "What do you mean, George, by saying this nonsense?" "What do you expect, a neat set of rules to meet all your problems?" George was getting uncomfortable. These were questions difficult for him to answer. Gradually he began to realize that a large part of the group disagreed with him; then he began to wonder why. He was learning something about people he hadn't known before. ". . . How does it feel, George, to have people disagree with you when you thought you had them behind you. . . ?"

Bob White was first annoyed with George and now with the discussion. He was getting tense, a bit shaky perhaps. Bob didn't like anybody to get a raw deal, and he felt that George was getting it. At first Bob tried to minimize George's outburst, then he suggested that the group get on to the real issues; but the group continued to focus on George. Finally Bob said, "Why don't you leave George alone and stop picking on him? We're not getting anywhere this way?"

With the help of the leaders, the group focused on Bob. "What do you mean, 'picking' on him?" "Why, Bob, have you tried to change the discussion?" "Why are you so protective of George?" Bob began to realize that the group wanted to focus on George; he also saw that George didn't think he was being picked on but he felt he was learning something about himself and how others reacted to him. "Why do I always get upset," Bob began to wonder, "when people start to look at each other? Why do I feel sort of sick when people get angry about each other?" . . . Now Bob was learning something about how people saw him, while gaining some insight into his own behavior.[29]

The passage illustrates something of both the function and form of the T-group and shows how it combined features of group therapy and progressive education. In a group characterized by egalitarian relationships, peers had little choice but to concentrate on democratic leadership skills and to solve problems through collaboration. If they resorted to authority or coercion, their peers criticized them; if they were too permissive, they found it difficult to learn anything. By not posing as an authority, the trainer offered himself as a model of the democratic leader who helped his group become self-steering and self-training. Moreover, the group itself challenged dominating members, encouraged passive ones, and rewarded democratic behavior.

The form of the T-group was also evident. Members directed their attention to the "here and now," providing immediate feedback on interpersonal events. The specific problems of "there and then," the difficulties faced back home, were ignored. The trainees could learn democratic leadership through an emotionally involving analysis of actions and feelings in the group. By being both subjects and scientists, they could discover how to deal with criticism from others and how to offer it constructively. Eventually authoritarianism and anarchism could seem maladaptive and be cast aside.[30]

The other activities at the training laboratory were supposed to intensify the experiences in the T-groups. Role playing was used both within the groups and in larger gatherings as a means to provide insight into typical organizational relationships. The cooperative capabilities of each T-group were also tested through competition with other groups. For instance, they manufactured a product out of Lego blocks based on customer specifications and written communications passed along a chain of command; the inevitable blunders showed the irrationality of bureaucracy. The T-groups were also asked to choose leaders, to replace them, or even to transfer them to other groups. In addition, they were asked to fire their least cooperative members and to hire the rejects of other groups. But only in the later stages of their training were they given advice on how to apply their new leadership style back home.[31]

This lack of attention to back home problems, however, soon produced difficulties for the sensitivity training movement, difficulties that were traced to use of stranger groups. The technique of isolating strangers on a cultural island away from their organizations, indeed often without the endorsement of their organizations, often caused graduates to have problems in transferring their new knowledge to unreformed, authoritarian institutions. Standing in the way were managers with traditional notions of bureaucratic rationality, who were often suspicious of democratic leadership and had the power to frustrate reform.[32]

In addition, even as the partisans of democratic leadership were finding that their techniques were inadequate, the business journalist William H. Whyte offered in The Organization Man the first major criticism of their whole project. To him they were essentially trying to re-create an integrated society like that of medieval Europe. Their new social ethic amounted to an attack on the old Protestant ethic of individualism, and their training laboratories were just one part of a wider quest by insecure white-collar workers for belonging in their immediate work group. The psychologists who spoke for them, Whyte noted, defined maladjustment as conflict with the group and justified their desire for consensus as an effort to subdue managerial tyrants. But the demand that people sublimate their egos to a group within a bureaucracy was dangerous. The quest for harmony mistook interaction and consensus in groups for results coming out of them, threatened the sort of leadership and individualism necessary for innovation, and legitimized conformity to the group in the here and now, thus assuming the long-term morality of the ends of the organization of which the group was a part.[33]

Whyte had hit on a basic problem. The stranger labs did tend to attract psychologists as trainers and professional people as trainees who were primarily interested in the technique's therapeutic and existential uses. In Benne's words, the language at the labs often became "more psychoanalytic or Rogerian and less sociological and Lewinian." Individuals often came to the labs to learn about their identity and values and to escape loneliness and alienation. Their interest in individual development led them to seek cathartic experiences in the here and now and to be satisfied with the interpersonal skills they learned in the groups. And once psychologists understood the problems and needs of this existential clientele, they established labs, like Michael Murphy's Esalen Center and Carl Rogers's Western Behavioral Science Institute, to cater to their demands. Sensitivity training thus gave birth to the encounter movement, whose leaders found the social climate more hospitable in California than in Maine. The psychologists at these institutes were not concerned with creating democratic leaders. They developed new touchy-feely techniques to induce catharsis, inspire trust of others, and restore the lost innocence of youth, techniques like stroking and fondling group members or passing them around the room. Not surprisingly, this "sort of bastard child" of the National Training Laboratories became associated with pop psychology and Eastern religion, the counterculture, and drug rehabilitation.[34]

Faced with criticism from within and from without, Lewin's heirs responded by trying to distinguish their goals from those of the encounter movement and by seeking to develop more effective methods of implementing democratic leadership. They increasingly acknowledged, from the late 1950s on, that the stranger group was too different from work groups to be an effective reform medium. Unlike work groups, it had no work agenda, technical focus, organizational limitations, or hierarchy. Hence stranger training should be supplanted by the training of actual work teams, teaching them understanding of organizational roles and relationships and improving their interpersonal skills so that they could use their technical skills more effectively. In addition, the

Lewinians now recognized that organizational development and reform back home was needed to provide a favorable environment for democratic leadership to survive and prosper. For this to happen, the top managers of business corporations had to be persuaded that the democratic change program did not threaten their goals and that lab training and organizational restructuring were rational.[35] Without the support of corporate officials, the movement would founder for lack of funds and properly positioned change agents.

As the movement responded to its critics, new leaders began to emerge, among them Chris Argyris and the team of Robert Blake and Jane Mouton. These leaders shaped the changes underway and provided more mature statements of its corporative premises.

Argyris, a social psychologist and disciple of Douglas McGregor, emerged as the leading spokesman for the technique in the 1960s because of his ability to explain its values and sociological presuppositions to the business community. An effective work team, he argued, needed not only "technical competence" but "interpersonal competence" as well. Someone with interpersonal competence had to be willing and able to accept others' ideas and to help them grow as persons. The key to this, he said, was giving and receiving "nonevaluative feedback," criticism without malice. When a whole team could do this, it could be open to new ideas, handle conflict constructively, and monitor its processes and performance objectively, which in turn meant that it could solve problems effectively and achieve the goals of both its members and the firm of which it was a part.[36]

Scientific management theory, Argyris went on to explain, endorsed an authoritarian style of leadership that eroded interpersonal competence. Superiors chose goals and adopted controls based on scientific management tenets, which forced rational bureaucrats to use one another as instruments, suppress their emotions, and act "dependent, subordinate, and submissive." Superiors then had to rely on formal power to settle conflicts and to motivate subordinates with promotions and pay raises. Such authoritarianism led to mistrust, conformity, inflexibility, apathy, and a general withdrawal of efficiency. It spawned work teams that were incompetent interpersonally and, by being so, became incompetent technically. Nor could the problem be solved merely by decentralizing authority. This did nothing to overcome the way people had been conditioned to submit to others and to suppress their emotions.[37] Truly effective work teams could only come through democratic reform of the organization combined with democratic reeducation of its members.

The answer, Argyris concluded, lay in building an alternative to "pyramidal" organization and "pyramidal values," an alternative that could be built through sensitivity training. The training showed that authoritarianism clobbered people and triggered defensive behavior, and it taught trainees how to discuss and understand emotions. And since "skills follow values," it also taught how to influence behavior through "self-actualization," "authentic relationships, internal commitment, psychological success, and the process of confirmation," thus teaching the trainees how to organize work that could fulfill individual needs and institutional goals. In short, sensitivity training taught corporative values and showed how "the rationality of feelings" was as important as the rationality of techniques.[38]

The sensitivity training that Argyris had in mind, however, no longer featured stranger groups and cultural islands. It featured instead "team" or "family" training within a company and was designed "for the sake of the business, not necessarily for the personal development of the individuals."[39] This new "instrumental" variety of training evolved from the criticisms of the late 1950s and from a growing demand by corporate customers for a technology that could train large numbers of employees.

Family training was first tried extensively at Humble Oil (later called Exxon). There between 1957 and 1959, in an effort to introduce cost-cutting measures without arousing union opposition, the company put 650 managers and scientific personnel at one of its refineries through one of the first examples of in-house sensitivity training. And when the training seemed successful, the company trained another 550 more white-collar employees at another refinery between 1959 and 1961. But because Humble Oil was training so many people and could not find enough trainers, it turned to managers who had already been through the program, provided them with instructional forms for running group sessions, and used them as training leaders.

In 1961, largely because top management felt that the earlier training had put too much emphasis on interpersonal rather than technical and task skills,[40] Humble Oil refined a new technique of in-house, family training. This was the "managerial grid" system, developed by Robert R. Blake and Jane S. Mouton, and it was supposed to produce a "9,9" leadership style concerned with both people and production. The system required, first of all, that management take a "diagonal slice" across the organizational chart in order to select an initial group of managerial trainees. This vanguard would then be taught "the best manner of achieving production through people." Next, beginning at the top of the organization and working down, these returning leaders would train their work teams in handling interpersonal and production problems. Training from the top down was supposed to insure the necessary concentration on organizational goals and improve the "integration between hierarchical levels in the organization." Then "linking pins," employees belonging to more than one team, were to be trained, which in theory would make certain that "individual and team, as well as organizational development, [took] place in an integrated manner" and were "mutually reinforcing." And finally, as the training took hold for the vertical and horizontal linking pins, all personnel in the firm could be reeducated, and the firm itself could be organized along corporatist lines.[41]

Once adopted, the grid system became the basis for the in-house training of approximately eight hundred Humble Oil managers. It provided a way for top management to direct the educational process toward improving work skills rather than toward changing total personality. And according to the company, the training program led away from "softness and compromise" toward "firmness and better integration of objectives"; employees were more cooperative, and the firm more productive and profitable. By the time the formal training programs ended, the company felt that democratic values had permeated the company. Humble Oil later went on to install a management by objectives system that it thought was based on the same values and could achieve the same results at less expense.[42]

When in the late 1950s the Lewinians turned to in-house and family training, they had admitted that they could only help individuals and firms become rational by resorting to bureaucracy. In effect, they made the training itself bureaucratic, with managers often leading the sessions of their teams and with interpersonal matters becoming relevant only so far as they affected technical problems. Turning to bureaucracy and coercing people into cooperating meant a denial that harmony could be achieved, a repudiation of their visions of work without stoicism, and an endorsement of the utility of authoritarian leadership and hence of Taylor's ideal of the scientific manager.

And whether in stranger or in family groups, sensitivity training was always more bureaucratic and corporatist rather than genuinely democratic. The Lewinians in the 1960s as in the 1940s were essentially liberal philosophes trying to counsel enlightened despots. A leftist psychologist or two might talk about changing managerial consciousness so drastically that managers would abdicate power.[43] But the vast majority of consultants had no intention of doing this. They expected managers to remain managers and subordinates to remain subordinates. Their role, as they saw it, was to train managers in a parental style of leadership that could eliminate the waste, irrationality, repression, and conflict endemic in authoritarian organizations. Accomplishing this, they would not need to destroy authoritarianism by overthrowing managers and empowering all members. In the process, of course, the consultants would make a good living trying to humanize and rationalize bureaucrats. They did not want to slaughter the geese who were laying golden eggs.

Nor did the advocates of sensitivity training wish to eradicate authoritarianism by changing the consciousness of blue-collar workers. They had never envisioned a training that would attack authoritarianism from below, teaching production employees to be sensitive to manipulation and coercion and to demand respect and autonomy. In their eyes, this would have been the road to dysfunctional class consciousness and conflict. Moreover, blue-collar workers could not afford the two weeks in a luxury hotel at a cultural island, and their employers were certainly not going to pay for in-house training.

Consequently, in a few cases production employees were trained only as a means to rationalize the collective bargaining process in unionized firms. Blake and Mouton, for example, experimented with a "union-management intergroup laboratory," in which managers and union officials were supposed to be sensitized together as a "strategy for resolving inter-group conflict." But the results of this were meager. Management learned that the union could be concerned with production, and the union leaders likewise learned that management could be concerned with people. But mainly they clarified their differences.[44] Whatever the uses of sensitivity training in mitigating interpersonal conflicts, it appeared to be of little help in resolving class conflict.

Still, as a palliative for interpersonal conflicts endemic in bureaucracies, the technique could be very appealing to managers. Top managers often saw it, particularly in its later family form, as a means to enhance communication and cooperation and hence to make relationships more transparent, predictable, and controllable. They also saw how it could help to get lower-level managers and knowledge workers to drop "the mask of manners" and set aside private agendas that might clog group gears, inhibit discussion, and reduce productivity and profitability.

By the same token, low-ranking bureaucrats probably thought the experience would help them climb the corporate ladder; by participating in it, they could pad their resumes and develop useful leadership skills.[45] The training offered opportunities in corporate "dramaturgy"[46] where in the safety of the T-group, inhibitions could be lowered and feelings expressed. The trainees could act out the interpersonal style that they used in their daily roles in the corporate drama. By receiving criticism from an audience of peers, they could learn how others saw them and then could experiment with new theatrical styles. White-collar workers also probably saw the training as a way to fulfill other middle-class expectations; the system promised to establish a social environment at work in which they could enjoy autonomy, respect, and collegiality. Moreover, both upper and lower officials were probably attracted by the promise that by imitating group therapists and progressive teachers they could become democrats who were at once moral and rational. Becoming democratic could both assuage guilt and grease the cogs of bureaucracy.

In any event, sensitivity training acquired a wide following among members of the business community, a following that increased as the stranger method gave way to the family mode. By the late 1950s, business leaders were the most frequent patrons of the National Training Laboratories. This patronage continued in the 1960s when the National Training Labs became a formal department of the NEA, began publishing *The Journal of Applied Behavioral Science* as the medium for discussion of the technique, and increased its budget ten times (up to $3 million annually by 1969). During the 1960s, thousands of managers were trained by the National Training Laboratories, by the American Management Association and similar organizations, or by their companies. A survey conducted by the Conference Board in 1964 revealed that 38 percent of the companies examined used sensitivity training and four of five of those expected to continue using it. In 1968, 76 percent of the companies surveyed were using it. About 35 percent used the National Training Labs, about 33 percent used the managerial grid system, and about 7 percent used in-house sensitivity training of other kinds.[47]

Even at the height of its influence during the late 1960s and early 1970s, however, sensitivity training seemed to have only mixed success in improving interpersonal effectiveness. A poll of 2,026 managers conducted in 1974 by the American Management Association showed that while 1 of 5 had received the training since 1971, only about 20 percent of the trainees thought it had helped them considerably, while another 20 percent of the trainees thought it had scarcely helped them at all.[48] Nor was the technique particularly successful in making business more democratic. Its dismal record was evident in the findings of a variety of mandarins and critics who were also active during the 1960s.

Rationality for What? for Whom?

When mandarins experimented with sensitivity training, they also attempted to determine how effective it had been in changing values and behavior and in aligning the firm with the new values. By 1970 they had conducted 149 studies on the technique.[49] These studies and other critical commentaries produced ambiguous evidence and contradictory conclusions. But many mandarins concluded that no simple correlation existed between the training and democratic leadership or between democratic leadership and organizational rationality. Describing corporatism was proven easier than teaching or practicing it.

Partisans of the technique conducted many case studies. In their research they often relied on the testimony of graduates of the programs and their untrained colleagues. From this evidence it appeared that the technique had helped produce democratic leadership. Typically researchers said that graduates of the training were better at listening and giving feedback and were more patient, considerate, and tolerant. Graduates were more aware of interpersonal conflicts and were less afraid to discuss them, more receptive to new ideas and more willing to express them, and more critical while decisions were being made but more conforming afterward. In addition, since they were better able to delegate authority and consult with others, they demanded less subservience and were less subservient themselves. Consequently graduates felt they had grown as individuals and as family members and that their work teams often cooperated better and became cohesive groups.[50]

Such findings, however, often rested on shaky research methods, and a variety of mandarins were quick to point this out. To them, proof of the effectiveness of sensitivity training required more than was being offered. It must be shown, first, that the training had led not merely to changes in values or language or perceptions but to changes in behavior. Second, it had to be shown that the training was better than other methods at inducing behavioral changes; and third, it had to be proved that the behavioral results were actually helpful to the individual, the team, and the firm. These kinds of proof, the critics said, were lacking, and eventually their arguments would convince some who had been partisans of the technique.

This controversy concerning the research done on the results of sensitivity training persisted from the early 1960s. The issues involved can be seen by examining a debate in 1968 between a partisan, Chris Argyris, and two skeptics, Marvin D. Dunnette and John P. Campbell, who avowed that their criticism was supposed to improve the technique. Most studies of the system, Dunnette and Campbell argued, bordered on charlatanism. Typically, case studies relied on questionnaires, completed before and after training, in which graduates reported changes in self-perception. But controls were generally not used to guard against the possibility that trainees would receive clues from their training on how to answer questionnaires afterward. As a result graduates often merely parroted the trainer. Since they knew that laboratory training had been designed to make certain changes, they tried to validate the cost of the training and to show that they were not dummies by reporting as changes attitudes that they may have held before or may never have held.[51]

Argyris had considerable difficulty refuting this criticism. In the end, he merely explained why control groups were not used and argued that using them could never fully clarify the impact of the training. Employees, he noted, resented being put in control groups because they were deprived of the training that was supposed to help them. Top management could also be impatient with controls and had a natural concern about their costs. And even if control groups could be set up, he said, they could not guarantee valid data because interpersonal competence could be raised within them through on-the-job experience or by organizational reforms that rewarded the desired behavior.[52]

Campbell and Dunnette also observed the almost complete lack of comparative studies that would show whether sensitivity training had done more than other methods to change people. So far as the critics could see, little or no evidence proved that a T-group changed anyone more than "the simple passage of time, or the mere act of filling out a self-description questionnaire." And in the eyes of another critic, spending two weeks in a submarine might be even better. Without such comparative studies the costs of various methods for helping people become sensitive, and effective leaders could not be known. Hence a strong possibility existed that the costs of sensitivity training to the firm and the individual were too high.[53]

Indeed, some psychoanalysts suggested that a T-group experience could be harmful. Sometimes the lowering of inhibitions and the evaluation of interpersonal skills in the T-group could trigger sadism, narcissism, or masochism. And sometimes graduates came away feeling that their privacy had been invaded, their self-images threatened, and their defense mechanisms destroyed. This was particularly troublesome since many trainees did not attend voluntarily but because their bosses ordered or suggested it. Defenders of the technique could cite studies showing that the T-group stimulated no more anxiety than a college exam and that its proportion of psychological casualties was no higher than that of the freshman class at Yale or Michigan. But such criticisms did eventually lead to the drafting of a code of ethics that set standards of professional competence and prescribed measures to prevent the training from becoming insensitive.[54]

Still other critics argued that the lessons learned by trainees were not necessarily democratic ones. Some research showed that trainees often learned very specific lessons and in effect chose what they wanted to learn. Rather than moving toward becoming ideal democratic leaders, they typically selected a few tricks that could enable them to better adapt to their job back home, such tricks, for example, as merely showing greater concern for others' problems or, more negatively, managing impressions to avoid criticism. The training, it seemed, could teach manipulation as well as participation.[55]

In the view of the critics, moreover, even successfully teaching democratic values might leave behavior and the firm unchanged. The task-oriented and autocratic manager might have his or her values transformed by the training. But this kind of manager was likely to work for a firm with a rigid hierarchy, a specialized division of labor, and standardized jobs. Such an individual would work in a setting, in other words, in which cooperative, interpersonal skills were less important than following the rules, meeting deadlines, pleasing autocratic superiors, cowing suspicious subordinates, and suppressing humane feelings. Hence one person's improved interpersonal skills, a critic pointed out, were "small advances compared to the powerful forces that maintain a status quo in organizations." Reeducating the individual apparently reduced authoritarianism less than did changing work goals and rewards to encourage participation. A democratic lamb thrown into an arena that demanded authoritarian wolves would either quickly revert to old habits or initiate conflicts that might well end in its leaving the field. And by the same logic, the person-oriented and participative manager was more likely to work in a more collaborative, nonroutine, and loosely structured firm. Often that manager had already developed interpersonal skills, which meant that training was of limited value.[56]

In contrast, research cited by critics revealed that sensitivity training that impelled individuals to successfully internalize new values and that stimulated democratic behavior could sometimes create leaders who put cohesiveness before productivity. The trainees could become democratic managers who encouraged their team members to be nice rather than honest, so that harmony became an end in itself rather than a means to greater productivity. The training could in effect create what had been defined in the boys' club experiments as laissez-faire leadership, which could raise morale and reduce turnover but was unlikely to establish the well-defined group roles, clear objectives, smooth flows of information, and coordinated work schedules that were needed for effective labor.[57] Harmony achieved in this way could undermine organizational rationality rather than enhance it and could thereby threaten the survival of the firm.

Meanwhile, as students of the technique were publishing both supportive and critical research, some Taylorist theoreticians were attacking the Lewinian system and arguing that democratic leadership would sabotage bureaucratic rationality. Typically these mandarins failed to appreciate the bureaucratic aspects of the technique. They took its democratic and corporative rhetoric at face value. And hence to them sensitivity training amounted to a variety of anarchism that challenged the existence of the managerial function and therefore threatened bureaucracy, free enterprise, and the American way of life.

The T-group people, so the argument ran, were mainly therapists. Because of this, they had unconsciously echoed anarchists like Bakunin and assumed that "all exercise of authority perverts and all submissiveness to authority humiliates." Their democratic reeducation was designed to undermine managers' will to power. As one critic said, the laboratory seminar caused managers to wander about mumbling to themselves, "I must not be a leader. I must not be a leader." Beyond this, the Lewinian program was based on a "utopian ideal of panacean democracy," an impossible dream that managers could enjoy individual autonomy, personal growth, and egalitarianism while at the same time maintaining labor discipline.[58] To survive in the marketplace, a business required a bureaucratic authority that could subordinate the interests of employees to the corporate interests of task performance, productivity, and profits. Hence the company president who had stopped a sensitivity training program because he thought it "seemed like communism" and was afraid that his subordinates would not "follow orders" seemed right to some.[59]

Another part of this critique of the anarchic side of sensitivity training stressed the threats posed to managerial consciousness. The psychologist Abraham H. Maslow, for instance, whose concept of self-actualization influenced job enrichment, thought that the "Pollyannish tendencies" of sensitivity training were irrational for managers. Upon attending a T-group session, he was impressed with the "spontaneity" and "intimacy" of members, who, he said, acted like people who had been in psychoanalysis for more than a year. But the resulting intimacy between the leader and the led could inhibit the leader's will to discipline and punish. A superior could not be open or loving with subordinates or make a team into "one big, happy family." Managers, Maslow apparently thought, should avoid the training for themselves but use it to teach subordinates to accept and express criticism; for them it could be "a kind of training in masculinity" that could help them overcome acting like a "fawning puppy dog."[60]

More central to the critique, however, was the contention that the Lewinians had been naive in thinking that collegial organization could replace pyramidal organization in business and in believing that such a change was desirable anyway. By eroding "aggressiveness and creativity," "entrepreneurial drive, competitiveness, respect for hierarchical authority, the work ethic, reward for achievement, and little sympathy for failure," the training could destroy the very personality traits that had made American business so successful. Following this logic to its conclusion, one advocate of management by objectives, George Odiorne, went so far as to argue that sensitivity training was so dangerous that it should be made illegal, much as revolutionary syndicalism had been.[61]

On the fringes of mandarin debates, some anticommunist conservatives and right-wing radicals also joined in the attack. They argued that the technique was a trick used by "the usual forces of the conspiratorial Left" to destroy the American way of life. In their accounts the technique had originated in Pavlovian psychology, in proletarian discussion circles in the Soviet Union, and in "psywar" methods used by the North Koreans to brainwash American prisoners of war. It had spawned the nefarious body awareness methods of the encounter movement in public schools and similar sorts of practices in industry, the Peace Corps, and the State Department. Accordingly it was another manifestation of the conspiracy by "Humanists" to undermine Judeo-Christian values, encourage criticism and permissiveness, erode authority, make "ideological war against the entire warp and woof of the American culture," and thus pave the way for a communist dictatorship. They insisted that the technique was contributing to the rise of drug abuse, sexual promiscuity and perversion, social conflict, and a general sense of "confusion, frustration, and wholesale disorientation."[62]

More within the mainstream of the this ongoing debate about sensitivity training were efforts to explain its popularity among managers. These explanations emphasized its capacity to salve the emotional wounds of white-collar workers rather than the way it lubricated the gears of bureaucracy. White-collar workers were said to be suffering from anomie and searching for belonging in face-to-face groups. The most developed piece along these lines was Kurt Back's polemic comparing sensitivity training to "a religiously oriented social movement." Like religion during the Middle Ages, he contended, sensitivity training had its conversion experiences, priests, icons, mythology, worldview, rituals, pilgrimages to holy places, and coterie of believers who maintained, without resort to scientific proof, their faith in a miraculous "regeneration" of individuals and society. People believed because the training promised commercial profit and personal salvation. And even if it did not fulfill its promises, it still offered the lonely and the bored an "intense emotional experience" in a group as a "value in itself." While Back doubted that the religious and therapeutic orientation of the T-group was consistent with the aims of business or that it improved productivity, he noted that it did ease frustrations and improve morale.[63]

Apparently critics like Back did not understand how the catharsis of a T-group experience could be useful to managers. Similar to the effects of nondirective counseling previously used by Mayoists, family training could, temporarily at least, create an intimate, face-to-face group and perhaps also could create the illusion that the firm itself was harmonious. This feeling was expressed by one trainee who explained that "in this group we are safe to reveal ourselves; it has a special feeling for me—maybe sacred is too strong a word, but it's something like that." Another noted that he felt "truly alive and so grateful and joyful and hopeful and healthy and giddy and sparkly," "as though my eyes and ears and heart and guts have been opened to see and hear and feel more deeply, more widely, more intensely." As some suggested, sensitivity training was the white-collar equivalent of pot, flower power, and rock and roll; it was an aesthetic rebellion against authoritarianism. But however much better it made participants feel, it did very little to eradicate bureaucracy, and some corporations even used T-groups to disguise authoritarianism and conflict.[64] In most respects, the training failed to transcend Mayoism, which had also used therapy to form, as C. Wright Mills had argued, "pseudo-gemeinschaft islands" in a gesellschaft swamp.[65]

Indeed, a few critics feared that cathartic experiences made the training, whatever its avowed goals, another Mayoist instrument for adjusting people to bureaucracy. Max Pagès, a French social psychologist, complained that T-groupers were as oppressive as the leaders they had intended to replace. Since they lacked a clear "theory," their thought had undergone an "unconscious contamination by the market ideology of . . . capitalist society" and led them to commodify techniques that could engineer harmony. They successfully taught methods useful as defenses against aggression and isolation. But by showing how to achieve harmony "cheaply" through manipulating techniques and suppressing conflicts, he said, they also inhibited communication, understanding, and democratic reform. Rather than teaching how to establish real relationships, they taught how to establish merely formal ones. Rather than creating an intimate, cooperative community of equals, they provided power for the manipulators and security for the manipulated; they established "an artificially united community devout in the cults of its norms under its benevolent rulers." By promoting notions of "a united society and the validity of a social hierarchy," Pagès concluded, the Lewinians had helped prop up American bureaucracies.[66]

Others agreed that the interpersonal skills learned in a T-group could be just as useful to dictators as to democrats. Authoritarian leaders could learn how to improve their skills in "Machiavellian manipulations," how to "secure a fuller personal commitment for the enterprise from its constituents," and how to establish in work teams a tyranny of the majority that kept all members in line. Furthermore, the sensitivity training movement was fostering the delusion that two weeks of training could so improve interpersonal competence that bureaucracy would wither away. As the job enricher Frederick Herzberg claimed, proponents failed to see that "interpersonal incompetence" was less often the source of conflict than was an oppressive organization of work. And William Gomberg, a labor arbitrator, argued that unions provided more effective defenses against authoritarian leaders than did psychotherapy.[67]

Pioneers of the training, not surprisingly, have objected to the notion that they were another set of democratic social engineers. Like their authoritarian critics, they have accepted their own rhetoric at face value, assuming that opposition to authoritarianism was tantamount to democracy. Ronald Lippitt, for instance, rejected as "one-sided" Graebner's idea that the technique was another "form of control" based on the "participation of the objects of control." While admitting that some managers had turned from "coercive to kid-gloved authoritarianism," he denied that the Lewinians had done so and saw them as having remained committed to "genuinely participatory democracy" concerned with "member-leader relations," "mutual decision making," "joint policy development," "reciprocal influence relationships," and "participative management."[68] Yet these phrases, rather than proving Lippitt's point, merely showed that the Lewinians wanted hierarchy to continue and superiors to cooperate with subordinates. Cooperation was to them a more rational form of control than coercion.

Indeed, the organization theorist William G. Scott has argued that Schmidt, Taylor's paradigmatic rational man, was "alive and enrolled in a sensitivity training program." In a brilliant parody of the technocratic style, Scott posed as an "elder" in the "Soviet of Technicians" and recalled how Taylor's scientific management had induced a stupid and phlegmatic ox like Schmidt to raise his productivity 350 percent in exchange for a 60 percent pay raise. But even though managers had convinced manual laborers that "rationality" was "the essence of freedom," they had continued to have trouble with the irrational "sons of Schmidt," the scientists, engineers, and technicians, and this had led to new forms of Taylorism. Managers had learned from the social sciences that people best coped with their emotional problems and identified with collective goals if they were given opportunities to express themselves and enjoy "the embrace of sustaining group relationships" like those in "the peasant farming communities of medieval Europe." They had also learned that the managerial responsibility for restraining the "coarser instincts" could be shared by everyone if all were trained in resolving interpersonal conflicts and that a combination of sensitivity training and organizational reform could "merge the satisfactions sought by the nonelite from work with the rational systems formulated by the elite to produce and distribute more and more goods and services."[69] If the social scientists that Scott burlesqued were right, managers could look forward to a rationality based on bureaucratic consensus and mutuality of interest between manager and managed.

Taken as a whole, criticism from the left and the right can probably be credited with changing the direction of the T-groupers in several ways. First, it seems to have reinforced the trend toward in-house and family training. By catering to the wishes of each client corporation and its top management, those involved could overcome the criticism that the training was too permissive and egalitarian. Second, it forced advocates of the technique to tone down some of their claims and advertise it more as a means of improving communication than as a means of wholesale reconstruction. And third, the criticism led some Lewinians to investigate which sets of circumstances in the training and organizational environment best created democratic managers. In doing so, they pursued very narrow, tightly controlled research programs, seeking better reeducation and reform technologies.[70]

The criticism can probably be credited also with inducing some early partisans of the training to distance themselves from its claims. In the mid-1960s, for example, Warren Bennis wrote several articles proclaiming that the triumph of democracy in industry was "inevitable." But these were then followed by articles in the early 1970s in which he recanted. After serving as a university administrator and dealing with student demonstrations, he recognized the difficulties of applying Lewinian ideas about group "micro-systems" to organizational "macro-systems." When the macro-goals of superiors conflicted with the micro-goals of subordinates, "consensus" and collaboration easily collapsed because leaders often could not reconcile "the cozy *gemütlichkeit* of a Theory Y orientation and the realities of macro-power." Unfortunately, he decided, the participative side of democratic leadership could unleash populist desires and undermine the bureaucratic authority that was often needed to impose discipline and integrate conflicting agendas.[71] For Bennis, the turmoil of the sixties showed that the sensitivity training technique and its ideal of democratic leadership were too permissive.

In contrast Chris Argyris dropped sensitivity training because it was too authoritarian. The moment of truth for him came when he acted as a consultant for several corporate executives who had all been through the training. He found that none of them would consider organizational reforms or even adopt a participative management style. T-groups, he concluded, could not change values. Although remaining committed to democratic leadership, Argyris no longer believed that a few hours of therapy and training were enough to teach interpersonal competence. Other ways would have to be found to integrate individual and organization and thereby achieve the apogee of rationality. In his subsequent work Argyris used tape recordings of actual meetings to help executives understand the values that determined their leadership style and its effects on others.[72]

Ironically then, the same sort of scientific research into the effects of management style on groups that had helped launch the sensitivity training movement in the 1930s had all but beached it by the 1970s. The research led many to conclude that the democratic leadership style that worked best in boys' clubs could be ineffective or dangerous in business. These people were doubtless happy that the T-group ship was dead in the water and probably felt that authoritarian leadership and bureaucratic rationality had been validated. Others still concerned with the dysfunctions of bureaucracy concluded that since group therapy had not been shown effective in reeducating authoritarians, they would have to abandon ship and find some other way of democratizing managers and organizations. But a few hardy (or foolhardy) scientists and trainers did not notice that the good ship T-group had floundered. Some thought by performing a few more studies they could determine the proper course toward democratic leadership; others missed the boat entirely and persisted in training that had taken the form that it had been designed to transform, a development that should not be surprising given the similarity of fostering harmony to imposing rationality. Its history seemingly testifies to the durability of bureaucracy and to the absurdity of expecting to create harmony merely by teaching bureaucrats to be nice and honest about their emotions.

Since the 1960s, sensitivity training has become less popular among managers, but the ideal of corporative leadership has persisted. Managers seldom shut themselves away so they can cry, hold hands, and be born again. Nonetheless the notion of a leader who was good for people and profits has become a permanent part of managerial culture. The ideal could be found in such seventies innovations as the quality control circle, a technique developed by the Japanese but growing in part from their adoption of Lewin's ideas.[73] The ideals of corporative leadership, its contradictory ideals of freedom and order, liberty and rationality, have been very attractive to American managers.

6

Capitalism
without Class?

Job Enrichment and the
Baby Boomers

In 1971 Elliot Richardson, President Nixon's secretary of health, education, and welfare, commissioned a task force of social scientists to report on the quality of working life. Their report, *Work in America*, condemned Taylorism for being an "anachronism" that ignored the "social needs" of manufacturing workers of the "baby boom generation"; for raising business costs by encouraging high rates of turnover, absenteeism, wildcat strikes, sabotage, and low rates of productivity; for burdening society with crime, alcoholism, and physical and mental illness; and for contributing to "alienation" that made people prone to "radical social or political movements." Nor had Mayoism met workers' "social needs"; it had merely used deception to adjust workers to oppressive jobs. The only solution, the report concluded, was for managers to repudiate Taylor and Mayo and redesign jobs so that work would be productively and socially efficient.[1]

Work in America sanctioned a corporative theory of management developed during the 1950s. Mandarins hoped to make every employee a manager and integrate individual and organization. Their promise of harmony on the shop floor had by the early 1970s led managers in such prominent firms as IBM, AT&T, General Mills, Polaroid, and Texas Instruments to find another best way.[2] But following the pattern of democratic leadership and other corporatisms, job enrichment provoked denunciations from the right and the left. Such criticism, however, would little tarnish the glitter of class harmony, and whatever luster was lost was subsequently restored by turning from the language of psychology to that of engineering.

The history of job enrichment ideas has not been told before.[3] Its story shows discontinuity and continuity in post-Mayoist theory. Job enrichment broke from human relations in the 1950s when mandarins came to believe that their new conceptions of human nature were incompatible with bureaucracy. Ironically, however, the new ideas often reinvented Mayoism and merely proposed using participation to change despotic rule into hegemonic rule.

Mind and Management

Corporatists did not develop job enrichment because of a new crisis in bureaucracy. Job enrichment originated from the psychological theories of Abraham H. Maslow, and all of its intellectual pioneers were social scientists at universities: Douglas McGregor at MIT, Chris Argyris at Yale, Rensis Likert at the Institute for Social Research at Michigan, and Frederick Herzberg at Case Western Reserve.

Before the 1950s, a few managerial systems existed that might be seen as forerunners to a blue-collar corporatism. During the First World War and in the 1920s, some of Taylor's disciples had thought that consultations with workers could reduce resistance to scientific management.[4] During the 1930s, Joseph N. Scanlon had developed the Scanlon Plan, which was based on the notion that teamwork between managers and workers, joint production committees, and profit-sharing arrangements could make firms more just, efficient, and profitable. In addition, Allen Morgenson's "work simplification" had called for workers to be trained in the methods of industrial engineering so they could help managers design jobs.[5] Yet none of the proposals went very far toward repudiating a very simplified and specialized division of tasks. This was true even of the Scanlon Plan, with which McGregor had been much impressed.[6] And for this reason, he and the other corporatists wanted to go beyond participative techniques for instituting specialization.

Other critiques of Taylorism also foreshadowed the developments in the 1950s. Some managers and writers, for example, used Lewin's theory of democratic leadership and developed such participation experiments as those conducted at the Harwood garment factory. Others pointed out the inefficiencies that emerged from worker frustration and publicized some alternatives that had been tried in manufacturing during World War II.[7] Peter Drucker, in particular, had described how managers at IBM had learned that extreme specialization of tasks and the separation of planning from doing fostered employee dissatisfaction and inefficiency. The planning of jobs, he argued, was necessary but did not require that "the planner and the doer" be "two classes of people." "Even the lowliest human job should have some planning; only it should be simple planning and there should not be too much of it." And workers, he said, should be changed from operators into controllers of machines. They should participate in the planning of new products at an early stage, become members of cooperating work teams, and have "meaningful" jobs in which they could develop "internal self-motivation" and "managerial vision" and hence "drive themselves." This sounded much like subsequent job enrichment theory.[8]

Some commentators have also seen the new developments as a response to changes in machinery and market forces. The sociologist Charles Sabel, for instance, has argued that job enrichment was designed to meet the demands of "specialized" or "flexible" production.[9] But what Sabel says applies more to its adoption in the 1970s than to its origins in the 1950s. At that time, writers justifying it said little about flexible production and a lot about worker psychology. Its originators were stimulated by new psychological ideas developed by Kurt Lewin, Erich Fromm, Bruno Bettelheim, Victor Frankl, Carl Rogers, Gordon Allport, and above all by Abraham H. Maslow.

In the 1940s and 1950s Maslow had asserted that everyone shared a "hierarchy of needs," which progressed from lower physiological and safety needs through higher social needs for love and esteem to the highest ego need for "self-actualization." Unsatisfied needs, he said, motivated people; satisfied needs ceased to motivate. And once people had satisfied their lower needs, they tried to gratify their desires for belonging, self-esteem, and personal fulfillment. The average American wanted greater satisfaction of his higher needs, and achieving this required opportunities to express individuality, feel a sense of competence and achievement, and earn and receive respect from others. Lacking such opportunities, a person would feel threatened and react defensively. And in Maslow's view, social arrangements that inhibited gratification were "sick" and had to be reformed.[10]

For mandarins Maslow's self-actualization seemed a way to make workers satisfied and motivated. It was the mainspring of self-actualizing man, a concept that differed from Taylor's economic man or Mayo's social man. Taylor had assumed that people worked only to earn a living, and because they wanted to expend as little effort as possible, their work had to be closely monitored and rewarded for performance. Mayo, by contrast, had presumed that nurturant managers could provide a social wage for which workers would exert themselves. Yet both Taylorism and Mayoism shared the assumption that people did not like work.[11] But Maslow's self-actualizing man could like working, could see it as more than merely a means to money or fellowship, and could value work in itself as an act of self-expression. The first principle of Douglas McGregor's corporatism, which he called Theory Y, stated that work which allowed self-development and affirmation was as natural and satisfying as play. Nothing inherent in human biology made people avoid work. Only tasks that did not satisfy needs were disliked.[12]

Accordingly, the idea of self-actualization became the foundation of a new theory of motivation. Real motivation, Frederick Herzberg asserted, came from inside the worker; a motivated worker performed effectively because he or she wanted to. Outside stimulation, meaning rewards and punishments from managers, could cause workers to perform. But it could not create motivation. And of course motivated employees were better workers because they had an internal "generator" and a manager did not periodically have to recharge their batteries.[13]

Accordingly, managers should set up tasks that were self-actualizing. Or in McGregor's agricultural metaphor, they should provide fertile conditions that would let employees "grow" themselves.[14] Argyris believed that "the door to happiness for every individual" was "locked from the inside," and since managers could not "unlock" it, they must create conditions in which workers could stimulate themselves. Managers should provide opportunities to participate in work teams, to define goals, to carry out plans and solve problems, and to overcome challenges, thus putting workers where they could experience success, feel competent and proud, and earn peer respect. As self-actualization and social acceptance accumulated, workers would exert themselves more, which in turn would provide greater opportunities for success and self-esteem and lead to even greater effort. Self-actualization would endlessly generate motivation.[15]

Of all the reformers, Herzberg would develop the most elaborate motivation theory. Beginning in 1959, he published what he was learning from interviews of accountants and engineers who were asked about situations in which they felt either satisfied or dissatisfied with work. His goal was to locate the sources that caused workers to be "happy" and "unhappy." The responses led to his "dual factor" theory, which held that "dissatisficers," the factors that caused unhappiness, could be found in the "job situation" rather than in the job itself. Such factors as company policy, supervision, relationships with coworkers, working conditions, job security, occupational status, and even pay could at worst cause dissatisfaction and at best "no job dissatisfaction." Managers, in other words, could manipulate such "maintenance" or "hygiene" factors so as to prevent unhappiness. But once workers met their basic needs, changing these variables could not inspire satisfaction or motivation. Pay raises, for instance, eventually stopped inducing performance, and manipulation of the job situation was inefficient. Like "heroin" it was addictive and took "more and more to produce less and less effect."[16]

To motivate and satisfy workers, Herzberg said, managers would have to enrich the content of work itself rather than the context in which work was done. Only work that was rewarding in itself could provide the "motivators" and "satisficers" that addressed the needs of the employee for "continuous psychological growth" and "self-actualization." Hence if managers wanted workers who were not constantly seeking more money, they should set up jobs that allowed opportunities for personal growth.[17]

Self-actualization also provided the basis of a continuing condemnation of scientific management and human relations ideas. Simplified, specialized work under close supervision was inefficient and immoral. It could satisfy neither industrial or individual needs. Herzberg and McGregor explained the inefficiency of Taylorism in different ways. Herzberg thought Taylorists had wrongly assumed that the employment contract was merely an exchange of labor and wages. Consequently they had ignored the higher needs of workers, organized tasks so as to use machines efficiently, and thus created boring jobs that encouraged workers to be money-hungry and uncooperative.[18] McGregor, on the other hand, contended that scientific managers had been wrong about human nature. They held that people disliked work, perceived it as a form of punishment, and needed direction. Their presumption, which he called Theory X, led to close supervision, which generated a self-fulfilling prophecy. Scientific management made work oppressive and workers hostile and lazy.[19]

Probably the most sophisticated critique of Taylorism came from Chris Argyris. Scientific managers, he thought, accepted bureaucracy as a given. They assumed that specialization and centralization could achieve efficiency by making workers "dependent upon, passive toward, and subordinate to" the manager and that workers were most productive when they had so little power that they could not choose personal goals.[20] But these assumptions had created frustrating jobs. Earlier in the century Taylorized jobs might have been suited to an ill-educated, deferential work force. But by the 1950s, Taylorism was only useful for managing "children," "morons," and the "mentally re-tarded." Its autocratic methods no longer suited well-educated workers with democratic values who wanted autonomy and meaningful work. When applied to the new work force, Taylorism spawned the conflicts it intended to eliminate.[21]

Argyris also explained that employees developed defense mechanisms. They

quit, became apathetic, resisted innovation, developed psychosomatic ill-
nesses, escaped in daydreams, reduced effort, lowered standards, formed work
groups that restricted output, harassed employees who accepted managerial
assumptions, joined unions, demanded high compensation for dull jobs,
taught their children to have low expectations, and isolated themselves from
the community. In general, they came to believe that "a deep and wide gulf"
divided them and "those who were in control." Their behavior was bad from a
managerial point of view. Yet managers could only blame themselves for failing
to meet their workers' needs.[22]

In addition, Argyris condemned Mayoists for failing to reform Taylorism.
Company recreation and participation programs, he thought, primarily functioned to "sugar coat" the bad taste, not fix the recipe. Personnel gimmicks,
like picnics and softball teams, incorrectly assumed that satisfaction could be
managed without reorganizing tedious work and that workers could be appeased "outside of the immediate job environment." Likewise "pseudo-
participation" did not empower employees and permit them to grow; it merely
allowed consent on trivial matters or on decisions already made.[23] On this
point, moreover, empirical support could be found in surveys Likert had
conducted. They confirmed that participation in recreation programs and
favorable attitudes toward the company had virtually no impact on job
performance.[24]

Herzberg, too, rejected Mayoism, concluding that it confused "hygienic"
with "motivational" factors and was based on the fallacious assumption that
benevolence motivated. At best, he said, it could only make workers feel
comfortable with their employer, not instill responsible work habits.[25] Motivation could only come through work that was self-actualizing in itself.

The need, then, was for a new philosophy beyond Taylorism and Mayoism.
And while initially the prescriptions were rather general and vague, they did
constitute a new agenda for managers.

Among the more modest proposals was job enlargement. Tedium could be
relieved, the job enrichers believed, if the number of simple tasks could be
increased and more abilities challenged. In some cases, Argyris thought, tasks
could be combined so as to give an assembly line worker ten rather than five
operations to carry out. In others, workers could be rotated from job to job.[26]
The reformers realized, however, that more was needed than increased numbers of specialized operations per worker. As Herzberg put it, rotating between
dull jobs or adding boring tasks to an already dull job was not enough because
"two or three meaningless activities" did not "add up to a meaningful one."[27]
Truly meaningful work demanded opportunities for workers to exercise

discretion and experience cooperation. In jobs that integrated planning and doing, workers could grow, create, learn, develop expertise, and express individuality. Moreover, such opportunities for self-realization could be multiplied by creating work teams. Workers could then enjoy fellowship and sustenance in the group, and the "excitement and meaning" of self-controlling and cooperative work could improve health and motivation.[28]

Workers in enriched jobs, however, were supposed to be as responsible as they were independent. Work should be set up so that its goal was, to borrow the title of Argyris's second book on job enrichment, integrating the individual and the organization. Performing redesigned jobs should automatically make workers productive.[29]

To ensure integration of individual and organization, the reformers believed, managers should maintain veto power over employee decisions. As the political scientist Carole Pateman correctly noted, job enrichment was a theory of management, not a theory of participatory democracy.[30] It did not prescribe that managers should abdicate and achieve corporate harmony through syndicalist democracy. That type of democracy at work, McGregor thought, could satisfy employees and reduce conflict. But it was naive because it could not ensure high productivity and the survival of the firm. Expressing the management theory of value, he argued that only professional managers could "organize human effort" and direct the individual to "sacrifice" and to serve "the economic objectives of the enterprise." McGregor's Theory Y, and job enrichment as a whole, was supposed to be an intermediate between industrial democracy and the bureaucracy of Theory X.[31]

Consequently, the discretion that job reformers allowed workers was necessarily limited. Discretion did not mean that workers were free to choose their goals, methods, rules, or leaders regardless of the wishes of management. And so job enrichment mandarins sought to convince managers of the rationality of rearranging tasks without significantly redistributing power.

The amount of participation that the work reformers thought permissible varied. At one extreme, Argyris believed that workers should set up jobs and select goals under the supervision of management.[32] At the other extreme, Herzberg argued that such "true participation" was "unrealistic" and "clearly impossible" given the need of the firm for "coordination"; hence workers should only be allowed to choose from a narrow range of means for "achieving the ends" given them by "centralized authority."[33] But all agreed that participation should be constrained. According to McGregor, participation should consist "basically in creating opportunities under suitable conditions for people to influence decisions affecting them." Depending on the limits imposed by the manager, that "influence" could "vary from a little to a lot." In any case, participation was merely "a special case of delegation" in which "the subordinate" gained "greater control, greater freedom of choice, with respect to his own responsibilities," and "greater influence over matters within the superior's responsibilities."[34]

Even Argyris, whose anti-Taylorism was most radical, admitted that he was not challenging the traditional pyramidal structure of American corporations. Managers, he believed, were still needed to plan and control. Nor did he expect that work could be so redesigned as to make people truly happy. He hoped managers could find a minimally satisfactory way for the firm and the individual to get what they needed, a way to mix autonomy and order so as to make decision making "more 'democratic,' 'participative,' 'collaborative,' 'employee-centered.'" Loosening the hold of authoritarianism would reduce the "defensive activities" hampering organizational effectiveness, make "relative" improvements in the workers' lot, and increase their opportunities to self-actualize. Echoing Drucker's corporatism, he thought that employees could then enjoy "freedom within the law."[35]

The fusion of freedom and fealty in a firm with enriched jobs was best articulated by Likert in his *New Patterns of Management* and *The Human Organization*. He suggested that in a "participative" firm, managers realized that the highest efficiency could be attained when workers were treated as "human beings" rather than as "cogs in a machine." They therefore designed "supportive" work that nurtured the employee. They ensured that each person "identified with the objectives of the organization and the goals of his work group" and saw "the accomplishment of them as the best way to meet his own needs and personal goals." This "integration," Likert said, could best come through participative decision making. Through participation, workers could influence corporate and team objectives and bring such objectives closer to individual goals. Moreover, each highly integrated, self-governing team had members who belonged to other similar teams. Members of at least two teams were linking-pins and communicated from one group to another. Thus at the managerial level, the linking-pins were superiors in their own group and subordinates in groups above them. Interlocked by linking-pins, corporate teams coordinated their activities without controlling each other. Coordination was less downward than "upward and sideward," with the expertise and needs of one group influencing the behavior of teams around it. And since each group was "supportive" and obeyed what Mary Follett had called "the law of the situation," the dictates of job-related facts, the corporation could be hierarchical without being dictatorial or exploitive.[36]

Although Likert and Argyris apparently felt that all jobs could eventually be enriched, Herzberg and McGregor were less certain. Herzberg doubted that some jobs could be redone. In such cases, he would either give the workers "sabbaticals" from meaningless tasks by temporarily moving them into meaningful jobs or encourage them to actualize themselves by finding "fruitful hobbies."[37] And McGregor excepted cases where employees would not commit themselves to the organization; there a Taylorist Theory X had to be used.[38] Nevertheless, the work reformers were, on the whole, optimistic.

These reformers were encouraged by what they were learning from similar notions developing in Europe, especially in Britain and Norway. They became particularly interested, in part because of the language barrier confronting the Norwegians and in part because of the more explicit theorizing of the British, in the work being done at the Tavistock Institute of Human Relations in London.[39] In particular, they studied the "socio-technical systems" theory of the Tavistock group, which initially included Eric Trist, K. W. Bamforth, Albert Rice, and Eliot Jacques. This idea too held that Taylorism was inefficient because it frustrated psychological needs. But unlike the Americans, the British endorsed the "responsible autonomy" associated with traditional craft organization and believed it superior to scientific management.[40] Whatever the differences, many American job enrichers believed that the Tavistock mandarins had independently confirmed their new ideas.[41]

The evidence, then, shows that job enrichment emerged from a new conception of human nature. Some scholars, to be sure, have denied its novelty and have completely ignored the Maslow influence. The sociologists Ivar Berg, Marcia Freedman, and Michael Freedman, for instance, have argued for continuity and asserted that job enrichment derived "almost entirely and in a straight line from the investigations, articles, and books by Harvard Business School professors, their associates, and their students in the period before and during World War II."[42] But in reality, Maslow not only came from outside the management community, but he also provided ideas that led work reformers away from Taylor and the human relations ideas developed by Mayo and his Harvard successors.

Indeed, their steps toward corporatism convinced some that job enrichment constituted a "third managerial revolution." From this perspective, the separation of planning from doing and the creation of the management function was the first revolution, the professionalization of management and the creation of management schools was the second, and the rejection of the claim that expert despots could and should dictate all the decisions was the third and latest.[43] Such an interpretation, however, overlooked how the proposed changes fell short of being revolutionary. The corporatist mandarins only proposed to allow some discretion and some participation for workers in manufacturing. This was not intended to eliminate bureaucratic divisions of labor or managers. On the contrary, it would help legitimate them.

According to a more satisfactory interpretation, the reformers believed that Taylorism had created conflicts that neither it nor Mayoism could solve. As sociologist Alan Fox has suggested, managers had centralized power and specialized jobs because they had not trusted workers. But management had been "hoist with its own petard" because making labor into a commodity, employment into a monetary transaction, and work into a confinement had taught employees to return distrust with distrust. And distrust could not be remedied by more of the same or by friendliness toward workers away from the point of production.[44] Only some sort of integration of planning and performing, corporatists came to believe, could bring harmony.

Of course, in their quest for harmonious corporative communities the job enrichers were partly inspired by earlier human relations theory. In particular, the reformers drew, as Mayo had before them, from Emile Durkheim and from his quest to explain and eradicate anomie.[45] At times, to be sure, they talked about eliminating alienation. But they were not using this term in the Marxist sense and never subscribed to a conception of alienation which held that workers could fulfill themselves only after they had buried capitalism. They would eliminate alienation by making industrial work fulfilling, reconciling labor and capital, and creating a capitalism without class, and so they often used *alienation* and *anomie* interchangeably. Argyris, for instance, defined alienation as "estrangement from a group" and implied that conflict in the corporation was pathological.[46] And Robert Blauner, a popularizer of job enrichment, interchanged the two concepts throughout an entire book. He thought alienation fostered feelings of powerlessness, meaninglessness, isolation, and self-estrangement and that it existed when workers were unable "to control their immediate work processes, to develop a sense of purpose and function which connects their jobs to the overall organization of production, to belong to integrated industrial communities, and when they fail to become involved in the activity of work as a mode of personal self-expression."[47] His solution, like that of all the work reformers, was to give workers some latitude at the point of production and thereby integrate them into the corporate community.[48]

Their anomic conception of alienation also led the job enrichers to view self-actualization less as an end and more as a means to solve managerial problems. Making this clear in statements of purpose in nearly all of their books, they said that their goals were to enhance both mental health and managerial efficiency. Herzberg labeled his profession Industrial Mental Health and described its purpose as reducing the number of "psychological casualties" and bolstering the work ethic. Argyris hoped to provide business leaders with knowledge that could be used to "control" workers, and McGregor felt he could help managers understand "human nature" so they could "predict and control" employee behavior for "economic ends."[49]

The corporatists assumed that helping managers rationalize and workers self-actualize were consistent. Consequently, they shunned any modes of individual liberation threatening to corporate integration. As sociologists George Strauss and Philip Selznick have noted, they proposed no liberal mechanisms that might enable workers to direct the firm or protect themselves against managers. They did not support a constitutional framework that would empower workers, provide for due process and redress of grievances, and defend individual dignity and influence. In essence, any autonomy would depend on the "goodwill or self-interest" of managers. And because participation was merely "administrative subordination" designed to eradicate interests alien to the goals of the firm, each employee would be treated as "a deployable instrument" rather than granted the rights of "an autonomous being" or a full-fledged citizen in a corporate polis.[50] Of course by continuing to see people as factors to be manipulated by managers, the corporatists were also perpetuating bureaucracy and precluding a capitalism without class. In effect their new psychology and philosophy were little more than Mayoism in high gear.

Sticking close to bureaucracy and steering wide of any potential radicalism, however, was just what the management community wanted to hear. It heard the call of class harmony, and the allure of that call, according to a late 1960s survey conducted by the Conference Board, made McGregor, Herzberg, Likert, Argyris, and Maslow the most influential writers in the management profession.[51]

Crisis and Panacea

Although the job enrichment idea originated in humanistic psychology, its subsequent history was shaped by wider social and economic forces. It became a way for managers to adapt to changes in the marketplace and the work force that were worsening the dysfunctions of bureaucracy.

One thing managers had to adapt to was the educational improvements of industrial workers. Average years of schooling for male blue-collar workers jumped from 8 years in 1948 to 12.2 in 1966 to 12.6 in 1976. The proportion of male craft and blue-collar workers with one or more years of college doubled between 1966 and 1978; by 1978 almost one-fifth of craft workers and one-tenth of other blue-collar workers had at least one year of college. At the same time, the gap in education between professional and blue-collar workers narrowed. In 1945 blue-collar workers had only half as many years of schooling as professionals, but by the 1970s they had three-fourths as much.[52]

Obviously the current generation was better schooled than the workers of the early twentieth century, who were often illiterate or immigrants without English skills. And it was for these uneducated and immigrant workers that Taylorized jobs had often been designed. Such jobs seemed less suited to the talents and adaptability of well-educated workers; more importantly, attitudinal measures showed that workers overeducated for their jobs usually expressed more dissatisfaction because they had access to more information, were more aware of other opportunities, and had higher expectations. As one mandarin put it, Taylorism had "created too many dumb jobs for the number of dumb people to fill them."[53]

The problem of managing more highly educated workers was compounded by the relative youthfulness of American workers by the late 1960s. In 1960 only 16 percent of the work force was under twenty-four years old. But by 1972, after much of the baby-boom generation found employment, 21 percent of workers were under twenty-four.[54] And most of them, like young workers generally, were concentrated in low-paying, low-skill, less desirable jobs. Like previous generations of rural and immigrant workers, moreover, they lacked "work discipline." They were almost twice as likely to express dissatisfaction with their jobs as the work force as a whole and were more likely to be absent and to quit.[55]

In addition, the frustration with Taylorized jobs was heightened by changing cultural expectations accompanying the emergence of an ethic of individual fulfillment and liberation. Managerial capitalism, the sociologist Daniel Bell would later argue, was becoming caught in a "cultural contradiction." By creating abundance, it had helped to discredit the older ethic of discipline, denial, and submission to authority that had helped make abundance possible. The consumption side of capitalism had encouraged a quest for gratification that its production side denied.[56]

Among the most important of the cultural influences were the Vietnam War, the New Left, the civil rights movement, and the counterculture. The "fragging" of officers by troops in Vietnam, the protests against the war, the plea of the New Left for participatory democracy, the demand by civil rights activists for respect for the individual, and the quest by hippies for satisfaction were all in part rebellions against bureaucratic authority. And similarly, the New Left, the civil rights movement, and the counterculture all challenged the notion that work and life were separate realms and that work was self-denying and leisure alone was satisfying.[57]

Attitudinal surveys, to be sure, continued to report that more than three of four American industrial workers expressed satisfaction with their jobs. But what this avowed satisfaction meant is open to question. Satisfaction with a job is not identical to commitment; a worker may be satisfied but not motivated. Moreover, reported satisfaction may not have measured attitudes toward the job itself; it may have measured satisfaction with the compensation attained from the job environment, leisure pursuits, or the way workers adjusted to routine. In such cases the work may have been less satisfying than cheating the boss, hanging out with the guys, or cruising in a bass boat on weekends. Alternatively, the satisfaction that workers expressed may have meant only that they were resigned to their jobs because they felt they lacked opportunity to get better ones. When asked if they would remain in their jobs if a different type were available, 60 percent of blue-collar workers answered that they preferred another. And in the late 1960s and early 1970s, workers expressed higher levels of interest in the content, meaning, and interest of jobs than before or after. But this did not mean that they were willing to sacrifice income and security for reformed work, and surveys showed the primary cause of dissatisfaction with work continued to be wages rather than work content.[58]

Those who would discount the impact of cultural changes could also point out that heightened disgust with Taylorized jobs did not show up in turnover rates. Quit rates in manufacturing continued to fluctuate inversely with levels of unemployment. During slack labor markets workers were unwilling to risk unemployment to seek better jobs.[59] Nor did the period witness any significant increase in absenteeism, although in some industries, especially auto, absentee rates were high.[60] But stability in such measures does not necessarily mean that workers were satisfied with specialized tasks; their behavior could have been influenced by many factors, including wage levels.[61]

The strike eruption of the late 1960s and early 1970s can also be interpreted economically rather than culturally. The inflation caused by the Vietnam War and the tight labor market gave workers reason to strike, and most of the strikes were over wages.[62] But again, evidence also indicates that economic explanations are not sufficient. An unusually high proportion of the strikes were over working conditions and control issues and were wildcat strikes not sanctioned by unions.[63] The rank-and-file, moreover, more frequently rejected contracts that did not improve working conditions.[64] Such evidence seems to indicate that cultural shifts in work attitudes fostered hostile reactions to fragmented work and to unions that supported it.

Indeed, the strike activity that became common by the late 1960s seemed symptomatic of a breach of the truce between business and labor that had existed during the previous two decades. This truce rested on a bargain between union leaders and managers in trend-setting manufacturing industries. The unions had conceded the right of management to institute bureaucracy and had helped to discipline workers while managers had bought union cooperation with legal recognition, long-term contracts, high wages, financial security, the seniority principle, improved working conditions, and elaborate grievance procedures. The truce had been successful throughout the 1950s and much of the 1960s. Production, profits, wages, and the ratio of supervisory to production employees rose while unemployment, industrial accidents, and workdays lost to strikes fell. But by the late 1960s both parties were finding it difficult to meet their commitments.

In part, contradictions in the bargain weakened it. High wages and job security used to convince workers to accept specialized work under close supervision raised labor costs. Long-term contracts, grievance procedures, and the seniority principle also restrained the whip of the market as an enforcer of work discipline. And unions had difficulty acting as disciplinary mechanisms. As rewards dwindled, cooperation with management often alienated leaders from the rank-and-file.

On their part, managers had less with which to buy cooperation. Momentous changes in world markets, particularly the reconstruction of Western European and Japanese manufacturing and the industrialization of the Third World, challenged American firms, and American managers often reacted in ways that triggered conflicts with labor. By maintaining or reducing real wage levels, laying off workers, increasing the supervisory ratio, instituting speed-ups, and letting working conditions deteriorate, they violated the bargain. In response workers turned to strikes and sabotage, often to challenge management prerogatives in defiance of union leaders.[65]

Conflicts from 1970 to 1972 in a General Motors plant at Lordstown, Ohio, symbolized for many the demographic, cultural, economic, and institutional developments that were subverting bureaucracy. The plant was new, created to make the compact *Vega* and to compete with imported small cars. GM engineers had designed very specialized tasks; all line jobs could be learned in half an hour and mastered in half a day. The workers, who averaged less than twenty-five years old and included many Vietnam veterans, had been specially screened to exclude troublemakers, and both wages and benefits were as high as any auto workers' in the world. Yet high pay was not enough, particularly for young workers. They refused to tolerate mindless jobs and militaristic authority and consequently withdrew their efficiency. On some Mondays the line at Lordstown had to be shut down because too many workers stayed home. And when they showed up, they worked slowly, refused to obey orders, and sabotaged thousands of cars. They also defied their leaders and engaged in wildcat strikes. Management made matters worse by introducing a major speedup that tried to accelerate production from one car a minute to one every thirty-six seconds, a rate at least 40 percent higher than any other auto plant. In response, workers sped up their sabotage, and subsequently 97 percent of the rank-and-file voted for a strike.[66]

Lordstown quickly became a symbol of what many called a crisis at work. The national television and print media analyzed the Lordstown syndrome. *Life*, *Newsweek*, and *Harper's* devoted cover stories to the blue-collar blues.[67] Numerous journalists and sociologists became fascinated with working-class life and wrote books about alienation and conflict at work. Studs Terkel's *Working* became a best-seller.[68] Politicians also got into the act. Liberal senators introduced a bill asking for appropriations to fund alienation research,[69] and the Nixon administration jumped on the bandwagon with the *Work in America* report. The common theme in the discussions of the crisis was the notion of the humanist psychologists that Taylorism was the problem and job enrichment the panacea.

Under these circumstances, many managers became attracted to the harmony promised by the job enrichers. Management mandarins and journalists drew their attention to efforts to mitigate the authoritarian direction of work by such companies as Texas Instruments, Polaroid, General Mills, Corning Glass, IBM, AT&T, Procter and Gamble, and Donelly Mirrors.[70] And in September 1972, at Harriman, New York, management mandarins and consultants from across the globe gathered to discuss common problems and to share the latest information on how to redesign jobs and improve the quality of working life.[71]

Managers at the Harriman conference and elsewhere were able to draw on literature that popularized the ideas of the pioneering mandarins and provided more clearly defined prescriptions for enriching jobs. The original psychological justification remained. But subsequent mandarins and managers—people like Scott Myers, Richard Walton, and Robert Ford—had conducted experiments in reforming work, and what they had learned from their efforts enabled them to publish practical guides.

Reforming work had come to mean not merely redesigning the job of the production employee but that of the manager as well. Reformers argued that managers had to surrender some of "the divine rights of 'King Supervisor,'" stop dictating all goals and methods, and cease closely evaluating performance. Employees should take on these functions, and managers should act less as commanders and more as helpers.[72]

The new agenda, as expressed in Myers's slogan, was to make "every employee a manager." At Donelly Mirrors, the manufacturer of mirrors for most American cars, job enrichers went so far as to give all employees the title of manager.[73] In redesigned jobs, they argued, workers should not merely be machine tenders. They should be planners who identified problems, selected some goals, innovated, and chose the methods of work. And, unlike the pioneering theorists, the later ones discussed how unions could participate in planning tasks and reorganizing work. They envisioned labor-management committees setting up specific jobs and guiding managers' efforts to help workers. But managers, they admitted, might have to keep employees focused on issues that they could solve and keep them away from matters outside their control.[74]

According to the new prescriptions, many of the control functions of managers should be made inherent in work itself. The jobs of special checkers or quality control inspectors whose primary job was supervision should be eliminated. In their place some sort of feedback system should be organized, one that gave frequent information about quality and quantity of performance so that employees could guide their own efforts. A particularly effective method, they suggested, would be to connect each employee or work team to a customer who received their product and informed them about performance. The customer could be other employees, teams, or even consumers outside the firm. Using feedback, workers could manage themselves.[75]

The work reformers also called for a "natural" organization of tasks. Enriched jobs would not only draw on a wide range of skills and abilities but would also include a "complete plan-do-control cycle." Tasks and workers would "nest" together, with work teams sharing a space, communicating easily with one another, and thus having an opportunity to develop a "natural, mutual dependence." Workers might then feel like they "owned" their jobs and could receive "motivation through the work itself." Managers could "integrate individual efforts into cohesive, purposeful, whole units" and thus create "synergy" between corporate performance and individual development.[76]

Nevertheless such endeavors were far from radical. By creating synergistic government, the sociologist Michael Burawoy has argued, managers were continuing a project begun by Taylor, an effort to make their authority less visible and less personal. Managers were relying less and less on simple coercion, personal orders, and direct control; instead they were trying to organize tasks that channeled workers toward the goals of the firm, to "manipulate rather than dominate," and to make their power less "despotic" than "hegemonic."[77] The central feature of hegemonic management, Burawoy noted, was its attempt to elicit consent by organizing work into a game. By playing the game and joining in teamwork, participants agreed to abide by corporate rules and gained relatively more satisfaction than not playing. But relative improvements in satisfaction did not mean that players found self-actualization or integration in a harmonious comity. At best the game provided some camaraderie and status; at worst it lessened fatigue and boredom. Employee consent derived not from acceptance of the legitimacy of managers; rather, consent came from participation in a relatively satisfying game that was also rational for the firm.[78]

By publicizing their successes, job enrichers sought to legitimize their theories. Judson Gooding visited several companies with reformed jobs and reported "a discernible mutuality of interest between management and the working force"; workers spoke less about what "they" (meaning managers) wanted, and more about what "we" were doing.[79] Reformers especially pointed to changes at AT&T, Texas Instruments, and a General Mills dog food plant. Managers at these places had found that job enrichment lowered turnover and absenteeism (thus reducing training and replacement costs) and improved quality. In some cases too, especially at the General Mills plant, productivity had risen. People either produced more or worked in ways that allowed supervisory, janitorial, and clerical jobs to be eliminated.[80]

By the mid-seventies, such corporative models were being imitated. A number, for instance, had decided to redesign their office work, partly because it, unlike manufacturing, could be reformed without technology costs. And as of 1974, a survey of 300 randomly chosen firms in the leading 1,000 *Fortune* industrials showed that 29 percent of the companies responding had some enriched jobs and that another 24 percent expected to try the system. Of the enrichers, 4 percent, all high technology firms, had endorsed the technique as a formal company policy, and of the remainder, individual managers had tried the system. They had changed from 3 to 10 percent of their total jobs, mostly in fields designated as clerical, technical, or low-level managerial. Such figures compared favorably with the early impact of Taylorism.[81]

Still, a majority of firms had not gone along with the fad, and two-thirds of these were not planning on doing so. Applications, moreover, affected only a few workers, and these were not usually in manufacturing jobs. Obviously many managers had not been persuaded to reform work.

Trial and Error

Ironically, while job enrichment was at the apex of its popularity and its advocates seemed most assured, critics were questioning it. The critics, a mix of mandarins, managers, psychologists, union leaders, and economists, thought that job enrichers had misunderstood human nature, the goals of American workers, the requirements of the firm, and the relationship of task organization to technology and the marketplace. Most detractors rebuffed corporatism and embraced Taylorism.

Perhaps the most embarrassing attack fell upon Maslow's psychology. His notion of a hierarchy of needs had implied that after wages had satisfied basic needs, wage increases ceased to motivate and managers should turn to enriching work. But the theory was difficult to verify. Research revealed that needs almost defied categorization, that they could seldom be ranked according to his hierarchy, and that the least satisfied were not necessarily the most dominant. Psychologists concluded, moreover, that the drive for self-actualization might not be a need at all; it could represent a cultural value, a wish of what people should be rather than what they are. And to some, Maslow's conception of needs was so vague as to be nontestable and of little use in explaining motivation.[82] Whatever the validity of the research on Maslow's ideas, many mandarins concluded that self-actualization was a thin reed on which to rest technique.

This became clear in criticisms of Frederick Herzberg's dual factor theory. He had claimed that job context influenced dissatisfaction and that job content affected satisfaction and motivation. But to critics, his logic, definitions, and data were faulty. One researcher distilled five versions of the dual factor thesis from Herzberg's publications, tested each, and found that none was an accurate description of employee attitudes. Others pointed to crucial methodological errors. Herzberg had arrived at his theory, in part, by asking white-collar workers to describe situations when they had felt dissatisfied and satisfied and had then categorized their responses into preconceived classifications. Hence, researchers discovered that they could verify his conclusions only by using his method; his answers were determined by the questions he asked and the categories in which he put the responses. Beyond this, the separation of dissatisficers and motivators amounted to a false dichotomy because sometimes what he defined as the job context could motivate and sometimes the content could dissatisfy. An obvious example that contradicted his theory was working on an automobile assembly line: the pay often satisfied, while the work dissatisfied. Finally, critics thought that Herzberg and the other job enrichers had used the conception of self-actualization to confuse satisfaction and motivation, which were neither theoretically nor behaviorally identical.[83]

To some critics, discrediting Maslow's and Herzberg's science also discredited job enrichment. But their charges were often off the mark. Some, for example, misunderstood the dual nature of self-actualization and thought job enrichers had simply wanted satisfying work, while others seemed to think job enrichment theory had no place for monetary rewards.[84] They refused to recognize that the job enrichers had not denigrated monetary rewards but had merely assumed that satisfactory wages and enriched jobs could go together and that job content was at least as significant a reward as wages.

More telling was the charge that enriched jobs did not enrich workers. Many believed that the workers who felt most motivated by reformed work had cultural backgrounds and personal goals that made them value jobs involving some discretion, cooperation, and personal responsibility. These workers tended to come from rural backgrounds or to express attitudes that ranked high on indices measuring the Protestant work ethic. But unfortunately for the job enrichers, such workers were said to be fast disappearing. A growing majority had urban outlooks and monetary orientations.[85]

And ironically, Maslow himself expressed doubts about whether such workers wanted self-actualizing jobs. Visiting a company with enriched jobs during the 1960s, he came away favorably impressed by the intentions of the reforms. But not only did he wonder whether managers would allow worker participation during hard times, he also questioned whether many workers had "the instinct of workmanship" and the desire for responsibility necessary for harmony to be achieved.[86]

By misunderstanding labor goals, other critics charged, job enrichers had wildly exaggerated the blue-collar blues. More than three of four workers said they were satisfied with their jobs, which was taken as clear evidence that most preferred boring, routine jobs. And the clincher for such critics was an experiment in which six autoworkers from Detroit spent several weeks at a Saab-Scania factory in Sweden, worked with semiautonomous work teams, and preferred the traditional assembly line five to one. They thought the Swedish jobs were not only just as tedious but also more quickly paced and anxiety ridden. As one worker said, "If I have to bust my ass to be meaningful, forget it; I'd rather be monotonous."[87]

In addition, some opponents argued that the labor market generally miti-gated frustration on the job by matching people to suitable jobs. Workers chose jobs that conformed to their skills, values, and goals. They avoided boring and unhealthy jobs, which drove wages up, because employees who took such jobs received more compensation, providing incentive to employers to eliminate those tasks.[88] Taylorized jobs, some went so far as to argue, were normally filled by unskilled people who wanted to avoid freedom and respon-sibility; for them centralized power and specialized tasks, far from being frustrating, were actually quite satisfying.[89] Job enrichment was thus less therapeutic than tyrannical.

Indeed, critics contended that the job enrichers were cultural imperialists, imposing their values on blue-collar workers. As academics, they had been socialized to value autonomy, personal development, and hard work at crea-tive tasks. Consequently they had incorrectly assumed blue-collar workers also wanted enriched jobs. But what the job enrichers had said that workers wanted was not the same as what workers said they wanted. So corporatist prescriptions told more about the values of the intellectuals who advocated them than about the problems of industrial workers, who were not alienated from specialized work but from middle-class values about work.[90]

Some union officials and sympathizers voiced similar charges and argued that unions better protected workers than any system introduced by man-agers. William Winpisinger, president of the International Association of Ma-chinists and Aerospace Workers, denied that Lordstown signified a new crisis at work and thought the conflict stemmed from traditional objections to speedup, unsafe working conditions, and unilateral decisions by management. If Americans wanted to enrich jobs, he said, they should "enrich the paycheck," shorten the workweek, extend vacations, lower the retirement age, improve working conditions, strengthen grievance procedures, and establish a seniority system to ensure that workers could move up to better jobs.[91]

Other labor leaders maintained that union demands for high wages could help eliminate boring jobs by providing an incentive to automate and mecha-nize. And the specific, practical objections of unions, it was said, provided a better guide to improving working life than abstract job enrichment theory. Union objections to Taylorism, extending back to 1915 and Robert F. Hoxie's *Scientific Management and Labor*, had helped make work more healthy. In contrast, managerial work reform was merely another cynical attempt to de-legitimize unions and included a sophisticated speedup designed to make fewer employees do more for less.[92]

In addition, labor leaders complained that harmony threatened the traditional adversarial role of unions. They were concerned that if they cooperated with management they could "become managers themselves." If unions went to bed with management, one official argued, two groups "would be screwing the workers instead of one"; a situation could develop like George Orwell's *Animal Farm*, where workers could look "from the pigs to the men, and from the men to the pigs" and would be unable to tell the difference. Or as another official asked, "who in the hell" would cooperative unions "be fighting against?" Not surprisingly, given such fears, few union contracts in the mid-1970s had clauses for enriching jobs.[93]

Some union officials, however, did disagree, believing that union participation in job redesign could become necessary to maintain membership. Leaders of the United Auto Workers (UAW) in particular were less afraid of work reform and were ready to consider it in an industry noted for its deadening tasks and declining competitiveness. In this case, the leaders' affiliations with liberal intellectuals and politicians and their more positive attitude to the social sciences may have been a factor. In any event, Irving Bluestone, a vice-president in the UAW, became the most prominent advocate of work reform among union leaders and insisted that participation in work reorganization, rather than being a threat to the adversarial role, offered a new means to better the lives of workers and extend union power. Hence as early as 1973 the UAW signed an agreement with Ford establishing committees to "seek joint answers to the difficult questions of job enrichment."[94]

For their part, bureaucratic mandarins were less concerned with how rational job enrichment was for workers than with how rational it was for business. They complained that reports on its productive efficiency rested on shaky evidence or unscientific methodology. The findings, they said, were often distorted by some "Hawthorne effect," in which the observers biased the experiment by their participation in it and did not control for the way that workers could have been affected by the attention managers lavished on them. Moreover, the scientists involved were typically consultants who had an interest in favorable reports, and many of the trials were not in representative businesses. The workers and managers at the General Mills dog food plant, for instance, had been specially selected, and its site had been chosen because of its isolation from industrial centers and unions. Those at Procter and Gamble could build on a tradition of paternalism, high pay, and skilled workers. And at Polaroid and Texas Instruments the reforms had been confined to a select few.

Beyond these flaws, critics thought that the experiments often contrasted poorly designed jobs with enriched ones; that control groups were inadequate or, more typically, nonexistent; and that studies were often short term, which could distort results since almost any escape from routine would temporarily improve productivity and attitudes. They also argued that job enrichment had often been accompanied by new compensation schemes or new machines, thus making it impossible to separate the effects of reformed work, better wages, and more efficient technology. At the General Mills plant, for example, much of the improvement could be attributed to the introduction of continuous-process technology. Given these flaws, they said, improvements attributed to job enrichment remained unproven.[95]

Bureaucratic mandarins also reproached the work reformers for failing to understand the necessity of centralization. Decentralization, they thought, could result in irrational choices. And surveys showed that most managers believed their workers lacked the intelligence, expertise, and responsibility needed to organize and plan production.[96] As one GM manager put it, "the girls on the carton-folding operation really" had "nothing to contribute to almost anything important about running a container company."[97] Or in the words of another manager, participation by workers was "a passing fancy created by unions for purposes of disruption and featherbedding, by consultants to create more clients, and by publishers and educators as a current fad to talk and write about. If properly used, [it was a] social improvement. But we still need to retain the ability to design, make, and sell widgets for profit or there won't be any jobs left to enrich."[98]

Still another manager, whose electronics company Maslow had visited and whose reforms had been held up as a model by job enrichers, returned to Taylorism during a sales slump; he admitted that he "may have lost sight of the purpose of business" and got too involved in developing "new theories of management."[99] Managers like him turned corporative rhetoric against itself and claimed that bureaucracy was the one best way to help society. Managers had to be "realistic" and recognize that the Golden Rule was an inappropriate guide in a market economy because "doing unto others as one would have others do unto him" did not typically result in "profitable and workable management." And failure in the market did not do anyone any good. It was really more altruistic to empower managers to protect the firm and the public.[100]

According to this line of criticism, the job enrichers had failed to understand that mandarinisms could not show managers how best to organize work. In practice managers could not and did not use social science to design tasks. Typically they did not even read mandarin publications. They had to act within the limits imposed by superiors and by structures and technology already in place, seeking to overcome specific problems, to use machines efficiently, to open bottlenecks, to minimize the number of workers, and to reduce short-term costs. And this meant that job structures emerged from many decisions guided by rules of thumb and years of trial and error. Every company had a considerable investment in its division of labor, and most had specialized tasks for a perfectly good reason: they had worked.[101]

Simplified and specialized tasks existed because they had raised profits and fulfilled consumer demand. Adam Smith had been right, economists Sar Levitan and William Johnston argued. He had correctly foreseen that specialized and standardized work had developed not from "the arbitrary decisions of engineers" or "the inevitable progression of technology" but from "a rational search for efficiency" in a market. "Industrial survival of the fittest" had "produced a species not easily changed for the better."[102] And ultimately jobs could be changed only if demand changed and exerted new evolutionary pressures on managers or if managers resisted market pressures.

It followed that resisting market pressures to help workers would lead to inefficiency. Managers who put the well-being of workers as laborers ahead of the interests of the firm, consumers, and workers as wage earners would end up with added costs. And when consumers refused to pay for the higher costs, the firm would be uncompetitive. According to Levitan and Johnston, specialization was an "inevitable" and "unavoidable" part of industrial life, and workers were doomed to be "cogs" in a machine. But at least American workers were rich. Workers "readily agreed with Marx that the jobs" were "bad," Levitan and Johnston quipped, but they "continued to work for Ford because the wage" was "good." And managers had recognized the dangers and costs inherent in a utopian pursuit of harmony. Accepting the inevitability of conflict, they had settled on bureaucratic forms that kept it at a "tolerable level."[103]

Judiciously enough, Marxists seconded the mandarinate's motion that bureaucracy was natural for capitalism. For instance, David F. Noble, the historian of technology, showed that when worker participation was introduced in a General Electric machine shop, it failed to produce harmony. The machinists used it to assert job control, and managers tried to circumvent union rules and extract job knowledge. But middle managers came to feel threatened, scuttled sincere cooperation, and caused a deterioration in production and morale that they then used to discredit the experiment. Corporatism withered away, and managers returned to running the shop based on "old-fashioned coercion," even though it was less productive. The episode showed, Noble thought, that job enrichment could not overcome the contradictions and class conflicts of capitalism, because the real end of capitalism was "domination," not industrial efficiency or social harmony. Management was quite willing to sacrifice participation, productivity, and profits in order to preserve its "private power and prerogatives."[104] All roads through capitalism, it seemed, led to bureaucracy.

As a sort of compromise view, some mandarins were willing to concede that job enrichment could be useful, although not for the blue-collar manufacturing workers that it had been intended to help. It was really appropriate only for white-collar knowledge workers and managers. Raymond Miles, for instance, argued that most managers wanted their own jobs enriched along corporatist lines but preferred to use old-fashioned human relations techniques on their subordinates. Managers, he said, felt they were as smart and as good as their bosses and should therefore be allowed to exercise "self-control" and share authority in "partnership." But they believed their subordinates were irrational and should be subject to "formal authority."[105] What was good for the goose was not good for the gander.

Toward the Quality Circle

The most significant trends since the early seventies have been efforts by corporatist work reformers to rebut the technological and economic determinism of opponents. In general, these rebuttals have proceeded along two lines, one questioning the validity of technological determinism and the efficiency of specialized jobs, the other asserting the efficiency of job enrichment and its similarity to previous theories. Ironically, as psychological justifications for integrating planning and performing gave way to engineering arguments, job enrichers who had originally contrasted their technique to Taylorism began comparing it to scientific management. In the process, sales people put new labels on old bottles and peddled job enrichment as task design or job redesign, a means of making efficient use of human resources.[106] And they began pointing to satisfied customers in Western Europe and Japan.

Some of the pioneers found it difficult to give up the older rhetoric. Herzberg responded to his critics by reprinting his previous articles, and his graduate students argued that their mentor's ideas had not been disproved. Evidently they assumed that his motivation-hygiene theory had not been understood and needed only to be explained one more time. And although Herzberg sought to dissociate himself from Maslow's hierarchy of needs and from Argyris's democratic leadership, he continued to argue that people had a need to grow, which managers could satisfy by integrating planning and doing.[107]

More novel ideas came from people who drew from the Tavistock sociotechnical systems theory in order to refute the determinism of the opponents of job enrichment. Along with James Taylor and Albert Cherns, for example, Louis Davis argued that technological determinism was conservative. It assumed that technology imposed a very narrow range of organizational alternatives and that the only efficient organizations of work could be, and should be, Taylorist. People, in other words, were but "parts of machines" and must be fitted to machines, and any attempt to repudiate Taylorism was to opt for inefficiency and failure. This assumption, he and his colleagues contended, was "dangerously simplistic." Its validity rested on the notion that technology developed autonomously, without influence from values. But this was incorrect. In reality, technology and organization were shaped by the goals and value judgments of their designers. The determinists had confused organizations with unalterable "natural biological entities," refusing to recognize that they were really human inventions that could be changed to address different goals.[108] They had also failed to see that choosing different goals would affect the choice of organizational technique and that managers could and should choose goals that were good for their employees.

In certain respects, however, this argument had missed the central point made by critics. The critics had not claimed that technology and organization developed independently, but rather that the market had imposed a Taylorist division of labor by requiring that business make a profit. To argue for a different choice of business goals implied either an escape from the market or a sacrifice of profits to enhance the quality of working life. And admitting this, whatever its merits as social policy, was unlikely to make job enrichment attractive to American managers.

Consequently, a more sensible rebuttal came from those who denied that market imperatives dictated Taylorism. As early as 1971, Edward Lawler and Richard Hackman rejected the presumption that Taylor's scheme of simplifying, standardizing, and specializing jobs maximized profits. His technique seemed economical, and managers assumed that its monetary benefits offset its many hidden costs. But dissatisfaction led to costs in turnover, recruitment, inexperienced replacements, absenteeism, high wages, low quality, underused employees, excessive administrative overhead, and "balancing" the assembly line. Maximizing profits required reducing the costs of Taylorism without reimposing the costs that centralization and specialization had been designed to eliminate. The choice between profits and satisfaction was a "pseudo-dilemma," and properly instituted work reform was the way to have both.[109]

Accordingly proponents began emphasizing production rather than psychology. In 1973 William Dowling, editor of *Organizational Dynamics*, visited three Western European manufacturing plants with redesigned jobs and was convinced that advantages came from greater flexibility and satisfaction. At the Volvo, Saab, and Philips plants, less money was tied up in expensive product-specific tools; workers were more adaptable; fewer administrative personnel were required; planning was easier because one bottleneck did not disrupt the whole plant; and production could be increased by hiring more workers. These advantages, Dowling thought, compensated for the slower production speed of man-paced work, and he believed that the European firms had earned "at least an economic draw" in the switch from standardized to flexible production.[110]

By the late 1970s and early 1980s the economist Robert Reich and the sociologist Charles Sabel had become prominent advocates of the strength through flexibility argument. They emphasized that after the 1960s significant changes had occurred in technology and market demand. A larger and larger portion of the market for manufacturers rested on a demand for high-quality goods and for products custom-tailored to specific buyers. The change could be seen in the rise of companies using small-batch, customized production to produce numerically controlled machine tools, industrial robots, specialty steels and chemicals, computers, and telecommunications and office equipment. And in the future they expected that more manufacturing would become technology-driven and would be characterized by rapid changes in process and product, as was now apparent in the electronics and ceramics industries. Because of the expansion of specialized as opposed to mass production, precision and flexibility were becoming more important than quantity and standardization, which meant that tasks were becoming difficult to routinize; general-purpose machines and skilled, adaptable workers more useful than special-purpose technology and unskilled machine tenders; and a collegial organization of work more sensible that a militaristic approach. Although neither Reich nor Sabel endorsed job enrichment, and in fact both doubted that most expressions of it went far enough to reintegrate planning and doing, they did point out that when workers participated in planning, production was more rapidly adjusted to the changing goals of the corporation and its customers. Indeed, they concluded that because Japanese and Western European firms had adopted a collegial organization, they had enjoyed great success in the new manufacturing sectors.[111]

The end-of-mass-production, rise-of-flexible-specialization argument, however, rested on some dubious propositions. Sabel and Reich overestimated the dependence of mass production on specialized equipment, long production runs, and uniform products; they ignored how manufacturers had learned from the way that Ford had driven his Model T into a cul-de-sac and had since the 1920s continually sought ways to increase both volume and flexibility. They also exaggerated the integration of planning and doing in computer-driven manufacture, overlooked how computer technology was often used to deprive workers of discretion, and basically blew out of proportion the market share taken by new industries. In addition, their notion that manufacturing workers were being given more autonomy and becoming more like nineteenth-century craft workers seemed unproven by reference to Japanese quality circles or Italian sweatshops.[112]

Corporatist reformers also began to emphasize their agreements with rather than their differences from scientific management. When the consultant Lyle Yorks, for example, moved from the usual psychological argument in *A Radical Approach to Job Enrichment* (1976) to an engineering one in *Job Enrichment Revisited* (1979), he began claiming that job enrichment was really intended to eliminate "disefficiencies" and "diseconomies" and so was not basically different from Taylorism. Seen as a means for making work efficient, it was much less "a revolutionary panacea for production problems and employee discontent" than "first and foremost a work analysis technique" dependent on sound engineering.[113]

Peter Drucker, who had helped start work reform in the 1950s, also argued that Taylor's ideas had always been similar to job enrichment. In a remarkable attempt to rewrite history, he claimed that Taylor had originated many of the notions later expressed by Herzberg and McGregor. Taylor had wanted to reorganize unhealthy and burdensome tasks, to replace the boss with servants of labor, and to develop the potentiality and personality of workers. And he had believed "above all" that managers should select, train, and develop individuals for the jobs they were "best fitted for" and help them become "first rate" workers by scientifically designing their tasks and providing them with appropriate information and tools.[114] By emphasizing Taylor's corporatist rhetoric and by ignoring how his prescriptions had called for people to be separated into planners and performers of very simplified jobs, Drucker tried to drape the bureaucrat with corporatist clothing.

In 1983 Yorks and David Whitsett greatly expanded Drucker's argument. They contended that effective jobs were necessarily designed to be efficient from both an "engineering" and a "behavioral" perspective but that this had been obscured by the way mandarins had overemphasized either one perspective or the other in order to gain attention. Such writers had been so interested in selling new ideas and in changing entrenched ways of thinking that they had used the strongest possible terms and unwittingly misreported or mis-represented the factual basis of their conclusions. In the process, their proofs had become more legend than science and had split the engineering and behavioral orientations into separate schools of management. The engineering school, created by Taylor, became associated with task orientation, technical efficiency, work simplification and specialization, monetary incentives, and fulfillment outside work through consumption. Taylor, however, was said to have sometimes combined tasks and had often expressed concern for health and growth at work. And the behavioral school, developed by Elton Mayo and his Harvard colleagues and continued by the early job enrichers, became associated with a people orientation, interpersonal efficiency, communication and participation schemes, sensitivity training, job enrichment, and psycho-logical satisfaction at work. But the behavioralists had always allowed for monetary incentives, specialized jobs, centralized power, and machinery im-provements. In short, engineering and behavioral mandarins had differed more in ideology than in practice.

Whitsett and Yorks concluded that management had yet to develop one best way for managing workers and designing organizations. Management was not a science; it was a craft, trade, or practice that rested on experience, intuition, academic knowledge, and value commitment. Hence mandarins and managers should be honest about the dysfunctions of their techniques and should be concerned with both satisfaction and production. Job reform should be under-stood less as a cure than as one important treatment in the managers' medicine bag.[115]

In the late seventies and early eighties, the psychological and engineering language coexisted in the literature promoting the Japanese way to class har-mony. Mandarins explained that through quality control circles, teams could cooperatively plan their work and help maximize quality and productivity. Yet ironically, when quality circle boosters searched for a usable past and for ways to discredit Taylorism, they turned to the psychological theories of early job enrichment and emphasized that self-actualizing work could integrate individ-ual and organization. Corporatism and bureaucratism were becoming more and more difficult to distinguish.

7

The American
Samurai

Japanizing
American Corporatism

In 1967 the French journalist Jean-Jacques Servan-Schreiber warned that a managerial gap was developing between European and American business, giving American firms advantages that could eventually make Europe into a glorified colony. He advised Europeans to protect themselves by imitating the "decentralized" management of American firms.[1] By the late 1970s and early 1980s many American managers and mandarins were expressing similar concerns about Japanese business. Worried by industrial stagnation and the Japanese invasion of domestic markets, they questioned American values and institutions. They too sought to learn from their rival and to import Japanese ideas in addition to Sonys and Toyotas.[2]

American managers wanted to imitate Japanese methods of corporate government. They flocked to seminars on Japan and went on pilgrimages to Japanese plants; they tried Zen meditation techniques and read medieval samurai texts.[3] They also became enthusiasts of the Japanese management system and its corporative philosophy, paternalism, consensual decision making, lifetime employment, seniority principles, enterprise unions, and quality control circles.

Indeed by the early 1980s, interest in Japanese management had exploded. The annual number of citations on Japanese management in *The Business Periodicals Index* tripled from 1979–80 to 1980–81 and doubled again in 1981–82 before leveling off at two to three times the annual number of the seventies.[4] Books recommending imitation of Japanese management became best-sellers.

This chapter discusses these publications and ways Americans have understood and used Japanese business ideas.[5] Many managers and mandarins sought to recover from the perceived crisis through "cross-fertilization of Japanese philosophy of management with American technology."[6] Unwittingly echoing the old slogan "Eastern values, Western technology" chanted by Asian modernizers a century earlier, they despaired over American individualism and bureaucracy and yearned for American samurai who could inspire loyalty in their employees. Seen in historical perspective, their quest to learn Japanese ways of managing nobly became the latest effort by American managers to transcend Taylor and Mayo through corporatism. Ironically, Japanese corporatism was often stamped "made in the USA" and was closer to Taylorism and Mayoism than they would admit.

Japan as Janus

American images of Japanese management in the 1980s drew from previous studies that had agreed that Japan had a unique management system but had disagreed about its rationality. These disagreements created a Janus-faced image of Japan, which persisted and helped produce differing perceptions in the American management community.

The "convergence" interpretation, prominent at the beginning of the "American Century," acknowledged that Japan had successfully industrialized but emphasized the inefficiency of Japanese firms compared with Western ones. Obviously this perception was influenced by the assumption that all roads to rationality went through Detroit, as proven by American military victory and material prosperity. Some Americans concluded that Japanese management was so irrational that it should not be studied. James Abegglen, later a respected authority on Japanese business, recalled that when he began his graduate work in the mid-1950s, he found no interest in such studies, either at Harvard or in Japanese universities.[7] And occupation officials believed understanding Japanese management was less important than Americanizing it. They sought to reform Japanese business by teaching Western techniques through lectures by American managers and tours of firms in the States.[8]

Convergence theorists mocked Japanese practices as feudal. Japanese business suffered, they said, from a rigid class hierarchy perpetuated by an educational system designed to separate managers from production workers. This encouraged elitism, inhibited communication, thwarted development of democratic institutions, and sometimes produced violent labor conflicts. Critics also faulted group recruitment and promotion. Large Japanese firms typically recruited an annual cadre of employees directly from school, hiring them for life, giving them in-house training, and promoting them automatically according to seniority. While acknowledging that such methods led to "a subordinated and loyal work force," American observers thought them inferior to the Western practice of hiring individuals for specific vacancies and rewarding them based on merit. Japanese practices rewarded conformity and complacency, caused businesses to become "tradition-bound and ingrown," stifled "individual initiative," and introduced rigidity.[9]

American critics also condemned Japanese consensual decision making. Japanese managers and professional workers had general tasks and rather diffuse responsibilities, which they coordinated by discussions and consultations. After discussion, everyone formalized their agreement in a ritual called *ringi* and fixed personal seals to a certificate. This procedure sometimes put initiative into the hands of lower ranks; at other times it only legitimized decisions of top managers. Americans familiar with a bureaucratic division of labor, characterized by individual responsibility and hierarchical authority, found it time consuming and irrational. They feared that a never-ending search for consensus would lead to paralysis.[10]

Convergence theory suggested that Japanese managers would have to westernize. They would be forced by competitive pressures to treat workers as factors of production and by the individualism that came with wealth and consumerism to reward individual initiative. They would have to abandon obsolete practices and adopt modern, that is, American, techniques. Failure to modernize would mean that Japan would inevitably "fall behind in the ranks of modern industrial nations."[11]

Not all American scholars, however, believed that Japan's system was irrational. The Japanese economy, after all, was successful, and many believed that Japanese management could claim at least some credit.

James Abegglen offered a path-breaking, culturalist explanation. He conducted field investigations and interviews in several factories of large Japanese companies in the mid-1950s. Industrialization in Japan, he concluded, combined feudalism with Western technology. Consequently, labor relations differed greatly from any Western pattern and were not based on contractual relationships, that is, on an impersonal exchange of labor and wage designed to minimize costs and maximize outputs and profits. Japanese managers had created a system based on traditional relationships and customs, especially on conceptions of family roles and ideals of social service and obligation.

Japanese managers, Abegglen said, founded their system on "feudalistic" relations intended to maintain loyalty and ensure worker identification with the firm. The firm was organized more like a family than a factory. Managers cared for workers through company welfare programs and maintained respect for elders through seniority promotion. Industrial clans sometimes sacrificed productivity to achieve harmony, but their success proved the compatibility of industrialization and feudalism.[12]

Other scholars developed some of the implications of Abegglen's culturalist interpretation. William Brown described the modern Japanese corporation as the social equivalent of the Tokugawa village and thought that commitment to preindustrial values was "the strength of Japanese organizations and the source of their efficiency."[13] Similarly, the anthropologist Thomas Rohlen, who lived, trained, worked, and socialized with employees of a Japanese bank, found that managers had adapted village culture to the needs of a modern white-collar organization. They treated permanent employees as members rather than as instruments; employees felt like members of a household and accepted a Confucian sense of obligation to perform for the clan.[14]

The culturalist interpretation, however, also had critics. Many Japanologists doubted the system was traditional. Many practices had been adopted only after the Second World War and could be attributed either to American occupation or to union demands for employment security. Before the war, paternalism had existed mostly as ideology or as a means of controlling turnover and training costs among white-collar and skilled workers. Even after the war, practices regarded as uniquely Japanese were applied only to the third of the work force considered members of the corporate clan. The rest, including virtually all women, were temporary and part-time employees exploited by elites. The whole notion of a traditional, unitary Japanese managerial system seemed to some social scientists "no more than a caricature of the corporate economy as a whole."[15]

The sociologist Robert Cole created a credible compromise between convergence and culturalist interpretations. Unlike Abegglen, Cole discounted managers' rhetoric, drawing instead on his experiences as an assembly line worker in two factories, and decided harmony came less from shared traditional values than from lack of employment opportunities and management cooption of opposition. Managers, he said, used a rhetoric of noblesse oblige but were pragmatic. Confronting a shortage of skilled workers, they found that they could best recoup training investments and reduce labor costs by promising lifetime employment and basing wages and status on length of service. This gave young workers considerable incentive to stay with the firm and view their job "as a stage in a career." Workers recognized that quitting usually meant loss of income and position. Lacking better options, they identified with the firm and resorted to traditional "household-kinship" metaphors, proclaiming loyalty to their "family circle."[16]

In addition, Cole claimed that Japanese practices were functional equivalents of modern Western practices. Western companies also based wages on seniority to retain skilled, experienced workers. The Japanese tied promotion and part of the wages to education and job performance. They also made exceptions to lifetime employment and sometimes badgered incompetent workers until they quit "voluntarily." And they used enterprise unions as "administrative apparatus" and as means to control workers. Practices might be justified with traditional metaphors and might differ somewhat from Western ways, but they could not be characterized as feudal or unique.[17]

American academics, then, offered differing interpretations of Japanese management. But prior to the mid-seventies, almost no one thought it was worth importing. Some considered it too irrational even to think about; others, like William F. Whyte, concluded that what was rational in Japan would not be in America.[18] "Successful management practices must be tailored to the customs and culture of the country," they assumed. Techniques based on deference to the group, which flourished in Japan's religious climate, would wither in America where Protestantism nourished individualism.[19] And others who accepted Cole's view that Japanese practices were functional equivalents of Western ones saw no need to imitate them. Western managers, they believed, already had solutions and so had little reason to try Eastern methods.

The only notable exceptions to the view that East and West would never meet came from the sociologist Ronald Dore and the management guru Peter Drucker. Dore developed a sort of reverse convergence theory and argued that Western patterns of labor relations, at least British ones, were evolving without conscious imitation toward those of Japan.[20] And Drucker was explaining to Americans by 1971 how the Japanese had succeeded in joining the harmony of corporatism with the riches of capitalism. His *Practice of Management* (1954) had been Japan's business "bible," read "zealously."[21] And he returned respect by praising their practices of consensual decision making, lifetime employment, and employee training. Their slowness in making decisions and building consensus, he said, was more than compensated by how quickly legitimized ideas were implemented. Lifetime employment worked well in conjunction with the flexibility provided by temporary labor. And their system of employee training helped them escape the dysfunctions of specialization, particularly in regard to overcoming boredom and "tunnel vision," improving workers' skills, and teaching corporate goals so that employees could become "responsible for the performance and results of the entire organization." He doubted that the West could copy Japan's system exactly but nonetheless suggested that its principles could "point the way to solutions for some of our most pressing problems."[22]

At the time, not many Americans were attracted to Drucker's arguments. A few business leaders agreed that Japan had been successful, but they wondered if America was ready for "a Commodore Perry in reverse."[23] And convergence theorists remained unpersuaded. Zbigniew Brzezinski noted that although consensual decision making had worked well during times of growth, it could easily lead to buck passing when confronted with difficult choices. Such problems, he said, had plagued the Japanese high command during the Second World War, and in his view the growth of the Japanese economy through the late fifties and the sixties had come "in spite of, and not because of" their management system. Japan's business community had benefited from fortuitous circumstances, including the low value of the yen; low defense costs; inexpensive raw material imports; a hard-working, well-educated work force; the willingness of America to open markets and sell technology; and wars in East Asia.[24]

The modernization theorists Robert M. Marsh and Hiroshi Mannari went so far as to argue that uniquely "Japanese" practices, like paternalism and lifetime employment, had far "less causal impact on performance" than such "universal" practices as job knowledge and rewards for performance. From their quantitative study of three Japanese firms they concluded that Japanese success could be attributed mainly to universal management techniques identical to those used by the West.[25] To them the effectiveness of Japanese practices was far from self-evident.

Still, even as some were arguing that Japanese methods were either irrational or inapplicable, managers of Japanese subsidiaries were bringing their methods across the Pacific and putting them to work in manufacturing operations. American observers saw a "yen for harmony" and a "tuning" of "both executives and workers to the corporate wavelength" in American plants like those of Sanyo or Matsushita. And they were amazed by the "egalitarianism" of Japanese managers, who periodically took a place on the assembly line or swept the floor. On their part, the Japanese found American workers were motivated by money more than status and were initially "befuddled" by the seemingly endless meetings that were part of consensual decision making. But once acclimated to foreign practices, Americans supposedly liked participating.[26]

The success of Japanese subsidiaries, especially their ability to outperform

American firms even when using identical machinery, surprised Americans and set off a scramble to understand what was happening. American firms had become plagued by too much individuality, according to Richard Johnson and William Ouchi. Too many managers wanted to play John Wayne, and capitalist cowboys had become so busy competing and corralling one another that collective effort was all but impossible. Japanese managers, on the other hand, were concerned with family obligation and social service, making them facilitators and molders rather dictators and macho men. They were suited to a "crowded organizational life."[27] Other observers thought that they also had superior production values, which were manifest in their concern with quality, meticulous attention to details, careful planning, and extensive efforts to do things right the first time.[28] Whatever the explanation, their success in subsidiaries in America undermined the claim that their management ideas were culture bound.[29]

During the same period, a few American firms began experimenting with manufacturing methods learned from Japan, especially with quality control circles designed to inspire initiative and cooperation from manufacturing workers. Lockheed Missile and Space Company, whose managers learned of the technique on a tour of Japan in 1973, became one of the first to try it the following year. Other aerospace companies, then pharmaceutical and electronics industries, followed suit.[30]

Still, cultural obstacles to importing Eastern techniques did not collapse until the hard times of 1979. The second oil shock, stagflation, and soaring interest rates made people in business desperate for any nostrum. And they could scarcely help but be charmed by Japanese management, since Japan's economy was booming while America's seemed to have gone bust. Feelings of crisis created a demand for fakirs who promised industrial peace and prosperity, and prophets marched forward with a supply of solutions said to have been made in Japan.

The Japanese Mirror

American business, boosters of Japanese management complained, suffered from individualism. They would have agreed with the Japanese manager in Ron Howard's movie *Gung Ho* who complained that Americans working for an Assan Motors subsidiary had "defects" because they "put themselves above the company" and were "selfish" and therefore "weak."[31] And so to cure America, Japanophiles prescribed Japan's familialism, groupism, or communalism. These prescriptions, however, were similar to, when not directly based upon, American corporative management. By celebrating "Japanese" practices consistent with their own corporative beliefs, "Japanizers" defined what was good and bad in American business, what should be copied and what should be cast off.

This tendency can be seen in the way Harvard Business School educator George C. Lodge influenced Ezra Vogel, author of the first major book prescribing Japanese cures. In his writings in the 1970s, Lodge argued that America's individualistic ideology directed people in business toward competitive and adversarial arrangements that were becoming ever more dysfunctional. Most managers assumed that firms were instruments of stockholders and should be operated to maximize profits. They felt no embarrassment in self-serving policies like Taylorism, even if such policies antagonized employees and undermined competitiveness. Only in recent years had some begun to learn from such mistakes and developed a new "communitarian" ideology that presumed firms belonged to employees and their communities. Communitarian managers, Lodge said, had introduced profit sharing and job enrichment, worked to create a cooperative work force, and pursued long-term strategies. The communitarian ideology of Japanese managers had caused their success.[32] Agreeing with this, Vogel, a distinguished Japanologist also at Harvard, acknowledged that he was "especially indebted" to Lodge.[33] Later they would edit an anthology based on Lodge's theories about the relationship of ideology to national competitiveness.[34]

In *Japan As Number One*, Vogel described those parts of "the Japanese national system" that offered "lessons for America." Studying the harmony of Japanese society, he thought, could furnish "a mirror" in which Americans could see how their own "egoism and nihilism" led to failure and how "communitarian values" and institutional arrangements had promoted "cohesiveness" and enabled the Japanese to become "number one." The Japanese had found ways to provide stability and security. Firms tried to increase market share and insure long-term growth, and they cared for people by offering lifetime employment, organizing work around groups, and basing promotions on seniority and ability to foster consensus. Their efforts made people identify with the firm and work hard for its goals, creating "a very effective modern corporatism." And from seeing this, Vogel thought Americans would understand how their failures came from their notion that the businessman was a "cowboy" who should act from "egoism and self-interest." They would see the need to restore the "communitarian vision" of the small town and recreate "the force of the moral community" so that people acted with sensitivity and restraint.[35]

The message and timing of Vogel's book made it a best-seller and a pattern for later writers. Like Vogel, subsequent authors generally began with statistics designed to show that Japanese business outperformed American business; then they argued that success rested on the unique parts of Japan's management system and described the Japanese practices that America should emulate.

A common contention was that Japanese management was more ethical and more effective than Taylorism. Richard Pascale and Anthony Athos in their best-selling *The Art of Japanese Management* (1981) contended that American managers used the same "tools" as the Japanese but guided them with a very different "vision." Agreeing with the founder of Honda that Japanese and American management were 95 percent alike but different in all important respects, they contrasted the management style of Harold S. Geneen, longtime chief executive at IT&T, and that of Konosake Matsushita, shogun of the Panasonic, National, Quasar, and Technics empire.

Geneen, they said, was representative of American managers who separated management from ethics and saw employees as factors of production. His dictatorial style, which included phoning underlings in the middle of the night and running meetings like an inquisition, centralized control and generated enormous profits. But by treating people as instruments, he stifled creativity, drove people from the organization, and made it difficult for IT&T to function effectively after he left. The failing of Geneen and managers like him, Pascale and Athos claimed, was rooted in their definition of firms as purely economic institutions designed to maximize profits and in their "engineer's view of individuals as primarily interchangeable parts and units of production." This led them to overemphasize the scientific, "hard" side of management and become overly concerned with controlling people and eliminating "ambiguity, uncertainty, and imperfection." As a result, they spent too much time manipulating strategy, structure, and information and decision-making systems and not enough nurturing people and developing consensus.[36]

In contrast, Matsushita and other Japanese managers were both willing to "play hard ball" and pursue "harmony." Their style, according to Pascale and Athos, balanced the American fetish with controls with a "soft" side of management that paid close attention to the staff, skills, superordinate goals, and style of the organization. Matsushita conceived of the company as a servant of the nation with goals transcending profit making. It had obligations to treat employees and customers as members of a community whose social needs were to be satisfied in the course of doing business. Given these premises, he established training programs and encouraged employees to initiate projects. Matsushita's approach led to "a kind of secular 'religious' system" that inspired employees to work together harmoniously, making him "a managerial genius of world caliber."[37]

The Japanese system, Pascale and Athos would concede, did have some dangerous fascist tendencies. But they urged American managers to imitate Matsushita by being both "hard-headed" and "soft-hearted." They should try to integrate the Eastern "art" of management with Western science, develop a new vision to guide old tools, and reform the national "management subculture." They needed to become less individualistic, independent, specialized, macho, and stoical and more cooperative, interdependent, well-rounded, feminine, and supportive. Although Pascale and Athos doubted that Americans could "ape the Japanese system," they could imitate "excellent companies" in the West that unified soft and hard. Several American firms—notably IBM, Boeing, Procter and Gamble, Delta Airlines, 3M, and Hewlett-Packard—had successfully combined "human values" with profit and efficiency.[38]

After 1981, these ideas became a staple, and American managers were accused of treating the worker as "a factor of production," a "robot," or just "another cog," which made employees reluctant to cooperate. Managers tried to cope by imposing tighter controls, which created a tangle of rules, or by offering monetary rewards, which caused more competition than cooperation. They did not seem to realize that to cut the Gordian knot, they would have to trust people, to treat the employee as "a member of the organization" rather than "an outsider," and to accept that everyone was entitled to manage his or her own work. They needed to learn the "professional code of ethics" that Japanese managers had derived from Confucian and samurai philosophy; this would lead them to abandon the premises of scientific management. By humanizing their methods, Americans could attain the harmonic relations of Japanese companies or of American firms like United Airlines, Intel, or Eastman Kodak.[39]

Several writers noted that this rhetoric was similar to language used by previous corporatists. It resurrected the refrain that managers had to go beyond Taylorism. It echoed Drucker's call for managers to shoulder social responsibilities and establish corporate communities, Lewin's plea for democratic leaders who were sensitive to feelings, and McGregor's cry for managers to become effective by helping people achieve their goals. The Japanese management style was said to be more comprehensive than its American counterparts and to have integrated all components into a unitary system.[40]

But management commentators often ignored the fact that the rhetoric of the Japan boosters was drawn from previous American corporatist theory more than from Japanese practices. For example, UCLA management professor William Ouchi was of Japanese ancestry and had made a three-week visit to Japan in 1974, but he was criticized for enhancing the appeal of his writings by "masquerading in a kimono."[41] Born and raised in Hawaii, he could not speak Japanese fluently. The prescriptions in Ouchi's best-selling *Theory Z* were based not so much on a study of Japan as on surveys and interviews of American workers, on his experiences as a consultant for Fortune 500 companies, and on Western sociological and managerial literature. Twenty-nine such works appeared in its bibliography (not including five of his own publications), with only five studies of Japanese management. He drew primarily from progenitors of modern corporatism Emile Durkheim, Ferdinand Tönnies, and Chester Barnard; from pioneers of corporative management Douglas McGregor, Chris Argyris, and Rensis Likert; and from two leading corporative consultants, Richard Walton and Edgar Schein.[42]

Durkheim's critique of capitalism informed Ouchi's belief that most American firms were bureaucracies crippled by a "rather extreme form of individualism." American managers and professionals expected rapid promotion or they would seek another job. To channel selfishness toward corporate goals, such firms used bureaucracy, specialized tasks, formal rules, rewards based on individual performance, and individual responsibility and decision making. But this only encouraged individualism and had harmful side effects. Specialists who lacked understanding of other parts of the firm worked against one another; without understanding the whole or trusting anybody, they often had little choice but to resolve disputes by using mathematical standards they privately acknowledged were bogus. And turnover, uncooperative behavior, elaborate systems for monitoring cheaters, and excessive reliance on numerical techniques hurt performance. Since business suffered from too much anomie, Ouchi thought that Durkheim's industrial clan was the remedy.

Such clans, Ouchi explained, were united by more than hierarchical controls and monetary contracts. They were communities of people whose shared ethical goals permitted "a balance between freedom and integration" going "beyond our current interpretation of individualism." Clans in Japanese society subordinated the individual to the group, because "industrial life" was "better suited to cooperation than to individualism." American firms, Ouchi said, should reorganize to spur "moral integration" and strengthen "societal bonds."[43]

He drew lessons for forming clans from the Japanese management system, America's "best" companies, and McGregor's Theory Y. The best American firms already shared certain characteristics with Japanese companies. Unbeknownst to them, managers of both were successful because they practiced the Theory Z management style, which, Ouchi admitted, was "related to" McGregor's Theory Y. Actually Z was virtually identical, and apparently the new label was as much for promotional purposes as anything else. Like McGregor, Ouchi believed that people were trustworthy and responsible and only needed proper guidance and incentive. His recommendations included some of McGregor's suggestions, including management by objectives, job enrichment and rotation, participative decision making, the Scanlon suggestion and profit-sharing plan, and sensitivity training.[44]

Since these ideas were already familiar, Ouchi explained the Japanese techniques consistent with Theory Y/Z. He suggested that copying the Japanese pattern of stable employment, corporate training, company welfare programs, seniority promotion, and teamwork would socialize employees to feel that they were members of a clan and were not just instruments for making a profit. They would share the goals of their employer, "trust" managers, and develop "disciplined unselfishness" and "a sense of community responsibility." They would accept slower promotion because they knew they would benefit in the long run. In addition, company-sponsored social activities would unify work and leisure, creating "intimacy" that would breed "egalitarian" relationships and stimulate cooperation. And job rotation would reduce specialization, make employees familiar with the goals of many units in the firm, and allow them to be "subtle" when making decisions.[45]

Ouchi also said that a formal company "philosophy," characteristic of Z firms, could socialize workers. Without a common "sense of mission" beyond maximizing profit, employees would be unable to integrate their efforts and unwilling to subordinate their interests to corporate goals. They needed to know that the "greatest sin" was "competitive" behavior, and they needed to have guidelines in cases where no rules or precedents existed. A philosophy would provide better direction than mathematical standards, since in the short run it was impossible to know what would pay off in the marketplace.[46] In short, Ouchi argued that American managers could benefit from corporatism and beat the Japanese at their own game.

The collectivism and antiindividualism of Ouchi and other Japan boosters were not the only ideas reminiscent of earlier corporative management theory. Old corporatist controversies were also replicated, especially the debate over how much power should be given to subordinates. This was most apparent in discussions of the *ringi* ritual and consensual decision making.

Some argued that the Japanese system was bottom-up management using initiatives originated in lower levels that moved up and across the organizational structure. This supplied fresh ideas, enabled people close to problems to propose solutions, allowed subordinates opportunities to be creative, and permitted action only after consensus had been reached. Harmony became as important as rationality.[47] But others saw a top-down arrangement in which superiors continued to set goals but also sought advice from subordinates, advice they could veto. Management professor Stephen Robbins thought Japanese managers were merely "consultative." He was attracted to Theory Z because it did not propose to make organizations "more democratic" or to equalize "power." Z-style managers, Robbins said, did not just give orders. Instead their consultations made subordinates more dependent and enhanced "managerial control." The whole system of Theory Z, including consultations, job security, and deskilling managers by converting them from specialists to generalists was effective because it promoted "psychological commitment to the organization."[48]

Another old debate was the issue of whether the participative techniques should be applied primarily to professionals or to production workers. Ouchi thought quality circles were a good idea but insisted implementation for managers and professionals should come first. People on the bottom could not initiate anything until invited by those on top. Starting participative reforms at the bottom could bring "revolution" and spawn "antagonistic" unions.[49] In contrast, Frank Gibney, a journalist and longtime manager of the Japanese division of *Encyclopedia Britannica*, thought that cooperative arrangements would not work with white-collar workers in the States. The commanding heights of American corporations, he said, were "authority-laden" and "not a little oppressive." They were staffed by bureaucrats who were overly concerned with "form and status" and with the "rites and ceremonies" of "protocol." Bureaucrats would interpret cooperation as a diminution of their standing and a dilution of their authority.[50]

Somewhat surprisingly, given the previous disposition to apply participative techniques primarily to white-collar employees, Gibney's ideas prevailed. The major import from Japan was not the white-collar *ringi* ritual but the blue-collar quality control circle. Managers in manufacturing probably were more desperate than others and more willing to try new solutions. Their acceptance of the quality circle was also influenced by its association with American corporative theories exported to Japan.

The beginnings of the quality circle in Japan can be traced to the influence of the statistician W. Edwards Deming, once described as "the high prophet of quality control." While working in Japan in 1950, Deming instructed some of Japan's leading industrialists and engineers in the use of statistics for discovering the source of defects, improving quality, and reducing costs. Statistical quality control, he had predicted, could dramatically increase national exports. He was proven right. Although ignored and virtually unknown in the States, he became a hero in Japan and received a medal from the emperor. The Japanese equivalent of the *Wall Street Journal* established an annual Deming Award for companies achieving high quality, an award so prized that the presentation ceremony was broadcast on national television.[51]

Another American contributing to the development of the quality circle was Joseph M. Juran, a former quality manager at Western Electric who taught his ideas to the Japanese in the early 1950s. Quality, Juran believed, could not be achieved in Taylorist fashion through imposing tighter controls on workers. Most defects resulted not from bad workers but from bad management and from faulty design of the product and production process. Improving quality meant that management would have to adopt new values and commit itself to improving design. The Japanese accepted this logic, and by the mid-fifties many companies had made this commitment.[52]

Finally, Japanese engineers were receptive to American writings on democratic leadership and job enrichment. Their Confucian values and desire to motivate permanent employees made them attentive to Drucker, McGregor, Likert, Argyris, and Herzberg. Indeed, they were perplexed when they learned Americans were ignorant of corporatism and were content with Taylorism.[53]

By adding participation to the quality control ideas of Deming and Juran, the Japanese invented the quality control circle. Production workers learned statistical techniques recommended by Deming and shouldered the managerial responsibility for quality recommended by Juran. With managers they formed groups of about ten. Participation was voluntary, but, typically, company policy and peer pressure made attendance mandatory. In brief group meetings, workers investigated and tried to resolve problems. They concentrated on quality control, production and design improvement, cost reduction, and sometimes on safety promotion. Sometimes, too, the circles were used for training workers.

Maintaining harmony in the circles preoccupied Japanese managers. They gave workers some latitude in choosing methods and encouraged their rotation from task to task within the group. But the system was not democratic. The presence of the shop supervisor helped keep people in line even if he had no formal authority. Moreover, management established production goals, determined the pace of work, allocated workers to various projects, helped link circles together, and maintained veto power. In some cases controls became so oppressive that the meetings degenerated into ceremonies for management to communicate with workers. Yet if their authoritarian and ritualistic tendencies could undermine their ability to create harmony, the circles also provided bureaucratic mechanisms that rewarded cooperation by offering status, recognition, and sometimes wage bonuses. These incentives inspired Japanese workers to contribute incredible numbers of suggestions.[54]

In 1967, Juran wrote one of the first articles endorsing the quality circle and explaining it to Americans. He claimed the superiority of the circle over Taylorism, correctly predicting that it would help Japan maintain productive advantages even as labor costs rose. He pointed out its similarities to the Scanlon Plan, which also included shop committees and group rewards.[55] Juran's prescriptions, however, were virtually ignored. Explaining this, he contended that American managers, unlike Japanese ones, assumed workers caused defects and lacked respect for their abilities. By isolating their quality departments from the manufacturing floor, they were often unaware of flaws in design. In addition, Americans tended to be experts in finance and marketing who lacked experience in manufacturing, resisted reforms that could empower engineers, and transferred costs for correcting defects to merchants and consumers. Their dispositions differed markedly from those of the Japanese.[56]

Not until the mid-1970s did the first American applications of the circles begin. Trials came in aerospace, pharmaceuticals, and electronics where the work force was often nonunion and where quality was particularly important. But use later spread to industries trying to cope with shrinking market shares and growing Japanese competition, especially steel and automobile manufacturing. By the late seventies, promoters of the technique formed organizations to recognize achievements and disseminate information. The International Association of Quality Circles, formed in San Francisco in 1978, served as a registering agency. And by the early 1980s there were over 8,000 sites with 135,000 circles, involving over 1 million workers and over 100 major corporate users, among them American Airlines, General Foods, Bethlehem Steel, Honeywell, Ford, General Motors, and Rockwell International.[57]

The rhetoric that promoted the circles repeated the claims that had been used in the sixties and seventies to legitimize job enrichment. Blissfully ignorant of the scientific challenges to previous theories, partisans explained anew that managers should understand Maslow's hierarchy of needs, Herzberg's dual factor theory of motivation, and McGregor's X and Y theories. Only self-actualizing work could fulfill workers and unleash their full potential. This was especially true for the "new generation" of "younger, better educated, and more demanding workers" who wanted to use their "minds" as well as manual skills on the job. "The traditional top-down school of management," by assuming that "workers should work and managers should think," stifled self-expression and stimulated conflict between individuals and organization. Clashing interests were undermining productivity and quality, suppressing wages and profits, and menacing firms and jobs.[58]

Reformers said that quality control circles could integrate classes. Problem-solving teams would allow workers some autonomy but would counter their individualism by encouraging them to identify with the firm and work with managers. This would eliminate "us versus them" consciousness. Participation would make workers feel "part of management" and convince them "to be more than just the hands that do the work" by asking them "to think and work out solutions that improve the quality of the company's product and increase productivity." The quality circle, one partisan said, could imitate the Japanese "way of organizational life" that benefited "productivity and people."[59]

The rhetoric promoting quality circles in the eighties perpetuated the notion of the seventies that participation was consistent with sound economic and engineering principles. Boosters of Japanese management helped enrich corporatism by including the engineering ideas of Deming and Juran. They also contrasted their views with older American assumptions that workers should be treated as factors of production and that growth came mainly through new hardware. Productivity increases could come through cooperative work relations that solved problems and motivated workers. By making everyone a manager, firms could draw on the experience and knowledge of more people and could eliminate waste and bottlenecks. By making everyone an inspector, they could improve quality. Accordingly, quality circles were "as dollar-and-cents practical" as they were "humanitarian." Judging from the number of articles on the technique that appeared in engineering journals, boosters were making their case credible.[60]

Promoters also pointed to success stories in Japanese subsidiaries and American firms. Juran described how a Motorola television assembly plant, managed by Americans, was plagued by 1.5 to 1.8 defects per set. But the same plant, after being purchased by Quasar, a Matsushita company, introduced organizational reforms that lowered the defect rate to 3 or 4 per 100 sets. A TRW plant that implemented quality circles claimed to have reduced absenteeism by two-thirds, cut turnover 80 percent, and boosted productivity 35 percent.[61]

As Robert Cole pointed out, however, such successes usually required adapting Japanese conceptions to American conditions. Japanese techniques were attuned to a society in which cooperation was rewarded, in which lack of opportunities to exit made permanent employees dependent on the firm and its career ladder, and in which enterprise unionism left workers without an organization through which they could voice resistance to managerial policy. In America, by contrast, middle managers received rewards based on short-term productivity. They lacked incentives to implement participation schemes and tended to see them as threats. Workers felt little peer pressure to cooperate and saw themselves as members of an occupation rather than a firm. Unions insured the independence of workers and protected their interests. The differences made implementing Japanese-style circles difficult; when reformers failed to take them into account, their efforts often led to failure. At Lockheed Missile and Space, for example, quality circles were sabotaged by the union because workers believed they were working harder for the same pay, and elsewhere middle managers scuttled circles that challenged their authority. Many managers, Cole believed, wrongly assumed that quality circles were "nice clean packages" that could be "plugged into operations with a minimum of disruption in the organizational hierarchy."[62]

Most promoters recognized these problems and recommended Americanizing Eastern ideas and Japanizing Western people. They believed middle managers could become "American samurai" who submerged their egos in collective endeavors. They could learn a participative style and lead through manipulating personality rather than by pulling rank. But they would have to be evaluated as much for their success in creating consensus and forming cooperative work teams as for maximizing the bottom line, or they would have no incentive to change. And blue-collar workers could be induced to cooperate if their companies would establish agreements with unions, pay workers for time spent in meetings, and grant an incentive system that went beyond the Japanese practice of ceremonial recognition and paid substantial group bonuses for useful suggestions and improvements.[63]

Most promoters of quality circles thought that the technique would work better if permanent employment was tried. They believed in both the American saying, "If you can be fired, you're part of the working class," and in the Japanese homily, "If you can't be fired, you're part of the company; be loyal to it." Job security, in other words, would help workers feel like members of the firm and identify with it. But boosters also acknowledged that lifetime employment would make labor a fixed cost, and many, including Cole, doubted that American managers would want to tie their own hands. Unions had long sought job security. But American managers had refused to give up their right to dispose of unwanted people, and American government had also failed to insure full employment.[64]

Generally, however, doubts were foreign to Japan boosters, and they often depicted Japan as a corporate capitalist utopia. Frank Gibney, who only a few years before had used his understanding of America to advise the Japanese,[65] now began using his experience as a manager in Japan to advise Americans. In his aptly titled paean, *Miracle by Design*, Gibney celebrated Japan's "Confucian capitalism, communal capitalism, or people-centered business" as somewhere between the state socialism that had ruined the Soviet Union and the free market capitalism that was ruining the United States.[66]

Retracing the Lodge line, Gibney claimed that too much individualism had impoverished and corrupted the land of the free. Americans had lost their traditional "community sense of values" and had taken up "the cult of doing one's thing" regardless of whether it was in the "public good." Antisocial individualism caused managers to see the firm as a "piece of property" and workers as "interchangeable parts" to be used as "mechanical pawns or counters in its numbers games." Managers pursued short-term profit at the expense of long-term national interest and practiced authoritarianism at the cost of antagonizing workers. As a result Americans thought work was "onerous" and labored only to earn enough to find "self-fulfillment" in leisure. In short, selfishness made managers too greedy and workers too lazy for their firms to succeed in a competitive market. And if Americans continued to shun their traditional Protestant work ethic and to avoid commitments to the commonweal, he warned, their "greed" and sloth would cause them to go the way of ancient Athens and Rome. Their only salvation lay in replacing antisocial individualism with "a collective virtue" composed of "shared aspirations, ethics, and morality."[67]

Americans, Gibney thought, were capable of constructing "a new capitalism" by copying the "miracle" of Japan's Confucian capitalism. That miracle had sprung from the concern of Japanese managers with "harmony between people," from their definition of the firm "in political terms" as a "community," and from their belief that people were "as much a part of capital as machines" and that managers should play the role of "community-builder" more than "profit-maker." They pursued long-term growth to preserve jobs, used participative and paternalistic techniques to improve the quality of life, and ran their firms like "medieval guilds." Their efforts gave workers a sense of membership in a "social organism" and inspired them to perform heroic labors for "their" corporate communities that were "the real-life embodiment of many socialist ideals of spontaneous fraternal cooperation." Such cooperation and harmony, Gibney argued, explained the prosperity of Japan's economy and the democracy of its society. And by copying the way Japanese managers had bound "Gesellschaft" and "Gemeinschaft" together and made the workplace into the "neighborhood," American managers could achieve their own miracle, especially since "the young worker of today" wanted to improve his "quality of life" and participate in "the company-as-community."[68]

By teaching the wisdom of the East, Japanophiles like Gibney expected to ennoble American managers and turn them into American samurai. They would invest knights of the corporate order, who would not covet treasure, seek glory at expense of the common good, deceive their peers with numerical necromancy, dictate tactics to vassals or bribe them with gold, make untidy battle, lay off soldiers between campaigns, or offer defective relics to the sovereign consumer. Instead they would restrain plebeian desires for immediate temporal satisfaction and would pursue lofty goals set by their lords, make eloquent declarations of collective purpose, lead dutiful peasants into righteous combat, vanquish the invading foes, rescue Lady Liberty from foreign mercenaries, and patiently await whatever humble reward might be bestowed upon them.

It seems likely that few who purchased such canon bought the samurai image itself. But the aristocratic ideal was as American as Peter Drucker.[69] He and other corporative mandarins had taken the first steps down the road to samurai management and had long contrasted regressive companies floundering for want of virtue and harmony with progressive ones. Because Americans already had ideas about managing nobly, they did not really import new "Japanese values" to guide "American technology." And for decades, particularly during the First and Second World Wars, Americans had established labor-management shop committees to solve problems.[70] Accordingly, some denied that the Japanese were doing anything original and suggested that they had learned everything from Americans. Drucker modestly suggested that the Japanese were simply practicing what he had preached.[71] And others merely brought in a few Japanese techniques that matched their values and decorated their own conceptions of management with a "japanned" finish.

Such East-West hybrids were viable enough to pass from management literature into popular culture, a phenomenon Howard illustrated in the final scene of Gung Ho, where he tried to show how wonderful work could be if Japanese and American ideas were combined. American workers participated in group calisthenics, but to the beat of rock and roll played on an imported blaster.

What was new about Japanophilia was the way boosters like Gibney went beyond contrasting the government of particular firms to contrasting national management styles. They claimed that a whole country across the Pacific had created a living and breathing industrial system that satisfied both managers and workers. Japan supplied the ultimate proof that corporatism worked.

Not surprisingly, when these writers looked in the Japanese mirror, they saw their own corporatism reflected back, albeit somewhat foreign looking around the edges. They were convinced that their imports of Japanese management were similar to domestic ideas already in use. Also, since the Japanese mirror only showed what was held before it, Japan boosters could show both the utility of American corporative techniques by citing Japanese experience and the utility of Japanese methods by invoking American corporative theory and practice.

Still, such circular flights of images back and forth across the Pacific proved nothing so much as that Japanophilia, indeed corporatism itself, was a closed system constricted in values and vision. Americans with different values could look in the mirror and see very different images.

Other Sides of Japan and America

Japanophiles were not matched by an equal number of Japanophobes, but every argument presented by boosters of Japanese management was countered by bashers. Social scientists, mandarins, and union activists less enamored with corporatism saw flaws in Japanophilia. They thought that boosters had manufactured historical, technical, and moral myths about Japanese and American business.

One such myth was the notion of a Japanese management system designed and deployed by Japanese managers. Labor historian Andrew Gordon discounted this myth by downplaying the role of managerial initiatives. He showed that Japanese labor relations had been shaped by the wartime government's stabilization policies, American occupational reforms designed to check managerial power, blue-collar demands for employment security and respect as citizens, and managerial concessions intended to coopt workers after union-busting campaigns.[72] Gordon drew no conclusions for managers, but his work implied that no system designed by management existed. Since what was called a management system was really a pattern of labor relations created by interplay of many actors, successful duplication of Japanese practices was beyond the power of managers alone.

Gordon also showed that so-called Japanese techniques had never been applied to all Japanese workers. Permanent employment, for instance, was a reality for managers but merely an "opportunity" for blue-collar workers; only a few employees in the largest companies were permanent, and turnover was at least 50 percent within the first six years after hiring. Japanese blue-collar workers, he found, were only "slightly more settled than their American counterparts," and the "myth" that had it otherwise was an ideological fiction created by managers and perpetuated by workers seeking "a tentative foothold in the new middle class." Furthermore, permanent employees were mainly younger males employed by big business whose security came at the expense of older, temporary male and part-time female workers in big business and all workers in small business. For nonpermanent workers, employment fluctuated with the business cycle.[73]

Again Gordon made no recommendations. But Robert Cole suggested that the discrimination in Japan's dual labor markets was scarcely a model to be copied by Americans complaining about disharmony and injustice.[74] And Torutomo Ozawa, an economist at Colorado State, found it ironic that some American managers wanted to adopt methods that were selectively practiced in Japan and were under challenge by "LIFO (last in, first out) employees" fed up with second-class citizenship.[75]

In addition, James Abegglen pointed out that many industries that were "managed in the Japanese style," including railways, nonferrous metals, petrochemicals and petroleum, and paper and pulp, were not doing well. The techniques had not "overcome dominating economic handicaps."[76] And beyond this, some attributed the competitive success of Japanese business less to the management system than to the use of "industrial policy," the impact of banks and internal sources of capital, the emphasis on long-term growth and production engineering, the "just-in-time" method of inventory control, and the commitment to "doing the basic things a little better, every day, over a long period of time." The Japanese success story, many writers suggested, could be attributed to many practices that were less exotic than their ways of managing harmony.[77]

Bashers also criticized the assertion that Japanese methods were compatible with American society and culture. Japanese personnel schemes could violate American civil rights laws. They could lead to age, sex, or racial discrimination; a suit that American managers brought against a subsidiary of the C. Itoh company, for instance, alleged illegal favoritism of Japanese employees.[78]

A graver problem was the unsuitability of Japanese methods to the professional training, customs, and values of American managers. The reward systems of American companies, rather than molding managers into industrial samurai motivated by noblesse oblige, had stressed quantitative techniques over corporative leadership, individual mobility over social responsibility, and short-term profit making over long-term growth.[79] Expecting such managers to change was unrealistic, or at least, as Juran realized, problematic.[80] And even if a few managers became samurai, they might not transform America's competitive corporate culture into the communal one called for in Theory Z.[81]

Other detractors believed that American workers posed an even greater obstacle to implementing Japanese techniques. They drew evidence from studies by the sociologists Shin-Ichi Takezawa and Arthur Whitehill, who had conducted attitudinal surveys of Japanese and American manufacturing workers in 1960 and 1976. They found large, widening differences. Americans were more distrusting of managers, more likely to distance themselves from work, and more disposed to exit. While Americans were as anxious as Japanese to participate in decision making, they were less willing to impose work values on others.[82]

Similarly, two management consultants with experience in Japan cast doubt on Americans' compatibility with corporatism. B. Bruce-Biggs argued that Theory Z was dangerously permissive and "feminine" and amounted to a "rehash" of job enrichment proposals for running firms "like New England town meetings." In Japan, participation worked because the people had a sound work ethic and knew "their place in the system," making it "unnecessary to kick people or shout at them." But American workers would just exploit the freedom and work less. "To imitate the Japanese," Bruce-Biggs said, Americans "would need a labor force disciplined by a social hierarchy controlled by an oligarchy," and while this oligarchy "should be copied," it would take "a thousand years."[83]

Agreeing with these sentiments, the consultant Frank Versagi complained that unions were a "nonprogressive, reactionary power block." American labor had an "automatically adversarial position" and was continually "dragging its feet," stuck in "a time-warp, unable to stop fighting past battles." He doubted that American union leaders would ever become like their Japanese counterparts, who thought like managers and sought to improve market share.[84]

Like proponents, critics were using selective images of Japan. Versagi overlooked the fact that Japanese labor organizations were not as autonomous as American ones, that instead they were "enterprise unions" led by young white-collar employees and formed "part of the administrative apparatus of the company."[85] And Bruce-Biggs assumed that the docility of Japanese workers stemmed from preexisting values rather than from the techniques he ridiculed, an assumption that not only downplayed the skill of Japanese managers and diverted attention from how they controlled people but also provided a van-tage from which to denigrate American workers. In the process, too, attention passed from the failures Japan boosters saw in American management and from the Theory Z of "excellent companies."

In addition, some critics focused not on whether the ideas could be imported but on whether they should be. Some Japanese ideas, like assigning tasks based on blood type, could be dismissed as ridiculous.[86] But others, like job rotation and seniority promotion, required more careful study.

The most empirical work criticizing such techniques was a Harvard dissertation done by Haruo Takagi, a Japanese scholar. Takagi investigated the effects of job rotation and seniority promotion on a cohort of forty-four- to forty-nine-year-old engineers in a single company, finding some evidence to support Ouchi's claim that these procedures propagated rational clansmen. In just as many cases, however, he discovered that the practices underutilized people and made them "passive." Arbitrary transfers moved talented people from their specialties and from technical tasks into supervisory positions for which they were unsuited. The Peter Principle was institutionalized, and promotions raised people above their level of competence; they became conservative superiors dependent on subordinates and protective of hierarchy. This led to apathy, lethargy, and bureaucratism, which the Japanese called "Large Company Disease" and ridiculed with the slogan "never fail to come, never be late, never do any work." In short, Takagi concluded, Theory Z was "one-sided and overly simplistic."[87]

Consensual decision making faced similar charges. Technical critics claimed that harmony was never spontaneous. It came from time-consuming struggle in which factionalism often developed; a few malcontents could exercise a Polish veto and delay or sabotage the whole process. Bunglers escaped responsibility, creating what one critic called "collective irresponsibility." And at least as often as initiatives came up from below, subordinates wasted time trying to figure out what their superiors wanted. By rewarding conformity and making harmony an end in itself, the system seemed likely to encourage even more conservatism.

Indeed, conservatism was the objection Americans most often voiced. They believed that Americans, unlike Japanese, were eager to make individual decisions and take risks. The process of forming consensus could stifle individual creativity and prove dangerous under rapidly changing conditions and in innovative industries. Making harmony an end in itself, they conceded, had helped Japanese industry improve Western technology. But it worked to Japan's disadvantage when it came to striking out in new directions. Some Japanese managers were recognizing this problem and imitating the Americans' autocratic styles. Bruce-Biggs sounded a common note when he said that

Americans could never "match the Japanese at corporatism" but could surpass them in innovation. Accordingly he and others defended Western bureaucracy and praised how individual responsibilities and rewards whipped up initiative and top-down authority harnessed it.[88]

While defending bureaucracy, technical critics also praised the market and expressed skepticism about the rationality of permanent employment. Withholding the whip of the market also led to passivity and conservatism. It could mean retention of incompetent and redundant workers, as in Japan where hundreds of thousands of "unproductive" workers were kept on the payroll as messengers, doorkeepers, and maintenance personnel. By making labor a fixed cost, permanent employment locked managers into yesterday's plans and encouraged companies to meet their payroll through overproduction and dumping, practices that irritated many of Japan's trading partners. It prevented managers from disposing of highly paid workers with obsolete skills, requiring young workers to subsidize older ones. Americans preferred to preserve flexibility by treating labor as a factor of production.[89]

The techniques were not only shown to be costly and dangerous for business but for society as well. "Moral" critics thought boosters had evaluated Japan according to managerial and material standards, according to its ability to make parts arrive on time. They claimed that the pressures to commit to the work group had forced Japanese workers to become "economic animals," who felt obliged to sacrifice personal development, individual health, family life, community infrastructure, and the environment to the god of industrial growth.[90]

Critics denied that Theory Z and quality circles redistributed power. Although in the early 1980s workers and their unions often accepted the promise from management that teamwork would bring benefits and security, their experiences left doubts. Quality circles were said to be "cosmetic," more "placebo" than "panacea," more "symbolic" than "substantive." Managers created the circles, constricted their focus to production problems, coordinated their activities, checked their authority, and evaluated their performance according to whether they improved the bottom line and disciplined workers. Workers often did not feel like members of a community but recognized that they were still used as instruments for meeting the goals of managers and stockholders. Rather than a means to achieve harmony between equal partners, circles were just another means for "motivating and manipulating" workers and "merely the same old attempts to increase workers' commitment to company goals without requiring managers to accept the burdens and risks of full participation."[91]

Mike Parker, a union activist and observer of circles in many industries, argued that the system was merely "a kind of super-Taylorism," scientific management modified in theory but maintained in spirit. Managers designed circles as forums for workers to offer suggestions and surrender job knowledge without giving them power to make important decisions. Consequently workers normally imposed time-and-motion study, stretchout, and speedup on themselves. Moreover, team members seldom had more interesting jobs but rotated from one boring, specialized job to another. Flexible work organization also undermined work rules and job classifications negotiated in union contracts, taking away hard-won rights and threatening seniority principles. It permitted managers to use workers "like interchangeable parts." And because the circles often eroded union prerogatives, encouraged workers to act like managers, and became collective bargaining forums dominated by managers, the National Labor Relations Board had in some cases ruled that circles amounted to company unions and violated the Wagner Act. Or at least the board had made such rulings until the Reagan administration packed it with circle sympathizers. The Reagan administration's endorsement and the technique's Taylorite essence, Parker thought, made the quality circle a weapon in a management offensive to cheapen labor costs, erode skills, and weaken unions.[92]

Hence American workers often came to regard the circles as shams and refused to participate. Studies of bargaining contracts showed limited interest in circles when compared with wages, hours, and job security. Parker noted that the interest shown in teamwork was sometimes intended to take advantage of the cooperative arrangements to heighten worker solidarity and power. As some critics said, until "corporate power structures" were transformed, until the separation between planners and doers was eliminated and the "dominance of professional managers" was thwarted, America's workers were likely to remain adversarial.[93]

By far the most vehement assault on the Japan boosters, indeed one that amounted to Japanophobia, came from Marvin Wolf. In *The Japanese Conspiracy*, he argued that a Japanese "Bureaucratic-Industrial Complex" had established a new version of "economic totalitarianism" intended to dominate world trade. Managers of this complex, moved by samurai values, racial ideology, and commitment to market share, believed that business competition was "a life-and-death mercantile war." They geared everything to win the "trade war," including enlistment in boot camps where business people could steel themselves for battle and learn samurai discipline. Corporate commanders treated workers as soldiers in "an industrial army." They controlled "usually obsequious" enterprise unions, using them as training grounds in which young white-collar employees could prove their mettle. Unions could also teach workers to be "members of a company 'family'" where "respect for authority" was "the highest virtue" and their value as individuals was less than their value as members of the group.

Although the mercantilist mentality and martial work organization had enabled the Japanese to become industrial leaders, Wolf said, the effects on their society had been appalling. Workers were impoverished by Western standards and were crowded into housing that lacked central heat and modern plumbing. Consumer loans were hard to get and expensive because capital was channeled into industry. Company dorms regimented young, unmarried workers. Retirees were degraded and forced to find menial jobs. Employees were discouraged from taking their full vacation time, and the pay of teams whose members reported accidents was docked. The resulting job pressures caused stress and illness. Moreover, management rigged union elections "Soviet-style" and thus corrupted democracy. Such a system, Wolf believed, could not and should not be imitated. America should defend itself from the Japanese trade invaders by establishing tariff and patent barriers and demanding access to Japanese markets.[94]

Wolf's indictment of Japanese management, like those of other bashers, reiterated many of the charges that had been made against previous incarnations of corporatism. Although critics were most unfamiliar with literature that presented arguments challenging corporatism, they reinvented standard objections by gazing in the Japanese mirror. They found corporatism in a kimono inconsistent with business dynamics and American traditions, either too permissive to be effective or too manipulative to be ethical. Seeing Japanese management did not lead to believing in it.

But because critics had been unfamiliar with the history of corporatism, they failed to point out that a contradiction existed in the samurai ideal much like that in democratic leadership. Samurai managers were supposed to be sensitive servants subject to employee desires and concurrently chivalric champions protecting the corporate realm from the selfishness of subordinates. Reconciling autonomy and control, self-governing workers and professional managers, depended on a spirit of self-sacrifice so that samurai managers could integrate labor and capital without coercion. But Japanophiles themselves pointed to the weak tradition of virtue in America. A long line of reformers who sought a new individualism and class harmony, a line stretching from Taylor to Hoover to Drucker, had been unable to transcend older interpretations of individualism. Given the improbability that virtue would emerge in an age of narcissism, their quest for corporatism seems as quixotic as their predecessors'. This may explain why the final scene from *Gung Ho* appeared so improbable, a scene showing workers exercising together in company uniforms, in perfect ranks, and happy as clams, the whole atmosphere reminiscent of Hollywood films about boot camp made during the Second World War. Howard's lesson, however unintentional, was that Americans could only cooperate during times of national crisis, when they were losing martial or mercantile wars.

As a final reflection, the distinctions the boosters saw between managing nobly and scientific management should not be taken at face value. Gibney's portrait of Japanese business might seem very different from Wolf's. For while Gibney saw Japanese firms as households run by Confucian parents caring for happy children and making decisions for their own good, Wolf saw them as armies dominated by feudal warriors using soldiers as pawns in games for personal prestige and racial status. But an ideology of enlightened management that proclaimed harmony between leaders and followers could disguise a reality of oriental despotism resting on manipulation of the weak by the strong. For this reason, the Japanophiles' belief that Geneen and Matsushita, Taylorism and the Japanese management system, were opposites seems dubious. After all, bureaucracy and corporatism were both forms of managerial government.

Conclusion

The Management
Theory of Value

The American bureaucratic and corporative schools were opposite sides of the same Taylorist coin. Seen separately, either side could seem quite different from the other. Bureaucracy could seem different from corporatism because each school apparently offered contrasting views on whether power should be centralized or decentralized and on whether planning should be separate from performing or synthesized with it. Seen together, however, the schools were fundamentally fungible. Both expressed interchangeable premises and both exchanged ideas in a common marketplace of managers. Accounting for the easy fungibility of bureaucracy and corporatism, registering some of the most recent bureaucratic manifestations of corporatism, and assessing the significance of these findings are the subjects of this concluding chapter.

Transcending Taylorism meant developing new ideas that could synthesize planning and performing and eliminate managers as a distinct class. But such a transvaluation of Taylorism was rarely achieved in corporatist theory and was even more rarely achieved in practice. Corporative mandarins, like bureaucratic ones, continued presuming Taylor's management theory of value and accepting existing socioeconomic arrangements as givens. To do otherwise, to reject centralized power and specialized production would have meant rejecting management itself. And a mandarin who rejected management (besides no longer being a mandarin) would have difficulty peddling ideas to managers. Thus the possibility of developing a genuine corporative theory that could unite planning and performing was largely foreclosed from the beginning. And bureaucratic premises, in turn, were shaped by the desires of managers, especially by their will to power. Hence managerial demand in the long run determined mandarin supply, with bureaucratic desires leading relentlessly to bureaucratic premises and on to bureaucratic practice, drawing a circle that bound American business.

The confines of the bureaucratic circle often proved uncomfortable, and especially in the 1980s, American mandarins longed for the world beyond. Their glorification of Japanese management expressed only part of the deep longing for corporatism. Indeed mandarins in the eighties were seldom more confident they were transcending Taylorism. They congratulated themselves for coming to a new understanding of the limitations of bureaucracy. They said managers showed more awareness of the needs of a better-educated work force as well as a new respect for the rationality of workers, autonomous teams, and individual creativity. International competitive challenges were forcing American companies to abandon rigid hierarchy for a more flexible, flat organization. And improvements in information technology, especially in computer-aided design, manufacturing, and accounting, facilitated decentralization while maintaining managerial control. Mandarins believed each of these changes brought managers and workers into the same team, fused planning and doing, and signified the ending of bureaucracy and the beginning of corporatism.[1]

Reports of the death of bureaucracy, however, were highly exaggerated. No matter how often corporative visions danced through mandarins' heads, managers kept awakening to a bureaucratic reality. That mix of corporative dream and bureaucratic reality in the eighties can be seen in two widely heralded reforms of business government—intrapreneurship and employee stock ownership plans.

Under pressure of increasing competition in the early 1980s, managers in many large corporations reorganized to stimulate innovation. Their philosophy was most clearly expressed in Gifford Pinchot's writings on "intrapreneurship." Pinchot blamed American business stagnation on too much bureaucracy. Divisional structures, he said, prevented specialists from cooperating with one another. Rather than cooperatively carrying new products and services to market, specialists engaged in a series of handoffs, passing a new idea from research and development to manufacturing to marketing. Each handoff led to delays, dilution of responsibility, and degeneration of quality. Isolation of planners from performers made specialization more irrational. Ivory-tower staff experts and top managers judged everything using abstract techniques. Although such isolation inhibited understanding and resulted in caution and conservatism, it also enhanced managerial control and enabled managers to be bureaucratic "barons." In short, Pinchot argued, American bureaucratism was as stultifying as that of a "socialist nation."[2]

Business bureaucracy could be escaped, he promised, through a new form of American freedom, freedom of "intraprise." He thought managers at

Kollmorgen, Du Pont, 3M, IBM, Lockheed, and other companies had achieved freedom by creating semiautonomous teams within corporate enterprise. In these teams, employees thought and acted less like bureaucrats and more like "intrapreneurs." They had the power and capital to develop, manufacture, and market their ideas. Such independence helped "employees feel like owners" and think like managers. Walls between specialties fell as researchers, engineers, and marketing experts worked together. And since each intraprise was semiautonomous and functionally complete, planners were integrated with performers; the doers were the deciders.[3]

Intrapreneurial government, Pinchot claimed, rested on the market rather than on managers. Each intraprise had to show a profit, either from selling to customers or to other groups in the corporation. Such an "internal marketplace" pushed "intrapreneurs and employees toward the objectives of the corporation." Top managers did not exercise direct control; they used methods much like management by objectives. They negotiated written contracts with intrapreneurs that designated resources, operational goals, and profit-shares. Managers provided the corporate "vision" and set the "rules of the game so that self-determined players end up serving their own interests best when they served the corporation." Their efforts made the corporation into a "confederation of entrepreneurs." Its government was founded more on "voluntary customer-vendor relationships than on commands." Accordingly Pinchot concluded, in a phrase reminiscent of Peter Drucker, that intrapreneuring was based on "responsible freedom."[4]

Indeed intrapreneuring sprang from the corporatist tradition. Its number of applications was new, but its ideas were not. Drucker had mixed entrepreneurial and corporative ideas for years. Tom Peters, probably the eighties leading prophet of entrepreneurship, expressed his "amazement" and "perhaps dismay" that Drucker had written "everything" on managing for innovation in 1954 in *The Practice of Management*.[5]

Given its similarities to management by objectives, intrapreneuring did not overthrow bureaucracy. As they had with previous corporative schemes, staff specialists and divisional managers feared loss of authority and resisted intrapreneurial teams.[6] Very few companies developed such teams for their whole organization or for manual workers. Most reserved teams for a few creative knowledge workers. As even Pinchot admitted, only a few "right people" should be permitted in the system.[7] The formation of corporative oases in a bureaucratic desert was evident in "skunk works," which isolated talented, often temperamental, employees away from company headquarters.[8] Skunk works and other intraprises were intended to keep dynamic, ambitious employees loyal and to discourage them from exiting to establish entrepreneurial ventures. And by preserving employeeship, the profit-sharing contracts amounted to a glorified incentive wage for independent workers. Moreover, forming intraprises was often a euphemism for forming temporary product-specific divisions rather than permanent function-specific ones. Since the structure of each intraprise typically duplicated in microcosm the bureaucracy of divisions and the larger enterprise, it did not stray far from Taylorist premises. It created "new-age fiefdoms" for managerial barons to command.[9] Intrapreneuring thus seemed more a confederation of petty bureaucrats than of autonomous entrepreneurs.

Similarly, the employee stock ownership plan (ESOP) promised more corporatism than it delivered. ESOPs, when accompanied by real participation, seemingly promised a revolution in American business; they pointed toward genuine syndicalism based on worker self-employment and self-government. Such plans originated in the early seventies during concern about blue-collar blues. But partisans of employee ownership did not want job enrichment. They wanted laws giving tax incentives to companies that encouraged worker investment. Their legislative sponsor was Louisiana Senator Russell Long, Huey's boy, who hoped that sharing the wealth would make workers into capitalists, eliminate class conflict, and stimulate productivity. The proposals appealed to both liberals and conservatives, who referred to it as an "'industrial' Homestead Act." The initial legislation passed in 1974 and was elaborated upon several times thereafter. The laws permitted various forms of stock trust funds in which employers could make investments in the name of employees. In return, employers would receive tax advantages on their contributions.[10]

Few companies, however, took advantage of the laws until the early 1980s. During the perceived economic crisis of the early eighties, managers used stock ownership plans partly to motivate employees but mostly to get tax breaks and financial benefits. Indeed the number of plans increased dramatically after Reagan tax legislation plugged many loopholes but ignored employee stock ownership laws. Managers also found other financial advantages in establishing employee stock trusts; they used ownership plans to extract wage concessions, limit medical and pension payments for retirees, expand the capital fund, and build barriers to keep out corporate raiders. Furthermore, government studies revealed that an ESOP accompanied by a participatory program increased productivity 50 percent faster than an ESOP alone. This excited many corporatists who thought worker ownership and participation would "elicit the American version of Japanese loyalty" and "forge a joint sense of partnership." But the vast majority of ESOP firms did not introduce participatory programs.[11]

In fact, the corporatist mandarin Joseph Blasi's careful study showed that managers overwhelmingly used the employee stock ownership laws to entrench and enrich themselves. The laws were either imprecise, allowing managers to enact self-serving plans, or antisyndicalist. The hierarchical bias in ESOPs showed in several ways. In membership, managers usually excluded young, nonprofessional employees and included only senior workers and professionals. So the plans reproduced rather than reversed income stratification.

Moreover, Blasi found that managers prevented even workers involved in the plans from becoming owner-citizens. They normally kept workers from earning dividends until after retirement and from controlling their stock. Managers used the vesting provisions of the law to control stock trusts. Therefore the workers' rights of ownership were separated from rights of control. Congress had separated these rights to preserve managerial autonomy, thinking full rights would be "unduly burdensome" and fearing that workers would check managers. So the possibility of codetermination by managers and workers, let alone genuine syndicalism by worker-manager-owners, was partly foreclosed by "the ideology of bureaucracy in American law" that assumed "the bureaucratic way was the only way." The corporative possibilities were also foreclosed by what Blasi called a "feudal ideology of business," a management theory of value that caused managers to convert ESOPs from potentially syndicalist reforms into manipulative bureaucratic techniques. In fact mandarins advertised them under such titles as "How Mr. Big Can Remove His Capital, Retain Control, and Perpetuate the Company" and "How to Sell Your Company and Still Keep It."[12] Normally then, employee stock ownership was a contradiction in terms. Rather than bringing employees into the management team, the plans left them the instruments of managers.

ESOPs and intrapreneuring thus fit into the corporatist pattern in American business history. Hopes of harmony rose and then were crushed by the weight of bureaucracy. But corporative ideas revived in some new guise, only to be smothered again. This pattern reveals the strengths and weaknesses of contemporary corporatism.

Post-Mayoist corporatism charmed managers and mandarins for many reasons. Basically corporatism appealed to those who believed that bureaucracy had problems with irrationality and illegitimacy. Of course these people were not revolutionaries; like most Americans, they valued individual mobility and voted for bureaucracy with their checkbooks and resumes every day. Thus from a Chandlerian view, the gears of bureaucracy kept grinding on. But so Olympian a perspective overlooked the difficulties managers experienced with bureaucratic machines and missed the breakdowns they continually struggled to fix. They knew that they and their companies could fail. Every day they confronted the competitive pressures of an economy with few state-protected cartels. Every day they faced the cultural pressures of a society with many individualists who hated bosses or wanted to be one. Every day they faced the organizational pressures of superiors who wanted to squeeze the last drop of productivity from subordinates. Faced with such pressures, managers always searched for a more rational government.

Managers in trouble found corporatist visions alluring. Corporatism became more popular when bureaucracy was in crisis. Job enrichment, for instance, became a fad when managers became concerned about strikes and the blue-collar blues, and quality circles became popular when foreigners began capturing American markets. When workers became unruly, managers could see that a little participation could restore legitimacy. When competitors became aggressive and when something had to be done beyond scheduling a staff meeting, managers needed help and so questioned the separation of planning from doing.

Moreover, corporatism offered theories of human nature and government consistent with the experiences and expectations of managers and mandarins. Corporatist mandarins were often trained in psychology or sociology and believed that Taylor and Mayo had been wrong about human nature. Corporatists' humanistic psychology presumed that people had desires to express individuality. In addition, the liberal ideologies of anticommunism, the civil rights movement, the counterculture, and an affluent society endorsed civil liberties, especially the right to self-government. Such optimistic ideas broke down distinctions between public democracy and private bureaucracy, making Taylorist government seem contrary to some traditional liberal values.

Many in the management community also thought that Taylorism was unsuited to a changing work force. They knew that the postwar generation was better off and better educated than before; whatever the color of their collar, all Americans wanted the respect owed to citizens of a middle-class republic and resented being treated like factors of production. In particular, managers recognized that Taylorism was inappropriate for governing the independent knowledge workers of a scientific and technologically advanced business. Managers found despotism uncomfortable when governing professional workers of their own class. And the separation of planning from doing prevented independent workers from using the expertise they had been hired to exercise.

Rather than producing efficiency, treating people like machines prevented managers from maximizing use of their human resources.

The academic background of managers and mandarins reinforced these perceptions. They typically trained or worked in universities that had many corporatist qualities. In academe, individual and organization often seemed in harmony. A primary goal of the university was self-development, and so professors and students, knowledge workers par excellence, produced for the organization by pursuing individual interests. This synergy meant that nobody was being oppressed, so little direct supervision was needed; performance was monitored by checking results. Moreover, collegial government, even if merely mythical, discredited managers. While business schools may not have been bastions of liberal humanism, they prompted the management community to pattern the enterprise after an idealized vision of the university. This explained why academic interest in corporatism so outweighed use in business.

Corporatists developed new theories about business government consistent with their conceptions of human nature and the good life. They envisioned the capitalist firm as a social institution, an industrial clan, whose managers had responsibilities beyond the bottom line and whose members had goals beyond the paycheck. Managers and members shared goals because improving productivity and raising profits depended on personnel fulfillment.

To achieve harmony, corporatists tried to go beyond Taylorism by calling for new management techniques. They wanted managers to act less like scientist-dictators and more like democratic leaders, orchestra conductors, samurai masters, parents, teachers, and therapists. Managers would still select goals and monitor performance but would be more sensitive to feelings and more encouraging of participation in decision making.

Participation in management was the central corporatist departure from Taylorism. Corporatists claimed that participation would unify planning and performing, thereby integrating individual and organization. It would create a middle-class organization of work in which everyone would think like a manager and cooperate in classless comity. It would reconcile ethics and efficiency, freedom and order, liberty and rationality. So reforms like management by objectives, job enrichment, and quality circles tried to make members governors and not merely objects of government. Members would not, however, become governors of the corporate hierarchy; they would simply participate in it. Although all corporatists sought limited participation, they disagreed on how to balance top-down consultations and bottom-up initiatives. This lack of precision undoubtedly enhanced the popularity of their methods; managers could define participation in as syndicalist or manipulative a way as they pleased. And eventually, in one form or another, many successful and respected companies applied corporative ideas.

Yet few managers applied corporatism to their whole work force, and many rejected it altogether. Frustrated by this, some sincere corporatists had concluded by the 1980s that the Gordian knot of bureaucracy could never be untangled by managers from within. Industrial policy advocates recognized that most managers doubted corporatist claims and were not going to change on their own. Most would govern in ways that perpetuated their rule, inhibited cooperation, and strangled entrepreneurship. Cutting the bureaucratic knot from the outside would require federal intervention.

Urging use of macrogovernment to reform microgovernment was unusual for mandarins. Knowing that statist plans antagonized American managers, they normally advised self-help. But industrial policy reformers pointed out that the success of corporatism overseas had come from sponsorship by powerful organizations and assistance from government. In Japan, for instance, the Union of Scientists and Engineers had helped companies set up quality circles. Similarly in Sweden, the Employer's Federation, the labor movement, and the Social Democratic Labor party had supported cooperative arrangements and lobbied for governmental assistance.[13]

By offering managers a carrot that could entice them to give up the stick, industrial policy advocates like Robert Reich thought America could duplicate foreign corporatism. Specifically, reforms of tax codes and capital structures would change the incentives operating on business and encourage the emergence of entrepreneurial firms that united planning and performing.[14] Similarly, ESOP advocates like Joseph Blasi wanted new legislation to exempt from taxation only employee stock ownership plans in participative firms.[15] Good laws and greed, proponents hoped, would teach corporatist virtue. Unfortunately for the reformers, however, the weaknesses of American corporatism have made it difficult to muster sufficient support to change federal legislation, let alone change business government. Failures by Gary Hart and Michael Dukakis, candidates who endorsed industrial policy, suggested that proponents would long struggle to overcome traditional bureaucratic definitions of managerial prerogatives.

Bureaucratic premises were so prevalent in managerial America that corporatists typically deluded themselves, mistaking Taylorism incognito for genuine corporative alternatives. Indeed, accounting for the disparity between corporative principles and corporative practices requires understanding the dominance of bureaucratic theory.

Most American managers and mandarins accepted bureaucracy as a given and assumed it was legitimate and generally rational. Bureaucracy had justified itself by satisfying consumers and producers. It had produced wealth, created jobs, and provided social mobility. These arguments were neither insubstantial nor completely self-serving. Obviously, however, success came easier to the assistant manager who accepted the rationality of his boss and to the consultant who accepted the legitimacy of his client.

Consenting to bureaucracy seemingly made governing easier. Managers did not have to waste time feeling guilty or negotiating. By believing in bureaucracy, they reduced governmental disputes to conflicts over efficiency rather than ethics, over means rather then ends. The search for good government was simplified to a search for the one best way to govern bureaucracy. Accepting bureaucracy led naturally to the dominant philosophy of management; it led to Taylorism.

Likewise, university life, however much it cultivated corporatism, undoubtedly taught Taylorism more. The modern American university, as Thorstein Veblen pointed out long ago, parodied the business enterprise; it had its board of directors, CEO, managers, public relations department, divisions, ranks, rules, struggles for power and status, specialization, and separation of planning from doing; and scholars and scientists labored under the staff and its secretariat.[16]

In fact the very purposes of the business school, training technocrats and advising managers, presumed Taylorism.[17] Students read textbooks of systematic methods and memorized codes of scientific principles, trying to become scientific managers. Professorial mandarins invented, researched, published, and taught standard procedures for governing bureaucracy. Their exaltation of science drew them toward positivism and toward value-free disciplines like mathematics, economics, cybernetics, and computer science. Knowledge in these disciplines was intended to promote apolitical expertise. And mandarins studied some of the same problems that Taylor had confronted; they also applied his approach to new problems in the bureaucracies his ideas had helped to create. So the business school, its organization, purposes, subjects, methods, disciplines, and ideals perpetuated Taylorism and the management theory of value.

The federal government also perpetuated bureaucratic thinking. Its labor law assumed managers and workers were separate classes, discouraged codetermination, and produced rules and regulators to mediate class relations.[18] Furthermore, it underwrote bureaucratic techniques in various ways. To be sure, the federal government subsidized corporatism as well; government grants funded corporative research and government agencies sometimes applied corporative ideas. But the shadow cast by corporative subsidies was shorter than that cast by bureaucratic ones.

Particularly, the military sponsored Taylorism. The military was bureaucratic and preferred centralized command and specialized operations. It subsidized development of numerically controlled machine tools as labor control devices.[19] It also pioneered operations research and management science and encouraged improvements in cybernetic, computerized management tools. And not only did the military underwrite development costs, it advertised them as well, lending credibility and prestige. Military techniques quickly filtered into business and the rest of government. Managers thought tools that worked in one bureaucracy would work in another.

Indeed, post-Taylorist bureaucrats assumed that governing well meant installing the right device. They wanted to fix breakdowns in bureaucracy without changing centralized management or specialized tasks. They wanted new equipment to plug into the bureaucratic machine. This inevitably narrowed the spectrum of management ideas because mandarins adjusted the supply of tools to managerial demand. They invented mechanisms to plan for planners, feedback devices to regulate performance, and quantitative and computerized methods to maximize rationality. These mechanical and mathematical decision-making techniques were their most important achievement. With these tools, bureaucrats believed they had achieved the age-old quest for an apolitical governor that regulated all parts of a smoothly running machine.

The bureaucrats' mechanistic thinking was much like Taylor's. His machine model of human nature persisted because bureaucrats desired to keep their psychology consistent with their sociology; since they believed in the legitimacy and rationality of bureaucracy, they did not worry much about employees and their values. They believed workers were essentially passive factors of production who could be deployed and used like any other instrument. In Herbert Simon's case, this involved some irony because he had begun his academic career trying to improve mechanistic organization theory with economics and its hedonistic notions. He had largely repudiated hedonism, however, when he concluded that superiors easily programmed subordinates, that subordinates welcomed programming, and that bureaucratic animals were in the same genus as computers. It was only natural that Simon's most practical ideas were his contributions to computerized expert systems, machines that parodied bureaucratic rationality.

Faith in the bureaucratic machine and its tools was the weak link in Taylorist theory. Technical and political problems emerged when managers assumed that bureaucracy was rational and legitimate. Assuming that profit was a simple goal and the ultimate standard for business ethics led them to ignore the difficulties of balancing the short-term success of a firm with its long-term survival. Assuming workers were machines led management scientists to overlook disagreements about values, goals, and methods and hence to impose policies that often intensified conflicts. Assuming their tools were rational fostered the illusion that techniques were ends in themselves and led managers to value bureaucracy and technique over practicality and profitability. Excessive faith in bureaucracy prevented bureaucrats from applying cost-benefit analysis to themselves and from believing that they caused irrationality.

When taken to its logical conclusion, Taylorism was, among other things, irrational. Its postulates demanded that planning be separated from performing and that superiors make all decisions. But if, as philosopher Michael K. Green suggested, its postulates obeyed the Kantian categorical imperative and were applied universally, no decisions would be made. Everyone, including top managers, would lack autonomy and would await orders. Taylorism could not hold as a universal moral law. Not only was it morally wrong to deprive others of autonomy, but it was stupid to try.[20] Business bureaucracy, like any other form of government, needed to allow people some freedom to create. Without creativity and innovation a business would stagnate and die.

Sometimes bureaucrats were honest enough to blame management for irrationality. Such honesty created demand for corporatism. Concern that mathematics and cybernetics could not fix political breakdowns and could not resolve disputes over values and struggles over power led management scientists like C. West Churchman and Russell Ackoff to corporatism. But as they envisioned it, corporatist negotiations would only change the process by which goals and quantitative standards were selected; mathematical tools would be left in place as would the experts who would use them.

Such compromises with bureaucracy almost always occurred, and each ultimately corrupted corporatism. Corporatists wanted management without bureaucracy, believing that worker participation in management would decentralize power, unify tasks, and bring harmony between individual and firm. But they did not want management to wither away; they sought management based on hegemony rather than tyranny. They never understood that management was bureaucracy. They never considered that transcending Taylorism required more than installing a few participative mechanisms; it required a revolution in American society as a whole, in its values, economic structures, educational institutions, and macrogovernment. So however much they talked about democracy and industrial clans, they still presumed the rightness of the management theory of value and the rationality of managers. They could scarcely do otherwise if they wanted to sell ideas in the manager market.

The management theory of value, whatever its form, amounted to a bureaucratic ethic. Empowering managers inevitably limited participation and autonomy, foreclosing real harmony; if cooperation came from centralized power, their corporatism was self-contradicting and chimerical. Centralizing power established a managerial will more important than any combination of individual wills. It allowed managers to establish collective goals transcending individual interests. In doing so, it imposed the rationality Weber had defined as central to bureaucracy. When swept out, bureaucratic ideas always crept back into microcorporatism.

Such had been the previous history of managerial corporatisms. Right-wing corporatism in Europe had centralized power, as seen particularly in fascist labor fronts. Macrocorporatism in the United States also fit this pattern. In his "associative state," Herbert Hoover as secretary of commerce and as president had tried to use apolitical experts to plan the economy and coordinate interest groups. His experts provided scientific advice and instructed private groups to follow it, combining coordination and voluntarism. But the private groups insisted on doing what they wanted and never showed the rationality that Hoover's experts requested. Hoover avoided using the state to compel cooperation, as that would have contradicted his corporatist voluntarism. Franklin Roosevelt and the New Dealers felt no such compunction and converted the associative institutions into a regulatory state.[21]

Like Hoover's macrocorporatism, Drucker's and McGregor's microcorporatism presumed harmony could be established between planners and performers. Their ideas predicted that participation in management would allow individuals to influence organizational goals and thus identify with such goals. The resulting coincidence of individual and organizational goals would lead to corporate harmony. Because individual and organization would be fulfilled, bureaucratic controls would be unnecessary. Such a synthesis of individual and organizational goals, however, was rarely, if ever, achieved. Nor were Americans willing to sublimate their desires and unquestioningly subordinate themselves to the organization. Accordingly, without harmony based on synthesis or on subordination, the application of corporatist theory in American business often failed to produce the new rationality it predicted.[22]

In the end, the search for corporatist harmony floundered on America's ageless rock of individualism. As generations of conservatives and radicals and dissenters from Henry Adams and Eugene Debs to John Galbraith and C. Wright Mills have recognized, American acquisitive individualism and capitalism ignored values other than material growth, money, and upward mobility. With a social system that rewarded selfishness and a public culture that lacked a common conception of virtue, Americans seldom cooperated in a harmonious community of ends. And the dearth of spontaneous cooperation led to a surplus of managed cooperation and bureaucracy.

Many managers and mandarins insisted that Americans were unsuited to communal work and condemned corporatism. Workers, they said, were too entranced with the rewards of leisure to become enthralled with the responsibilities of leadership. Managers were better with numbers than with people and wanted individual mobility more than social responsibility. In this context, Maslow's hierarchy of needs seemed less operational, two mandarins complained, than the me-generation's "hierarchy of greeds." Rather than desiring solidarity and self-actualization, Americans suffered from "money-nucleosis," "sue-bonic plague," "belonging Beri-Beri," "ego-addiction," and "staff-actualization." Such greeds raised wages and built empires without shaping corporatist teamwork.[23] Performing the corporatist tango required two willing dancers, and both American workers and managers were wallflowers.

Reluctance to cooperate was especially evident in American managers' aversion to surrendering power. Wanting wealth, status, and dominion, they feared that sharing power and treating employees as members of a community would impose extra costs, limit their freedom, prevent them from treating workers as factors of production, and limit their chances of success. So superiors demanded freedom for themselves but denied it to their subordinates. But for corporatist power sharing to succeed, managerial autonomy needed to be balanced by some institutional check that would permanently, formally empower subordinates. Corporatists typically relied on managers to check themselves, which was a naive idea in a narcissistic culture and capitalist economy. Managers easily converted corporatist institutions into Taylorism and Mayoism under new names, if a conversion was even necessary.

So although real differences separated bureaucratic and corporative theories, they were really two schools of Taylorism. Their disputes were analogous to those between liberals and conservatives that the consensus historian Louis Hartz thought characteristic of America's predominantly liberal culture.[24] Debates between the schools, like quarrels within families, sometimes became ferocious. Bureaucrats accused corporatists of being closet anarchists intent on sapping managerial power and spurring worker populism, and corporatists accused bureaucrats of being despots who were restraining democratic and material progress. But really their differences were usually over means rather than ends. Their common premises expressed a new twentieth-century consensus, a shared commitment to managerial government and a management theory of value.

Their common premises showed in several ways. Both schools provided tools for managers. So when bureaucrats accused corporatists of being soft on anarchism, they overlooked the affinity between controlling a hierarchy and fostering harmony in it. Imposing rationality on an organization and integrating individual and organization led toward the same end, a fact acknowledged by corporatists and verified by labor leaders, union sympathizers, and leftist intellectuals.[25] And if corporatism had contradictions between harmony as an end in itself and harmony as a means to bureaucratic rationality, between liberation and adjustment, and between participation and manipulation, the contradictions were normally resolved in favor of rationality, adjustment, and manipulation. Management by objectives obliged employees to adopt their manager's goals; sensitivity training taught bureaucrats to be rational with feelings; job enrichment imbued workers with managerial habits; quality circles obliged workers to impose time-and-motion study and speedups on themselves. In addition, engineering rhetoric eventually legitimized participative management. Similarly some management scientists recognized problems in authoritarianism and recommended corporatist negotiations. Simon, who realized that bureaucratic rationality depended on the legitimacy of managerial premises, sometimes used corporatist metaphors to describe harmony between superiors and subordinates.

Besides serving managers, both bureaucratism and corporatism emerged at about the same time and attempted to solve problems that Taylorism had helped create but could not solve. Scientific management had helped bureaucracies grow, but these organizations encountered problems in synthesizing specialized operations and in integrating independent experts. Help could not come from Mayoism, since it sought harmony by manipulating the social environment away from the point of production. Hence managers and mandarins sought to transcend the techniques of Taylorism. Their quest for new ways to engineer harmony led to post-Taylorite bureaucratic theory for integrating specialized operations and post-Mayoist corporatism for integrating specialists. Of course harmonious productive operations and rational social relations were not distinct, and both were desired by managers.

Another similarity between bureaucrats and corporatists could be seen in the faith both schools had in science. Bureaucrats were not alone in their attraction to positivist rituals and rhetoric. They were joined by the corporatists, who as liberal social scientists were also attracted to apolitical ideology; they presumed that evidence spoke for itself and assumed that systematic theory, statistical methods, and appropriate controls led to objective proofs and apolitical policy. If corporatists questioned aspects of the legitimacy and rationality of bureaucratic forms of managerial capitalism, they also sanctioned end-of-ideology values and did not question managerial capitalism itself. They wanted participative management rather than participatory democracy. Accordingly corporatism also exalted the scientific manager who accepted capitalist ends and sought the one best way, testing participative methods in the same manner that Taylor had tested metal-cutting techniques.

Corporatism was thus within the bureaucratic spectrum of Taylorism. By acknowledging the dominance of bureaucracy, my ideas superficially match the views of the business historian Alfred Chandler. As I explained in the Introduction, he too had argued that bureaucracy persisted. But really my political description differs from Chandler's technological one. Describing the persistence of bureaucracy as a consequence of choice and power is different from describing it as an inevitable outcome of technological and market forces. A political description denies Chandler's notion that management had progressed to bureaucratic perfection.

Chandler's notion of perfection rested on his assumption that bureaucracy was rational and legitimate. This view, of course, expressed the positivism and avowedly apolitical perspective of bureaucratic mandarins. Like them, he accepted bureaucracy as a given. He therefore studied it as a fact of nature rather than as an artifact of culture. This perspective helped him see relationships between technological and organizational change but led him to ignore how managers continually sought control.

Particularly, Chandler overlooked the political consequences inherent in the shift from the invisible hand to the visible hand. With the shift, business leaders became petty despots. In their new dominions, they struggled for power and wrangled over policy like politicians. And their counselors, business mandarins, debated one another like philosophers, offering advice and solutions, and championing and challenging various ideas.

Such conflicts and debates disproved Chandler's iron law of bureaucracy, discrediting his notion that bureaucracy could be understood without studying politics. Managers had no choice but to participate in political debates and make choices about government. They could not separate technical decisions from political ones. They had to choose political alternatives and were anxious for help in making choices. Given their demand for advice, mandarins were eager to supply it.

Even within the bureaucratic spectrum, managers had latitude to choose among various governmental forms. Their choices were not completely limited by technology or markets. They selected alternatives ranging from Taylor and Simon to Drucker and Argyris. Their selections were based as much on value preference as anything else.

This is not to imply that technology and markets were unimportant and that managers made history just as they pleased. Contingency theorists like Paul R. Lawrence and Jay W. Lorsch have generalized that formal bureaucracy was more characteristic of firms with stable markets and technologies; under stable conditions, centralized command, written rules, specialized operations, and clear demarcations between planners and doers were easier to establish. Conversely, corporatist forms of bureaucracy were probably more common in unstable situations; where markets and technologies changed rapidly, formal bureaucracy was too rigid, and flexibility demanded greater teamwork and closer cooperation between planners and doers.[26] The dominance of bureaucratic forms, however, indicates the conservatism of managers and their desires to preserve power.

Of course, students of management should put mandarinism in economic and technological perspective. Theorists were competitors in the knowledge and value industry. Bureaucrats were would-be monopolists protecting their market, and corporatists were entrepreneurs peddling old gizmos with new bells and whistles. The competitive nature of management discourse, the claims and counterclaims, and the fact that mandarins could see other's failings but not their own showed that management advice was more commercial than scientific. Indeed, mandarins often acted less like seekers of truth than like sellers of technique. Their commodity was some standardized technique designed to be packaged and sold to managers. Each intellectual commodity was marketed through advertisements in the marketplace of ideas that exposed the dysfunctions of other techniques and promised that new tools could do the job. Mandarins commodified themselves when they became management consultants; they sold theories and techniques, customizing each to fit the problems and goals of particular managers and firms. And some sellers doubled as consumer advocates, who measured the cash value of the products and determined that their competitors were selling defective goods. In the end the measures proved that all techniques had defects, and this meant, as the neoclassical economist Donald McCloskey has argued, that management experts were more likely to become "rich by selling advice" than "by using it."[27]

At least in terms of fulfilling their advertisements, Taylor's disciples failed to make management into a positive science. In practical terms, mandarins promised managers a science of government, a technology of power with which they could realize their will by applying the appropriate device. The promise rested on what the philosopher William Barrett has called "the illusion of technique," the illusion that they had "only to find the right method, the definite procedure, and all problems in life must inevitably yield before it."[28] But in each case other mandarins asserted contradictory claims. Critics showed that the techniques were incapable of fully predicting and programming behavior and hence were incomplete, inconsistent, and normally self-defeating. And in philosophical terms, mandarins promised managers a science that was apolitical and progressive. But their techniques were founded on choices of ends and means, and these choices were less empirical than existential. Hence the techniques were not value-free facts of nature but rather value-laden devices developed and driven by managers and their will to power. So even if the techniques were practical, technical progress for managers and bureaucracy was not necessarily equivalent to moral progress for society. A rational managerial society is not the same thing as a happy, virtuous, or free one.[29]

Mandarins' failure to make governing a science did not mean that managers were impotent. Quite the contrary, the irrationality of mandarin ideas forced managers to judge values and to exercise power. To maintain their rule, managers continued to depend on bureaucracy; if bureaucracy failed, they could resort to pre-Taylorite drive methods.

Thus changes in management ideas never led significantly beyond Taylorism. New ideas helped new cohorts of professional managers climb up the bureaucratic ladder; mathematicians, natural scientists, economists, computer programmers, artificial intelligentsia, and even humanistic psychologists came to influence. They brought new tools with them. Mathematical and mechanical technologies provided new means of making decisions. Corporatist systems sometimes established the appearance of harmony, if seldom the reality of it, in parts of some prominent organizations. New groups and ideas mitigated some old problems and left successors with new ones.

But the theory of good business government remained essentially the same as in Taylor's day. Management experts were still shoveling the same stuff, although with at least ten new kinds of shovels. Whether mandarins were boosting the operations researcher or the democratic leader, they exalted the same management theory of value. They still believed that the best government was that ruled by the scientific manager. Taylor's bureaucratic and corporatist successors transcended his techniques but not his premises.

Notes

Introduction

1. Kaufman, "Organization Theory and Political Theory."
2. See D. Vogel, "Corporation As Government." Vogel pointed out that growing awareness of the interdependence of business and government in the sixties changed reform behavior. The civil rights, women's rights, consumer rights, pacifist, and environmental movements treated corporations as governments. They held firms to the same standards, expected business to carry out social responsibilities, and used tactics traditionally reserved for influencing governments, like protests and petitions, to pressure business leaders to change their ways.
3. Jay, *Management and Machiavelli*.
4. Nader and Taylor, *Big Boys*.
5. Chandler, *Visible Hand*, esp. pp. 1–12, 484–500, quote p. 490. See also Cuff, "From Market to Manager."
6. Chandler, *Visible Hand*, chaps. 1, 2, 3, quote pp. 6, 12, 14.
7. Chandler, *Visible Hand*, pp. 498–500, quote p. 497; Chandler, "Emergence of Managerial Capitalism."
8. Chandler, *Visible Hand*, pp. 94–120, 8–10, quote, 120, 95.
9. See Duboff and Herman, "Chandler's New Business History"; Perrow, "Markets, Hierarchies and Hegemony," pp. 371–86, 403–4; Dellobuono, "Markets and Managers."
10. McCraw, "Introduction," pp. 6, 19–21; Chandler, "Comment"; Chandler, "Business History As Institutional History." See also Galambos, "Parsonian Sociology and Post-Progressive History."
11. Chandler, *Visible Hand*, pp. 75, 82, 92, 104, 117, 143, 145, 253, 378, 411, 412, 417, 448, 449, 450, 454, 456, 463.
12. The exception is Weber, who unfairly has been given a reputation as an efficiency expert, largely due to inaccurate translations and interpretations by Talcott Parsons. See Weiss, "Weber on Bureaucracy"; Brubaker, *Limits of Rationality*.
13. For a summary of this literature, see Goldman and Van Houten, V"Bureaucracy and Domination."

14. Braverman, *Labor and Monopoly Capital*, quote p. 87; see also pp. 68, 82, 88, 107, 114–18, 126. For a similar view, see Stone, "Origins of Job Structures."

15. Edwards, *Contested Terrain*. See also Gordon et al., *Segmented Work, Divided Workers*.

16. Edwards, "Social Relations of Production," p. 156.

17. Bendix, *Work and Authority*.

18. Koontz, "Management Theory Jungle"; Koontz, "Making Sense of Management Theory," quote p. 25.

Chapter 1

1. Locke, "Ideas of Frederick W. Taylor." See also Fry, "Maligned F. W. Taylor."

2. See Chandler, *Visible Hand*; Clawson, *Bureaucracy and the Labor Process*; Goldman and Van Houten, "Bureaucracy and Domination"; Hounshell, *From the American System*; D. Nelson, "Scientific Management, Systematic Management"; D. Nelson, *Managers and Workers*, esp. pp. 49–78; B. Palmer, "Class, Conception and Conflict"; Stone, "Origins of Job Structures"; Noble, *America by Design*; Jacoby, *Employing Bureaucracy*; Gordon et al. *Segmented Work, Divided Workers*, chap. 4.

3. See Gordon et al., *Segmented Work, Divided Workers*, pp. 116–18, 128–41; Jacoby, *Employing Bureaucracy*, esp. pp. 1–8, quote p. 280.

4. See esp. Gordon, Edwards, and Reich, *Segmented Work, Divided Workers*, chap. 4. Also see Goldman and Van Houten, "Bureaucracy and Domination," pp. 189–209; D. Nelson, "New Factory System and the Unions."

5. B. Palmer, "Class, Conception and Conflict," pp. 35–38; Nelson and Campbell, "Taylorism Versus Welfare Work"; D. Nelson, "Scientific Management, Systematic Management."

6. Stabile, *Prophets of Order*, esp. pp. 47–50.

7. See B. Palmer, "Class, Conception and Conflict"; D. Nelson, "Scientific Management, Systematic Management."

8. F. W. Taylor, *Principles of Scientific Management*, p. 128. For the popularity of Taylor's philosophy, see Haber, *Efficiency and Uplift*; Stabile, *Prophets of Order*; Merkle, *Management and Ideology*.

9. F. W. Taylor, *Principles of Scientific Management*, pp. 100, 140–41. The best biography of Taylor is D. Nelson, *Frederick W. Taylor*.

10. Haber, *Efficiency and Uplift*; Bell, *Work and Its Discontents*; Merkle, *Management and Ideology*.

11. Drucker, *Practice*, p. 280.

12. Montgomery, *Workers' Control*, pp. 9–27, 34–44, 91–112, 113–34; Montgomery, "Labor and the Republic of Industrial America," pp. 201–15; B. Palmer, "Class, Conception and Conflict," pp. 41–44; M. Davis, "Stop Watch and the Wooden Shoe"; Aitken, *Taylorism at Watertown Arsenal*; Mathewson, *Restriction of Output*; Gordon et al., *Segmented Work, Divided Workers*, pp. 147–64.

13. Jacoby, *Employing Bureaucracy*, pp. 1–8, 280.

14. Gordon et al., *Segmented Work, Divided Workers*, pp. 147–64, esp. pp. 162–64; Meyer, *Five Dollar Day*, esp. chap. 5.

15. Stabile, *Prophets of Order*, chaps. 3 and 4, quote pp. 78, 104.

16. Nadworny, *Scientific Management*, pp. 98–146; Haber, *Efficiency and Uplift*, pp. 128–33; Fraser, "Dress Rehearsal"; McKelvey, *AFL Attitudes*.

17. Brody, "Rise and Decline of Welfare Capitalism"; Brandes, *American Welfare Capitalism*; Harris, *Right to Manage*, pp. 159–68, 172–75; Jacoby, *Employing Bureaucracy*, chaps. 2–5.

18. Baritz, *Servants of Power*.

19. Roethlisberger and Dickson, *Management and the Worker*; Roethlisberger, *Elusive Phenomena*.

20. See Trahair, *Humanist Temper*.

21. Mayo, *Human Problems*, quote pp. 131, 165, 100, 69, 79.

22. C. W. Mills, "Contributions of Sociology," quote pp. 22–23.

23. See, among many things, Gilson, "Review"; Landsberger, *Hawthorne Revisited*; Bendix, *Work and Authority*, pp. 308–26; Baritz, *Servants of Power*, pp. 77–114; Sykes, "Economic Interest and the Hawthorne Researcher"; Carey, "The Hawthorne Studies"; Franke and Kaul, "Hawthorne Experiments"; Schlaifer, "Relay Assembly Test Room"; Bramel and Friend, "Hawthorne, the Myth of the Docile Worker, and Class Bias in Psychology"; Sonnenfeld, "Clarifying Critical Confusion," pp. 904–9; Friend and Bramel, "More Harvard Humbug."

24. By this, I mean corporatism on the "micro" level, the theories intending to explain conflicts within the firm between individuals, classes, and units as well as the techniques seeking to eliminate them. Other historians have written on corporatism on the "macro" level; see particularly Hawley, "Discovery and Study of a 'Corporate Liberalism'"; Hogan, "Corporatism," pp. 363–72; Sklar, *Corporate Reconstruction*.

25. See Schmitter, "Still the Century of Corporatism?"; Golob, *The Isms*, pp. 540–44; R. H. Bowen, *German Theories*, pp. 1–5, 11–23, 210–19; Elbow, *French Corporative Theory*, pp. 11–12, 197–204. Corporative thinkers who influenced American management are discussed in E. S. Mason, "Saint-Simonism and the Rationalization of Industry," and Nisbet, *Emile Durkheim*.

26. For corporative practice, see, in addition to the works cited above, Sewell, *Work and Revolution in France*; Stearns, *Revolutionary Syndicalism and French Labor*; Mazgaj, *Action Française and Revolutionary Syndicalism*; Martin, *Count Albert de Mun*; Diamant, *Austrian Catholics and the First Republic*; Fine, "Toward Corporatism"; Kuisel, *Capitalism and the State in Modern France*; Kuisel, *Ernest Mercier*; Maier, "Between Taylorism and Technocracy," pp. 27–60; Maier, *Recasting Bourgeois Europe*; Tannenbaum, "Goals of Italian Fascism"; Roberts, *Syndicalist Tradition and Italian Fascism*; Sarti, *Fascism and the Industrial Leadership in Italy*; Schoenbaum, *Hitler's Social Revolution*; Paxton, *Vichy France*; Levinson, *Industry's Democratic Revolution*.

27. See especially Stabile, *Prophets of Order*; Wiebe, *Search for Order*, chaps. 5 and 6; Weinstein, *Corporate Ideal in the Liberal State*; Gilbert, *Designing the Industrial State*;

Noble, *America by Design*; Hawley, *Great War*; Gerber, "Corporatism in Comparative Perspective"; Alchon, *Invisible Hand of Planning*.

28. See Lipow, *Authoritarian Socialism in America*; Segal, *Technological Utopianism in American Culture*.

29. F. W. Taylor, *Principles of Scientific Management*, p. 140.

Chapter 2

1. See Kline, *Mathematics*; Davis and Hersh, *Descartes' Dream*.

2. See Blackett, "Operational Research"; Crowther and Whiddington, *Science at War*; E. C. Williams, "Origin of the Term 'Operational Research'"; Waddington, *O.R. in World War 2*; Lardner, "Origin of Operational Research"; Daniel, "Half a Century of Operational Research in the RAF."

3. Trefethen, "History of Operations Research"; Steinhardt, "Role of Operations Research"; Kittel, "Nature and Development of Operations Research"; Morse and Kimball, *Methods of Operations Research*.

4. See notes 2 and 3.

5. Woolsey, "Where the War Stories Began," quote p. 37.

6. Wooldridge, "Operations Research"; on "the whiz kids" at Ford, who were also called "shiny-ass Harvard bookkeepers," "bean-counters," or "beanies," see Halberstam, *The Reckoning*, esp. chap. 11.

7. See Rinehart, "Threats to the Growth"; Wooldridge, "Operations Research."

8. Solow, "Operations Research," quote pp. 105–6; Morse and Kimball, *Methods of Operations Research*, esp. Preface; P. M. Morse, "Trends in Operations Research," pp. 159–60, 163–64; Churchman et al., *Introduction to Operations Research*, esp. pp. 3–6. See also citations in note 3.

9. Churchman et al., *Introduction to Operations Research*, pp. 3–6, 20, quote p. 6. See also Hurni, "Operation Research and Synthesis in General Electric," pp. 28–33.

10. Hurni, "Operation Research and Synthesis in General Electric," quote pp. 28–33; Hurni, "Purpose of Operations Research and Synthesis," quote pp. 2–7; Wooldridge, "Operations Research"; Churchman et al., *Introduction to Operations Research*, pp. 11, 20, 3–6; Solow, "Operations Research," pp. 106–7, 146.

11. See references in note 10 and Herrmann and Magee, "Operations Research for Management," pp. 110–12. For discussions of systems theory as related to management, see Churchman, *Systems Approach*, esp. chaps. 2 and 3; also an entire journal issue devoted to the subject, *Academy of Management Journal* 15 (December 1972). For a critique of the assumptions and mathematics in systems theory, see Berlinski, *On Systems Analysis*.

12. See Churchman et al., *Introduction to Operations Research*, chap. 4.

13. Lilienfeld, *Rise of Systems Theory*, esp. chap. 9, quote pp. 263.

14. For a description of the steps common to OR projects, see Churchman et al., *Introduction to Operations Research*, esp. pp. 13–15, 105–55.

15. Drucker, "Management Science and the Manager." See also Drucker's *Practice*, pp. 62–63.

16. Ackoff and Rivett, *Manager's Guide*, pp. 32, 34.

17. The most readable early OR/MS texts include Churchman et al., *Introduction to Operations Research*; Miller and Starr, *Executive Decisions and Operations Research*; Churchman, *Prediction and Optimal Decision*; Ackoff, *Scientific Method*; Eddison et al., *Operational Research in Management*; Ackoff and Rivett, *Manager's Guide*. See also R. Dorfman, "Operations Research."

18. See Ackoff, "Development of Operations Research."

19. See "Constitution and By-Laws"; W. W. Cooper, "Presidential Address to TIMS"; Rinehart, "Threats to the Growth," pp. 229–34; J. R. Cooper, "An Issue-Oriented History of TIMS."

20. On business school education, see Schlossman et al., "The 'New Look,'" pp. 11–27; Sass, *Pragmatic Imagination*, chaps. 8–10. For the literature, see Wooley and Pidd, "Problem Structuring."

21. For early business attitudes and applications, see Goodeve, "The Growth of Operational Research in the Civil Sector"; Caminer and Andlinger, "Operations Research Roundup"; Malcolm, "Status of Operations Research"; Solow, "Operations Research in Business"; American Management Association, "Progress in Industrial Operations Research"; Hovey and Wagner, "Sample Survey"; Schumacher and Smith, "Sample Survey." For a listing of early corporate users in Britain and America, see Ackoff and Rivett, *Manager's Guide*, pp. 87–93. On production management, see Bowman and Fetter, *Analysis for Production Management*; Buffa, *Modern Production Management*.

22. Solow, "Operations Research," pp. 148; Solow, "Operations Research in Business," pp. 155–56; Ackoff and Rivett, *Manager's Guide*, pp. 93–96; Malcolm, "On the Need for Improvement"; Howard, "The Practicality Gap." See also Watson and Marett, "Survey of Management Science Implementation Problems."

23. Drucker, "Management Science and the Manager."

24. Koopman, "Fallacies in Operations Research."

25. Radnor and Neal, "Progress of Management-Science"; Thomas and DaCosta, "Sample Survey," statistics from p. 103; Gaither, "Adoption of Operations Research Techniques," statistics from p. 803.

26. American Management Association, "Progress in Industrial Operations Research."

27. Radnor and Neal, "Progress of Management-Science"; Thomas and DaCosta, "Sample Survey," statistics from pp. 104, 107.

28. Ranyard, "History of OR and Computing."

29. Radnor and Neal, "Progress of Management-Science"; Thomas and DaCosta, "Sample Survey," statistics from pp. 104, 107.

30. Baritz, *Backfire*, pp. 245–50; Cohen, "Systems Paralysis"; G. Palmer, *McNamara Strategy and the Vietnam War*. See also B. L. R. Smith, *RAND Corporation*; Hitch, "An Appreciation of Systems Analysis."

31. Gibson, *The Perfect War*.

32. Baritz, *Backfire*, pp. 245–50, quote p. 247.

33. See Cohen, "Systems Paralysis"; Bonder, "Changing the Future of Operations Research"; Enthoven and Smith, *How Much Is Enough?*

34. Doty, "Science Advising and the ABM Debate," pp. 185–204; Klein and Butkovich, "Can the Professions of Operations Research/Management Science Change and Survive?"; Caywood et al., "Guidelines for the Practice," quote pp. 1134, 1127, 1128.

35. *Planning-Programming-Budgeting*, p. 6.

36. Hoos, *Systems Analysis in Public Policy*, esp. pp. 241–47, quote p. xiv.

37. Dando and Bennett, "Kuhnian Crisis." See also Keys, "Traditional Management Science and the Emerging Critique."

38. Bevan, "Language of Operational Research"; Bevan and Bryer, "On Measuring the Contribution of OR"; Dando et al., "Could OR Be a Science?"; Dando and Sharp, "Operational Research in the U.K. in 1977," quote pp. 445–46, 447.

39. Grayson, "Management Science and Business Practice," quote pp. 43–44.

40. Drucker, "Performance Gap."

41. Levitt, "Heretical View of Management Science."

42. H. J. Leavitt, "Beyond the Analytic Manager."

43. Ackoff, "Future of Operational Research," quote pp. 93, 94, 95, 100; Ackoff, "Resurrecting the Future," p. 195.

44. Ackoff, "Resurrecting the Future," esp. pp. 195–99; Grayson, "Management Science and Business Practice," pp. 46–48. For references to dozens of articles suggesting reforms in OR education, research, and practice during this period, see Zahedi, "A Survey of Issues in the MS/OR Field," esp. pp. 59–63; H. J. Leavitt, "Beyond the Analytic Manager: Part II."

45. Grayson, "Management Science and Business Practice," pp. 46–48; Drucker, "Performance Gap," pp. 24–29; Ackoff, "Resurrecting the Future," pp. 189–92; Ackoff, "Future of Operational Research," p. 100; Ackoff, *Creating the Corporate Future*. For other articles along these lines, see Radford, "Decision-Making in a Turbulent Environment"; Hall and Hess, "OR/MS, Dead or Dying?"

46. See note 45.

47. Eden and Sims, "On the Nature of Problems in Consulting Practice." Among Eden's other works, see Eden et al., "Policy Analysis and Organizational Politics."

48. Churchman, "OR As a Profession."

49. See R. O. Mason, "Dialectical Approach to Strategic Planning"; Mitroff et al., "Assumptional Analysis"; Mason and Mitroff, *Challenging Strategic Planning Assumptions*.

50. Woolsey, "Reflections on the Past."

51. Ackoff, *Creating the Corporate Future*, esp. pp. 34, 44, 48–50, 52; Ackoff, "Resurrecting the Future," pp. 189–95; Ackoff, "Future of Operational Research," pp. 98–103; Ackoff, "Art and Science of Mess Management."

52. The hard-soft distinction was created by a British ORer, Peter B. Checkland; see his *Systems Thinking, Systems Practice*. Especially see Jackson, "Social Systems Theory and Practice."

53. Rosenhead and Thunhurst, "Materialist Analysis"; Rosenhead, "From Management Science." See also Rosenhead, "Why Does Management Need Management Science?"; Jackson, "Nature of 'Soft' Systems Thinking"; Jackson, "Social Systems Theory and Practice." For an early view of this type, see Hales, "Management Science and 'The Second Industrial Revolution.'"

54. Rosenhead and Thunhurst, "Materialist Analysis," pp. 115–20; Rosenhead, "From Management Science," pp. 117–22; Rosenhead, "Why Does Management Need Management Science?"

55. Jackson, "Nature of 'Soft' Systems Thinking," pp. 17–19; Jackson, "Social Systems Theory and Practice."

56. Rosenhead and Thunhurst, "Materialist Analysis," pp. 120–22; Rosenhead, "From Management Science," pp. 122–28.

57. Hayes and Abernathy, "Managing Our Way to Economic Decline"; Magaziner and Reich, *Minding America's Business*, pp. 4–5, 65–66, 106–46, 191–94; Reich, *Next American Frontier*, esp. parts 2 and 3.

58. See chart in Hayes and Abernathy, "Managing Our Way to Economic Decline," p. 75; Reich, *Next American Frontier*, pp. 158–59.

59. Hayes and Abernathy, "Managing Our Way to Economic Decline," pp. 70, 73.

60. Hayes in Wayne, "Management Gospel Gone Wrong," p. C21. See also Magaziner and Reich, *Minding America's Business*, pp. 109–17.

61. Magaziner and Reich, *Minding America's Business*, pp. 4–5, 65–66; Reich, *Next American Frontier*, esp. pp. 140, 141, 145, 166.

62. Reich, *Next American Frontier*, pp. 164, 183, 160. The dichotomy was also central in Melman, *Profits without Production*.

63. Halberstam, *The Reckoning*; contrast, for instance, his portrayal of George Vincent and Ed Lundy.

64. See Wayne, "Management Gospel Gone Wrong," p. C1.

65. Melman, *Profits without Production*, pp. 68, 134, 169, 177, 246, 272, 224 and n.; also see Melman, *Permanent War Economy*.

66. Veblen, *Portable Veblen*, pp. 364–75.

67. See, for instance, Morrison, "Job-Hopping at the Top."

68. Lewis, "Technology, Enterprise, and American Economic Growth," esp. pp. 1209–10. Japanese managers denigrated the way Americans depended on quantitative techniques and stock market investment, a dependence that intensified during inflationary times; see Lohr, "Overhauling America's Business Management."

69. Bluestone and Harrison, *Deindustrialization of America*, esp. chap. 6.

70. Hayes and Abernathy, "Managing Our Way to Economic Decline," pp. 70–77; Reich, *Next American Frontier*, chaps. 11, 12, quote pp. 246, 282.

71. Reich, *Next American Frontier*, p. 280.

Chapter 3

1. Simon, *Models of Man*, p. vii; J. Williams, "Herbert A. Simon."

2. Royal Swedish Academy of Sciences, "Nobel Memorial Prize," p. 73. For a partial listing of his publications, see Simon, "Bibliography."

3. Newell and Simon, *Human Problem Solving*, pp. 10–11.

4. Simon, "My Life Philosophy," p. 17. See also March, "Nobel Prize," p. 858.

5. Neuhaus, "He Has the Nobel," pp. 54, 56; Cyert, "Herbert Simon," pp. 62–63.

6. Simon, "My Life Philosophy," quote p. 17; Simon, "Rational Decision Making," p. 500. On the Chicago school, see Reder, "Chicago Economics."

7. Ridley and Simon, *Measuring Municipal Activities*; Simon, *Models of Discovery*; "Herbert A. Simon," *Current Biography* (1979), pp. 358–59.

8. Newell and Simon, *Human Problem Solving*, p. 880 n. 4; Simon, *Administrative Behavior*, chap. 3, esp. p. 45.

9. For discussions of positivism in economics, see Caldwell, *Beyond Positivism*, esp. chap. 7; McCloskey, *Rhetoric of Economics*, esp. chap. 1.

10. Simon, *Administrative Behavior*, p. 62 n. 2, pp. 220, 45–47, 253.

11. Ibid., pp. 3, 37–39, 41, 43, 47–49, 65, 240–41, Appendix.

12. Gulick and Urwick, *Papers on the Science of Administration*; Urwick, *Elements of Administration*.

13. Simon, *Administrative Behavior*, pp. 20, 28–35, 36, xiv.

14. March and Simon, *Organizations*, pp. 13–21, 29, 30, 33–34, 36, also pp. 39–46. I have assumed that ideas from works on which Simon collaborated with others expressed his opinions as much as works he authored alone.

15. Simon, "Formal Theory of the Employment Relation." See also Simon, "Comparison of Organization Theories."

16. Simon, "Rational Decision Making," p. 499; Simon, *Administrative Behavior*, p. 136.

17. Commons, *Institutional Economics*; Chamberlain, "Institutional Economics of John R. Commons"; J. Dorfman, *Economic Mind in American Civilization*, 3:276–94, 4:377–95, 5:664–73.

18. Barnard, *Functions of the Executive*, esp. pp. 163–65, 170–75, 182–84. See also W. B. Wolf, *Basic Barnard*; Perrow, *Complex Organizations*, pp. 74–93.

19. For his early ideas, see following discussion.

20. See Simon's introduction to the 1957 edition of *Administrative Behavior*, esp. pp. xxiii and 62; also see Simon, *Models of Man*, pp. 3, 198. He made the same charges about "game theory"; see *Models of Man*, pp. 201–3.

21. Simon, "Behavioral Model"; Simon, "Rational Choice and the Structure of the Environment," reprinted as chaps. 14 and 15 of his *Models of Man*. Simon has claimed that these essays were written *before* he and Allan Newell decided in the summer of 1954 to test his ideas through computer simulation; see Simon, *Models of Thought*, p. 5.

22. Simon, "Behavioral Model of Rational Choice," chap. 14 of *Models of Man*, pp. 241–52, quote p. 256.

23. Ibid., pp. 252, 199; Simon, "Rational Choice and the Structure of the Environment," in *Models of Man*, pp. 261, 263, 270–71, 272; the needle story is from March and Simon, *Organizations*, p. 141. Searching for a label to distinguish his theory of choice from maximizing, Simon found *satisficing* in the *Oxford English Dictionary* in the early 1950s; see Roach, "Simon Says," p. 8.

24. Simon, "Formal Theory of the Employment Relation"; Simon, *Administrative Behavior*, pp. 8, 79–84, xxiv–v, 102.

25. Simon, *Administrative Behavior*, pp. 8–9, 66, 79, 98–103, esp. pp. 102–3.

26. Ibid., pp. 8–10, 50, 53, 61, 62, 65, 118, 172–73, 179.

27. Ibid., pp. 16–18, 110–19, 12, 204. See Barnard, *Functions of the Executive*, chaps. 11 and 16, esp. pp. 56–59.

28. Simon, *Administrative Behavior*, pp. 11–12, 22, 125–28.

29. Ibid., pp. xxxiv–xxxv, 11–12, 154.

30. Ibid., pp. 138, 198–99, 202–5, 210, 228–31, 242, 204, 39, 11–16.

31. Ibid., pp. 11–12, 131–33, 232–35, 146.

32. Ibid., pp. 134, 114–15.

33. Simon, *Models of Man*, pp. 3, 75, 167–68.

34. For an admiring appraisal of Simon as a "Neo-Weberian" sociologist, see Perrow, *Complex Organizations*, pp. 145–63, 175–76.

35. Simon, *Administrative Behavior*, p. 62.

36. Alchian, "Uncertainty, Evolution and Economic Theory."

37. Margolis, "Analysis of the Firm"; Haire, "Psychological Problems Relevant to Business and Industry"; Day, "Profits, Learning and the Convergence of Satisficing to Marginalism"; Horowitz, *Decision Making*, pp. 315–17.

38. Stigler, "Economics of Information."

39. Stigler and Becker, "*De Gustibus non est Disputandum.*"

40. Alchian and Demsetz, "Production, Information Costs, and Economic Organization."

41. M. Friedman, *Essays in Positive Economics*, pp. 3–43; Machlup, "Theories of the Firm."

42. March, "Nobel Prize," pp. 859–61.

43. Ando, "On the Contribution of Herbert A. Simon," p. 84 n. 1. See Ando's and the identically titled article by Baumol in the same issue for essays summarizing Simon's work in economics.

44. Neuhaus, "He Has the Nobel," p. 53.

45. Machlup, "Theories of the Firm," p. 32. See also Horowitz, *Decision Making*, pp. 322–31.

46. Simon, *Reason in Human Affairs*, pp. 38–39.

47. Simon, "Theories of Decision-Making," pp. 253–83, quote p. 255; Simon, "Rational Decision Making," quote p. 498. See also Cyert et al., "Observation of a Business Decision"; Simon, "Administrative Decision Making," pp. 31–37; Cyert and Simon, "Behavioral Approach," pp. 95–108.

48. Waldo, "Development of a Theory," pp. 81–103; Waldo, "Replies and Comments"; Wolin, *Politics and Vision*, chap. 10, esp. pp. 380–81, 410–11; S. Krupp, *Pattern in Organization Analysis*, esp. chaps. 6 and 8; Storing, *Essays*, pp. 63–105. See also Gouldner, "Metaphysical Pathos and the Theory of Bureaucracy," pp. 496–507.

49. Storing, *Essays*, p. 150.

50. Simon et al., *Public Administration*, p. 22.

51. See Storing, *Essays*, pp. 70–83, 95–96, 99–103, 147–48; Waldo, "Development of a Theory," pp. 87–88; Waldo, "Replies and Comments"; S. Krupp, *Pattern in Organization Analysis*, pp. 92–96.

52. Simon et al., *Public Administration*, p. 502.

53. Storing, *Essays*, pp. 93–96, quote p. 103. See also S. Krupp, *Pattern in Organization Analysis*, pp. 182–83, 92–96.

54. Wolin, *Politics and Vision*, pp. 380–81, 410–11, 368, 403, quote p. 389. See also Storing, *Essays*, pp. 87–89.

55. See S. Krupp, *Pattern in Organization Analysis*, p. 96; Storing, *Essays*, pp. 89–93, 105.

56. Storing, *Essays*, pp. 105–9, 132–35; Wolin, *Politics and Vision*, pp. 382–93; S. Krupp, *Pattern in Organization Analysis*, pp. 96–116, quote pp. 99, x. The rationality of Simon's "administrative man" can be profitably contrasted with C. Wright Mills's "Cheerful Robot"; see C. W. Mills, *Sociological Imagination*, chap. 9.

57. S. Krupp, *Pattern in Organization Analysis*, pp. 142, 185.

58. Simon, "Development of a Theory."

59. Ibid., pp. 501–3.

60. See Simon, *Administrative Behavior*, pp. 18, 119–20.

61. McCorduck, *Machines Who Think*, pp. 115–16.

62. Simon quote in Gardner, *Mind's New Science*, pp. 22–23. See also Newell and Simon, *Human Problem Solving*, pp. 874–76, 878–89.

63. Bolter, *Turing's Man*, esp. pp. 8–12, chap. 11. See also Goldstine, *The Computer from Pascal to von Neumann*.

64. See Heims, *John von Neumann and Norbert Wiener*, pp. 203–19; the posthumous work by von Neumann, *The Computer and the Brain*; Wiener, *Cybernetics*; Dechert, "Development of Cybernetics."

65. See Gardner, *Mind's New Science*, pp. 6–7, 38–45, chap. 2.

66. McCorduck, *Machines Who Think*, pp. 126, 132; Newell and Simon, *Human Problem Solving*, p. 880 n. 4; Simon, "Theory of Automata." See also Simon, "Application of Servomechanism Theory."

67. McCorduck, *Machines Who Think*, chap. 6, quote p. 127; Newell and Simon, *Human Problem Solving*, pp. 873–82.

68. McCorduck, *Machines Who Think*, pp. 136–40; Gardner, *Mind's New Science*, pp. 60–65, esp. pp. 64–65; Newell and Simon, *Human Problem Solving*, pp. 882–85, quote p. 884.

69. McCorduck, *Machines Who Think*, pp. 134–40; Gardner, *Mind's New Science*, pp. 64–65; Newell and Simon, *Human Problem Solving*, pp. 882–85.

70. Newell and Simon, "Logic Theory Machine"; Gardner, *Mind's New Science*, pp. 145–47. See also Newell, Simon, and Shaw, "Problem Solving in Humans and Computers."

71. In addition to *Human Problem Solving*, see Newell, Simon, and Shaw, "Report on a General Problem Solving Program."

72. Newell and Simon, *Human Problem Solving*, pp. 5, 9–10, 870.

73. Simon, "Thinking by Computers," pp. 3–5.

74. Simon, "Modeling Human Mental Processes"; Simon, "Thinking by Computers"; Simon, "The Logic of Heuristic Decision Making."

75. See note 74.

76. Newell, Shaw, and Simon, "General Problem Solving Program," p. 12.

77. See "Challenges to Cybernetic Simonism" in this chapter.

78. Simon, "Motivational and Emotional Controls of Cognition," pp. 29–39.

79. Simon, "Thinking by Computers," pp. 19–21. For the influence of behaviorism on Simon, see Newell and Simon, *Human Problem Solving*, pp. 874–76. See also Bolter, *Turing's Man*, pp. 219–20.

80. Simon, "My Life Philosophy," pp. 15–17.

81. Simon, *Reason in Human Affairs*, pp. 43–44, 54–66.

82. Ibid., pp. 55, 65–66.

83. Simon, *Sciences of the Artificial*, pp. 24–26, 52–53; Simon, *New Science* (1960), p. 23.

84. Simon, *Sciences of the Artificial*, p. 52; "Decision Doctor."

85. Newell and Simon, "Heuristic Problem-Solving," p. 6.

86. Kobler, "The Flip-Flop Machines," p. 46.

87. Simon, *New Science* (1977).

88. "Herbert A. Simon," *Current Biography* (1979), pp. 360–61.

89. For interpretations of Simon as an artificial intelligencer and cognitive scientist, especially see previous citations of McCorduck, Gardner, and Bolter.

90. Simon, "Organization of Complex Systems"; Simon, *New Science* (1960), quote pp. 40–41, 43.

91. Simon, *New Science* (1960), pp. 5–10; March and Simon, *Organizations*, esp. pp. 169–79, also pp. 139–57; Simon, *Sciences of the Artificial* (1981), pp. 31–61; Simon, *Reason in Human Affairs*, pp. 79, 87–89.

92. Simon, "On the Concept of Organizational Goal." See also March and Simon, *Organizations*, pp. 141–51.

93. Simon, *Models of Man*, pp. 204, 219–20, chap. 13; March and Simon, *Organizations*, p. 157, also pp. 145–51.

94. Simon, "On How to Decide What to Do," pp. 494–96. See also Simon, "Logic of Rational Decision."

95. See Simon, "How Managers Express Their Creativity"; Simon, "Making Management Decisions"; Simon, "Experts in Your Midst."

96. March, "Nobel Prize," pp. 859–61.

97. Cyert and March, *Behavioral Theory of the Firm*, esp. chap. 6. For a description of the Carnegie-Mellon approach, see D. W. Taylor, "Decision Making and Problem Solving," pp. 30–63; Cyert and Hedrick, "Theory of the Firm"; C. E. Weber, "Decision Making in Business"; Simon, "Rational Decision Making," pp. 493–511.

98. Weber, "Decision Making in Business."

99. Urwick, "Why the So-Called 'Classicists' Endure"; Urwick, "Papers in the Science of Administration."

100. See essays in Cyert and Welsch, *Management Decision Making*, especially D. W. Taylor, "Decision Making and Problem Solving," pp. 30–63. See also Newell and Simon, "Heuristic Problem-Solving"; Simon, *New Science* (1960), pp. 21–34; Michael, "A Review of Heuristic Programming."

101. A search of *expert system* on the computerized ABI/INFORM business journal index covering May 1984 to April 1989 retrieved 1,405 items. See Harmon and King, *Expert Systems*; Silverman, *Expert Systems for Business*; Kriz, *Knowledge-based Expert Systems in Industry*; Chorafas, *Applying Expert Systems in Business*; Fordyce et al., "Artificial Intelligence and the Management Science Practitioner."

102. Simon, "Two Heads Are Better Than One."

103. "Making a Business School More Relevant"; Cohen et al., *Carnegie Tech Management Game*, quote pp. 3, 26, 149; D. W. Taylor, "Decision Making and Problem Solving," pp. 30–63. Harvard MBAs were not impressed with this approach; they joked that corporate presidents were Harvard generalists who had a staff of Carnegie-Mellon specialists. See "Making a Business School More Relevant."

104. Schlossman et al., "The 'New Look,'" pp. 11–27, esp. pp. 15, 27; Gordon and Howell, *Higher Education for Business*.

105. Emmerman, "Decisions, Decisions."

106. For other discussions of the psychological challenges, see McCorduck, *Machines Who Think*, chaps. 8–9; Gardner, *Mind's New Science*, pp. 150–51, 161–63, 175–76, also pp. 167, 318–22, 385–87.

107. Dreyfus, *Alchemy and Artificial Intelligence*; Dreyfus, *What Computers Can't Do*; Weizenbaum, *Computer Power and Human Reason*; Searle, "Minds, Brains and Programs"; Searle, *Minds, Brains and Science*.

108. Dreyfus, *What Computers Can't Do*, esp. part 2.

109. Searle, *Minds, Brains and Science*, chaps. 2 and 3, esp. pp. 48–49. For an important mathematical critique of the cybernetic model of the mind, see Lucas, "Minds, Machines and Gödel."

110. Weizenbaum, *Computer Power and Human Reason*, chap. 6, quote p. 266. See also Berlinski, *On Systems Analysis*, pp. 32–34.

111. Dreyfus and Dreyfus, *Mind over Machines*, chap. 6, quote pp. 161, 177.

112. Dreyfus, *What Computers Can't Do*, part 3, pp. 168–71, 183–84, 192, 194; Weizenbaum, *Computer Power and Human Reason*, chap. 8; Searle, *Minds, Brains and Science*, chaps. 1, 2, 3, esp. chap. 4.

113. Andreski, *Social Sciences As Sorcery*, pp. 174–86, quote pp. 174–75, 181.

114. Boguslaw, *New Utopians*, pp. 13–15, 71–81, 95–98, 2, 188–92.

115. Argyris, "Some Limits of Rational Man Organization Theory."

116. McCorduck, *Machines Who Think*, pp. 194, 202.

117. See discussion in previous section, "Computers and Cybernetics."

118. Simon, "Organization Man," pp. 346–53.

Chapter 4

1. Bender, "Consulting Guru"; Clarkson, "Drucker," p. 23.

2. A. Bennett, "Management Guru."

3. Kantrow, "Why Read Peter Drucker," quote p. 76.

4. O'Toole, "Peter Drucker."

5. See, however, Odiorne, "MBO"; McConkey, "MBO"; Greenwood, "Management by Objectives."

6. Lustig, *Corporate Liberalism*, pp. 255–56.

7. Two studies have mentioned Drucker's corporatism, one by a political scientist, Auerbach, *The Conservative Illusion*, pp. 211–12, and another by a journalist, Tarrant, *Drucker*, pp. 53–59. Neither traced corporatism to Europe nor showed how management by objectives was a technique designed to synthesize corporatism and capitalism.

8. On corporatism in general, see Schmitter, "Still the Century of Corporatism?," pp. 86–131; R. H. Bowen, *German Theories*, pp. 1–5, 111–18, 210–19; Elbow, *French Corporative Theory*, pp. 11–22, 29–96, 197–204; Golob, *The Isms*, pp. 540–44, 548–60. For the Austrian thinkers, see Ringer, *German Mandarins*, p. 232; and Diamant, *Austrian Catholics and the First Republic*, pp. 11–14, 22, 24, 29–30, 36, 54–57, 61, 72, 160–64, 168, 194, 203–7.

9. Diamant, *Austrian Catholics and the First Republic*, esp. pp. 238, 286–87.

10. Drucker, *End of Economic Man*, pp. 106–7, chap. 4. See also Drucker, *Friedrich Julius Stahl*.

11. Freyberg, "Genesis of Drucker's Thought."

12. McLuhan and Nevitt, "The Man Who Came to Listen," p. 36; Diamant, *Austrian Catholics and the First Republic*, p. 90; Ringer, *German Mandarins*, pp. 75–76; "Peter Ferdinand Drucker"; O'Toole, "Peter Drucker," pp. 18, 24, 32.

13. Drucker, *Age of Discontinuity*, pp. 145–15; Drucker, "Schumpeter and Keynes"; Schumpeter, *Capitalism, Socialism, and Democracy*, part 2, esp. pp. 132, 141–42, 156.

14. Drucker, *Future of Industrial Man*, pp. 184–86; Drucker, *Landmarks*, pp. 45, 59, xii; Drucker, *New Society*, pp. 351–52; Drucker, "Epilogue," p. 365; Drucker, *Adventures of a Bystander*, p. 140.

15. Richman, "Interview," p. 10.

16. Drucker, *Adventures of a Bystander*, p. 135; Drucker, *End of Economic Man*, pp. 55, 77, 242, 268. For more on "the lessons of fascism" for Drucker, see Kantrow, "Why Read Peter Drucker," p. 81.

17. Drucker, *Future of Industrial Man*, pp. 78–85; Drucker, *Concept of the Corporation*, pp. 114–38; Drucker, *New Society*, pp. 47–49, 229, 151, 153, chaps. 15, 25.

18. See Hartmann, *Authority and Organization in German Management*, esp. pp. 8–10.

19. See Barnard, *Functions of the Executive*, esp. pp. 215–34.

20. Drucker, *Practice*, pp. 119, 126–27; Drucker, *Management*, pp. 398–99; Drucker, *Age of Discontinuity*, p. 235. This symphonic analogy, Fritz Ringer has argued, was a "sort of mental habit" among German university professors in the early twentieth century. These mandarins adopted the metaphor to protect themselves from "mob rule" and promote themselves in a hierarchical order. They saw society as an organic whole within which each person had a role. They believed that people experienced real freedom within their roles and in submitting to the community. They thought that submission by workers to legitimate authority would lead to social harmony and solve the "social question." Their conductor analogy was profoundly antidemocratic. See Ringer, *German Mandarins*, pp. 108, 114–19, 122–23, 128–29, 234–35, 446–47.

21. Drucker, *Future of Industrial Man*, p. 15; Drucker, *New Society*, pp. 5–7, 20–26, 343, 350; Drucker, *Practice*, p. 4.

22. Drucker, *New Society*, pp. 47, 50, 52, 61, 204, 314; Drucker, *Practice*, pp. 35–37, 47, 60, 91, 46, 76; Mohri, "Neo-Fordism," pp. 196–99.

23. Drucker, *New Society*, p. 99.

24. Drucker, *Future of Industrial Man*, pp. 35, 36.

25. Ibid.

26. Drucker, *New Society*, pp. 99, 103, 100; Drucker, *Concept of the Corporation*, pp. 35–36, 42.

27. Drucker, *Future of Industrial Man*, pp. 62, 109–11, 115; Drucker, *New Society*, pp. 160, 49, 157.

28. Drucker, *New Society*, pp. 106–13, 146, 150, 282–88.

29. Ibid., pp. 42–43.

30. Gordon et al., *Segmented Work, Divided Workers*, pp. 202, 211, 222, 224. See also Edwards, *Contested Terrain*, pp. 88–89, 174–77, 192–93.

31. Drucker, *Effective Executive*, p. 173.

32. Ibid., pp. 3, 61; Drucker, *Age of Discontinuity*, pp. 276–77; Drucker, *People and Performance*, pp. 24, 74–78.

33. Drucker, *Management*, pp. 450–51, 454; Drucker, *Managing in Turbulent Times*, p. 131.

34. Drucker, *Effective Executive*, p. 34; Drucker, *Management*, pp. 32–33, 183; Drucker, *Landmarks*, pp. 60–73.

35. See DeMott, "Here Come the Intrapreneurs."

36. Drucker, *Practice*, pp. 274–80.

37. Drucker, *Managing in Turbulent Times*, pp. 132–33; Drucker, *Landmarks*, pp. 78–82, 106; Drucker, *Effective Executive*, pp. 173–74. See also Drucker, "Coming of the New Organization."

38. Follett, *Dynamic Administration*, pp. 50–70.

39. Richman, "Interview," p. 10.

40. Tarrant, *Drucker*, p. 77; Drucker, *Concept of the Corporation*, esp. pp. 49–50, 64, 67, 78, 121; Drucker, *Adventures of a Bystander*, p. 272. For information on GM and Sloan, see also Chandler, *Strategy and Structure*, chap. 3; Sloan, *My Years with General Motors*, chap. 23.

41. Greenwood, "Management by Objectives," pp. 225–30.

42. Drucker, *Practice*, pp. 60–61; Drucker, *Management*, pp. 81, 91, 94, chap. 7; Drucker, *Managing for Results*, pp. 5, 94, 127, chap. 11.

43. Drucker, *Managing for Results*, pp. 222–26; Drucker, *Management*, pp. 99–100, chap. 8; Drucker, *Age of Discontinuity*, pp. 42–57; Drucker, *Landmarks*, p. 52; Drucker, *Practice*, pp. 62–81, 88; Drucker, *Technology, Management, and Society*, pp. 132–33, 136.

44. Drucker, *Frontiers of Management*, chap. 27.

45. Drucker, *Management*, pp. 257, 466–70; Drucker, *Men, Ideas and Politics*, pp. 203–10; Drucker, *Toward the Next Economics*, p. 188.

46. Drucker, *Management*, p. 309; Drucker, *Toward the Next Economics*, pp. 87–89; Drucker, *Practice*, pp. 126–30; also Drucker, *People and Performance*, pp. 63–70.

47. Drucker, *Practice*, pp. 129.

48. See Buttrick, "Inside Contract System"; Clawson, *Bureaucracy and the Labor Process*, chap. 3; Braverman, *Labor and Monopoly Capital*, chap. 2.

49. Drucker, *New Society*, p. 195; Drucker, *Management*, pp. 490–93; Drucker, *Practice*, p. 136.

50. Drucker, *Management*, pp. 494–504, 218; Drucker, *Practice*, pp. 131–32.

51. Drucker, *Practice*, pp. 133, 147, 150, 303, 304, 310, 267; Drucker, *Managing in Turbulent Times*, pp. 67–71; Drucker, *Management*, pp. 460–61.

52. Drucker, *Management*, pp. 284, 441–42; Drucker, *People and Performance*, p. 78; Drucker, *Practice*, pp. 131, 135–36.

53. See Abrahamson, "Corporate Capitalism," pp. 35–36, 87–88, 90–91.

54. Vogel, "The 'New' Social Regulation," pp. 155–85.

55. Drucker, *Practice*, pp. 382–83, 391; Drucker, *Concept of the Corporation*, pp. 27–29, 206, 214.

56. Drucker, *Practice*, pp. 9–10, 382–83; Drucker, *Management*, pp. 319–25, 348, 350, 366; Drucker, *People and Performance*, pp. 28, 299. See also M. Friedman, *Capitalism and Freedom*, pp. 133–34; T. Leavitt, "Dangers of Social Responsibility," pp. 41–50.

57. Drucker, *People and Performance*, pp. 293; Drucker, *Management*, pp. 325, 348–49; Drucker, "Converting Social Problems into Business Opportunities"; Drucker, *Age of Discontinuity*, chap. 10.

58. Drucker, "Behind Japan's Success," pp. 83–90.

59. Drucker, *Practice*, pp. 383–86, 389–91; Drucker, "Converting Social Problems into Business Opportunities," pp. 53–63; Drucker, *People and Performance*, pp. 307–10.

60. Drucker, *People and Performance*, pp. 301–5; Drucker, *Management*, pp. 368–69, 325–29.

61. Drucker, "What Is 'Business Ethics'?," esp. pp. 32–35.

62. Drucker, *Managing in Turbulent Times*, pp. 206–21, 229–30; Drucker, *Management*, pp. 334, 362–63; Drucker, *Age of Discontinuity*, chap. 10.

63. Drucker, *Concept of the Corporation*, pp. 27–28; Drucker, *Practice*, p. 391.

64. Richard Mansell, "A Management by Objectives Bibliography," mimeograph (Waterloo, Ontario: University of Waterloo, 1977) cited in Odiorne, "MBO," p. 14.

65. See Chandler, *Visible Hand*, pp. 476–83; Fligstein, "Spread of Multidivisional Form."

66. Gordon et al., *Segmented Work, Divided Workers*, p. 211. See also Wright and Martin, "Transformation of American Class Structure."

67. McConkey, "MBO," p. 26.

68. McGregor, "An Uneasy Look at Performance Appraisal"; McGregor, *Leadership and Motivation*, chaps. 3, 4, 5, 10; McGregor, *Human Side of Enterprise*. See also Odiorne, "MBO," p. 20; McConkey, "MBO," pp. 26–27.

69. McConkey, "MBO," p. 27.

70. Schuster and Kindall, "Management by Objectives."

71. See Edwards, *Contested Terrain*, pp. 146–47.

72. Tosi and Carroll, "Managerial Reactions to Management by Objectives"; Tosi and Carroll, *Management by Objectives*, pp. 14, 15, 26–31, 44, 50–51, 74–75.

73. Tosi and Carroll, *Management by Objectives*, pp. 3–5, 7–10, 36, 39–41, 43, 64, 66, 76. See also Villarreal, "Management by Objectives Revisited," pp. 28–30; Dyer and Weyrauch, "MBO and Motivation"; McConkie, "Clarifying and Reviewing."

74. Levinson, "Management by Whose Objectives?" The sociologist Alan Fox has made a similar evaluation, pointing out its similarity to Soviet-style techniques and noting that middle managers sometimes referred to management by objectives as a "Do-It-Yourself Hangman's Kit"; see Fox, *Beyond Contract*, p. 358. See also G. Strauss, "Management by Objectives."

75. Levinson, "Management by Whose Objectives?" See also Molander, "Management by Objectives in Perspective."

76. Fitzgerald, "Why Motivation Theory Doesn't Work."

77. Wrapp, "Management by Objectives"; see also West, "Bureaupathology and the Failure of MBO"; McCaskey, "Contingency Approach to Planning."

78. See Mintzberg, *Nature of Managerial Work*.

79. Dowling, "Conversation," p. 36; Maslow, *Eupsychian Management*, pp. xi, xii, 165.

80. "Where Being Nice to Workers Didn't Work." Managers abandoned participative techniques so they could impose tougher performance standards. See also Malone, "Non-Linear Systems Experiment."

81. Maslow, *Eupsychian Management*, pp. 7, 41, 139–40, 150–53.

82. Ibid., pp. 88–91, 103.

83. Dowling, "Conversation," pp. 36, 46; Drucker, *Management*, pp. 231–45, 526, 192, 268.

84. Drucker, *Unseen Revolution*, p. 114.

85. Drucker, *Landmarks*, pp. 252–54; Drucker, *Management*, p. 811.

86. Corbin, "Impact of Drucker on Marketing."

87. See Hayes and Abernathy, "Managing Our Way to Economic Decline"; Reich, *Next American Frontier*, esp. parts 2 and 3; Magaziner and Reich, *Minding America's Business*, pp. 4–5, 65–66, 109–46, 191–94.

88. See Drucker, *Practice*, pp. 62–63, and also Drucker, *Technology, Management and Society*, pp. 149–65; Drucker, "Performance Gap," pp. 41–48; Drucker, "Management Science and the Manager."

89. See Drucker, *Innovation and Entrepreneurship*, esp. Introduction and pp. 254, 139–40, 258.

90. Drucker, "Coming of the New Organization," pp. 45–53.

91. Ibid.

92. See Business Week, *Reindustrialization of America*, pp. 57.

93. W. A. Williams, *Contours of American History*, pp. 376, 352, 358, 373, 379, 384–85, 391.

94. See Gibbons, "Interview with Drucker," p. 319.

95. See O'Toole, "Peter Drucker."

96. Kanter, "Drucker."

Chapter 5

1. M. Weber, *From Max Weber*, pp. 214–16, 228, 261–62.

2. Kanter, *Men and Women of the Corporation*, pp. 20–23.

3. Ibid., pp. 24–25.

4. Graebner, "Small Group and Democratic Social Engineering," esp. pp. 137–38.

5. Graebner, *Engineering of Consent*, pp. 78–87.

6. Mayo, *Human Problems*; C. R. Rogers, *Counselling and Psychotherapy*.

7. Dewey, *Education and Democracy*; Dewey, "Science As Subject-Matter"; Cremin, *Transformation of the School*.

8. Bradford, "Biography."

9. Benne, "Democratic Ethics in Social Engineering."

10. Moreno, *Who Shall Survive?*, p. 11.

11. Moreno, *Who Shall Survive?*; Moreno, *Psychodrama and Sociodrama*; Bradford, "Biography"; Bradford and Lippitt, "Roleplaying."

12. Back, *Beyond Words*, pp. 9–10.

13. Marrow, *Practical Theorist*, pp. 14–16, chap. 17; Lewin, *Dynamic Theory of Personality*; Lewin, *Field Theory in Social Science*. Also see the essays in the *Journal of the History of the Behavioral Sciences* 14 (July 1978): 223–46.

14. Lewin et al., "Patterns of Aggressive Behavior"; Lippitt and Bradford, "Building a Democratic Work Group." See also White and Lippitt, *Autocracy and Democracy*.

15. C. W. Mills, *Sociological Imagination*, pp. 12, 67–68.

16. See Napoli, *Architects of Adjustment*, esp. pp. 35–41.

17. Whatever their intentions, they could not have designed a setting in which anarchy would be more likely to be a productive failure. Selecting children as subjects, neglecting to teach them how to govern themselves, and refusing to train them in their relatively complex task would almost guarantee that they would produce little. How would the scientists have reacted to, say, a revolution among the boys aimed at converting the club project into fingerpainting?

18. Pells, *Radical Visions and American Dreams*.

19. Lewin, *Resolving Social Conflicts*, quote pp. 50, 39, 65; also see pp. 52, 58–59, 67, 116–17, 135–41.

20. Back, *Beyond Words*, pp. 100–102; Benne, "History of the T-Group," pp. 81–82; Lippitt, *Training in Community Relations*, pp. ix–x; Marrow, "Events."

21. Lippitt, *Training in Community Relations*, pp. ix–x, 2, 36, 263.

22. Benne, "History of the T-Group," pp. 82–83; Bradford, "Biography," p. 136.

23. Lippitt, *Training in Community Relations*, chap. 12; Back, *Beyond Words*, pp. 7–10.

24. Coghill, *Sensitivity Training*, pp. 8–9.

25. Bradford, *Explorations in Human Relations Training*, pp. 13, 28, 14; Benne, "History of the T-Group," pp. 83–86.

26. Bradford, *Explorations in Human Relations Training*, pp. 4–5, 15–17.

27. Benne, "History of the T-Group," p. 84; Bradford, *Explorations in Human Relations Training*, pp. 14, 27, 29–30. See also Bennis and Schein, *Personal and Organizational Change*, chap. 2.

28. A summary of the educational theory behind lab training can be found in Bennis and Schein, *Personal and Organizational Change*, part 4.

29. Tannenbaum et al., *Leadership and Organization*, p. 123.

30. Benne, "History of the T-Group," p. 84; Bradford, *Explorations in Human Relations Training*, pp. 14, 27, 29–30. See also Bennis and Schein, *Personal and Organizational Change*, chap. 2.

31. Bradford, *Explorations in Human Relations Training*, pp. 35–46; "Where Executives Tear Off the Masks."

32. Benne, "History of the T-Group," pp. 99–100; Bennis and Schein, *Personal and Organizational Change*, pp. 201–3. See also Golembiewski, *Renewing Organizations*, pp. 319–24.

33. W. H. Whyte, *Organization Man*, part 1, esp. pp. 61, 54.

34. Benne, "History of the T-Group," pp. 92–99, 117–18; Bradford et al., "Two Educational Innovations," pp. 6–7; Back, *Beyond Words*, chaps. 9 and 10.

35. Bradford, "Biography," pp. 142–43; Benne, "History of the T-Group," pp. 117–18, 125–35; Bradford et al., "Two Educational Innovations," pp. 7–11. See also Golembiewski, *Renewing Organizations*, pp. 326, 328, 331.

36. Argyris, *Interpersonal Competence*, pp. 1–26, 50–51.

37. Ibid., pp. 36–37, 40–48; Argyris, "T-Groups for Organizational Effectiveness," pp. 60–61.

38. Argyris, *Interpersonal Competence*, pp. 131–44, 154–57; Argyris, "T-Groups for

Organizational Effectiveness," pp. 60–65, quote p. 61. See also Argyris, "Interpersonal Barriers to Decision-Making."

39. Kuriloff and Atkins, "T-Group for a Work Team," p. 64.

40. Rush, *Organization Development*, pp. 59–60.

41. Blake and Mouton, *Managerial Grid*, esp. pp. 265–85. Also see Blake and Mouton, "Instrumental Training Lab."

42. Rush, *Organization Development*, pp. 60–61.

43. Hampden-Turner, *Radical Man*.

44. Blake et al., "Union-Management Intergroup Laboratory."

45. Marrow, *Behind the Executive Mask*, p. 101; Bennis and Schein, *Personal and Organizational Change*, chap. 10. For the application of this type of training at TRW, see Poppy, "It's OK to Cry in the Office," pp. 68–76; S. Davis, "Organic Problem-Solving Method."

46. Thompson, *Modern Organization*, chap. 7; Goffman, *Presentation of Self*.

47. Klaw, "Two Weeks in a T-Group," p. 160; Back, *Beyond Words*, p. 70; Rush, *Behavioral Science*, statistics p. 44.

48. Pearse, *Manager to Manager*, pp. 2–3, 32–34.

49. Back, *Beyond Words*, pp. 192–93.

50. Argyris, *Interpersonal Competence*, pp. 239–56, 285; Buchanan, *Evaluating the Effectiveness of Laboratory Training*, p. 65; House, "T-Group Education," p. 23; Buchanan, "Laboratory Training and Organization Development," p. 472; Stogdill, *Handbook of Leadership*, p. 181; Stogdill and Bass, *Stogdill's Handbook of Leadership*, p. 561.

51. Dunnette and Campbell, "Laboratory Education," pp. 7, 8, 11–16.

52. Argyris, "Issues in Evaluating Laboratory Education."

53. Campbell and Dunnette, "Effectiveness of T-Group Exercises," pp. 99–101; Odiorne, "Trouble with Sensitivity Training," pp. 9–20. See also Stogdill, *Handbook of Leadership*, pp. 194–96. Argyris and Dunnette tried to resolve their disagreements with T-group methods; see Alderfer, "Conflict Resolution among Behavioral Scientists."

54. Gottschalk, "Psychoanalytic Notes on T-Groups"; Gottschalk and Pattison, "Psychiatric Perspectives on T-Groups"; Lubin and Zuckerman, "Level of Emotional Arousal in Laboratory Training"; Argyris, "In Defense of Laboratory Education"; National Training Laboratories, *Standards*.

55. Bunker, "Individual Applications of Laboratory Training."

56. Buchanan, "Laboratory Training and Organization Development," quote pp. 472, 476–77; Tannenbaum et al., *Leadership and Organization*, pp. 22–23; House, "T-Group Education," pp. 24–25; Stogdill, *Handbook of Leadership*, pp. 183, 192; Berger, "Selection and Training Effectiveness"; Steele, "Can T-Group Training Change the Power Structure?"

57. Powell and Stinson, "Worth of Laboratory Training," pp. 87–95; House, "T-Group Education," pp. 7–13; Stogdill, *Handbook of Leadership*, pp. 191–92, 198–99; Stogdill and Bass, *Stogdill's Handbook of Leadership*, p. 563.

58. Bass, "Anarchist Movement and the T-Group," quote pp. 215, 216 n. 3; Odiorne, "Trouble with Sensitivity Training," quote p. 19. See also Horwitz, "Training in Conflict Resolution"; Drotning, "Sensitivity Training Doesn't Work Magic."

59. Bennis, *Changing Organizations*, pp. 157, 160.

60. Maslow, *Eupsychian Management*, pp. 154–86.

61. L. A. Allen, "The T-Group," quote pp. 59–60; Odiorne, "Trouble with Sensitivity Training," pp. 18–19.

62. G. Allen, "Hate Therapy"; Steinbacker, *Child Seducers*; U.S. Congress, House, *Congressional Record*, 91st Cong., 1st sess., 10 June 1969, pp. 15322–35.

63. Back, *Beyond Words*, pp. 3–6, 14–16, 19, 47, 77–79, 82, 85–86, 96, 160–66, 170–73, 190, 204. See also Harvey, "Organization Development As a Religious Movement."

64. Klaw, "Two Weeks in a T-Group," quote p. 156; C. R. Rogers, "Process of the Basic Encounter Group"; Thomas and Smith, "T-Grouping"; Perrow, *Complex Organizations*, pp. 117–18.

65. C. W. Mills, "Contributions of Sociology," quote pp. 22–23.

66. Pagès, "Bethel Culture," pp. 267–84.

67. Dubin, "Psyche, Sensitivity, and Social Structure"; Herzberg, *Work and the Nature of Man*, pp. 185–87; Gomberg, "'Titillating Therapy.'"

68. Lippitt, "Small Group and Participatory Democracy."

69. Scott, "Schmidt Is Alive."

70. See Back, *Beyond Words*, p. 106; P. B. Smith, "Controlled Studies of the Outcome of Sensitivity Training"; P. B. Smith, "Why Successful Groups Succeed."

71. Bennis and Slater, "Democracy Is Inevitable"; Bennis, "Organizational Developments"; Bennis, "A Funny Thing Happened on the Way to the Future," esp. pp. 599–604; Bennis, "Who Sank the Yellow Submarine?"

72. Dowling, "Conversation with Chris Argyris," pp. 52–56.

73. In the late 1950s Japanese social scientists and managers duplicated the boys' club experiments in democratic leadership and came up with identical results; their findings influenced their use of corporatist management methods. See Blumberg, *Industrial Democracy*, pp. 47–48, 244 n. 7. See also S. Krupp, "Quality Circle Phenomenon," chap. 3.

Chapter 6

1. Special Task Force, *Work in America*, pp. 13, 17, 18–19, 22, chaps. 1 and 4.

2. See ibid., Appendix.

3. Although the history has not been traced, I have benefited from excellent studies by social scientists Carole Pateman, George Strauss, Philip Selznick, Rosabeth Moss Kanter, Alan Fox, and Michael Burawoy as well as by the social historian David F. Noble.

4. See Muhs, "Worker Participation in the Progressive Era"; Stabile, *Prophets of Order*.

5. Lesieur, *Scanlon Plan*; Goodwin, "Work Simplification"; Morgenson, *Common Sense Applied to Time and Motions Study*.

6. McGregor, *Human Side of Enterprise*, pp. 110–24.

7. See Walker, "Problem of the Repetitive Job"; Walker and Guest, *Man on the Assembly Line*. See Blumberg, *Industrial Democracy*, pp. 78–95, 102–19, 124–28.

8. Drucker, *Practice*, part 4, quote pp. 258, 270, 262, 280, 283–84, 296, 303–4, 310.

9. Sabel, *Work and Politics*, pp. 213–17. See following section, "From Job Enrichment to Quality Circle."

10. Maslow, "Theory of Human Motivation"; Maslow, *Motivation and Personality*.

11. See Levinson, "Various Approaches to Understanding Man at Work," pp. 618–28; Vroom and Deci, "Overview of Work Motivation."

12. McGregor, *Human Side of Enterprise*, pp. 46–48. Chris Argyris denied that self-actualization was a physiological need and thought it was a Western cultural imperative; see Argyris, *Personality and Organization*, pp. 48–52.

13. Herzberg, "One More Time."

14. McGregor, *Human Side of Enterprise*, pp. 191–92.

15. Argyris, *Integrating the Individual*, pp. 23–34, quote p. 157.

16. Herzberg et al., *Motivation to Work*, chaps. 3, 8, quote pp. 63, 113, 114–19; Herzberg, *Work and the Nature of Man*, chaps. 6, 7, quote pp. 85, 170, 178; Herzberg, "One More Time," pp. 366–67.

17. Herzberg, *Work and the Nature of Man*, chap. 4, quote p. 56; Herzberg et al., *Motivation to Work*, pp. 114–15, chaps. 3, 8; Herzberg, "One More Time," pp. 366–67.

18. Herzberg, *Work and the Nature of Man*, pp. 24–25, 29, 36–37; Herzberg et al., *Motivation to Work*, pp. 123–25.

19. McGregor, *Human Side of Enterprise*, pp. 33–35, 40–43.

20. Argyris, *Personality and Organization*, pp. 54–74, 123–37, quote p. 60.

21. Ibid., pp. 66–68, 123–36.

22. Ibid., chap. 4, quote pp. 122, 139.

23. Ibid., pp. 46, 141–43, 152–57, quote pp. 110, 155.

24. Likert, *New Patterns of Management*, pp. 14–15.

25. Herzberg et al., *Motivation to Work*, pp. 126–27, 115; Herzberg, *Work and the Nature of Man*, pp. 34–38.

26. Argyris, *Personality and Organization*, pp. 177–81.

27. Herzberg, *Work and the Nature of Man*, p. 177; see also Herzberg, "One More Time," pp. 367–76.

28. Herzberg, "One More Time," 367–76; Herzberg et al., *Motivation to Work*, pp. 135–38; Herzberg, *Work and the Nature of Man*, pp. 172–83, quote p. 175; Argyris, *Personality and Organization*, pp. 177–98, esp. p. 181; McGregor, *Human Side of Enterprise*, pp. 68, 103, 115, 124–31, 138.

29. Argyris, *Integrating the Individual*, esp. pp. 4–6, 194–96; Argyris, *Personality and Organization*, pp. 181, 188; McGregor, *Human Side of Enterprise*, pp. 46–50, 68.

30. See Pateman, *Participation and Democratic Theory*, esp. chap. 4. See also Jenkins, *Job Power*, pp. 5, 241–43.

31. McGregor, *Human Side of Enterprise*, pp. 107, 158, 69, 46, 24, 3.

32. Argyris, *Personality and Organization*, pp. 178–88.

33. Herzberg et al., *Motivation to Work*, pp. 136–37; see also Herzberg, "One More Time," pp. 53–62.

34. McGregor, *Human Side of Enterprise*, pp. 126–30.

35. Argyris, *Integrating the Individual*, pp. 3–4, 194–96; Argyris, *Personality and Organization*, pp. 177, 188.

36. Likert, *New Patterns of Management*, pp. 99–116; 166–72, 182–87; 212–13; see also Likert, *Human Organization*.

37. Herzberg, *Work and the Nature of Man*, pp. 182–83; Herzberg et al., *Motivation to Work*, p. 138.

38. McGregor, *Human Side of Enterprise*, p. 56.

39. See Jenkins, *Job Power*, chaps 11, 13. Corporative mandarins could have learned from the Western European experience with codetermination and management-union cooperation. That they did not shows their lack of concern with unions and reforms that managers could not unilaterally apply. Like the managers to whom they were selling ideas, they believed unions were unfortunate, unnatural creations of Taylorized jobs; unions were symptoms of the problem, not part of the solution. They apparently expected unions to fade away when managers achieved harmony.

40. See ibid. Also see Rice, *Productivity and Social Organization*, pp. 3–4, 250–53; Trist et al., *Organizational Choice*, pp. xii–xiii, 6–7, 294; Trist and Bamforth, "Some Social and Psychological Consequences."

41. See Likert, *New Patterns of Management*, pp. 37–38, 93. For ideas in the Tavistock mode, see Davis and Taylor, *Design of Jobs*.

42. Berg, Freedman, and Freeman, *Managers and Work Reform*, pp. 11, 8–14.

43. Preston and Post, "Third Managerial Revolution."

44. Fox, *Beyond Contract*, esp. pp. 25–37, 74–79, 82–83, 336–37, 116–17, 338–43. See also A. Friedman, *Industry and Labour*, pp. 6–7, 77–102.

45. See Watson, *Sociology, Work and Industry*, pp. 41–44; Hill, *Competition and Control at Work*, pp. 86–88, 90.

46. Argyris, *Personality and Organization*, pp. 83–84. Argyris quotes Robert A. Merton's definition of alienation; Merton had been one of the Harvard group that rediscovered Durkheim during the 1930s and had written some of the first American articles on anomie. See Merton, "Durkheim's Division." See also Argyris, "Is Capitalism the Culprit?"

47. Blauner, *Alienation and Freedom*, chap. 2, quote p. 15. Blauner's book was a popular college text. The passage here was quoted in Special Task Force, *Work in America*, p. 22.

48. Blauner, *Alienation and Freedom*, esp. pp. 183–86; Hill, *Competition and Control at Work*, pp. 101–2.

49. Herzberg, *Work and the Nature of Man*, p. vii; Herzberg et al., *Motivation to Work*, pp. ix, 6; Likert, *New Patterns of Management*, pp. 1–3; Argyris, *Personality and Organization*, p. 5; McGregor, *Human Side of Enterprise*, pp. 10, 11.

50. Strauss, "Human Relations"; Selznick, *Law, Society and Individual Justice*, pp. 116–20.

51. Rush, *Behavioral Science*, pp. 9–10.

52. Kanter, "Work in a New America," pp. 72, 49; Levitan and Johnston, *Work Is Here to Stay*, pp. 56–57, 73–74. These two works provide useful information about work and workers during the postwar era.

53. See note 52. See also Strauss, "Job Satisfaction," p. 24; quote from *New York Times* (April 2, 1972), as cited in Braverman, *Labor and Monopoly Capital*, p. 35.

54. Levitan and Johnston, *Work Is Here to Stay*, p. 62.

55. Kanter, "Work in a New America," p. 49; see also Gutman, *Work, Culture and Society*, pp. 3–78.

56. Bell, *Cultural Contradictions of Capitalism*.

57. Matusow, *Unraveling of America*, chaps. 10, 11; Kanter, "Work in a New America," pp. 60–64, 67; Jenkins, *Job Power*, pp. 9–53.

58. Kanter, "Work in a New America," pp. 49–60; Kanter, *Men and Women of the Corporation*, pp. 161–62; Strauss, "Job Satisfaction, Motivation, and Job Design," pp. 28–34; Levitan and Johnston, *Work Is Here to Stay*, pp. 17–18, 77, chap. 4.

59. Kanter, "Work in a New America," p. 68; Levitan and Johnston, *Work Is Here to Stay*, pp. 69–70.

60. Levitan and Johnston, *Work Is Here to Stay*, pp. 16–17, 67, 69–70.

61. Kilbridge, "Turnover, Absence, and Transfer Rates."

62. Levitan and Johnston, *Work Is Here to Stay*, p. 77.

63. Naples, "Industrial Conflict," esp. chart p. 38.

64. Zernan, "Organized Labor."

65. See Edwards, *Contested Terrain*, pp. 152–59; Burawoy, *Manufacturing Consent*, p. 175; Naples, "Industrial Conflict"; Zernan, "Organized Labor." Especially see Gordon et al., *Segmented Work, Divided Workers*, pp. 215–22; Weir, "Rebellion in American Labor's Rank and File."

66. "Sabotage at Lordstown?"; "Spreading Lordstown Syndrome"; Widick, "Men Won't Toe the Vega Line"; Garson, "Luddites in Lordstown"; Kremen, "Lordstown"; Aronowitz, *False Promises*, pp. 21–50.

67. "Boredom on the Assembly Line"; "Who Wants to Work?"; Garson, "The Hell with Work."

68. See Terkel, *Working*; Jenkins, *Job Power*; Sheppard and Herrick, *Where Have All the Robots Gone?*; Garson, *All the Livelong Day*; Serrin, *Company and the Union*; Gooding, *Job Revolution*; Sennett and Cobb, *Hidden Injuries of Class*; Barkin, *Worker Militancy and Its Consequences*.

69. S. 3916 92d Cong., 2d sess., proposal for "Worker Alienation Research and Technical Assistance Act of 1972."

70. Janson, "Job Enrichment"; Walton, "How to Counter Alienation"; Gooding, "Wake Up the Blue-Collar Worker," pp. 133–35, 158–68; L. Davis, "Coming Crisis for Production Management."

71. Davis and Cherns, *Quality of Working Life.*

72. See esp. Myers, "Every Employee a Manager."

73. Gooding, "Wake Up the Blue-Collar Worker," p. 162.

74. Myers and Gomersall, "Break Through in On-the-Job Training"; Myers, "Every Employee a Manager"; Myers, *Every Employee a Manager*; Myers, "Overcoming Union Opposition"; Myers, "Adapting to the New Work Ethic"; Roche and MacKinnon, "Motivating People with Meaningful Work," p. 101.

75. Lawler, "Job Design and Employee Motivation"; J. W. Anderson, "Impact of Technology"; Whitsett, "Unenriched Jobs"; Ford, "Job Enrichment Lessons."

76. Myers, "Every Employee a Manager," quote p. 73. See also Whitsett, "Unenriched Jobs," pp. 74–75, 80; Ford, "Job Enrichment Lessons," p. 105; Myers, "Overcoming Union Opposition."

77. The plant Burawoy investigated was a machine shop in which individual workers set up their own machines and control was indirect; he believed that his findings shed light on job enrichment. See Burawoy, *Manufacturing Consent*, pp. 94, 180–83, 194.

78. Ibid., pp. xii, 5, 27, 64, 72, 81, 85–86, 92–93.

79. Gooding, "Wake Up the Blue-Collar Worker," p. 133.

80. Walton, "How to Counter Alienation"; Myers, "Who Are Your Motivated Workers?"; Ford, *Motivation through Work*, pp. 13–23, 188–89; Jenkins, *Job Power*, chap. 12; Rush, *Job Design for Motivation.*

81. *Wall Street Journal* (August 21, 1972), cited in Braverman, *Work and Monopoly Capital*, pp. 36–37; Reif et al., "Job Enrichment"; Luthans and Reif, "Job Enrichment."

82. The literature on Maslow is extensive; esp. see Wahba and Bridwell, "Maslow Reconsidered."

83. Again the literature is vast. Esp. see Luthans and Knod, "Critical Factors in Job Enrichment"; Vroom, *Work and Motivation*, pp. 127–29; Lawler, *Pay and Organizational Effectiveness*, pp. 32–33, 38–42. See also C. N. Green, "The Satisfaction-Performance Controversy"; Perrow, *Complex Organizations*, pp. 106–15.

84. See Perrow, *Complex Organizations*, pp. 106–15; Lawler, "Job Design and Employee Motivation."

85. See Hulin and Blood, "Job Enlargement"; Pierce and Dunham, "Task Design." See also Strauss, "Job Satisfaction," pp. 24–34; Fein, "Job Enrichment"; Steinmetz and Greenridge, "Realities."

86. Maslow, *Eupsychian Management*, pp. 7, 41, 139–40, 150–53. See section "For and against MBO" in Chapter 4.

87. Goldman, *Work Experiment*, quote p. 31. Actually, careful reading of this interesting little book shows that the experiment did not necessarily prove the incompatibility of Americans and job enrichment.

88. Fein, "Job Enrichment," pp. 69–88; Levitan and Johnston, *Work Is Here to Stay*, pp. 153–54.

89. McMurray, "Management's Achilles Heel."

90. Strauss, "Notes On Power Equalization," pp. 41–55; Fein, "Job Enrichment," pp. 69–88; Reif and Luthans, "Does Job Enrichment Really Pay Off?," p. 36; Kaplan et al., "Job Enrichment."

91. Winpisinger, "Job Enrichment."

92. Gomberg, "Job Satisfaction."

93. Quotation from Zwerdling, *Workplace Democracy*, pp. 167–70; see also Schappe, "Twenty-Two Arguments against Job Enrichment"; Blum et al., "Effects of Motivational Programs."

94. Zwerdling, *Workplace Democracy*, pp. 168, 175; White, "Innovations in Job Design"; Bluestone, "Comments on Job Enrichment"; UAW, "Summary of Agreement."

95. See Pierce and Dunham, "Task Design"; Fein, "Job Enrichment."

96. Strauss, "Notes on Power Equalization," p. 55; Derber, "Crosscurrents in Worker Participation"; Haire, Ghiselli, and Porter, "International Study."

97. Fitzgerald, "Why Motivation Theory Doesn't Work," p. 43.

98. Luthans and Reif, "Job Enrichment," pp. 34–35.

99. "Where Being Nice to Workers Didn't Work."

100. Steinmetz and Greenridge, "Realities," pp. 25, 26, 32; see also Wilcox, "Hierarchy, Human Nature and the Participation Panacea."

101. Duncan, "Transferring Management Theory to Practice"; Durand, "Citation Count Analysis"; Bowman, "Behavioral Sciences"; J. C. Taylor, "Job Design Criteria." See also Piore, "Impact of the Labor Market."

102. Levitan and Johnston, *Work Is Here to Stay*, p. 148.

103. Ibid., pp. 145–51, 79; Bowman, "Behavioral Sciences," p. 397.

104. Noble, *Forces of Production*, chap. 13, quote p. 321. See also Zimbalist, "Limits of Work Humanization."

105. Miles, "Human Relations or Human Resources?"; see also J. J. Morse, "Contingency Look at Job Design."

106. Such changes have also been noted by Whitsett and Yorks, *From Management Theory to Business Sense*, p. 230.

107. Herzberg, *Managerial Choice*.

108. L. Davis, "Job Design"; Davis and Taylor, *Design of Jobs*, pp. 104–18; Davis and Cherns, *Quality of Working Life*, 1:12–54.

109. Lawler and Hackman, "Corporate Profits and Employee Satisfaction." See also T. Mills, "Human Resources."

110. Dowling, "Job Redesign on the Assembly Line."

111. Sabel, *Work and Politics*, pp. 194–225; Reich, *Next American Frontier*, pp. 127–30, 133–36. See also Piore and Sabel, *Second Industrial Divide*, esp. chaps. 7, 10, 11; Sabel and Zeitlin, "Historical Alternatives to Mass Production."

112. See esp. Williams et al., "End of Mass Production?" Also see Hounshell, *From the American System*, chap. 7; Shaiken, *Work Transformed*.

113. Yorks, *Radical Approach to Job Enrichment*, pp. 195–96, chaps. 1–2; Yorks, *Job Enrichment Revisited*, pp. 7–8, 11–12, 32–36.

114. Drucker, "Coming Rediscovery of Scientific Management."

115. Whitsett and Yorks, *From Management Theory to Business Sense*, esp. pp. 4–10, 223–33, chaps. 11–14. See also Penzer, "Bridging the Industrial Engineering/Behavioral Science Gap," pp. 696–701.

Chapter 7

1. Servan-Schreiber, *American Challenge*.

2. Historian John W. Dower, overlooking recent attempts to imitate the Japanese, mistakenly argued that persistent racism has caused Americans to denigrate them as "economic animals" whose success rested on "some nondiscursive realm of intuition and quasi-mystical bonding unique to the Japanese"; see Dower, *War without Mercy*, pp. 312–17, quote p. 312.

3. They read the samurai Clauswitz, Musashi, *Book of Five Rings*. See also the samurai Dale Carnegie, D. J. Rogers, *Fighting to Win*.

4. See "Management—Japan," *Business Periodicals Index* (New York, 1969–86); the annual issues run from August to July.

5. Since this chapter is about American perceptions, I do not intend to offer new truths about the "real" nature of Japanese management. I relied primarily on the work of Robert Cole and, to a lesser degree, Andrew Gordon as a guide to Japanese labor relations. Moreover, other important subjects in the enormous American literature on Japan, such as how industrial policy affected Japan's economic growth or how to do business with the Japanese, are more or less ignored.

6. Rehder, "What American and Japanese Managers Are Learning," p. 70.

7. Abegglen, *Strategy of Japanese Business*, pp. xvii, 71.

8. See Noda, *How Japan Absorbed American Management*, pp. 22–23.

9. Harbison, "Management in Japan," quote pp. 254, 264; Yoshino, *Japan's Managerial System*, pp. 226–27, 230. Herman Kahn has said that publishers were initially reluctant to print Abegglen's book because they could not believe the seniority system existed, let alone that it worked; see Kahn, *Emerging Japanese Superstate*, p. 84.

10. See Yoshino, *Japan's Managerial System*, pp. 258–69.

11. Harbison, "Management in Japan," pp. 249, 264. See also, Yoshino, *Japan's Managerial System*, p. 274, chap. 9; Bennett, "Japanese Economic Growth."

12. Abegglen, *Japanese Factory*, esp. pp. 70, 98–100, chaps. 8, 7.

13. Brown, "Japanese Management," pp. 428–42, quote pp. 440, 442.

14. Rohlen, *For Harmony and Strength*, esp. pp. 13–16, 58–60, 261–68.

15. See Fruin, "Japanese Company Controversy." Fruin lists the literature in the controversy on pp. 268–69. These sorts of criticisms caused Abegglen to downplay the traditional origins of Japanese practices in the second edition of his book; see Abegglen, *Management and Worker* (1973).

16. Cole, *Japanese Blue Collar*, pp. 116–17, 218, 79–80, quote pp. 175, 103, 172.

17. Ibid., pp. 116–25, chaps. 3, 8.

18. W. F. Whyte, *Men at Work*, pp. 65–67.

19. Long and Seo, *Management in Japan and India*, pp. vii, 255–56. See also Oh, "Japanese Management."

20. Dore, *British Factory*.

21. Noda, *How Japan Absorbed American Management*, p. 24.

22. Drucker, "What We Can Learn."

23. Goldston, "What We Can Learn from Japan"; Diebold, "Management Can Learn from Japan," quote p. 14.

24. Brzezinski, *Fragile Blossom*, chap. 3., quote pp. 50–51.

25. Marsh and Mannari, *Modernization and the Japanese Factory*, chap. 12, esp. pp. 336–37.

26. Kraar, "Japanese Are Coming."

27. Johnson and Ouchi, "Made in America."

28. "Japan's Ways Thrive in the U.S.," pp. 156, 160.

29. Cole, "Learning from the Japanese," pp. 22–23.

30. Cole, "Learning from the Japanese," p. 28; Schleicher, "Quality Control Circles"; Ross and Ross, *Japanese Quality Circles*, pp. 14–17.

31. Ron Howard's *Gung Ho* (Paramount, 1986) is a misleading film of mainly historical interest; it portrays the contemporary love-hate for Japanese business, presents popular caricatures of Japanese managers and American workers, and uses sports metaphors to describe both corporatism and class consciousness.

32. See Lodge, "Top Priority," and his *New American Ideology*. For his recent ideas, see *American Disease* and Lodge and Vogel, *Ideology and National Competitiveness*.

33. E. F. Vogel, *Japan As Number One*, p. xi, also pp. 129, 234.

34. Lodge and Vogel, *Ideology and National Competitiveness*.

35. E. F. Vogel, *Japan As Number One*, esp. chaps. 6 and 10, quote pp. x, 3, 129, 157, 234–36.

36. Pascale and Athos, *Art of Japanese Management*, esp. chaps. 3 and 5, also pp. 23–25, 79–86, quote pp. 20, 23, 86.

37. Ibid., esp. chaps. 2 and 4, quote pp. 39, 53, 57.

38. Ibid., chap. 5, also pp. 198–99, 79–84, quote pp. 205, 206. They helped develop the idea of "excellent companies" while working for the consulting firm of McKinsey and Company; for more on this, see Peters and Waterman, *In Search of Excellence*.

39. See Pegels, *Japan vs. the West*, quote pp. 26, 45, 67, also chap. 11; Alston, *American Samurai*, pp. 87–108, quote pp. 89, 90, 92; Sours, "Influence of Japanese Culture," quote p. 29; Lange, "Participative Management."

40. See Hall and Leidecker, "Is Japanese-Style Management Anything New?"; Mai-Dalton, "Traditional Japanese Management"; Hatvany and Pucik, "Integrated Management System."

41. Ouchi, *Theory Z*; W. Bowen, "Lessons from Behind the Kimono," pp. 247–48.

42. Ouchi, *Theory Z*, pp. vii–ix, 230–36.

43. Ibid., esp. chap. 3, quote pp. 56, 166–67. See also Ouchi, "Markets, Bureaucracies, and Clans."

44. Ouchi, *Theory Z*, esp. pp. 58–59, 89–95, 27–29.

45. Ibid., chaps. 1 and 2, esp. pp. 5–9, 29–31, 49–59, 67–70.

46. Ibid., pp. 112, 133–34, 135.

47. For instance, see Moran, "Japanese Participative Management." Ezra Vogel used the phrase *bottoms-up management*, which conjures up a very different image of superior-subordinate relations; see E. F. Vogel, *Japan As Number One*, p. 134.

48. Robbins, "Theory Z Organization." See also Hatvany and Pucik, "Integrated Management System."

49. Ouchi, *Theory Z*, pp. 105–6, 229.

50. Gibney, *Miracle by Design*, pp. 193–94.

51. Ringle, "The American Who Remade 'Made in Japan'"; Halberstam, *The Reckoning*, chap. 17; Deming, "What Can American Manufacturers Learn?"; Lohr, "Consultant on Quality."

52. See note 51. Juran outlined his ideas in "QC Circle Phenomenon," "Japanese and Western Quality," "Product Quality," and *Juran on Planning*.

53. Cole, *Work, Mobility, and Participation*, chap. 7; Takezawa, "Quality of Working Life." See also Imaizumi, "Past and Present Status"; Yamamoto, "Tradition and Management."

54. The best sociology on quality circles in Japan was done by Robert Cole, who studied their operation in a Toyota plant. See Cole, *Work, Mobility, and Participation*, chap. 7; also his "Learning from the Japanese."

55. Juran, "QC Circle Phenomenon."

56. Juran, "Japanese and Western Quality"; Juran, "Product Quality."

57. Cole, "Learning from the Japanese," p. 28; Cole, "Japanese Management Import"; Sethi et al., *False Promise*, chap. 9; Parker, *Inside the Circle*, p. 8.

58. Ross and Ross, *Japanese Quality Circles*, pp. 27–28, 100–102, 102–4, quote pp. 37, 102; Dreyfack, *Making It in Management*, pp. 145–46, 157–58, chaps. 4, 7; Barra, *Putting Quality Circles to Work*, chaps. 2, 3, quote p. 42. See also Hranac and Brannen, "What, Where, and Whys"; Callahan, "Quality Circles."

59. Ross and Ross, *Japanese Quality Circles*, chaps. 1, 2, quote pp. xiii–iv, 34; Dreyfack, *Making It in Management*, quote p. 104; Barra, *Putting Quality Circles to Work*, chaps. 2, 3.

60. Dreyfack, *Making It in Management*, chap. 5, quote p. 114; Barra, *Putting Quality Circles to Work*, chap. 1; Ross and Ross, *Japanese Quality Circles*, chaps. 3–4; Konz, "Quality Circles"; Amsden and Amsden, "A Look at QC Circles"; McClenahen, "Bringing Home Japan's Lesson," pp. 56–65.

61. Juran, "Japanese and Western Quality," p. 42; Pegels, *Japan vs. the West*, chap. 5. For other examples, see Ross and Ross, *Japanese Quality Circles*; Barra, *Putting Quality Circles to Work*; J. Nelson, "Quality Circles Become Contagious."

62. Cole, *Work, Mobility, and Participation*, chaps. 4, 8, and esp. 7; Cole, "Learning from the Japanese," pp. 27–28, 38–41; Cole, "Japanese Management Import," quote p. 30.

63. Alston, *American Samurai*, pp. 31–32, 38–47, 56–59, 108–14, 117–18, 121, 216–24; Alston, "Awarding Bonuses the Japanese Way"; Ross and Ross, *Japanese Quality Circles*, chaps. 7, 8; Barra, *Putting Quality Circles to Work*, chaps. 5–7.

64. See Alston, *American Samurai*, chap. 7, quote p. 229; Cole, *Work, Mobility, and Participation*, pp. 255–63.

65. Gibney, *Japan*. See Schuppener, "Rehabilitation of the Corporatist Model," pp. 139–43.

66. Gibney, *Miracle by Design*, pp. 6, 11.

67. Ibid., pp. 12, 14–15, 20, 76, 151–53, 219–20, 222–23.

68. Ibid., pp. 7–9, 10, 12, 15–16, 20, 31–33, 53–54, 70, 88, 161, 202, 187–88.

69. David Tucker, a historian of contemporary Japan, has suggested to me that Americans have been most attracted to the aristocratic parts of Japanese culture and have felt none of the embarrassment in mimicking samurai that they would have felt imitating European nobles; karate, for instance, was not ridiculous like jousting. Perhaps this helps explain why mandarins turned to Japan rather than a dynamic Western European economy. Not only did Japan have far fewer independent unions than Germany and Italy, but sushi was higher class than beer and pizza.

70. See Ron Mitchell, "Rediscovering Our Roots."

71. Drucker, *Frontiers of Management*, pp. 220–21, 226. See also Leflufy, "Secret of Japanese Management"; Nadler, "What Japan Learned from the U.S."

72. Gordon, *Evolution of Labor Relations in Japan*, pp. 1–8, chaps. 9, 10.

73. Ibid., pp. 395–97, 400–401, 411, 432.

74. Cole, *Work, Mobility, and Participation*, p. 263.

75. Ozawa, "Japanese Chic."

76. Abegglen, *Strategy of Japanese Business*, pp. 76–77.

77. For a brief explanation of Japanese growth, see Hirschmeier and Yui, *Development of Japanese Business*, pp. 292–99. For these sorts of lessons drawn by Americans, see Abegglen and Stalk, *Kaisha*; Keys and Miller, "Japanese Management Theory Jungle"; Hayes, "Why Japanese Factories Work," quote p. 66; Wheelwright, "Japan"; Davidson, *Amazing Race*; Hall, *Zero Inventories*; Schonberger, *Japanese Manufacturing Techniques*. On industrial policy, see Schuppener, "Rehabilitation of the Corporatist Model," chaps. 6 and 7.

78. Sethi et al., *False Promise*, chap. 4.

79. England, "Japanese and American Management"; Sethi et al., *False Promise*, chaps. 5 and 6, esp. pp. 119–20, 125–28, 139, quote p. 138. See also Sullivan and Kameda, "Concept of Profit."

80. Juran, "Japanese and Western Quality," pp. 59–60.

81. Sullivan, "Critique of Theory Z."

82. Takezawa and Whitehill, *Work Ways*, pp. 178, 5–6, chaps. 3, 5, 6. See also

Pascale, "Personnel Practices and Employee Attitudes"; Lincoln et al., "Cultural Orientations and Individual Reactions."

83. Bruce-Biggs, "Dangerous Folly."

84. Versagi, "What American Labor/Management Can Learn."

85. See Cole, *Japanese Blue Collar*, chap. 7, quote p. 257; Rohlen, *For Harmony and Strength*, chap. 8.

86. According to this, "Type Os are born achievers, Type As are deep thinkers, Type Bs are highly creative, and Type ABs are natural problem solvers." Ouchi, strangely suspicious of Western social science, said this "sounds as good as anything we have got in psychology." See "Now from Japan."

87. Takagi, *Flaw in Japanese Management*, chaps. 5, 6, 7, esp. pp. 3, 86, 89, 93.

88. See Schein, "Does Japanese Management Style Have a Message?"; Woronoff, *Japan*, chap. 2, esp. pp. 37–50, quote pp. 44–50; Bruce-Biggs, "Dangerous Folly," quote p. 53; L. Smith, "Japan's Autocratic Managers"; Maitland, "Organizational Structure and Innovation," pp. 55–64.

89. Sethi et al., *False Promise*, pp. 48–52, chap. 10.

90. Ibid., pp. 201–26, esp. pp. 207–9, 212; Briggs, "Japanese at Work."

91. Reich, "Profession of Management," quote pp. 30, 31; Levitan and Johnson, "Labor and Management," quote p. 8.

92. Parker, *Inside the Circle*, esp. part 1, chaps. 12 and 15, quote pp. 24, 29; Parker and Slaughter, *Choosing Sides*, chaps. 1–3, 8–9, quote pp. 19, 48–49. The latter book has several case studies of the circles' use in Japanese subsidiaries, American companies, and joint American and Japanese ventures. For the legal issues, see Sockell, "Legality of Employee-Participation Programs"; Ferguson and Gaal, "Codetermination."

93. Reich, "Profession of Management," pp. 30, 31; Parker and Slaughter, *Choosing Sides*, esp. chap. 5; Levitan and Johnson, "Labor and Management."

94. M. J. Wolf, *Japanese Conspiracy*, quote pp. 15, 16, 104, 115, 231, 233, 234, 246, 247. For a similar portrait of a Toyota plant written by a Japanese journalist who worked there, see Kamata, *Japan in the Passing Lane*.

Conclusion

1. See Halpern et al., "Taylorism Revisited and Revised"; Austin, "How to Position Yourself"; Hummel, "Behind Quality Management"; Chanaron and Perrin, "Science, Technology, and Work Organization"; Helfgott, "Moving beyond Taylorism."

2. Pinchot, *Intrapreneuring*, pp. 202–11, 298, 320, 317.

3. Ibid., pp. 9, 207, 217, 234–35, 244.

4. Ibid., pp. 247–48, 309, 311–15, 320.

5. Peters, "Drucker," p. 16.

6. Russell Mitchell, "Managing Innovation."

7. Pinchot, *Intrapreneuring*, p. 310.

8. See Wolff, "Managers at Work"; McPherson, "Innovation and Creativity"; Rich, "'Skunk Works' Management Style."

9. Lee and Zemke, "'Intrapreneuring.'"

10. Blasi, *Employee Ownership*, pp. 24, 17, chaps. 1–2.

11. Ibid., pp. xi–xii; Farrell and Hoerr, "ESOPs."

12. Blasi, *Employee Ownership*, pp. 160–61, 114, 124, 132, 135–36, 179–80, 208, 241. See also Frug, "Ideology of Bureaucracy."

13. Hoerr, "Payoff from Teamwork," p. 62.

14. Reich, *Next American Frontier*, chaps. 11, 12.

15. Blasi, *Employee Ownership*, pp. 169–70, chap. 9.

16. Veblen, *Higher Learning in America*.

17. See Sass, "Managerial Ideology."

18. See Frug, "Ideology of Bureaucracy in American Law," pp. 1277–1388; Jacoby, *Employing Bureaucracy*.

19. Noble, *Forces of Production*.

20. Green, "Kantian Evaluation."

21. Hawley, "Herbert Hoover"; Hawley, *Great War*; Alchon, *Invisible Hand of Planning*.

22. See Overvold, "Imperative of Organizational Harmony."

23. Matejka and Ashworth, "Employee's Hierarchy of Greeds."

24. Hartz, *Liberal Tradition*.

25. See Gomberg, "Historical Roots."

26. Lawrence and Lorsch, *Organization and Environment*.

27. McCloskey, "Limits of Expertise," quote p. 399.

28. Barrett, *Illusion of Technique*, see esp. chap. 2, quote p. 25.

29. See McCloskey, "Limits of Expertise," esp. pp. 402–5, and Barrett, *Illusion of Technique*, esp. pp. 113–16, 117, 242. Also see MacIntyre, *After Virtue*, esp. chaps. 7, 8.

Bibliography

Primary Sources

Ackoff, Russell L. "The Art and Science of Mess Management." *Interfaces* 17 (1981): 20–26.

——. *Creating the Corporate Future: Plan or Be Planned For.* New York: Wiley, 1981.

——. "The Development of Operations Research As a Science." *Operations Research* 4 (1956): 265–95.

——. "The Future of Operational Research Is Past." *Journal of the Operational Research Society* 30 (1979): 93–104.

——. "Resurrecting the Future of Operational Research." *Journal of the Operational Research Society* 30 (1979): 189–99.

——. *Scientific Method.* New York: Wiley, 1962.

Ackoff, Russell L., and Patrick Rivett. *A Manager's Guide to Operations Research.* New York: Wiley, 1963.

Alderfer, Clayton P. "Conflict Resolution among Behavioral Scientists." *Professional Psychology* 3 (Winter 1972): 41–47.

Allen, Gary. "Hate Therapy: Sensitivity Training for Planned Change." *American Opinion*, January 1968, pp. 73–86.

Allen, Louis A. "The T-Group: Short Cut or Short Circuit." *Business Horizons* 16 (August 1973): 53–64.

Alston, Jon P. *The American Samurai: Blending American and Japanese Managerial Practices.* New York: Walter de Gruyter, 1986.

——. "Awarding Bonuses in the Japanese Way." *Business Horizons* 25 (September–October 1982): 46–50.

American Management Association. "Progress in Industrial Operations Research, Results of a Survey." *Management News*, December 1957, pp. 12–17.

Amsden, David M., and Robert T. Amsden. "A Look at QC Circles." *Tooling and Production* (June 1980): 102–6.

Anderson, J. W. "The Impact of Technology on Job Enrichment." *Personnel* 47 (September–October 1970): 29–37.

Anderson, William S. "What We Are Learning from Japan." *Nation's Business* 69 (March 1981): 39–41.

Argyris, Chris. "In Defense of Laboratory Education." *Training Directors Journal* 17 (October 1963): 21–23.

———. *Integrating the Individual and the Organization.* New York: Wiley, 1964.

———. "Interpersonal Barriers to Decision-Making." *Harvard Business Review* 44 (March 1966): 84–97.

———. *Interpersonal Competence and Organizational Effectiveness.* Homewood, Ill.: Dorsey, 1962.

———. "Is Capitalism the Culprit?" *Organizational Dynamics* 6 (Spring 1978): 2–19.

———. "Issues in Evaluating Laboratory Education." *Industrial Relations* 8 (October 1968): 28–40.

———. *Personality and Organization: The Conflict between the System and the Individual.* New York: Harper and Row, 1957.

———. "Some Limits of Rational Man Organization Theory." *Public Administration Review* 33 (May–June 1973): 253–67.

———. "T-Groups for Organizational Effectiveness." *Harvard Business Review* 42 (March 1964): 60–74.

Austin, Nancy K. "How to Position Yourself As a Leader." *Working Woman,* November 1988, pp. 140–44.

Barnard, Chester I. *The Functions of the Executive.* Cambridge, Mass.: Harvard University Press, 1938.

Barra, Ralph. *Putting Quality Circles to Work: A Practical Strategy for Boosting Productivity and Profits.* New York: McGraw-Hill, 1983.

Bass, Bernard M. "The Anarchist Movement and the T-Group: Some Possible Lessons for Organizational Development." *Journal of Applied Behavioral Science* 3 (April 1967): 211–27.

√ Benne, Kenneth D. "Democratic Ethics in Social Engineering." *Progressive Education* 26 (May 1949): 201–7.

√ ———. "History of the T-Group in the Laboratory Setting." In *T-Group Theory and Laboratory Method: Innovation in Re-education,* edited by Leland P. Bradford, Jack R. Gibb, and Kenneth D. Benne, pp. 80–135. New York: Wiley, 1964.

Bennis, Warren G. *Changing Organizations.* New York: McGraw-Hill, 1966.

———. "A Funny Thing Happened on the Way to the Future." *American Psychologist* 25 (July 1970): 595–608.

———. "Organizational Developments and the Fate of Bureaucracy." *Industrial Management Review* 7 (1966): 41–55.

———. "Who Sank the Yellow Submarine?" *Psychology Today,* November 1972, p. 120.

Bennis, Warren G., and Edgar H. Schein. *Personal and Organizational Change through Group Methods.* New York: Wiley, 1965.

Bennis, Warren G., and Philip E. Slater. "Democracy Is Inevitable." *Harvard Business Review* 42 (March–April 1964): 45–57.

Berger, Melvyn. "Selection and Training Effectiveness." In *Group Training Techniques*, edited by Melvyn Berger and Pam Berger, pp. 148–54. New York: Wiley, 1972.

Bevan, R. G. "The Language of Operational Research." *Operational Research Quarterly* 27 (1976): 305–13.

Bevan, R. G., and R. A. Bryer. "On Measuring the Contribution of OR." *Journal of the Operational Research Society* 29 (1978): 409–19.

Blackett, P. M. S. "Operational Research." *Advancement of Science* 5 (April 1948): 26–37.

Blake, Robert R., and Jane S. Mouton. "The Instrumental Training Lab." In *Issues in Human Relations Training*, edited by I. R. Weschler and Edgar H. Schein, pp. 61–76. Washington, D.C.: National Training Laboratories, 1962.

———. *The Managerial Grid*. Houston: Gulf, 1964.

Blake, Robert R., Jane S. Mouton, and Richard L. Sloma. "The Union-Management Intergroup Laboratory: Strategy for Resolving Intergroup Conflict." *Journal of Applied Behavioral Science* 1 (January 1965): 25–57.

Blasi, Joseph R. *Employee Ownership: Revolution or Ripoff?* Cambridge, Mass.: Ballinger, 1988.

Blauner, Robert. *Alienation and Freedom: The Factory Worker and His Industry*. Chicago: University of Chicago Press, 1964.

Bluestone, Irving. "Comments on Job Enrichment." *Organizational Dynamics* 2 (Winter 1974): 46–47.

Blum, Albert, Michael Moore, and B. Parker Fairey. "The Effects of Motivational Programs on Collective Bargaining." *Personnel Journal* 52 (July 1973): 633–41.

Bonaparte, Tony H., and John E. Flaherty, eds. *Peter Drucker: Contributions to Business Enterprise*. New York: New York University Press, 1970.

Bonder, Seth. "Changing the Future of Operations Research." *Operations Research* 27 (March–April 1979): 209–24.

"Boredom on the Assembly Line." *Life*, September 1, 1972, pp. 30–38.

Bowen, William. "Lessons from Behind the Kimono." *Fortune*, June 15, 1981, pp. 247–50.

Bowman, Edward H., and Robert B. Fetter. *Analysis for Production Management*. Homewood, Ill.: Irwin, 1957.

Bowman, James S. "The Behavioral Sciences: Fact and Fantasy in Organizations." *Personnel Journal* 55 (August 1976): 395–97.

Bradford, Leland P. "Biography of an Institution." *Journal of Applied Behavioral Science* 3 (April 1967): 127–34.

———. *Explorations in Human Relations Training: An Assessment of Experience, 1947–53*. Washington, D.C.: National Education Association, 1953.

Bradford, Leland P., Jack R. Gibb, and Kenneth D. Benne. "Two Educational Innovations." In *T-Group Theory and Laboratory Method: Innovation in Re-education*, edited by Leland P. Bradford, Jack R. Gibb, and Kenneth D. Benne, pp. 1–14. New York: Wiley, 1964.

———, eds. T-Group Theory and Laboratory Method: Innovation in Re-education. New York: Wiley, 1964.

Bradford, Leland P., and Ronald Lippitt. "Roleplaying in Supervisory Training." Personnel 22 (1946): 358–69.

Briggs, Pamela. "The Japanese at Work: Illusions of the Ideal." In Choosing Sides: Unions and the Team Concept, edited by Mike Parker and Jane Slaughter, chap. 6. Boston: Labor Notes—South End Press, 1988.

Bruce-Biggs, B. "The Dangerous Folly Called Theory Z." Fortune, May 17, 1982, pp. 41–44.

Buchanan, Paul C. Evaluating the Effectiveness of Laboratory Training in Industry. Washington, D.C.: National Training Laboratories, 1965.

———. "Laboratory Training and Organization Development." Administrative Science Quarterly 14 (September 1969): 466–80.

Buffa, Elwood S. Modern Production Management. New York: Wiley, 1961.

Bunker, David R. "Individual Applications of Laboratory Training." Journal of Applied Behavioral Science 1 (April 1965): 131–48.

Business Week. The Reindustrialization of America. New York: McGraw-Hill, 1982.

Callahan, Robert E. "Quality Circles: A Program for Productivity Improvement through Human Resources Development." In Management by Japanese Systems, edited by Sang Lee and Gary Schwendiman, pp. 76–110. New York: Praeger, 1982.

Caminer, John J., and Gerhard R. Andlinger. "Operations Research Roundup." Harvard Business Review 32 (November–December 1954): 132–33, 135.

Campbell, John P., and Marvin D. Dunnette. "Effectiveness of T-Group Exercises in Managerial Training and Development." Psychological Bulletin 70 (1968): 73–104.

Caywood, T. E., H. M. Berger, J. H. Engel, J. F. Magee, H. J. Miser, and R. M. Thrall. "Guidelines for the Practice of Operations Research." Operations Research 19 (September 1971): 1123–37.

Chanaron, Jean J., and Jacques Perrin. "Science, Technology and Work Organization." International Journal of Technology Management (Switzerland) 2 (1987): 377–89.

Checkland, Peter B. Systems Thinking, Systems Practice. New York: Wiley, 1981.

Chorafas, Dimitris N. Applying Expert Systems in Business. New York: McGraw-Hill, 1987.

Churchman, C. West. "OR As a Profession." Management Science 17 (1970): B37–B53.

———. Prediction and Optimal Decision: Philosophical Issues of a Science of Values. Englewood Cliffs, N.J.: Prentice-Hall, 1961.

———. The Systems Approach. New York: Dell, 1968.

Churchman, C. West, Russell L. Ackoff, and E. Leonard Arnoff. Introduction to Operations Research. New York: Wiley, 1957.

Clarkson, William. "Drucker: Closing the Theory/Practice Gap." New Management 2 (Winter 1985): 21–23.

Coghill, Mary Ann. *Sensitivity Training: A Review of the Controversy*. Ithaca, N.Y.: Cornell University Press, 1967.

Cohen, Kalman J., William R. Dill, Alfred A. Kuehn, and Peter R. Winters. *The Carnegie Tech Management Game: An Experiment in Business Education*. Homewood, Ill.: Irwin, 1964.

Commons, John R. *Institutional Economics: Its Place in the Political Economy*. Madison: University of Wisconsin Press, 1934, 1959.

"Constitution and By-Laws of The Institute of Management Sciences." *Management Science* 1 (October 1954): 97–102.

Cooper, J. R. "An Issue-Oriented History of TIMS [The Institute of Management Science]." *Interfaces* 13 (August 1983): 9–19.

Cooper, W. W. "Presidential Address to TIMS [The Institute of Management Science]." *Management Science* 1 (January 1955): 183–86.

Corbin, Alfred. "The Impact of Drucker on Marketing." In *Peter Drucker: Contributions to Business Enterprise*, edited by Tony Bonaparte and John Flaherty, pp. 147–65. New York: New York University Press, 1970.

Crowther, James, and R. Whiddington. *Science at War*. New York: Philosophical Library, 1948.

Cyert, Richard M., and C. L. Hedrick. "Theory of the Firm: Past, Present, and Future." *Journal of Economic Literature* 10 (June 1972): 398–412.

Cyert, Richard M., and James G. March. *A Behavioral Theory of the Firm*. Englewood Cliffs, N.J.: Prentice-Hall, 1963.

Cyert, Richard M., and Herbert A. Simon. "Behavioral Approach: With Emphasis on Economics." *Behavioral Science* 28 (April 1983): 95–108.

Cyert, Richard M., Herbert A. Simon, and D. B. Trow. "Observation of a Business Decision." *Journal of Business* 29 (1956): 237–48.

Cyert, Richard M., and L. A. Welsch, eds. *Management Decision Making*. Baltimore, Md.: Penguin, 1970.

Dando, M. R., and P. G. Bennett. "A Kuhnian Crisis in Management Science?" *Journal of the Operational Research Society* 32 (1981): 91–104.

Dando, M. R., A. Defrenne, and R. G. Sharp. "Could OR Be a Science?" *Omega* 5 (1977): 89–92.

Dando, M. R., and R. G. Sharp. "Operational Research in the U.K. in 1977: The Cause and Consequences of a Myth?" *Journal of the Operational Research Society* 29 (1978): 939–50.

Daniel, D. W. "Half a Century of Operational Research in the RAF." *European Journal of Operational Research* 31 (September 1987): 271–75.

Davidson, William H. *The Amazing Race: Winning the Technorivalry with Japan*. New York: Wiley, 1984.

Davis, Louis. "The Coming Crisis for Production Management." *International Journal of Production Management* 9 (1971): 65–82.

———. "Job Design: Overview and Future Direction." *Journal of Contemporary Business* 6 (1977): 85–102.

Davis, Louis, and Albert Cherns, eds. *The Quality of Working Life.* 2 vols. New York: Free Press, 1975.

Davis, Louis, and James C. Taylor. *Design of Jobs.* Baltimore: Penguin, 1972; Santa Monica, Calif.: Goodyear, 1979.

Davis, Sheldon. "An Organic Problem-Solving Method of Organizational Change." *Journal of Applied Behavioral Science* 3 (1967): 3–21.

"Decision Doctor." *Time,* October 30, 1978, p. 123.

Deming, W. E. "What Can American Manufacturers Learn from the Japanese?" *Iron Age,* October 6, 1980, p. 51.

DeMott, J. S. "Here Come the Intrapreneurs." *Time,* February 4, 1985, pp. 36–37.

Derber, Milton. "Crosscurrents in Worker Participation." *Industrial Relations* 9 (February 1970): 123–36.

Dewey, John. *Education and Democracy.* New York: Free Press, 1916, 1966.

———. "Science As Subject-Matter and As Method." *Science* 31 (January 28, 1910): 121–27.

Diebold, John. "Management Can Learn from Japan." *Business Week,* September 29, 1973, pp. 14, 19.

Dorfman, Robert. "Operations Research." *American Economic Review* 50 (1960): 575–623.

Doty, Paul. "Science Advising and the ABM Debate." In *Controversies and Decisions,* edited by Charles Frankel, pp. 185–203. New York: Russell Sage, 1976.

Dowling, William F. "Conversation: An Interview with Peter F. Drucker." *Organizational Dynamics* 3 (Spring 1974): 35–53.

———. "Conversation with Chris Argyris." *Organizational Dynamics* 3 (Summer 1974): 45–62.

———. "Job Redesign on the Assembly Line." *Organizational Dynamics* 2 (1973): 51–67.

Dreyfack, Raymond. *Making It in Management the Japanese Way.* Rockville Centre, N.Y.: Farnsworth, 1982.

Drotning, John E. "Sensitivity Training Doesn't Work Magic." *Management of Personnel Quarterly* 7 (Summer 1968): 14–20.

Drucker, Peter F. *Adventures of a Bystander.* New York: Harper and Row, 1978.

———. *The Age of Discontinuity: Guidelines to Our Changing Society.* New York: Harper and Row, 1968.

———. *America's Next Twenty Years.* New York: Harper, 1955.

———. "Behind Japan's Success." *Harvard Business Review* 59 (January–February 1981): 83–90.

———. *The Changing World of the Executive.* New York: Truman Talley, 1982.

———. "The Coming of the New Organization." *Harvard Business Review* 66 (January–February 1988): 45–53.

———. "The Coming Rediscovery of Scientific Management." *Conference Board Record* (June 1976): 23–27.

———. *Concept of the Corporation*. New York: John Day, 1946; Mentor, 1972.

———. "Converting Social Problems into Business Opportunities: The New Meaning of Corporate Social Responsibility." *California Management Review* 26 (Winter 1984): 53–58.

———. *The Effective Executive*. New York: Harper and Row, 1966.

———. *The End of Economic Man: The Origins of Totalitarianism*. New York: John Day, 1942; Harper and Row, 1969.

———. "Epilogue." In *Peter Drucker: Contributions to Business Enterprise*, edited by Tony Bonaparte and John Flaherty, pp. 362–65. New York: New York University Press, 1970.

———. *Friedrich Julius Stahl: Konservative Staatslehre & Geschichtliche Entwicklung Morttueringan*. Tuebingen: J. C. Mohr, 1933.

———. *The Frontiers of Management: Where Tomorrow's Decisions Are Being Shaped Today*. New York: Truman Talley, 1986.

———. *The Future of Industrial Man: A Conservative Approach*. New York: John Day, 1942; New American Library, 1965.

———. *Innovation and Entrepreneurship: Practice and Principles*. New York: Harper and Row, 1985.

———. *Landmarks of Tomorrow*. New York: Harper and Row, 1957.

———. "Management Science and the Manager." *Management Science* 1 (1955): 115–26.

———. *Management: Tasks, Responsibilities, Practices*. New York: Harper and Row, 1974.

———. *Managing for Results: Economic Tasks and Risk-Taking Decisions*. New York: Harper and Row, 1964.

———. *Managing in Turbulent Times*. New York: Harper and Row, 1980.

———. *Men, Ideas and Politics: Essays by Peter F. Drucker*. New York: Harper and Row, 1971.

———. *The New Society: The Anatomy of the Industrial Order*. New York: Harper, 1949.

———. *People and Performance: The Best of Peter Drucker on Management*. New York: Harper and Row, 1977.

———. "The Performance Gap in Management Science." *Organizational Dynamics* 2 (Autumn 1973): 19–29.

———. *The Practice of Management*. New York: Harper, 1954.

———. "Schumpeter and Keynes." *Forbes*, May 23, 1983, pp. 126–28.

———. *Technology, Management and Society: Essays by Peter F. Drucker*. New York: Harper and Row, 1970.

———. *Toward the Next Economics and Other Essays*. New York: Harper and Row, 1981.

———. *The Unseen Revolution: How Pension Fund Socialism Came to America*. New York: Harper and Row, 1976.

————. "What Is 'Business Ethics'?" *The Public Interest* 63 (Spring 1981): 18–36.

————. "What We Can Learn from Japanese Management." *Harvard Business Review* 49 (March–April 1971): 110–22.

Dubin, Robert. "Psyche, Sensitivity, and Social Structure." In *Leadership and Organization: A Behavioral Science Approach*, edited by Robert Tannenbaum, Irving R. Weschler, and Fred Massarik, pp. 401–15. New York: McGraw-Hill, 1961.

Duncan, W. Jack. "Transferring Management Theory to Practice." *Academy of Management Journal* 17 (December 1974): 724–38.

√ Dunnette, Marvin D., and John P. Campbell. "Laboratory Education: Impact on People and Organizations." *Industrial Relations* 8 (October 1968): 1–27.

Durand, Douglas E. "Citation Count Analysis of Behavioral Science Journals in Influential Management Literature." *Academy of Management Journal* 17 (September 1974): 579–82.

Dyer, L., and W. Weyrauch. "MBO and Motivation: An Empirical Study." *Academy of Management Proceedings* (1975): 134–36.

Eddison, Roger T., K. Pennycuick, and R. H. P. Rivett. *Operational Research in Management.* New York: Wiley, 1962.

Eden, Colin, and D. Sims. "On the Nature of Problems in Consulting Practice." *Omega* 7 (1979): 119–27.

Eden, Colin, D. Sims, and S. Jones. "Policy Analysis and Organizational Politics." *European Journal of Operational Research* 3 (1979): 207–25.

Emmerman, L. "Decisions, Decisions." *Chicago Tribune Tempo*, April 10, 1987, pp. 1–2.

England, George W. "Japanese and American Management: Theory Z and Beyond." *Journal of International Business Studies* 14 (Fall 1983): 131–42.

Enthoven, Alain C., and K. Wayne Smith. *How Much Is Enough?* New York: Harper and Row, 1971.

Ericsson, K. Anders, and Herbert A. Simon. *Protocol Analysis: Verbal Reports As Data.* Cambridge, Mass.: MIT Press, 1984.

Farrell, Christopher, and John Hoerr. "ESOPs: Are They Good for You?" *Business Week*, May 15, 1989, pp. 116–23.

Fein, Mitchell. "Job Enrichment: A Re-evaluation." *Sloan Management Review* 14 (Winter 1974): 69–88.

√ Fitzgerald, Thomas H. "Why Motivation Theory Doesn't Work." *Harvard Business Review* 49 (July–August 1971): 37–44.

√ Follett, Mary. *Dynamic Administration: The Collected Papers of Mary Follett.* Edited by Henry C. Metcalf and Lyndall Urwick. New York: Harper and Row, 1942.

√ Ford, Robert N. "Job Enrichment Lessons from AT&T." *Harvard Business Review* 51 (January–February 1973): 96–106.

————. *Motivation through Work Itself.* New York: AMA, 1969.

Fordyce, K., P. Norden, and G. Sullivan. "Artificial Intelligence and the Management Science Practitioner." *Interfaces* 17 (July–August 1987): 34–40.

Freyberg, Berthold. "The Genesis of Drucker's Thought." In *Peter Drucker: Contributions to Business Enterprise*, edited by Tony Bonaparte and John Flaherty, pp. 17–22. New York: New York University Press, 1970.

Fry, Louis W. "The Maligned F. W. Taylor: A Reply to His Many Critics." *Academy of Management Review* 1 (1976): 124–29.

Gaither, Norman. "The Adoption of Operations Research Techniques by Manufacturing Organizations." *Decision Sciences* 6 (October 1975): 797–813.

Gibbons, John F. "An Interview with Drucker on the Role of a Consultant." In *Peter Drucker: Contributions to Business Enterprise*, edited by Tony Bonaparte and John Flaherty, pp. 315–36. New York: New York University Press, 1970.

Gibney, Frank. *Japan: The Fragile Super Power*. New York: New American Library, 1975.

———. *Miracle by Design: The Real Reasons behind Japan's Economic Success*. New York: Times Books, 1982.

Goldman, Robert B. *A Work Experiment: Six Americans in a Swedish Plant*. New York: Ford Foundation, 1976.

Goldston, Eli. "What We Can Learn from Japan." *Fortune*, October 1971, pp. 137–38.

Golembiewski, Robert T. *Renewing Organizations: The Laboratory Approach to Planned Change*. Itasca, Ill.: F. E. Peacock, 1972.

Gomberg, William. "The Historical Roots of the Democratic Challenge to Authoritarian Management." *Human Resource Management* 24 (Fall 1985): 253–69.

———. "Job Satisfaction: Sorting out the Nonsense." *AFL-CIO American Federationist* 80 (June 1973): 14–19.

———. "'Titillating Therapy': Management Development's Most Fashionable Toy." *Personnel Administrator* 12 (July–August 1967): 30–33.

Goodeve, Charles. "The Growth of Operational Research in the Civil Sector in the United Kingdom." *Operational Research Quarterly* 19 (1968): 113–16.

Gooding, Judson. "It Pays to Wake Up the Blue-Collar Worker." *Fortune*, September 1970, pp. 133–35.

———. *The Job Revolution*. New York: Walker, 1972.

Goodwin, H. G. "Work Simplification." *Factory Management and Maintenance*, July 1958, pp. 72–106.

Gordon, Robert A., and J. E. Howell. *Higher Education for Business*. New York: Columbia University Press, 1959.

Gottschalk, Louis A. "Psychoanalytic Notes on T-Groups at the Human Relations Laboratory, Bethel, Maine." *Comprehensive Psychiatry* 7 (December 1966): 472–87.

Gottschalk, Louis A., and E. M. Pattison. "Psychiatric Perspectives on T-Groups and the Laboratory Movement: An Overview." *American Journal of Psychiatry* 126 (December 1969): 823–39.

Grayson, C. Jackson. "Management Science and Business Practice." *Harvard Business Review* 51 (1973): 41–48.

Green, Charles N. "The Satisfaction-Performance Controversy." *Business Horizons* 15 (October 1972): 31–41.

Gulick, Luther, and Lyndall Urwick, eds. *Papers on the Science of Administration.* New York: Institute of Public Administration, 1937.

Haire, Mason. "Psychological Problems Relevant to Business and Industry." *Psychological Bulletin* 56 (May 1959): 169–94.

Haire, Mason, Edwin Ghiselli, and Lyman W. Porter. "An International Study of Management Attitudes and Democratic Leadership." In *Proceedings CIOS XIII, International Management Conference*, pp. 101–14. New York: Council for International Progress in Management, 1963.

Hall, James L., and Joel K. Leidecker. "Is Japanese-Style Management Anything New? A Comparison of Japanese-Style Management with U.S. Participative Models." In *Management by Japanese Systems*, edited by Sang Lee and Gary Schwendiman, pp. 256–72. New York: Praeger, 1982.

Hall, John R., and Sidney W. Hess. "OR/MS, Dead or Dying? RX for Survival." *Interfaces* 8 (1978): 42–44.

Hall, Robert W. *Zero Inventories.* Homewood, Ill.: Dow Jones-Irwin, 1983.

Halpern, David, Stephen Osofsky, and Myron I. Peskin. "Taylorism Revisited and Revised for the 1990s." *Industrial Management* 31 (January–February 1989): 20–23.

Hampden-Turner, Charles. *Radical Man: The Process of Psycho-Social Development.* Cambridge, Mass.: Schenkman, 1970.

Harmon, Paul, and David King. *Expert Systems: Artificial Intelligence in Business.* New York: Wiley, 1985.

Harvey, J. B. "Organization Development As a Religious Movement." *O.D. Practitioner* 5 (Winter 1967): 4–5.

Hatvany, Nina, and Vladimir Pucik. "Integrated Management System: Lessons from the Japanese Experience." *Academy of Management Review* 6 (July 1981): 469–80.

Hayes, Robert H. "Why Japanese Factories Work." *Harvard Business Review* 59 (July–August 1981): 55–66.

Hayes, Robert, and William Abernathy. "Managing Our Way to Economic Decline." *Harvard Business Review* 58 (July–August 1980): 67–77.

Helfgott, Roy B. "Moving Beyond Taylorism." *International Journal of Technology Management* (Switzerland) 2 (1987): 459–71.

Herrmann, Cyril C., and John F. Magee. "Operations Research for Management." *Harvard Business Review* 31 (July–August 1953): 100–112.

Herzberg, Frederick. *The Managerial Choice: To Be Efficient and to Be Human.* Homewood, Ill.: Dow Jones-Irwin, 1976.

———. "One More Time: How Do You Motivate Employees?" *Harvard Business Review* 46 (January 1968): 53–62.

———. *Work and the Nature of Man.* Cleveland: World, 1966.

Herzberg, Frederick, Bernard Mausner, and Barbara Synderman. *The Motivation to Work.* New York: Wiley, 1959.

Hitch, Charles J. "An Appreciation of Systems Analysis." In *Systems Analysis,* edited by S. L. Optner, pp. 19–36. Harmondsworth: Penguin, 1973.

Hoerr, John. "The Payoff from Teamwork." *Business Week,* July 10, 1989, pp. 56–62.

Horowitz, Ira. *Decision Making and the Theory of the Firm.* New York: Holt, Rinehart and Winston, 1970.

Horwitz, Murray. "Training in Conflict Resolution." In *T-Group Theory and Laboratory Method: Innovation in Re-education,* edited by Leland P. Bradford, Jack R. Gibb, and Kenneth D. Benne, pp. 365–78. New York: Wiley, 1964.

House, Robert J. "T-Group Education and Leadership Effectiveness: A Review of the Empirical Literature and a Critical Evaluation." *Personnel Psychology* 20 (Spring 1967): 1–32.

Hovey, Ronald W., and Harvey M. Wagner. "A Sample Survey of Industrial Operations Research Activities." *Operations Research* 6 (November–December 1958): 876–79.

Howard, Ronald A. "The Practicality Gap." *Management Science* 14 (1968): 503–7.

Hranac, Jo Ann, and Kathleen C. Brannen. "The What, Where, and Whys of Quality Control Circles." In *Management by Japanese Systems,* edited by Sang Lee and Gary Schwendiman, pp. 67–75. New York: Praeger, 1982.

Hulin, Charles L., and Milton R. Blood. "Job Enlargement, Individual Differences, and Worker Responses." *Psychological Bulletin* 69 (1968): 41–55.

Hummel, Ralph P. "Behind Quality Management." *Organizational Dynamics* 16 (Summer 1987): 71–78.

Hurni, Melvin L. "Operation Research and Synthesis in General Electric." *Management Consultation Services of the General Electric Company,* 1954, pp. 28–33.

———. "The Purpose of Operations Research and Synthesis in Modern Business." *Management Consultation Service of the General Electric Company,* 1955, pp. 2–7.

Imaizumi, Masumasa. "Past and Present Status of Quality Management in Japan." *Management Japan* (Japan) 17 (Spring 1974): 18–22.

Janson, Robert. "Job Enrichment: Challenge of the '70s." *Training and Development Journal* 24 (June 1970): 7–9.

"Japan's Ways Thrive in the U.S." *Business Week,* December 12, 1977, pp. 156–60.

Johnson, Richard, and William Ouchi. "Made in America (under Japanese Management)." *Harvard Business Review* 52 (September–October 1974): 61–69.

Juran, Joseph M. "Japanese and Western Quality: A Contrast in Methods and Results." *Management Review* 67 (1978): 26–28, 39–45.

———. *Juran on Planning for Quality.* New York: Free Press, 1988.

———. "Product Quality—A Prescription for the West. Part 2." *Management Review* 70 (July 1981): 57–61.

———. "The QC Circle Phenomenon." *Industrial Quality Control* 23 (1967): 329–36.

Kamata, Satoshi. *Japan in the Passing Lane: An Insider's Account of Life in a Japanese Auto Factory*. Translated by Tatsuru Akimoto. New York: Pantheon, 1982.

Kantrow, Alan M. "Why Read Peter Drucker." *Harvard Business Review* 58 (January–February 1980): 74–82.

Kaplan, Roy, Curt Tausky, and Bolaria Bhopinder. "Job Enrichment." *Personnel Journal* 48 (October 1969): 791–98.

Keys, J. Bernard, and Thomas R. Miller. "The Japanese Management Theory Jungle." *Academy of Management Review* 9 (April 1984): 342–53.

Kilbridge, Maurice D. "Turnover, Absence, and Transfer Rates As Indicators of Employee Dissatisfaction with Repetitive Work." *Industrial and Labor Relations Review* 15 (1961): 21–32.

Kittel, Charles. "The Nature and Development of Operations Research." *Science* 105 (January 1947): 150–53.

✓ Klaw, Spencer. "Two Weeks in a T-Group." *Fortune*, August 1961, pp. 114–17, 155.

Klein, Dieter, and Paul Butkovich. "Can the Professions of Operations Research/Management Science Change and Survive?" *Interfaces* 6 (May 1976): 47–51.

Kobler, John. "The Flip-Flop Machines." *Saturday Evening Post*, May 4, 1968, pp. 32–39, 42–55.

Konz, Stephen. "Quality Circles: Japan's Success Story." *Industrial Engineering* 11 (October 1979): 24–27.

Koopman, B. O. "Fallacies in Operations Research." *Operations Research* 4 (1956): 422–26.

Kraar, Louis. "Japanese Are Coming—with Their Own Style of Management." *Fortune*, March 1975, pp. 116–21, 160–64.

Kremen, B. "Lordstown—Searching for a Better Way of Work." *New York Times*, September 9, 1973, sec. 3, p. 1.

Kriz, Jiri, ed. *Knowledge-based Expert Systems in Industry*. New York: Halsted, 1987.

✓ Krupp, Steven. "The Quality Circle Phenomenon." In *The Lewin Legacy: Field Theory in Current Practice*, edited by E. Stivers and S. Wheelan, chap. 3. Berlin: Springer-Verlag, 1986.

✓ Kuriloff, A. H., and S. Atkins. "T-Group for a Work Team." *Journal of Applied Behavioral Science* 2 (1966): 63–94.

Lange, Robert. "Participative Management As a Reflection of Cultural Contingencies: A New Way to Reevaluate Our Ethic." In *Japanese Management: Cultural and Environmental Considerations*, edited by Sang Lee and Gary Schwendiman, pp. 117–34. New York: Praeger, 1982.

Lardner, Harold. "The Origin of Operational Research." *Operations Research* 32 (March–April 1984): 465–75.

Lawler, Edward E. "Job Design and Employee Motivation." *Personnel Psychology* 22 (1969): 426–35.

———. *Pay and Organizational Effectiveness: A Psychological View*. New York: McGraw-Hill, 1971.

Lawler, Edward E., and J. Richard Hackman. "Corporate Profits and Employee Satisfaction: Must They Be in Conflict?" *California Management Review* 14 (Fall 1971): 46–55.

Lawrence, Paul R., and Jay W. Lorsch. *Organization and Environment.* Homewood, Ill.: Irwin, 1969.

Leavitt, Harold J. "Beyond the Analytic Manager." *California Management Review* 17 (Spring 1975): 5–12.

———. "Beyond the Analytic Manager: Part II." *California Management Review* 17 (Summer 1975): 11–21.

Leavitt, Theodore. "The Dangers of Social Responsibility." *Harvard Business Review* 36 (September–October 1958): 41–50.

Lee, Chris, and Ron Zemke. "'Intrapreneuring': New-Age Fiefdoms for Big Business?" *Training* 2 (February 1985): 27–41.

Lee, Sang M., and Gary Schwendiman, eds. *Japanese Management: Cultural and Environmental Considerations.* New York: Praeger, 1982.

———. *Management by Japanese Systems.* New York: Praeger, 1982.

Leflufy, Bob. "The Secret of Japanese Management Isn't Rice Diets—It's Practicing What We Preached." *Canadian Business,* December 1982, pp. 143.

Lesieur, Fred G. *The Scanlon Plan: A Frontier in Labor Management Cooperation.* Cambridge, Mass.: MIT Press, 1958.

Levinson, Harry. "Management by Whose Objectives?" *Harvard Business Review* (July–August 1970): 125–34.

———. "Various Approaches to Understanding Man at Work." *Archives of Environmental Health* (May 1971): 612–18.

Levitan, Sar A., and Clifford M. Johnson. "Labor and Management: The Illusion of Cooperation." *Harvard Business Review* 61 (September–October 1983): 8–16.

Levitan, Sar A., and William B. Johnston. *Work Is Here to Stay, Alas.* Salt Lake City: Olympus, 1973.

Levitt, Theodore. "A Heretical View of Management Science." *Fortune,* December 18, 1978, pp. 50–52.

Lewin, Kurt. *A Dynamic Theory of Personality: Selected Papers.* Translated by D. K. Adams and K. E. Zener. New York: McGraw-Hill, 1935.

———. *Field Theory in Social Science: Selected Theoretical Papers.* New York: Harper and Row, 1951.

———. *Resolving Social Conflicts: Selected Papers on Group Dynamics.* New York: Harper and Row, 1948.

Lewin, Kurt, Ronald Lippitt, and Ralph K. White. "Patterns of Aggressive Behavior in Experimentally Created 'Social Climates.'" *Journal of Social Psychology* 10 (1939): 271–99.

Lewis, Jordan D. "Technology, Enterprise, and American Economic Growth." *Science* 215 (March 1982): 1204–11.

Likert, Rensis. *The Human Organization: Its Management and Value.* New York: McGraw-Hill, 1967.

———. *New Patterns of Management.* New York: McGraw-Hill, 1961.

Lincoln, J. R., J. Olsen, and M. Hanada. "Cultural Orientations and Individual Reactions to Organizations: A Study of Employees of Japanese-Owned Firms." *Administrative Science Quarterly* 26 (1981): 93–115.

Lippitt, Ronald. "The Small Group and Participatory Democracy: Comment on Graebner." *Journal of Social Issues* 42 (Spring 1986): 155–56.

——. *Training in Community Relations: A Research Exploration toward New Group Skills.* New York: Harper and Row, 1949.

Lippitt, Ronald, and Leland Bradford. "Building a Democratic Work Group." *Personnel* 22 (1945): 142–52.

Locke, Edwin A. "The Ideas of Frederick W. Taylor: An Evaluation." *Academy of Management Review* 7 (1982): 7–24.

Lodge, George C. *The American Disease.* New York: Knopf, 1984.

——. *The New American Ideology.* New York: Knopf, 1976.

——. "Top Priority: Renovating Our Ideology." *Harvard Business Review* 48 (1970): 43–55.

Lodge, George C., and Ezra F. Vogel. *Ideology and National Competitiveness: An Analysis of Nine Countries.* Boston: Harvard Business School, 1987.

Lohr, Steve. "Overhauling America's Business Management." *New York Times Magazine,* January 4, 1981, pp. 14–17.

Lubin, Bernard, and M. Zuckerman. "Level of Emotional Arousal in Laboratory Training." *Journal of Applied Behavioral Science* 5 (1969): 483–90.

Lucas, J. R. "Minds, Machines, and Gödel." *Philosophy* 36 (1961). Reprinted in *Minds and Machines,* edited by A. R. Anderson, pp. 43–59. Englewood Cliffs, N.J.: Prentice-Hall, 1964.

Luthans, Fred, and Edward Knod. "Critical Factors in Job Enrichment." *Atlanta Economic Review,* May–June 1974, pp. 6–11.

Luthans, Fred, and William E. Reif. "Job Enrichment: Long on Theory, Short on Practice." *Organizational Dynamics* 2 (Winter 1974): 30–39.

McCaskey, Michael B. "A Contingency Approach to Planning: Planning with Goals and Planning without Goals." *Academy of Management Journal* 17 (June 1974): 281–91.

McClenahen, John S. "Bringing Home Japan's Lesson." *Industry Week,* February 23, 1981, pp. 69–73.

McConkey, Dale D. "MBO: Twenty Years Later." *Business Horizons* 16 (August 1973): 25–36.

McConkie, M. L. "Clarifying and Reviewing the Empirical Work on MBO." *Group and Organization Studies* 4 (December 1979): 461–75.

McGregor, Douglas. *The Human Side of Enterprise.* New York: McGraw-Hill, 1960.

——. *Leadership and Motivation: Essays of Douglas McGregor.* Edited by Warren G. Bennis, Edgar H. Schein, and Caroline McGregor. Cambridge, Mass.: MIT Press, 1966.

——. "An Uneasy Look at Performance Appraisal." *Harvard Business Review* 35 (1957): 89–94.

McLuhan, Marshall, and Barrington Nevitt, "The Man Who Came to Listen." In *Peter Drucker: Contributions to Business Enterprise*, edited by Tony Bonaparte and John Flaherty, pp. 35–55. New York: New York University Press, 1970.

McMillan, Charles J. *The Japanese Industrial System*. Berlin: Walter de Gruyter, 1985.

McMurray, Robert N. "Management's Achilles Heel." *Michigan Business Review*, November 1973, p. 14.

McPherson, Joseph. "Innovation and Creativity: Make Room for Your Own 'Skunk Works.'" *International Management* 39 (June 1984): 79.

Magaziner, Ira C., and Robert B. Reich. *Minding America's Business: The Decline and Rise of the American Economy*. New York: Harcourt Brace and Jovanovich, 1982.

Mai-Dalton, Renate R. "Traditional Japanese Management versus Likert's System 4." In *Management by Japanese Systems*, edited by Sang Lee and Gary Schwendiman, pp. 281–87. New York: Praeger, 1982.

Maitland, Ian. "Organizational Structure and Innovation: The Japanese Case." In *Management by Japanese Systems*, edited by Sang M. Lee and Gary Schwendiman, pp. 55–64. New York: Praeger, 1982.

"Making a Business School More Relevant." *Business Week*, December 5, 1970, pp. 58–60.

Malcolm, D. G. "On the Need for Improvement in Implementation of OR." *Management Science* 4 (February 1965): B48–B58.

———. "The Status of Operations Research in Industry." *Operations Research* 2 (1954): 211–13.

Malone, Erwin L. "The Non-Linear Systems Experiment in Participative Management." *Journal of Business* 48 (January 1975): 52–64.

March, James G. "The 1978 Nobel Prize in Economics." *Science* 202 (November 24, 1978): 858–61.

March, James G., and Herbert A. Simon. *Organizations*. New York: Wiley, 1958.

Margolis, Julian. "The Analysis of the Firm: Rationalism, Conventionalism, and Behaviorialism." *Journal of Business* 31 (July 1958): 187–99.

Marrow, Alfred J. *Behind the Executive Mask*. New York: AMA, 1964.

———. "Events Leading to the Establishment of the National Training Laboratories." *Journal of Applied Behavioral Science* 3 (April 1967): 144–50.

Maslow, Abraham H. *Eupsychian Management: A Journal*. Homewood, Ill.: Irwin-Dorsey, 1965.

———. *Motivation and Personality*. New York: Harper and Row, 1954.

———. "A Theory of Human Motivation." *Psychological Review* 50 (1943): 370–96.

Mason, R. O. "A Dialectical Approach to Strategic Planning." *Management Science* 15 (1969): B403–16.

Mason, R. O., and Mitroff, I. I. *Challenging Strategic Planning Assumptions*. New York: Wiley, 1981.

Matejka, J. Kenneth, and D. Neil Ashworth. "The Employees' Hierarchy of Greeds." *Administrative Management* 46 (October 1985): 24–25.

Mayo, Elton. *The Human Problems of an Industrial Civilization.* New York: Viking, 1933.

Melman, Seymour. *The Permanent War Economy: American Capitalism in Decline.* New York: Simon and Schuster, 1974.

———. *Profits without Production.* New York: Knopf, 1983.

Merton, Robert A. "Durkheim's Division of Labor in Society." *American Journal of Sociology* 40 (1934): 319–28.

Michael, G. C. "A Review of Heuristic Programming." *Decision Sciences* 3 (1972): 74–100.

Miles, Raymond E. "Human Relations or Human Resources?" *Harvard Business Review* 43 (July–August 1965): 148–63.

Miller, D. W., and M. K. Starr. *Executive Decisions and Operations Research.* Englewood Cliffs, N.J.: Prentice-Hall, 1960.

Mills, Ted. "Human Resources—Why the New Concern?" *Harvard Business Review* 53 (March–April 1975): 120–34.

Mitchell, Ron. "Rediscovering Our Roots: Quality Circles in the US, 1918–48." *Journal for Quality and Participation* 10 (December 1987): 56–66.

Mitchell, Russell. "Managing Innovation." *Business Week,* June 16, 1989, special issue, pp. 104–18.

Mitroff, Ivan I., James R. Emshoff, and R. H. Kilmann. "Assumptional Analysis: A Methodology for Strategic Problem Solving." *Management Science* 85 (1979): 583–93.

Mohri, Shigetaka. "Neo-Fordism." In *Peter Drucker: Contributions to Business Enterprise,* edited by Tony Bonaparte and John Flaherty, pp. 194–211. New York: New York University Press, 1970.

Molander, C. F. "Management by Objectives in Perspective." *Journal of Management Studies* 9 (February 1972): 74–81.

Moran, Robert T. "Japanese Participative Management—Or How Ringi Seido Can Work for You." *S. A. M. Advanced Management Journal* 44 (Summer 1979): 14–21.

Moreno, Jacob L. *Psychodrama and Sociodrama.* Boston: Beacon Press, 1946.

———. *Sociodrama: A Method for the Analysis of Social Conflicts.* Beacon, N.Y.: Beacon House, 1955.

———. *Who Shall Survive?* Beacon, N.Y.: Beacon House, 1934.

Morgenson, Allen. *Common Sense Applied to Time and Motions Study.* New York: n.p., 1932.

Morrison, Anne. "Job-Hopping at the Top." *Fortune,* May 4, 1981, pp. 127–30.

Morse, John J. "A Contingency Look at Job Design." *California Management Review* 16 (Fall 1973): 67–75.

Morse, John J., and Jay W. Lorsch. "Beyond Theory Y." *Harvard Business Review* 48 (May–June 1970): 61–68.

Morse, Philip M. "Trends in Operations Research." *Operations Research* 1 (1953): 159–65.

Morse, Philip M., and George F. Kimball. *Methods of Operations Research*. New York: Wiley, 1951.

Musashi, Miyamoto. *A Book of Five Rings*. Translated by Victor Harris. London: Allen and Unwin, 1974.

Myers, M. Scott. "Adapting to the New Work Ethic." *Business Quarterly* 38 (1973): 48–58.

————. "Every Employee a Manager." *California Management Review* 10 (Spring 1968): 9–20.

————. *Every Employee a Manager*. New York: McGraw-Hill, 1970.

————. "Overcoming Union Opposition to Job Enrichment." *Harvard Business Review* 49 (May–June 1971): 37–49.

————. "Who Are Your Motivated Workers?" *Harvard Business Review* 42 (January–February 1964): 73–88.

Myers, M. Scott, and Earl R. Gomersall. "Break Through in On-the-Job Training." *Harvard Business Review* 44 (July–August 1966): 123–31.

Nadler, Leonard. "What Japan Learned from the U.S.—That We Forgot to Remember." *California Management Review* 26 (Summer 1984): 46–61.

National Training Laboratories. *Standards for the Use of the Laboratory Methods in N.T.L. Institute Programs*. Washington, D.C.: National Training Laboratories, 1969.

Nelson, Joani. "Quality Circles Become Contagious." *Industry Week*, April 14, 1980, pp. 99–103.

Newell, Allen, J. C. Shaw, and Herbert A. Simon. "A General Problem Solving Program for a Computer." *Computers and Automation* 8 (July 1959): 10–17.

Newell, Allen, and Herbert A. Simon. "Heuristic Problem-Solving: The Next Advance in Operations Research." *Operations Research* 6 (January–February 1958): 1–10.

————. *Human Problem Solving*. Englewood Cliffs, N.J.: Prentice-Hall, 1972.

————. "The Logic Theory Machine." *IRE Transactions on Information Theory* IT-2 (September 1956): 61–79.

Newell, Allen, Herbert A. Simon, and J. C. Shaw. "Problem Solving in Humans and Computers." *Carnegie Technical Journal* 21 (March 1957): 34–38.

————. "Report on a General Problem Solving Program." *Proceedings of the International Conference on Information Processing*. Paris, June 15–20, 1959. London: Buttersworth, 1960.

Noda, Nobuo. *How Japan Absorbed American Management Methods*. Tokyo: Asian Productivity Organization, 1969.

"Now from Japan: Intravenous Management." *International Management* 40 (July 1985): 7, 11.

Odiorne, George S. "MBO: A Backward Glance." *Business Horizons* 21 (October 1978): 14–24.

————. "The Trouble with Sensitivity Training." *Training Directors Journal* 17 (October 1963): 9–20.

Oh, Tai K. "Japanese Management: A Critical Review." *Academy of Management Review* 1 (January 1976): 14–25.

O'Toole, James. "Peter Drucker: Father of the New Management, Retrospective." *New Management* 2 (Winter 1985): 4–32.

Ouchi, William G. "Markets, Bureaucracies, and Clans." *Administrative Science Quarterly* 25 (March 1980): 129–40.

———. *Theory Z: How American Business Can Meet the Japanese Challenge*. New York: Avon, 1981.

Ozawa, Torutomo. "Japanese Chic." *Across the Board* 19 (October 1982): 6–13.

Pagès, Max. "Bethel Culture, 1969: Impressions of an Immigrant." *Journal of Applied Behavioral Science* 7 (1971): 267–84.

Parker, Mike. *Inside the Circle: A Union Guide to QWL*. Boston: Labor Notes—South End Press, 1985.

Parker, Mike, and Jane Slaughter. *Choosing Sides: Unions and the Team Concept*. Boston: Labor Notes—South End Press, 1988.

Pascale, Richard T. "Personnel Practice and Employee Attitudes: A Study of Japanese and American-Managed Firms in the United States." *Human Relations* 31 (July 1978): 597–615.

Pascale, Richard T., and Anthony G. Athos. *The Art of Japanese Management: Applications for American Executives*. New York: Simon and Schuster, 1981.

Pearse, Robert F. *Manager to Manager: What Managers Think of Management Development*. New York: AMACOM, 1974.

Pegels, Carl. *Japan vs. the West: Implications for Management*. Boston: Kluwer-Nijhoff, 1984.

Penzer, William. "Bridging the Industrial Engineering/Behavioral Science Gap." *Personnel Journal* 52 (August 1973): 669–701.

Peters, Thomas J. "Drucker: The Other Half of the Message." *New Management* 2 (Winter 1985): 14–17.

Peters, Thomas J., and Robert H. Waterman. *In Search of Excellence: Lessons from America's Best-Run Companies*. New York: Harper and Row, 1982.

Pierce, Jon L., and Ronda Dunham. "Task Design: A Literature Review." *Academy of Management Review* 1 (1976): 83–97.

Pinchot, Gifford. *Intrapreneuring: Why You Don't Have to Leave the Corporation to Become an Entrepreneur*. New York: Harper and Row, 1985.

Piore, Michael. "The Impact of the Labor Market upon the Design and Selection of Productive Techniques within the Manufacturing Plant." *Quarterly Journal of Economics* 82 (November 1968): 602–20.

Planning-Programming-Budgeting. Official Documents, prepared by the Subcommittee on National Security and International Operations of the Committee on Government Operations. Washington, D.C.: Government Printing Office, 1967.

Poppy, John. "It's OK to Cry in the Office." *Look*, July 9, 1968, pp. 64–76.

Powell, Reed M., and John F. Stinson. "The Worth of Laboratory Training." *Business Horizons* 14 (August 1971): 87–95.

Preston, Lee S., and James E. Post. "The Third Managerial Revolution." *Academy of Management Review* 17 (September 1974): 476–86.

Radford, K. J. "Decision-making in a Turbulent Environment." *Journal of the Operational Research Society* 29 (1978): 677–82.

Radnor, Michael, and Rodney D. Neal. "The Progress of Management-Science Activities in Large US Industrial Organizations." *Operations Research* 21 (March–April 1973): 427–50.

Ranyard, J. C. "A History of OR and Computing." *Journal of the Operational Research Society* 39 (December 1988): 1073–86.

Rehder, Robert R. "What American and Japanese Managers Are Learning from Each Other." *Business Horizons* 24 (March–April 1981): 63–70.

Reich, Robert B. *The Next American Frontier.* New York: Times Books, 1983.

———. "The Profession of Management." *New Republic,* June 27, 1981, pp. 27–32.

Reif, William E., David N. Ferrazzi, and Robert J. Evans. "Job Enrichment: Who Uses It and Why?" *Business Horizons* 17 (February 1974): 73–78.

Reif, William E., and Fred Luthans. "Does Job Enrichment Really Pay Off?" *California Management Review* 15 (Fall 1972): 30–37.

Rice, Albert K. *Productivity and Social Organization: The Ahmedabad Experiment.* London: Tavistock, 1958.

Rich, Ben R. "The 'Skunk Works' Management Style—It's No Secret." *Executive Speeches* 3 (November 1988): 1–11.

Richman, Tom. "Interview: A Talk with a Wide-Ranging Mind." In *The Frontiers of Management: Where Tomorrow's Decisions Are Being Shaped Today,* edited by Peter F. Drucker, pp. 1–17. New York: Truman Talley, 1986.

Ridley, Clarence E., and Herbert A. Simon. *Measuring Municipal Activities: A Survey of Suggested Criteria for Appraising Administration.* Chicago: International City Managers Association, 1938.

Rinehart, Robert F. "Threats to the Growth of Operations Research in Business and Industry." *Operations Research* 2 (1954): 229–30.

Ringle, William F. "The American Who Remade 'Made in Japan' [W. E. Deming]." *Nation's Business* 69 (February 1981): 67–70.

Roach, John M. "Simon Says: Decision Making Is a 'Satisficing' Experience." *Management Review* 68 (January 1979): 8–17.

Robbins, Stephen P. "The Theory Z Organization from a Power-Control Perspective." *California Management Review* 25 (January 1983): 67–75.

Roche, W. J., and N. L. MacKinnon. "Motivating People with Meaningful Work." *Harvard Business Review* 48 (1970): 97–110.

Roethlisberger, Fritz J. *The Elusive Phenomena.* Edited by G. F. Lombard. Cambridge, Mass.: Harvard University Press, 1977.

Roethlisberger, Fritz J., and W. J. Dickson. *Management and the Worker*. Cambridge, Mass.: Harvard University Press, 1939.

Rogers, Carl R. *Counselling and Psychotherapy*. Boston: Houghton Mifflin, 1942.

———. "Process of the Basic Encounter Group." In *Challenges of Humanistic Psychology*, edited by James F. T. Bugental, pp. 262–76. New York: McGraw-Hill, 1967.

Rogers, David J. *Fighting to Win: Samurai Techniques for Your Work and Life*. Garden City, N.Y.: Doubleday, 1984.

Ross, Joel E., and William C. Ross. *Japanese Quality Circles and Productivity*. Reston, Va.: Reston, 1982.

Rush, Harold M. F. *Behavioral Science, Concepts and Management Applications*. New York: Conference Board, 1969.

———. *Job Design for Motivation: Experiments in Job Enlargement and Job Enrichment*. New York: Conference Board, 1971.

———. *Organization Development: A Reconnaissance*. New York: Conference Board, 1973.

"Sabotage at Lordstown?" *Time*, February 7, 1972, p. 76.

Schappe, Robert H. "Twenty-Two Arguments against Job Enrichment." *Personnel Journal* 53 (February 1974): 116–23.

Schein, Edger H. "Does Japanese Management Style Have a Message for American Managers?" *Sloan Management Review* 23 (Fall 1981): 55–68.

Schleicher, William. "Quality Control Circles Save Lockheed Nearly $3 Million in Two Years." *Quality*, May 1977, pp. 14–17.

Schonberger, Richard J. *Japanese Manufacturing Techniques: Nine Hidden Lessons in Simplicity*. New York: Free Press, 1982.

Schumacher, Charles C., and Barnard E. Smith. "A Sample Survey of Industrial Operations Research Activities II." *Operations Research* 13 (December 1965): 1023–27.

Schumpeter, Joseph A. *Capitalism, Socialism, and Democracy*. New York: Harper, 1942.

Schuster, Fred E., and Alva F. Kindall. "Management by Objectives: Where We Stand. A Survey of the Fortune 500." *Human Resources Management* 13 (Spring 1974): 8–11.

Scott, William G. "Schmidt Is Alive and Enrolled in a Sensitivity Training Program." *Public Administration Review* 30 (November 1970): 621–25.

Sethi, S. Prakash, Nobuaki Namiki, and Carl L. Swanson. *The False Promise of the Japanese Miracle: Illusions and Realities of the Japanese Management System*. Boston: Pitman, 1984.

Silverman, Barry G. *Expert Systems for Business*. Reading, Mass.: Addison-Wesley, 1987.

Simon, Herbert A. *Administrative Behavior: A Study of Decision-Making Processes in Administrative Organization*. New York: Macmillan, 1946.

———. "Administrative Decision Making." *Public Administration Review* 25 (1965): 31–37.

———. "Application of Servomechanism Theory to Production Control." *Econometrica* 20 (April 1952): 247–68.

———. "A Behavioral Model of Rational Choice." *Quarterly Journal of Economics* 69 (February 1955): 99–118.

———. "Bibliography." *Scandinavian Journal of Economics* 81 (1979): 94–114.

———. "A Comparison of Organization Theories." *Review of Economic Studies* 20 (1952–53): 40–48.

———. "Development of a Theory of Democratic Administration: Replies and Comments." *American Political Science Review* 46 (June 1952): 494–96.

———. "The Experts in Your Midst." *Harvard Business Review* 67 (January–February 1989): 120–24.

———. "A Formal Theory of the Employment Relation." *Econometrics* 19 (July 1951): 293–305.

———. "How Managers Express Their Creativity." *Across the Board* 23 (March 1986): 11–16.

———. "The Logic of Heuristic Decision Making." In *The Logic of Decision and Action*, edited by N. Rescher, pp. 1–20. Pittsburgh: University of Pittsburgh Press, 1967.

———. "The Logic of Rational Decision." *British Journal for the Philosophy of Science* 16 (1965): 169–86.

———. "Making Management Decisions: The Role of Intuition and Emotion." *Academy of Management Executive* 1 (February 1987): 57–64.

———. "Modeling Human Mental Processes." *Proceedings of the Western Joint Computer Conference, May 9–11* (1961): 114.

———. *Models of Discovery and Other Topics in the Methods of Science*. Boston: D. Reidel, 1977.

———. *Models of Man, Social and Rational: Mathematical Essays on Rational Human Behavior in a Social Setting*. New York: Wiley, 1957.

———. *Models of Thought*. New Haven: Yale University Press, 1979.

———. "Motivational and Emotional Controls of Cognition." *Psychological Review* 74 (January 1967): 29–39.

———. "My Life Philosophy." *American Economist* 29 (Spring 1985): 15–20.

———. *The New Science of Management Decision*. New York: Harper and Row, 1960, 1977.

———. "On How to Decide What to Do." *Bell Journal of Economics* 9 (Autumn 1978): 494–507.

———. "On the Concept of Organizational Goal." *Administrative Science Quarterly* 9 (June 1964): 1–22.

———. "Organization Man: Rational or Self-Actualizing." *Public Administration Review* 33 (July–August 1973): 346–53.

———. "The Organization of Complex Systems." In *Hierarchy Theory*, edited by H. H. Pattee, pp. 3–27. New York: G. Braziller, 1973.

———. "Rational Choice and the Structure of the Environment." *Psychological Review* 63 (March 1956): 129–38.

⋁ ———. "Rational Decision Making in Business Organizations." *American Economic Review* 69 (March 1979): 493–513.

———. *Reason in Human Affairs.* Stanford: Stanford University Press, 1983.

———. *The Sciences of the Artificial.* Cambridge, Mass.: MIT Press, 1969, 1981.

———. *The Shape of Automation for Men and Management.* New York: Harper and Row, 1965.

⋁ ———. "Theories of Decision-Making in Economics and Behavioral Science." *American Economic Review* 49 (June 1959): 253–83.

———. "Theory of Automata: Discussion." *Econometrica* 19 (1961): 72.

———. "Thinking by Computers." In *Mind and Cosmos: Essays in Contemporary Science and Psychology*, edited by R. Colodny, pp. 3–21. Pittsburgh: University of Pittsburgh Press, 1966.

———. "Two Heads Are Better Than One: The Collaboration between AI and OR." *Interfaces* 17 (July–August 1987): 8–15.

⋁ Simon, Herbert A., Donald W. Smithburg, and Victor A. Thompson. *Public Administration.* New York: Knopf, 1956.

Sloan, Alfred. *My Years with General Motors.* Garden City, N.Y.: Doubleday, 1964.

Smith, Lee. "Japan's Autocratic Managers." *Fortune*, January 7, 1985, pp. 56–65.

⋃ Smith, Peter B. "Controlled Studies of the Outcome of Sensitivity Training." *Psychological Bulletin* 82 (1975): 597–622.

⋁ ———. "Why Successful Groups Succeed: The Implications of T-Group Research." In *Developing Social Skills in Managers*, edited by C. L. Cooper, pp. 63–76. New York: Wiley, 1976.

Solow, Herbert. "Operations Research." *Fortune*, April 1951, pp. 105–7, 146–48.

———. "Operations Research in Business." *Fortune*, February 1956, pp. 128–31, 148, 151.

Sours, Martin H. "The Influence of Japanese Culture on the Japanese Management System." In *Japanese Management*, edited by Sang Lee and Gary Schwendiman, pp. 27–38. New York: Praeger, 1982.

Special Task Force to the Secretary of Health, Education, and Welfare. *Work in America.* Cambridge, Mass.: MIT Press, 1973.

"Spreading Lordstown Syndrome." *Business Week*, March 4, 1972, pp. 69–70.

√ Steele, Fred I. "Can T-Group Training Change the Power Structure?" *Personnel Administration* 33 (November–December 1970): 48–53.

Steinbacker, John. *The Child Seducers.* Fullerton, Calif.: Educator Publications, 1971.

Steindhardt, Jacinto. "The Role of Operations Research in the Navy." *United States Naval Institute Proceedings* 72 (May 1946): 649–55.

Steinmetz, Lawrence L., and Charles D. Greenridge. "Realities That Shape Managerial Style." *Business Horizons* 13 (October 1970): 23–32.

Stogdill, Ralph M. *The Handbook of Leadership.* New York: Free Press, 1974.

Stogdill, Ralph M., and Bernard M. Bass. *Stogdill's Handbook of Leadership: A Survey of Theory and Research.* New York: Free Press, 1981.

Strauss, George. "Human Relations, 1968 Style." *Industrial Relations* 7 (May 1968): 262–76.

————. "Job Satisfaction, Motivation, and Job Design." In *Organizational Behavior: Research and Issues,* edited by George Strauss, Raymond E. Miles, Charles C. Snow, and Arnold S. Tannenbaum, pp. 19–49. Belmont, Calif.: Wadsworth, 1974.

————. "Management by Objectives: A Critical View." *Training and Development Journal* 26 (April 1972): 10–15.

————. "Notes on Power Equalization." In *The Social Science of Organizations,* edited by Harold J. Leavitt, pp. 41–48. Englewood Cliffs, N.J.: Prentice-Hall, 1963.

Sullivan, Jeremiah. "A Critique of Theory Z." *Academy of Management Review* 8 (January 1983): 132–42.

Sullivan, Jeremiah, and N. Kameda. "The Concept of Profit and Japanese-American Managerial Communications." *Journal of Business Communications* 19 (1982): 33–40.

Takagi, Haruo. *The Flaw in Japanese Management.* Ann Arbor, Mich.: UMI Research, 1985.

Takezawa, Shin-Ichi. "The Quality of Working Life: Trends in Japan." *Labour and Society* 1 (1976): 29–48.

Takezawa, Shin-Ichi, and Arthur Whitehill. *Work Ways: Japan and America.* Tokyo: Japan Institute of Labor, 1983.

Tannenbaum, Robert, Irving R. Weschler, and Fred Massarik. *Leadership and Organization: A Behavioral Science Approach.* New York: McGraw-Hill, 1961.

Taylor, D. W. "Decision Making and Problem Solving." In *Management Decision Making,* edited by Richard M. Cyert and L. A. Welsch, pp. 40–86. Baltimore, Md.: Penguin, 1970.

Taylor, Frederick W. *Scientific Management: Comprising Shop Management, the Principles of Scientific Management, Testimony before the Special House Committee.* New York: Harper, 1947.

Taylor, James C. "Job Design Criteria Twenty Years Later." In *Design of Jobs,* edited by Louis Davis and James C. Taylor, pp. 54–63. Santa Monica, Calif.: Goodyear, 1979.

Thomas, D., and Smith, T. "T-Grouping: The White Collar Hippie Movement." *National Association of Secondary Schools Bulletin,* February 1968, pp. 1–9.

Thomas, George, and Jo-Anne DaCosta. "A Sample Survey of Corporate Operations Research." *Interfaces* 9 (August 1979): 102–10.

Thompson, Victor A. *Modern Organization.* Montgomery: University of Alabama, 1977.

Tosi, Henry L., and Stephen J. Carroll. *Management by Objectives.* New York: MacMillan, 1973.

————. "Managerial Reactions to Management by Objectives." *Academy of Management Journal* (December 1968): 514–26.

Trefethen, Florence N. "A History of Operations Research." In *Operations Research for Management*, edited by Florence N. Trefethen and Joseph F. McCloskey, pp. 3–35. Baltimore: Johns Hopkins University Press, 1954.

Trist, Eric L., and K. W. Bamforth. "Some Social and Psychological Consequences of the Longwall Method of Coal-Getting." *Human Relations* 4 (1951): 6–24, 37–38.

Trist, Eric L., G. W. Higgin, H. Murray, and A. B. Pollock. *Organizational Choice: Capabilities of Groups at the Coal Face under Changing Technologies.* London: Tavistock, 1963.

United Automobile Workers. "Summary of Agreement with Ford Motor Company." *Daily Labor Report*, November 5, 1973.

Urwick, Lyndall F. *The Elements of Administration.* New York: Harper and Row, 1944.

————. "Papers in the Science of Administration." *Academy of Management Review* 13 (December 1970): 361–71.

————. "Why the So-Called 'Classicists' Endure." *Management International Review* 2 (1971): 3–14.

Versagi, Frank J. "What American Labor/Management Can Learn from Japanese Unions." *Management Review* 71 (June 1982): 24–28.

Villarreal, John J. "Management by Objectives Revisited." *S.A.M. Advanced Management Journal* 39 (April 1974): 28–33.

Vogel, Ezra F. *Japan As Number One: Lessons for America.* Cambridge, Mass.: Harvard University Press, 1979.

von Neumann, John. *The Computer and the Brain.* New Haven: Yale University Press, 1958.

Vroom, Victor H. *Work and Motivation.* New York: Wiley, 1964.

Vroom, Victor H., and Edward L. Deci. "An Overview of Work Motivation." In *Management and Motivation*, edited by Victor H. Vroom and Edward L. Deci, pp. 9–19. London: Penguin, 1970.

Waddington, Conrad H. *O.R. in World War 2.* London: Elek Science, 1973.

Wahba, Mahmoud A., and Lawrence G. Bridwell. "Maslow Reconsidered: A Review of Research of the Need Hierarchy Theory." *Organizational Behavior and Human Performance* 15 (1976): 212–40.

Walker, Charles R. "The Problem of the Repetitive Job." *Harvard Business Review* (May 1950): 54–58.

Walker, Charles R., and Robert H. Guest. *The Man on the Assembly Line.* Cambridge, Mass.: Harvard University Press, 1952.

Walton, Richard E. "How to Counter Alienation in the Plant." *Harvard Business Review* 50 (November–December 1972): 70–81.

Watson, Hugh J., and Patricia Gill Marett. "A Survey of Management Science Implementation Problems." *Interfaces* 9 (August 1979): 124–28.

Wayne, Leslie. "Management Gospel Gone Wrong." *New York Times*, May 30, 1982, pp. C1, C21.

Weber, C. Edward. "Decision Making in Business: A Behavioral Approach." In *Encyclopedia of Economics*, edited by Douglas Greenwald, pp. 227–31. New York: McGraw-Hill, 1982.

Weizenbaum, Joseph. *Computer Power and Human Reason: From Judgment to Calculation*. San Francisco: W. H. Freeman, 1976.

West, George E. "Bureaupathology and the Failure of MBO." *Human Resource Management* 16 (Summer 1977): 33–40.

Wheelwright, Steven C. "Japan—Where Operations Really Are Strategic." *Harvard Business Review* 59 (July–August 1981): 67–74.

"Where Being Nice to Workers Didn't Work." *Business Week*, January 20, 1973, pp. 98–100.

"Where Executives Tear Off the Masks." *Business Week*, September 3, 1966, pp. 76–83.

White, B. J. "Innovations in Job Design: The Union Perspective." *Journal of Contemporary Business* 6 (1977): 23–35.

White, Ralph K., and Ronald Lippitt. *Autocracy and Democracy*. New York: Harper and Row, 1960.

Whitehill, Arthur, and Shin-Ichi Takezawa. *The Other Worker: A Comparative Study of Industrial Relations in the United States and Japan*. Honolulu: East-West Center, 1968.

Whitsett, David A. "Making Sense of Management Theories." *Personnel* 52 (May–June 1975): 44–52.

———. "Where Are Your Unenriched Jobs?" *Harvard Business Review* 53 (January–February 1975): 74–80.

Whitsett, David A., and Lyle Yorks. *From Management Theory to Business Sense: The Myths and Realities of People at Work*. New York: AMACOM, 1983.

"Who Wants to Work?" *Newsweek*, March 26, 1973, pp. 79–89.

Widick, B. J. "The Men Won't Toe the Vega Line." *Nation*, March 27, 1972, pp. 403–4.

Wiener, Norbert. *Cybernetics, or Control and Communication in the Animal and the Machine*. Cambridge, Mass.: MIT Press, 1948.

Wilcox, Herbert G. "Hierarchy, Human Nature and the Participation Panacea." *Public Administration Review* 29 (January–February 1969): 53–63.

Williams, E. C. "The Origin of the Term 'Operational Research' and the Early Development of the Military Work." *Operational Research Quarterly* 19 (June 1968): 111–13.

Williams, J. "Herbert A. Simon: A Life Spent on One Problem." *New York Times*, November 26, 1978.

Winpisinger, William W. "Job Enrichment: A Union View." *Monthly Labor Review* 96 (April 1973): 54–56.

Wolf, Marvin J. *The Japanese Conspiracy: The Plot to Dominate Industry Worldwide—and How to Deal with It*. New York: Empire, 1983.

Wolff, M. F. "Managers at Work: To Innovate Faster, Try the Skunk Works." *Research Management* 30 (September–October 1987): 7–8.

Wooldridge, Dean E. "Operations Research: The Scientists' Invasion of the Business World." *Journal of Industrial Engineering* 7 (September–October 1956): 230–35.

Wooley, R. N., and M. Pidd. "Problem Structuring—A Literature Review." *Journal of the Operational Research Society* 32 (1981): 197–206.

Woolsey, Gene. "Reflections on the Past of Scientific Management and the Future of Management Science." *Interfaces* 6 (May 1976): 3–4.

——, ed. "Where the War Stories Began—Some Founding Fathers Reminisce." *Interfaces* 11 (1981): 37–44.

Woronoff, Jon. *Japan: The Coming Economic Crisis*. Tokyo: Lotus, 1979.

Wrapp, H. E. "Management by Objectives—Or Wheel and Deal?" *Steel*, May 29, 1967, pp. 46–47.

Yamamoto, Shichihei. "Tradition and Management." *International Studies of Management and Organization* 15 (Fall–Winter 1985–86): 69–88.

Yorks, Lyle. *Job Enrichment Revisited*. New York: AMACOM, 1979.

——. *A Radical Approach to Job Enrichment*. New York: AMACOM, 1976.

Zahedi, Fatemeh. "A Survey of Issues in the MS/OR Field." *Interfaces* 14 (March–April 1984): 57–86.

Secondary Sources

Abegglen, James C. *The Japanese Factory: Aspects of Its Social Organization*. Glencoe, Ill.: Free Press, 1958.

——. *Management and Worker: The Japanese Solution*. Tokyo: Sophia, 1973.

——. *The Strategy of Japanese Business*. Cambridge, Mass.: Ballinger, 1984.

Abegglen, James C., and George Stalk. *Kaisha, the Japanese Corporation*. New York: Basic Books, 1985.

Abrahamson, Brant W. "Corporate Capitalism: An Analysis of Peter Drucker's Conception of Industrial Society." M.A. thesis, University of Iowa, 1961.

Aitken, Hugh. *Taylorism at Watertown Arsenal*. Cambridge, Mass.: Harvard University Press, 1960.

Alchian, Armen. "Uncertainty, Evolution and Economic Theory." *Journal of Political Economy* 58 (June 1950): 211–21.

Alchian, Armen, and Harold Demsetz. "Production, Information Costs, and Economic Organization." *American Economic Review* 62 (December 1972): 777–95.

Alchon, Guy. *The Invisible Hand of Planning: Capitalism, Social Science and the State in the 1920s*. Princeton, N.J.: Princeton University Press, 1985.

Ando, Albert. "On the Contribution of Herbert A. Simon to Economics." *Scandinavian Journal of Economics* 81 (1979): 83–93.

Andreski, Stanislav. *Social Sciences As Sorcery.* London: Andre Deutsch, 1972.

Aronowitz, Stanley. *False Promises: The Shaping of American Working Class Consciousness.* New York: McGraw-Hill, 1973.

Auerbach, M. Morton. *The Conservative Illusion.* New York: Columbia University Press, 1959.

Back, Kurt W. *Beyond Words: The Story of Sensitivity Training and the Encounter Movement.* New York: Russell Sage, 1972.

Baritz, Loren. *Backfire: A History of How American Culture Led Us into Vietnam and Made Us Fight the Way We Did.* New York: William Morrow, 1985.

————. *The Servants of Power: A History of the Use of Social Science in American Industry.* Middletown, Conn.: Wesleyan University Press, 1960.

Barkin, Solomon, ed. *Worker Militancy and Its Consequences, 1969–1975: New Directions in Western Industrial Relations.* New York: Praeger, 1975.

Barrett, William. *The Illusion of Technique: A Search for Meaning in a Technological Civilization.* Garden City, N.Y.: Doubleday, 1978.

Baumol, William J. "On the Contribution of Herbert A. Simon to Economics." *Scandinavian Journal of Economics* 81 (1979): 74–82.

Bell, Daniel. *The Cultural Contradictions of Capitalism.* New York: Basic Books, 1976.

————. *Work and Its Discontents: The Cult of Efficiency in America.* Boston: Beacon Press, 1956.

Bender, Marylin. "Consulting Guru for Managers." *New York Times,* April 14, 1974.

Bendix, Reinhard. *Work and Authority in Industry: Ideologies of Management in the Course of Industrialization.* New York: Wiley, 1956.

Bennett, Amanda. "Management Guru: Peter Drucker Wins Devotion of Top Firms with Eclectic Counsel." *Wall Street Journal,* July 28, 1987, p. 1.

Bennett, John. "Japanese Economic Growth: Background for Social Change." In *Aspects of Social Change in Modern Japan,* edited by Ronald Dore, pp. 411–53. Princeton, N.J.: Princeton University Press, 1967.

Berg, Ivar, Marcia Freedman, and Michael Freeman. *Managers and Work Reform: A Limited Engagement.* New York: Free Press, 1978.

Berlinski, David. *On Systems Analysis.* Cambridge, Mass.: MIT Press, 1976.

Bluestone, Barry, and Bennett Harrison. *The Deindustrialization of America: Plant Closings, Community Abandonment, and the Dismantling of Basic Industry.* New York: Basic Books, 1982.

Blumberg, Paul. *Industrial Democracy: The Sociology of Participation.* New York: Schocken, 1969.

Boguslaw, Robert. *The New Utopians: A Study of System Design and Social Change.* Englewood Cliffs, N.J.: Prentice-Hall, 1965.

Bolter, J. David. *Turing's Man: Western Culture in the Computer Age.* Chapel Hill: University of North Carolina Press, 1984.

Bowen, Ralph H. *German Theories of the Corporative State with Special Reference to the Period 1870–1919*. New York: Whittlesey, 1947.

Bramel, Dana, and Ronald Friend. "Hawthorne, the Myth of the Docile Worker, and Class Bias in Psychology." *American Psychologist* 36 (August 1981): 867–78.

Brandes, Stuart D. *American Welfare Capitalism, 1880–1940*. Chicago: University of Chicago Press, 1976.

Braverman, Harry. *Labor and Monopoly Capital: The Degradation of Work in the Twentieth Century*. New York: Monthly Review Press, 1974.

Brody, David. "The Rise and Decline of Welfare Capitalism." In *Workers in Industrial America: Essays on the Twentieth Century Struggle*, edited by David Brody, pp. 48–81. New York: Oxford University Press, 1980.

Brown, William. "Japanese Management—The Cultural Background." In *Culture and Management*, edited by Ross A. Webber, pp. 428–42. Homewood, Ill.: Irwin, 1969.

Brubaker, Rogers. *The Limits of Rationality: An Essay on the Social and Moral Thought of Max Weber*. London: Allen and Unwin, 1984.

Brzezinski, Zbigniew. *The Fragile Blossom: Crisis and Change in Japan*. New York: Harper and Row, 1972.

Burawoy, Michael. *Manufacturing Consent: Changes in the Labor Process under Monopoly Capitalism*. Chicago: University of Chicago Press, 1979.

Buttrick, John. "The Inside Contract System." *Journal of Economic History* 12 (1952): 205–21.

Caldwell, Bruce J. *Beyond Positivism: Economic Methodology in the Twentieth Century*. London: Allen and Unwin, 1982.

Carey, Alex. "The Hawthorne Studies: A Radical Criticism." *American Sociological Review* 32 (June 1967): 403–16.

Chamberlain, Neil W. "The Institutional Economics of John R. Commons." In *Institutional Economics: Veblen, Commons, and Mitchell Reconsidered*, edited by Joseph Dorfman, C. E. Ayres, Neil W. Chamberlain, Simon Kuznets, and R. A. Gordon, pp. 63–94. Berkeley: University of California Press, 1963.

Chandler, Alfred D. "Business History As Institutional History." In *Approaches to American Economic History*, edited by George R. Taylor and L. F. Ellsworth, pp. 17–24. Charlottesville: University Press of Virginia, 1971.

———. "Comment [on the New Economic History]." *Explorations in Entrepreneurial History*, Second Series (Fall 1968): 66–74.

———. "The Emergence of Managerial Capitalism." *Business History Review* 58 (Winter 1984): 473–503.

———. *The Essential Alfred Chandler: Essays toward a Historical Theory of Big Business*. Edited by Thomas McCraw. Boston: Harvard Business School, 1988.

———. *Strategy and Structure*. Cambridge, Mass.: MIT Press, 1962.

———. *The Visible Hand: The Managerial Revolution in American Business*. Cambridge, Mass.: Harvard University Press, 1977.

Clawson, Dan. *Bureaucracy and the Labor Process: The Transformation of U.S. Industry, 1860–1920.* New York: Monthly Review Press, 1980.

Cohen, Eliot. "Systems Paralysis." *American Spectator,* November 1980, pp. 23–27.

Cole, Robert E. *Japanese Blue Collar: The Changing Tradition.* Berkeley: University of California Press, 1971.

————. "A Japanese Management Import Comes Full Circle." *Wall Street Journal,* February 22, 1983, p. 30.

————. "Learning from the Japanese: Prospects and Pitfalls." *Management Review* 69 (September 1980): 22–28.

————. *Work, Mobility, and Participation: A Comparative Study of American and Japanese Industry.* Berkeley: University of California Press, 1979.

Cremin, Lawrence A. *The Transformation of the School: Progressivism in American Education, 1876–1957.* New York: Vintage, 1961.

Cuff, Robert D. "From Market to Manager." *Canadian Review of American Studies* 10 (1979): 47–54.

Cyert, Richard M. "Herbert Simon." *Challenge* 22 (September 1979): 62–64.

Davis, Mike. "The Stop Watch and the Wooden Shoe: Scientific Management and the Industrial Workers of the World." *Radical America* 9 (1975): 69–95. ✓

Davis, Philip J., and Reuben Hersh. *Descartes' Dream: The World According to Mathematics.* New York: Harcourt Brace Jovanovich, 1986.

Day, Robert H. "Profits, Learning and the Convergence of Satisficing to Marginalism." *Quarterly Journal of Economics* 81 (May 1967): 302–11.

Dechert, C. R. "The Development of Cybernetics." *The American Behavioral Scientist* 8 (June 1965): 5–10.

Dellobuono, Richard. "Markets and Managers: A Critique of Two Points of View." *Contemporary Crisis* 5 (October 1981): 403–15.

Diamant, Alfred. *Austrian Catholics and the First Republic: Democracy, Capitalism, and the Social Order, 1918–34.* Princeton, N.J.: Princeton University Press, 1960.

Dore, Ronald P. *British Factory—Japanese Factory: The Origins of National Diversity in Industrial Relations.* Berkeley: University of California Press, 1973.

Dorfman, Joseph. *The Economic Mind in American Civilization.* 5 vols. Vol. 1–2, *1606–1865.* Vol. 3, *1865–1918.* Vol. 4–5, *1918–1933.* New York: Viking, 1946–1959.

Dower, John W. *War without Mercy: Race and Power in the Pacific War.* New York: Pantheon, 1986.

Dreyfus, Hubert L. *Alchemy and Artificial Intelligence,* P-3244. Santa Monica, Calif.: RAND Corporation, 1965.

————. *What Computers Can't Do: A Critique of Artificial Intelligence.* New York: Harper and Row, 1972.

Dreyfus, Hubert L., and Stuart E. Dreyfus. *Mind over Machines: The Power of Human Intuition and Expertise in the Era of the Computer.* New York: Free Press, 1986.

Duboff, Richard B., and Edward S. Herman. "Alfred Chandler's New Business History: A Review." *Politics and Society* 10 (1980): 87–110.

Edwards, Richard. *Contested Terrain: The Transformation of the Workplace in the Twentieth Century.* New York: Basic Books, 1979.

————. "The Social Relations of Production at the Point of Production." In *Complex Organizations: Critical Perspectives,* edited by Mary Zey-Ferrell and Michael Aiken, pp. 156–82. Glenview, Ill.: Scott, Foresman, 1981.

Elbow, Matthew H. *French Corporative Theory, 1789–1948: A Chapter in the History of Ideas.* New York: Octagon, 1966.

Ferguson, Tracy H., and John Gaal. "Codetermination: A Fad or a Future in America?" *Employee Relations Law Journal* 10 (Autumn 1984): 176–99.

Fine, Martin. "Toward Corporatism: The Movement for Capital-Labor Collaboration in France, 1914–36." Ph.D. dissertation, University of Wisconsin, 1971.

Fligstein, Neil. "The Spread of the Multidivisional Form among Large Firms, 1919–1979." *American Sociological Review* 50 (June 1985): 377–91.

Fox, Alan. *Beyond Contract: Work, Power and Trust Relations.* London: Faber and Faber, 1974.

✓ Franke, R. H., and J. D. Kaul. "The Hawthorne Experiments: First Statistical Interpretation." *American Sociological Review* 43 (October 1978): 623–43.

Fraser, Steve. "Dress Rehearsal for the New Deal." In *Working Class America,* edited by Michael Frisch and Daniel Walkowitz, pp. 212–28. Urbana: University of Illinois Press, 1983.

Friedman, Andrew. *Industry and Labour.* London: MacMillan, 1977.

Friedman, Milton. *Capitalism and Freedom.* Chicago: University of Chicago Press, 1962.

————. *Essays in Positive Economics.* Chicago: University of Chicago Press, 1953.

Friend, Ronald, and Dana Bramel. "More Harvard Humbug." *American Psychologist* 37 (December 1982): 1399–1401.

Frug, G. E. "The Ideology of Bureaucracy in American Law." *Harvard Law Review* 97 (April 1984): 1277–1388.

Fruin, W. Mark. "The Japanese Company Controversy." *Journal of Japanese Studies* 4 (Summer 1978): 267–300.

Galambos, Louis. "Parsonian Sociology and Post-Progressive History." *Social Science Quarterly* 50 (June 1969): 25–45.

Gardner, Howard. *The Mind's New Science: A History of the Cognitive Revolution.* New York: Basic Books, 1985.

Garson, Barbara. *All the Livelong Day: The Meaning and Demeaning of Routine Work.* Garden City, N.Y.: Doubleday, 1975.

————. "The Hell with Work." *Harper's,* August 1972, pp. 8–9.

————. "Luddites in Lordstown." *Harper's,* June 1972, pp. 68–70.

Gerber, Larry G. "Corporatism in Comparative Perspective: The Impact of the First World War on American British Labor Relations." *Business History Review* 62 (Spring 1988): 93–127.

Gibson, James W. *The Perfect War: Technowar in Vietnam.* Boston: Atlantic Monthly, 1986.

Gilbert, James. *Designing the Industrial State: The Intellectual Pursuit of Collectivism in America, 1880–1940.* Chicago: Quadrangle, 1972.

Gilson, M. B. "Review of *Management and the Worker.*" *American Journal of Sociology* 46 (1940): 98–101.

Goffman, Erving. *The Presentation of Self in Everyday Life.* Garden City, N.Y.: Doubleday, 1959.

Goldman, Paul, and Donald R. Van Houten. "Bureaucracy and Domination: Managerial Strategy in Turn-of-the-Century American Industry." In *Complex Organizations: Critical Perspectives,* edited by Mary Zey-Ferrell and Michael Aiken, pp. 189–216. Glenview, Ill.: Scott, Foresman, 1981.

Goldstine, Herman H. *The Computer from Pascal to Von Neuman.* Princeton, N.J.: Princeton University Press, 1972.

Golob, Eugene. *The Isms.* New York: Harper, 1954.

Gordon, Andrew. *The Evolution of Labor Relations in Japan: Heavy Industry, 1853–1955.* Cambridge, Mass.: Council on East Asian Studies, Harvard University, 1985.

Gordon, David M. "Capitalist Efficiency and Socialist Efficiency." *Monthly Review* 28 (July–August 1976): 19–39.

Gordon, David M., Richard Edwards, and Michael Reich. *Segmented Work, Divided Workers: The Historical Transformation of Labor in the United States.* London: Cambridge University Press, 1982.

Gouldner, Alvin W. "Metaphysical Pathos and the Theory of Bureaucracy." *American Political Science Review* 49 (1955): 496–507.

Graebner, William. *The Engineering of Consent: Democracy and Authority in Twentieth-Century America.* Madison: University of Wisconsin Press, 1987.

————. "The Small Group and Democratic Social Engineering, 1900–1950." *Journal of Social Issues* 42 (Spring 1986): 137–54.

Green, Michael K. "A Kantian Evaluation of Taylorism in the Workplace." *Journal of Business Ethics* (Netherlands) 5 (April 1986): 165–69.

Greenwood, Ronald G. "Management by Objectives: As Developed by Peter Drucker, Assisted by Harold Smiddy." *Academy of Management Review* 6 (April 1981): 225–30.

Gutman, Herbert G., ed. *Work, Culture and Society in Industrializing America.* New York: Vintage, 1977.

Haber, Sam. *Efficiency and Uplift: Scientific Management in the Progressive Era.* Chicago: University of Chicago Press, 1964.

Halberstam, David. *The Reckoning.* New York: William Morrow, 1986.

Hales, Mike. "Management Science and 'The Second Industrial Revolution.'" *Radical Science Journal* 1 (January 1974): 5–28.

Harbison, Frederick. "Management in Japan." In *Management in the Industrial World: An International Analysis,* edited by Frederick Harbison and Charles A. Myers, chap. 13. New York: McGraw-Hill, 1959.

Harris, Howell John. *The Right to Manage: Industrial Relations Policies of American Business in the 1940s.* Madison: University of Wisconsin Press, 1982.

Hartmann, Heinz. *Authority and Organization in German Management.* Princeton, N.J.: Princeton University Press, 1959.

Hartz, Louis. *The Liberal Tradition in America: An Interpretation of American Political Thought since the Revolution.* New York: Harcourt, Brace and World, 1955.

Hawley, Ellis W. "The Discovery and Study of a 'Corporate Liberalism.'" *Business History Review* 52 (Autumn 1978): 309–20.

————. *The Great War and the Search for a Modern Order.* New York: St. Martins, 1979.

————. "Herbert Hoover, the Commerce Secretariat, and the Vision of the 'Associative State.'" *Journal of American History* 61 (June 1974): 116–40.

Heims, Steve J. *John von Neumann and Norbert Wiener: From Mathematics to the Technologies of Life and Death.* Cambridge, Mass.: MIT Press, 1980.

Hill, Stephen. *Competition and Control at Work: The New Industrial Sociology.* Cambridge, Mass.: MIT Press, 1981.

Hirschman, Albert O. *Exit, Voice, and Loyalty: Responses to Decline in Firms, Organizations, and States.* Cambridge, Mass.: Harvard University Press, 1970.

Hirschmeier, Johannes, and Tsunehiko Yui. *The Development of Japanese Business: 1600–1980.* London: Allen and Unwin, 1981.

Hogan, Michael J. "Corporatism: A Positive Appraisal." *Diplomatic History* 10 (Fall 1986): 363–72.

Hoos, Ida R. *Systems Analysis in Public Policy: A Critique.* Berkeley: University of California Press, 1972; rev. ed., 1983.

Hounshell, David A. *From the American System to Mass Production, 1800–1932: The Development of Manufacturing Technology in the United States.* Baltimore: Johns Hopkins University Press, 1984.

Jackson, Michael C. "The Nature of 'Soft' Systems Thinking: The Work of Churchman, Ackoff, and Checkland." *Journal of Applied Systems Analysis* 9 (1982): 17–29.

————. "Social Systems Theory and Practice: The Need for a Critical Approach." *International Journal of General Systems* 10 (1985): 135–51.

Jacoby, Sanford M. *Employing Bureaucracy: Managers, Unions and the Transformation of Work in American Industry, 1900–1945.* New York: Columbia University Press, 1985.

Jay, Anthony. *Management and Machiavelli: An Inquiry into the Politics of Corporate Life.* New York: Holt, Rinehart and Winston, 1968.

Jenkins, David. *Job Power: Blue and White Collar Democracy.* Garden City, N.Y.: Doubleday, 1973.

Kahn, Herman. *The Emerging Japanese Superstate: Challenge and Response.* Englewood Cliffs, N.J.: Prentice-Hall, 1970.

Kanter, Rosabeth Moss. "Drucker: The Unsolved Puzzle." *New Management* 2 (Winter 1985): 10–13.

————. *Men and Women of the Corporation.* New York: Basic Books, 1977.

————. "Work in a New America." *Daedalus* 107 (Winter 1978): 47–78.

Kaufman, Herbert. "Organization Theory and Political Theory." *American Political Science Review* 58 (March 1964): 5–14.

Keys, Paul. "Traditional Management Science and the Emerging Critique." In *New Directions in Management Science*, edited by Paul Keys and Michael C. Jackson, pp. 1–25. Aldershot: Gower, 1987.

Kline, Morris. *Mathematics: The Loss of Certainty.* Oxford: Oxford University Press, 1980.

Koontz, Harold. "Making Sense of Management Theory." *Harvard Business Review* 40 (July–August 1962): 24–44.

————. "The Management Theory Jungle." *Academy of Management Journal* 4 (December 1961): 174–88.

Krupp, Sherman. *Pattern in Organization Analysis.* New York: Holt, Rinehart, and Winston, 1961.

Kuisel, Richard. *Capitalism and the State in Modern France.* London: Cambridge University Press, 1981.

————. *Ernest Mercier, French Technocrat.* Berkeley: University of California Press, 1967.

Landsberger, Henry A. *Hawthorne Revisited.* Ithaca, N.Y.: New York State School of Industrial and Labor Relations, 1958.

Levinson, Charles, ed. *Industry's Democratic Revolution.* London: Allen and Unwin, 1974.

Lilienfeld, Robert. *The Rise of Systems Theory: An Ideological Analysis.* New York: Wiley, 1978.

Lipow, Arthur. *Authoritarian Socialism in America: Edward Bellamy and the Nationalist Movement.* Berkeley: University of California Press, 1982.

Lohr, Steve. "Consultant on Quality: W. Edwards Deming—He Taught the Japanese." *New York Times*, May 10, 1981, p. 6.

Long, William A., and K. K. Seo. *Management in Japan and India with Reference to the United States.* New York: Praeger, 1977.

Lustig, R. Jeffrey. *Corporate Liberalism: The Origins of Modern American Political Theory, 1890–1920.* Berkeley: University of California Press, 1982.

McCloskey, Donald M. "The Limits of Expertise: If You're So Smart, Why Ain't You Rich?" *American Scholar* 57 (Summer 1988): 393–406.

————. *The Rhetoric of Economics.* Madison: University of Wisconsin Press, 1985.

McCorduck, Pamela. *Machines Who Think: A Personal Inquiry into the History and Prospects of Artificial Intelligence.* San Francisco: W. H. Freeman, 1979.

McCraw, Thomas K. "Introduction: The Intellectual Odyssey of Alfred Chandler, Jr." In *The Essential Alfred Chandler: Essays toward a Historical Theory of Big Business*, edited by Thomas K. McCraw, pp. 1–21. Boston: Harvard Business School, 1988.

Machlup, Fritz. "Theories of the Firm: Marginalist, Behavioral, Managerial." *American Economic Review* 57 (1967): 1–33.

MacIntyre, Alastaire. *After Virtue: A Study in Moral Theory*. Notre Dame: Notre Dame University Press, 1981.

McKee, J. B. "Status and Power in the Industrial Community: A Comment on Drucker's Thesis." *American Journal of Sociology* 58 (January 1953): 65–93.

McKelvey, Jean. *AFL Attitudes Toward Production, 1900–32*. Ithaca, N.Y.: Cornell Studies in Industrial and Labor Relations, 1952.

Maier, Charles S. "Between Taylorism and Technocracy: European Ideologies and the Vision of Industrial Productivity in the 1920s." *Journal of Contemporary History* 5 (1970): 27–60.

———. *Recasting Bourgeois Europe*. Princeton, N.J.: Princeton University Press, 1975.

Marrow, Alfred J. *The Practical Theorist: The Life and Work of Kurt Lewin*. New York: Basic Books, 1969.

Marsh, Robert M., and Hiroshi Mannari. *Modernization and the Japanese Factory*. Princeton, N.J.: Princeton University Press, 1976.

Martin, B. *Count Albert de Mun*. Chapel Hill: University of North Carolina Press, 1978.

Mason, E. S. "Saint-Simonism and the Rationalization of Industry." *Quarterly Journal of Economics* (1931): 640–83.

Mathewson, Stanley B. *Restriction of Output among Unorganized Workers*. New York: Viking, 1931.

Matusow, Alan J. *The Unraveling of America: A History of Liberalism in the 1960s*. New York: Harper and Row, 1984.

Mazgaj, Paul. *The Action Française and Revolutionary Syndicalism*. Chapel Hill: University of North Carolina Press, 1979.

Merkle, Judith A. *Management and Ideology: The Legacy of the International Scientific Management Movement*. Berkeley: University of California Press, 1980.

Meyer, Stephen. *The Five Dollar Day: Labor Management and Social Control in the Ford Motor Company, 1908–1921*. Albany: State University of New York, 1981.

Mills, C. Wright. "The Contributions of Sociology to Studies of Industrial Relations." *Berkeley Journal of Sociology* 15 (1970, reprint from 1948): 10–32.

———. *The Sociological Imagination*. New York: Oxford University Press, 1959.

Mintzberg, Henry. *The Nature of Managerial Work*. New York: Harper and Row, 1973.

Montgomery, David. "Labor and the Republic of Industrial America, 1860–1920." *Le Mouvement Social* 111 (1980): 210–15.

———. *Workers' Control in America*. Cambridge: Cambridge University Press, 1979.

Muhs, William F. "Worker Participation in the Progressive Era: An Assessment by Harrington Emerson." *Academy of Management Review* 7 (January 1982): 99–102.

Nader, Ralph, and William Taylor. *The Big Boys: Power and Position in American Business*. New York: Pantheon, 1986.

Nadworny, Milton J. *Scientific Management and the Unions, 1900–32: A Historical Analysis.* Cambridge, Mass.: Harvard University Press, 1955.

Naples, Michele I. "Industrial Conflict and Its Implications for Productivity Growth." *American Economic Review* 71 (May 1981): 36–41.

Napoli, Donald S. *Architects of Adjustment: The History of the Psychological Profession in the United States.* Port Washington, N.Y.: Kennikat, 1981.

Nelson, Daniel. *Frederick W. Taylor and the Rise of Scientific Management.* Madison: University of Wisconsin Press, 1980.

———. *Managers and Workers: Origins of the New Factory System in the United States, 1880–1920.* Madison: University of Wisconsin Press, 1975.

———. "The New Factory System and the Unions: The National Cash Register Dispute of 1901." *Labor History* 15 (1974): 163–78.

———. "Scientific Management, Systematic Management, and Labor, 1880–1915." *Business History Review* 48 (1974): 479–500.

Nelson, Daniel, and Stuart Campbell. "Taylorism Versus Welfare Work in American Industry: H. L. Gantt and the Bancrofts." *Business History Review* 46 (Spring 1972): 1–16.

Neuhaus, Cable. "He Has the Nobel in Economics, but Prof. Simon Is More Interested in How Humans Think." *People,* January 15, 1979, pp. 52–54, 56.

Nisbet, Robert A. *Emile Durkheim.* Englewood Cliffs, N.J.: Prentice-Hall, 1965.

Noble, David F. *America by Design: Science Technology, and the Rise of Corporate Capitalism.* New York: Knopf, 1977.

———. *The Forces of Production: A Social History of Industrial Automation.* New York: Knopf, 1984.

Overvold, Gary E. "The Imperative of Organizational Harmony: A Critique of Contemporary Human Relations Theory." *Journal of Business Ethics* (Netherlands) 6 (October 1987): 559–65.

Palmer, Bryan. "Class, Conception and Conflict: The Thrust for Efficiency, Managerial View of Labor and the Working Class Rebellion, 1903–1922." *Review of Radical Political Economics* 7 (1975): 31–49.

Palmer, Gregory. *The McNamara Strategy and the Vietnam War: Program Budgeting in the Pentagon.* Westport, Conn.: Greenwood, 1978.

Pateman, Carole. *Participation and Democratic Theory.* New York: Cambridge University Press, 1970.

Paxton, Robert. *Vichy France.* New York: Knopf, 1972.

Pells, Richard. *The Liberal Mind in a Conservative Age.* New York: Harper and Row, 1985.

———. *Radical Visions and American Dreams: Culture and Social Thought in the Depression Years.* New York: Harper and Row, 1973.

Perrow, Charles. *Complex Organizations.* Glenview, Ill.: Scott, Foresman, 1972.

———. "Markets, Hierarchies and Hegemony." In *Perspectives on Organization Design and Behavior*, edited by Andrew H. Van de Ven and William F. Joyce, pp. 371–86. New York: Wiley, 1981.

"Peter Ferdinand Drucker." *Current Biography* (1964): 112.

Piore, Michael J., and Charles F. Sabel. *The Second Industrial Divide: Possibilities for Prosperity*. New York: Basic Books, 1984.

Reder, Melvin W. "Chicago Economics: Permanence and Change." *Journal of Economic Literature* 20 (March 1982): 1–38.

Ringer, Fritz K. *The Decline of the German Mandarins: The German Academic Community, 1890–1933*. Cambridge, Mass.: Harvard University Press, 1969.

Roberts, David D. *The Syndicalist Tradition and Italian Fascism*. Chapell Hill: University of North Carolina Press, 1979.

Rohlen, Thomas P. *For Harmony and Strength: Japanese White-Collar Organization in Anthropological Perspective*. Berkeley: University of California Press, 1974.

Rosenhead, Jonathan. "From Management Science to Workers' Science." In *New Directions in Management Science*, edited by Paul Keys and Michael C. Jackson, pp. 109–31. Aldershot: Gower, 1987.

———. "Why Does Management Need Management Science?" In *A General Survey of Systems Methodologies*, edited by L. Troncale, pp. 834–39. Louisville, Ky.: Society for General Systems Research, 1982.

Rosenhead, Jonathan, and Colin Thunhurst. "A Materialist Analysis of Operational Research." *Journal of the Operational Research Society* 33 (1982): 111–22.

Royal Swedish Academy of Sciences. "The Nobel Memorial Prize in Economics 1978." *Scandinavian Journal of Economics* 81 (1979): 73.

Sabel, Charles F. *Work and Politics: The Division of Labor in Industry*. London: Cambridge University Press, 1982.

Sabel, Charles F., and Jonathan Zeitlin. "Historical Alternatives to Mass Production." *Past and Present* 108 (1985): 13–76.

Sarti, Roland. *Fascism and the Industrial Leadership in Italy*. Berkeley: University of California Press, 1971.

Sass, Steven. "The Managerial Ideology in Collegiate Business Education." *Business and Economic History* 14 (1985): 199–212.

———. *The Pragmatic Imagination: A History of the Wharton School, 1881–1981*. Philadelphia: University of Pennsylvania Press, 1982.

Schlaifer, R. "The Relay Assembly Test Room: An Alternative Statistical Interpretation." *American Sociological Review* 43 (December 1980): 995–1005.

Schlossman, S., M. Sedlak, and H. Wechler. "The 'New Look': The Ford Foundation and the Revolution in Business Education." *Selections*, 1983, pp. 229–34.

Schmitter, Phillippe. "Still the Century of Corporatism?" *Review of Politics* (January 1974): 85–131.

Schoenbaum, David. *Hitler's Social Revolution*. Garden City, N.Y.: Doubleday, 1966.

Schuppener, Linda L. "The Rehabilitation of the Corporatist Model." Ph.D. dissertation, University of Iowa, 1987.

Searle, John. "Minds, Brains and Programs." *Behavioral and Brain Sciences* 3 (1980): 417–57.

———. *Minds, Brains and Science*. Cambridge, Mass.: Harvard University Press, 1984.

Segal, Howard P. *Technological Utopianism in American Culture*. Chicago: University of Chicago Press, 1985.

Selznick, Philip. *Law, Society and Individual Justice*. New York: Russell Sage, 1970.

Sennett, Richard, and Jonathan Cobb. *The Hidden Injuries of Class*. New York: Knopf, 1972.

Serrin, William. *The Company and the Union*. New York: Knopf, 1972.

Servan-Schreiber, Jean-Jacques. *The American Challenge*. Translated by Ronald Steel. New York: Atheneum, 1968.

Sewell, William. *Work and Revolution in France*. New York: Cambridge University Press, 1980.

Shaiken, Harley. *Work Transformed: Automation and Labor in the Computer Age*. Lexington, Mass.: Lexington Books, 1984.

Sheppard, Harold L., and Neal Q. Herrick. *Where Have All the Robots Gone? Worker Dissatisfaction in the Seventies*. New York: Free Press, 1972.

Sklar, Martin J. *The Corporate Reconstruction of American Capitalism, 1890–1916*. New York: Cambridge University Press, 1988.

Smith, B. L. R. *The RAND Corporation: Case Study of a Non-Profit Advising Corporation*. New York: Harvard University Press, 1966.

Sockell, Donna. "The Legality of Employee-Participation Programs in Unionized Firms." *Industrial and Labor Relations Review* 37 (July 1984): 541–56.

Sonnenfeld, Jeff. "Clarifying Critical Confusion in the Hawthorne Hysteria." *American Psychologist* 37 (December 1981): 1397–99.

Stabile, Donald. *Prophets of Order: The Rise of the New Class, Technocracy and Socialism in America*. Boston: South End Press, 1984.

Stearns, Peter N. *Revolutionary Syndicalism and French Labor*. New Brunswick, N.J.: Rutgers University Press, 1970.

Stigler, George. "The Economics of Information." *Journal of Political Economy* 69 (June 1961): 213–15.

Stigler, George, and Gary Becker. "*De Gustibus non est Disputandum*." *American Economic Review* 67 (March 1977): 76–90.

Stone, Katherine. "The Origins of Job Structures in the Steel Industry." *Review of Radical Political Economics* 6 (1974): 113–73.

Storing, Herbert J., ed. *Essays in the Scientific Study of Politics*. New York: Holt, Rinehart, and Winston, 1962.

Sykes, A. J. M. "Economic Interest and the Hawthorne Researcher." *Human Relations* 18 (August 1965): 253–63.

Tannenbaum, Edward J. "The Goals of Italian Fascism." *American Historical Review* 74 (1969): 1183–1204.

Tarrant, John J. *Drucker: The Man Who Invented the Corporate Society.* Boston: Cahner, 1976.

Terkel, Studs. *Working.* New York: Pantheon, 1972.

Trahair, R. C. S. *The Humanist Temper: The Life and Work of Elton Mayo.* New Brunswick, N.J.: Transaction, 1984.

Veblen, Thorstein. *The Higher Learning in America: A Memorandum on the Conduct of Universities by Businessmen.* Stanford, Calif.: Academic Reprints, 1918, 1954.

―――. *The Portable Veblen.* Edited by Max Lerner. New York: Viking, 1948.

Vogel, David. "The Corporation As Government." *Polity* 8 (Fall 1975): 5–37.

―――. "The 'New' Social Regulation in Historical and Comparative Perspective." In *Regulation in Perspective: Historical Essays,* edited by Thomas K. McGraw, pp. 155–85. Cambridge, Mass.: Harvard University Business School, 1981.

Waldo, Dwight. "Development of a Theory of Democratic Administration." *American Political Science Review* 46 (March 1952): 253–83.

―――. "Development of a Theory of Democratic Administration: Replies and Comments." *American Political Science Review* 46 (June 1952): 501–2.

Watson, Tony J. *Sociology, Work and Industry.* London: Routledge and Kegan Paul, 1980.

Weber, Max. *From Max Weber: Essays in Sociology.* Translated and edited by Hans H. Gerth and C. Wright Mills. New York: Oxford University Press, 1946.

Weinstein, James. *The Corporate Ideal in the Liberal State, 1900–1918.* Boston: Beacon Press, 1968.

Weir, Stanley. "Rebellion in American Labor's Rank and File." In *Workers' Control: A Reader on Labor and Social Change,* edited by Gerry Hunnius, G. David Garson, and John Case, pp. 45–61. New York: Vintage, 1967, 1973.

Weiss, Richard M. "Weber on Bureaucracy: Management Consultant or Political Theorist?" *Academy of Management Review* 8 (April 1983): 242–48.

Whyte, William F. *Men at Work.* Homewood, Ill.: Irwin, 1961.

Whyte, William H. *The Organization Man.* Garden City, N.Y.: Doubleday, 1956.

Wiebe, Robert H. *The Search for Order: 1877–1920.* New York: Hill and Wang, 1967.

Williams, Karel, Tony Cutler, John Williams, and Colin Haslam. "The End of Mass Production?" *Economy and Society* 16 (August 1987): 405–38.

Williams, William A. *The Contours of American History.* New York: New Viewpoints, 1961.

Wolf, William B. *The Basic Barnard: An Introduction to Chester I. Barnard and His Theories of Organization and Management.* Ithaca, N.Y.: NYSSILR, 1974.

Wolin, Sheldon. *Politics and Vision.* Boston: Little, Brown, 1960.

Wright, Eric O., and Bill Martin. "The Transformation of the American Class Structure, 1960–1980." *American Journal of Sociology* 93 (July 1987): 1–29.

Yoshino, Michael Y. *Japan's Managerial System: Tradition and Innovation.* Cambridge, Mass.: MIT Press, 1968.

Zernan, John. "Organized Labor Versus 'The Revolt against Work': The Critical Contest." *Telos* 21 (Fall 1974): 194–206.

Zimbalist, Andrew. "The Limits of Work Humanization." *Review of Radical Political Economics* 7 (1975): 50–60.

Zwerdling, Daniel. *Workplace Democracy*. Washington, D.C.: Association for Self-Management, 1979.

Index

Abegglen, James, 162–63, 180, 230 (nn. 9, 15)
Abernathy, William, 43, 101
Ackoff, Russell L., 24, 38, 39, 41, 197
Adams, Henry, 198
Admiralty, the, 21
Alchian, Armen, 58, 59
Algorithms, 66, 72
Alienation, 141
American Jewish Congress, 111
American Management Association, 122
Anarchism, 16, 19, 54, 109, 125, 126, 199, 222 (n. 17). *See also* Corporatism
Ando, Albert, 60
Andreski, Stanislav, 75
Anomie, 15, 141. *See also* Durkheim, Emile
Antiballistic missile (ABM), 34
Antisubmarine methods, 21–22
Argyris, Chris, 15–16, 170, 173, 201, 223 (n. 53), 226 (n. 46); criticism of Herbert A. Simon, 76; and sensitivity training, 118–19, 130–31; and job enrichment, 133–42, 155
Arnold, Thurman, 2
Artificial intelligence, 50, 64. *See also* Computers; Simon, Herbert A.
Associationalism, 198
Athos, Anthony, 168–69

Austria, 79–80, 81
Autoworkers, 145–46, 152

Baby-boom generation, 132, 142–44
Back, Kurt, 127
Bakunin, Michael, 126
Bamforth, K. W., 140
Barnard, Chester I., 4, 53, 57, 82, 87, 170
Barrett, William, 202
Basic skills training group. *See* T-Group
Becker, Gary, 59
Behavioral approach to management, 159
Bell, Daniel, 143
Bellamy, Edward, 17–18
Bendix, Reinhard, 6
Benne, Kenneth D., 107, 111, 112
Bennis, Warren, 130
Berg, Ivar, 140
Bethel, Maine, 113
Black and Decker, 96–97
Blackfeet Indians, 100
Blake, Robert R., 118, 119–20, 121
Blasi, Joseph, 191, 194
Blauner, Robert, 141, 226 (n. 47)
Blue-collar workers, 121, 142–46, 172, 173, 183–84. *See also* Job enrichment; Quality control circles
Bluestone, Barry, 46

Bluestone, Irving, 152
Boguslaw, Robert, 75–76
Bolter, John, 63–64
Bonald, Vicomte de, 80
Boys' clubs, 109–10, 220 (n. 17), 224 (n. 73)
Bradford, Leland P., 107, 111, 112
Brady, Robert A., 2
Braverman, Harry, 5
Brown, Donaldson, 87
Brown, William, 163
Bruce-Biggs, B., 181
Brzezinski, Zbigniew, 165
Burawoy, Michael, 147–48, 228 (n. 77)
Bureaucracy: rise of, 2–4, 9–12; rationality of, 92, 104; structure of, 96, 110–11. *See also* Post-Taylorism; Taylorism
Bureaucratic management. *See* Post-Taylorism; Taylorism
Burke, Edmund, 81
Business history, 2–5, 201
Business Round Table, 94
Business schools, 193, 195

Campbell, John D., 123–24
Capitalism: cultural contradictions of, 143
Carnap, Rudolf, 51, 65
Carnegie, Andrew, 93
Carnegie Institute of Technology and Carnegie-Mellon University, 63, 65, 73–74, 216 (n. 103). *See also* Simon, Herbert A.
Carroll, Stephen J., 96–97
Case study method, 73
Categorical imperative of Immanuel Kant, 40, 197
Chandler, Alfred D., 2–5, 192, 201
Change agents, 105, 118. *See also* Sensitivity training
Cherns, Albert, 156

Chicago, University of, 50
Chicago school of economics, 50
Chinese room, parable of, 74–76
Churchman, C. West, 24, 40–41, 42, 197
Civil rights movement, 143–44, 192
Codetermination, 17, 226 (n. 39)
Cognitive science, 64. *See also* Simon, Herbert A.
Cole, Robert, 163, 175–76, 180, 230 (n. 5)
Commons, John R., 52–53, 57
Company unions, 14, 160, 181, 184–85
Computers, 31, 72, 73, 188, 196. *See also* Expert Systems; Operations research and management science; Simon, Herbert A.
Conference Board, 122
Conglomerates, 95
Connecticut, 111
Conservatism, 26, 79–80, 81. *See also* Corporatism
Contingency theory, 202
Corporatism: definition of, 7, 16; and Mayoism, 15, 200; European theory and practice, 16–17, 79–80, 226 (n. 39); in American professions, 17–18; and bureaucracy, 8, 19, 188, 191, 198–201; debates with post-Taylorists, 18–19; behavioral approach to management, 159; sources of, 191–93; criticisms of Taylorism, 192–93; and participation, 193; and industrial policy, 194; macro- versus micro-, 198; and individualism, 198–99. *See also* Anarchism; Codetermination; Democratic management; Drucker, Peter F.; ESOP; Intrapreneurship; Japanizers; Job enrichment; Management by Objectives; Sensitivity training

Cost-benefit analysis, 47
Counterculture, 143–44, 192
Craft workers, 85
Cryptoarithmetic problems, 66
Cybernetics, 18, 25–26, 49, 50, 63–71.
    See also Simon, Herbert A.
Cyert, Richard, 71

Davis, Louis, 156
Debs, Eugene, 198
Deming, W. Edwards, 172–73
Democratic management, 14, 19, 98,
    105, 109–11, 133, 173, 176, 193.
    See also Corporatism; Drucker, Peter
    F.; Japanizers; Job enrichment; Man-
    agement by Objectives; Sensitivity
    training
Demsetz, Harold, 59
Dewey, John, 106–7
Discounted cash flow, 43–44
Dissatisficers, 135–36, 149–50. *See also*
    Herzberg, Frederick; Job enrichment
Donelly Mirrors, 146, 147
Dore, Ronald, 164
Double-entry bookkeeping, 20
Dower, John W., 230 (n. 2)
Dowling, William, 157
Dreyfus, Hubert, 74, 75
Dreyfus, Stuart, 75
Drive system, 10, 203
Drucker, Peter F.: and post-Mayoism, 8,
    78–79; and Taylorism, 12, 86, 158;
    and management science, 27, 30, 37,
    38, 47; as management "guru," 78;
    impact of, 78, 94–96, 101; combin-
    ing corporatism and capitalism, 79–
    81; early life, 79–81; and Hegeli-
    anism, 80, 92; and Schumpeter's
    entrepreneur, 80–81; ideal of the
    corporation, 82–83, 217 (n. 7); and
    legitimacy, 83–85; and unions, 85;
    and knowledge workers, 85–86, 87;

criticism of Mayoism, 86–87, 88; as
    consultant, 87–88; and management
    by objectives, 88–93; and Japanese
    management, 89–90, 93, 94, 164,
    173, 178, 185; criticism of free mar-
    ket, 93; and business social responsi-
    bility, 93–94; criticisms of, 95–100;
    criticism of sensitivity training, 100;
    response to critics, 100–101; and en-
    trepreneurship, 101–2, 189; and job
    enrichment, 133–34. *See also* Cor-
    poratism; Management by Objectives;
    Post-Mayoism
Druckerism, 85
Dukakis, Michael, 48, 194
Dunnette, Marvin D., 123–24, 223
    (n. 53)
Durkheim, Emile, 4, 14, 16, 17, 141,
    170, 226 (n. 46). *See also* Corpora-
    tism; Mayoism; Post-Mayoism

Economics, 18, 32, 58–61, 154. *See*
    also Simon, Herbert A.
Eden, Colin, 39
Edwards, Richard, 5, 96
Eisenhooverian, 54
Encounter movement, 117. *See also* Sen-
    sitivity training
End-of-ideology theory, 12, 201
Engineering rhetoric, 155, 156–59, 175,
    200. *See also* Japanizers; Job enrich-
    ment; Quality control circles
Entrepreneurship, 37, 43–44, 81, 101–
    2. *See also* Drucker, Peter F.; Intra-
    preneurship; Risk aversion
Esalen Center, 117
ESOP (employee stock ownership plan):
    and corporatism, 190; applications of,
    190–91; as bureaucracy, 191
Expert Systems, 73, 196, 216 (n. 101).
    See also Computers; Simon, Herbert
    A.

Fair Employment Practices Act, 111
Fascism, 16, 17, 79–80, 82, 108, 198,
  217 (n. 16). *See also* Corporatism
Fayol, Henri, 87
Fitzgerald, Thomas, 98
Flexible production, 46, 134, 157–58,
  184, 188
Follett, Mary Parker, 87
Ford, Henry, 13, 93, 158
Ford, Robert, 146
Ford Motor Company, 23, 32, 44, 152,
  208 (n. 6)
Foremen's clubs, 106. *See also* Demo-
  cratic management; Sensitivity
  training
Fox, Alan, 141, 220 (n. 74)
Freedman, Marcia, 140
Freedman, Michael, 140
Freudian psychology, 53, 86, 108, 117
Freyberg, Berthold, 80
Friedman, Milton, 60, 93

Galbraith, John K., 2, 198
Gantt, H. L., 13
Geneen, Harold S., 168, 186
General Electric, 88, 154
General Mills, 95, 148, 152, 153
General Motors, 87–88, 98, 145–46
General Problem Solver, 66. *See also*
  Simon, Herbert A.
German management ideas, 3, 79,
  82–83, 92. *See also* Corporatism;
  Drucker, Peter F.; Lewin, Kurt
Gestalt psychology, 108. *See also* Lewin,
  Kurt
Gibney, Frank, 172, 177–78, 186
Gooding, Judson, 148
Gordon, Andrew, 179–80, 230 (n. 5)
Graebner, William, 105
Grayson, C. Jackson, 37, 38, 39
Great Britain, 3, 21–22, 29, 35–36,
  42–43

Guild socialism, 13
Gulick, Luther, 51
Gung Ho (film), 166, 178, 186, 231
  (n. 31)

Hackman, Richard, 156
Halberstam, David, 44, 45
Harrison, Bennett, 46
Hart, Gary, 45, 48, 194
Hartz, Louis, 199
Harvard Business Review, 44–45
Harvard University and Business School,
  14–15, 43, 73, 140, 167, 208 (n. 6),
  216 (n. 103), 226 (n. 46)
Harwood garment factory, 133
Hawley, Ellis, ix, 2
Hawthorne experiments, 14–15, 51,
  152. *See also* Mayo, (George) Elton
Hayes, Robert, 43, 44, 45, 101
Hegelianism, 40, 41, 80, 92
Hegemonic management, 147–48, 197.
  See also Corporatism; Post-Mayoism
Herzberg, Frederick, 173, 174; and job
  enrichment, 133–42, 149–50, 155,
  158
Heuristics, 65, 66–67, 72. *See also* Ex-
  pert Systems; Simon, Herbert A.
High technology firms, 148, 202
Homogenization of labor, 11, 13
Hoos, Ida, 35
Hoover, Herbert, 185, 198
Howard, Ron, 166, 178, 186, 231
  (n. 31)
Hoxie, Robert F., 151
Human relations theory, 14–16, 53. *See
  also* Corporatism; Mayo, (George)
  Elton; Mayoism; Post-Mayoism
Humble Oil (Exxon), 119–20

IBM, 132, 133
Ideology and management theory, 5–6,
  26, 57–58

Illinois Institute of Technology, 51, 63
Independent workers. *See* Knowledge
   workers; White-collar workers
Industrial clans, 163–64, 170–71. *See
   also* Corporatism; Durkheim, Emile
Industrial policy, 46–47, 194
Inside contracting system, 10, 91
Institutional economics, 50, 52–53. *See
   also* Simon, Herbert A.; Veblen,
   Thorstein
Institutional history, ix
Interactive planning, 40–41
International Association of Quality Cir-
   cles, 174
Intrapreneurship: and corporatism,
   188–89; similarity to management by
   objectives, 189; as bureaucracy, 189–
   90. *See also* Drucker, Peter F.; Entre-
   preneurship; Management by
   Objectives
Iowa City, Iowa, 108, 109
IT&T (International Telephone and Tele-
   graph), 168

Jackson, Michael, 42
Jacques, Eliot, 140
Japan boosters. *See* Japanizers
Japanese management, 3, 8, 89–90, 93,
   145, 157–58, 159, 179–80, 188,
   190, 221 (n. 68), 230 (n. 2), 233
   (n. 69); Kurt Lewin's influence on,
   131, 224 (n. 73); periodical citations
   of, 160; and lifetime employment,
   160, 161–62, 164, 179–80; and seniority system, 160, 161–62, 182;
   and consensual decision making, 160,
   165, 182; and company unions, 160,
   181, 184–85; and convergence theory, 161–62; and culturalist theory,
   162–63; and industrial clans, 163–
   64; American corporatism's influence
   on, 164, 173; and modernization the-

ory, 165; and subsidiaries in America,
   165–66; antiindividualism of, 166;
   and quality control circles, 166, 172–
   74, 194; American criticism of, 179–
   85; and blood types, 182
Japanizers: corporatism of, 166, 167,
   168–69, 177–79; criticism of Taylorism, 167, 168, 169, 173; and post-
   Mayoism, 169–71, 173, 174–75,
   178, 184–86; and participation, 171–
   72; and white-collar workers, 172;
   and blue-collar workers, 172, 173;
   and quality control circles, 172–77;
   and American adaptations, 174–76;
   bureaucratic criticism of, 181–82; labor criticism of, 183–84. *See also*
   Corporatism; Japanese Management;
   Post-Mayoism; Quality control circles
Japanophiles/Japanophilia. *See* Japanizers
Japanophobes/Japanophobia, 184–85.
   See also Japanizers
Job enlargement, 137
Job enrichment, 8; and Taylorism, 132,
   134, 136–37; and Mayoism, 132,
   134, 136, 137, 140, 141; and post-
   Mayoism, 132–33, 137, 141–42; and
   Abraham Maslow's theories, 133,
   134–35, 149; origins of, 133–35;
   early theories of, 134–38; and participation, 138–39; techniques of,
   138–40, 147; and European ideas,
   140; anomie versus alienation, 141;
   and socioeconomic change, 142–46;
   and blue-collar blues, 145–46; and
   Lordstown strike, 145–46; and
   unions, 145–46, 151–52, 226
   (n. 39); and hegemonic management,
   147–48; applications of, 148–49;
   motivation theory criticized, 149–50;
   labor criticism of, 151–52; bureaucratic criticism of, 152–54; Marxist criticism of, 154–55; and white-

collar workers, 155; economic and engineering rhetoric of, 155, 156–59. *See also* Corporatism; Japanizers; Post-Mayoism; Quality control circles

Job redesign, 155. *See also* Job enrichment

Job rotation, 137

Johnson, Lyndon, 34

Johnson, Richard, 166

Johnston, William, 154

Juran, Joseph M., 173, 175

Kant, Immanuel, 40, 197

Kanter, Rosabeth Moss, 103, 104, 105

Kaufman, Herbert, 1

Kill-ratios, 33

Knowledge workers, 8, 79, 85–86, 91, 95, 100, 192–93. *See also* Drucker, Peter F.; Management by Objectives; Sensitivity training; White-collar workers

Kolko, Gabriel, 2

Koontz, Harold, 7, 8

Koopman, B. O., 30

Krupp, Sherman, 61, 62

Kuhnian crisis in operations research and management science, 35

Labor history, ix, 5

Latham, Earl, 2

Lawler, Edward, 156

Lawrence, Paul R., 202

Leavitt, Harold J., 37–38

Levinson, Harry, 97–98

Levitan, Sar, 154

Levitt, Theodore, 37

Lewin, Kurt, 8; criticism of Taylorism, 108; psychological theories of, 108–9; studies of groups and leaders, 109–10; invention of sensitivity training, 112; death of, 113; influence on Japanese management, 131, 224

(n. 73); influence on job enrichment, 133–34. *See also* Democratic management; German management ideas; Post-Mayoism; Sensitivity training

Lewinians, 117. *See also* Lewin, Kurt; Sensitivity training

Lewis, Jordan D., 45–46

Likert, Rensis, 170, 173; and job enrichment, 133, 137, 139

Lilienfeld, Robert, 26

Linking-pins, 120, 139. *See also* Likert, Rensis

Lippitt, Ronald, 108, 111

Lockheed Missile and Space Company, 166, 176

Lodge, George C., 167, 177

Logical positivism, 50, 51. *See also* Positivism

Logic Theorist, 65. *See also* Simon, Herbert A.

Long, Russell, 190

Lordstown, Ohio, 145–46

Lorsch, Jay W., 202

McCloskey, Donald, 202

McConnell, Grant, 2

McGregor, Douglas, 15, 86, 95, 111, 118, 170–71, 173, 174, 198; and job enrichment theory, 135, 136, 141, 158. *See also* Democratic management; Job enrichment; Theory X; Theory Y

Machlup, Fritz, 60

MacIntyre, Alasdair, ix

McNamara, Robert, 32, 38, 44, 47

Macrocorporatism, 198

Macrogovernment, 197

Magaziner, Ira C., 43, 101

Maistre, Joseph de, 80

Management by Objectives (MBO), 171, origins of, 79–88; techniques of, 88–92; impact of, 94–96; criticisms of,

96–100. *See also* Drucker, Peter F.; Intrapreneurship

Management science. *See* Operations research and management science

Management theory of value, 19, 187, 197–98, 199, 203

Managerial capitalism, 4, 10, 42. *See also* Bureaucracy; Chandler, Alfred D.

Managerial grid, 105, 119–20, 122. *See also* Sensitivity training

Mandarins: definition, 6; and management theory of value, 187, 197–98; and business schools, 193, 195; as commercial group, 201–2

Mannari, Hiroshi, 165

March, James, 60, 71

Margolis, Julian, 59

Marsh, Robert M., 165

Marxism, 82, 154

Maslow, Abraham, 103, 153, 155, 174, 199; criticism of management by objectives, 99–100; criticism of sensitivity training, 126; influence on job enrichment, 134–35, 140; self-actualization idea criticized, 149. *See also* Job enrichment

Massachusetts Institute of Technology (MIT), 111

Mass production, 29, 47. *See also* Flexible production; Ford, Henry

Mathematics: relationship to management theory, 20; mathematicians in management, 21, 30–31. *See also* Operations research and management science

Matsushita, Konosake, 168–69, 186

Maximizing theory of choice, 50–53, 58–61. *See also* Simon, Herbert A.

Mayo, (George) Elton, 104; as organization theorist, 4; theories of, 14–15, 106; and behavioral approach to management, 159. *See also* Corporatism; Mayoism; Post-Mayoism

Mayoism: and personnel management, 14; and Elton Mayo, 14–15; differences from post-, 15, 200; and Herbert A. Simon, 55; and Peter F. Drucker, 85, 86–88, 90, 98; similarity to sensitivity training, 128; and job enrichment theory, 132, 134, 136, 137, 140, 141. *See also* Corporatism; Democratic management; Human relations theory; Post-Mayoism

Melman, Seymour, 45

Merton, Robert A., 226 (n. 46)

Microcorporatism, 198, 207 (n. 24)

Microgovernment, 198

Miles, Raymond, 155

Military: influence on management, 3, 20, 21–22, 24, 32–34, 45, 64, 196

Mills, C. Wright, 2, 15, 47, 110, 128, 198

Montgomery, David, ix

Moreno, Jacob L., 108

Morgenson, Allen, 133

Motorola, 175

Mouton, Jane S., 118, 119–20, 121

Multidivision firms, 87–88, 95

Murphy, Michael, 117

Myers, M. Scott, 146

Nader, Ralph, 2

National Education Association (NEA), 107, 122. *See also* Sensitivity training

National Labor Relations Board, 184

National Training Laboratory for Group Development, 113, 117, 122. *See also* Sensitivity training

Nazism. *See* Fascism

Neo-classical economics, 50, 58–61. *See also* Simon, Herbert A.

Neo-royalists, 80
New Britain State Teachers College, 111, 113
New Deal, 198
Newell, Allen, 64, 76, 212 (n. 21). See also Simon, Herbert A.
New Left, 143
Nissan Motor Company, 44
Nixon, Richard, 132, 146
Nobel Prize, 8, 49, 60
Noble, David F., 154–55
Nondirective counseling, 15, 106. See also Mayo, (George) Elton; Mayoism; Sensitivity training
Norway, 140

Odiorne, George, 127
Office of Program Analysis and Evaluation (Department of Defense), 32
Office of Systems Analysis (Department of Defense), 32
Open-shop campaigns, 13
Operations research and management science: and positivism, 20–21, 24–25, 30, 33–34, 35–36; in Britain, 21–22, 29, 35–36; origins in military, 21–23; problems of, 22–23, 29–30; and tactics vs. strategy, 23, 31–32; promotion of, 24; and Taylorism, 24, 25, 43, 47; and systems theory, 25–27; steps of, 26–27; mathematical techniques of, 27, professionalization of, 28, 30–31; use in business, 28–29, 30–31; and computers, 31; organization of, 31; and Vietnam War, 32–34; and antiballistic missile debate, 34; use in government, 34–35; "Kuhnian crisis" in, 35; scientific critique of, 35–36; practical critique of, 36–39; political critique of, 39–41; and corporatism, 40–41, 42, 47–48; hard vs. soft forms, 41,

42, 211 (n. 52); radical critique of, 41–43; entrepreneurial critique of, 43–47; and risk aversion, 43–47, 211 (n. 68). See also Post-Taylorism; Simon, Herbert A.
Organization theory, classical, 51, 72. See also Taylorism
ORSA (Operations Research Society of America), 28, 34
Orwell, George, 152
Ouchi, William, 166, 170–71, 234 (n. 86)
Ozawa, Torutomo, 180

Pagès, Max, 128
Pareto, Vilfredo, 53
Parker, Mike, 183
Parsons, Talcott, 4
Participatory democracy, 138. See also Anarchism
Pascale, Richard, 168–69
Pateman, Carole, 138
Pells, Richard, 111
Personnel management, 13, 106; influence on Mayoism, 14. See also Mayoism; Post-Mayoism
Pesch, Heinrich, 79
Peters, Tom, 189
Physiocrats, 20
Pinchot, Gifford, 188–89
Political interpretation of management theory, ix–x, 1–8
Political science, 50, 61–62, 138, 142. See also Simon, Herbert A.
Positivism, 18, 21, 62–63, 195, 200, 201, 202–3. See also Logical positivism
Positivists, 20
Postbureaucratic theory. See Post-Taylorism
Post-Mayoism: and Peter F. Drucker, 8, 78–83, 86–88; differences with Mayoism, 15, 200; and corporatism,

15–19; and debates with post-Taylorists, 18–19; and management by objectives, 88–92; and sensitivity training, 104–5, 109–11, 130–31; and job enrichment, 132–33, 137, 141–42; and Japanizers, 169–71, 173–75, 178, 184–86; criticisms of Taylorism, 192–93; and industrial policy, 194. *See also* Anarchism; Corporatism; Democratic management; Drucker, Peter F.; ESOP; Intrapreneurship; Japanizers; Job enrichment; Management by Objectives; Sensitivity training

Post-Taylorism: similarities to Taylorism, 7, 18, 20; debates with post-Mayoist corporatists, 18–19; and operations research and management science, 24, 25, 43, 47; and Herbert A. Simon, 49, 57–58, 62, 68, 77; criticism of management by objectives, 98–99; criticism of sensitivity training, 125–27; criticism of job enrichment, 152–54; criticism of Japanizers, 181–82; similarities to corporatism, 187; sources of, 194–96; positivism of, 195; and the federal government, 195–96; and mechanistic thinking, 196–97. *See also* Operations research and management science; Simon, Herbert A.; Taylor, Frederick W.; Taylorism

Procter and Gamble, 152

Progressive education, 106–8. *See also* Sensitivity training

Protestant work ethic, 45, 116

Psychoanalysis, 117. *See also* Freudian psychology

Psychodrama, 108. *See also* Sensitivity training

Psychology, 14, 18, 51, 53. *See also* Job enrichment; Lewin, Kurt; Sensitivity training; Simon, Herbert A.

Quality control circles, 131, 159; origins of, 172–74; and job enrichment theory, 174–75; as Taylorism, 183–84. *See also* Japanese management; Japanizers

Quasar, 175

RAND Corporation, 32, 64, 65, 75

Reagan, Ronald, 184

Reeducation. *See* Sensitivity training

Reich, Robert B., 43, 101, 157, 194

Research Center for Group Dynnamics, 111

Restoration Era, 80

Rice, Albert, 140

Richardson, Elliot, 132

Right, political, 127

Ringer, Fritz, 218 (n. 20)

Ringi ritual, 162, 171, 172. *See also* Japanese management

Risk aversion, 23, 43–47, 101–2, 211 (n. 68). *See also* Drucker, Peter F.; Entrepreneurship; Intrapreneurship; Management by Objectives

Robbins, Stephen, 172

Rogers, Carl, 106, 117

Rohlen, Thomas, 163

Role playing, 108. *See also* Sensitivity training

Roosevelt, Franklin, 198

Rosenhead, Jonathan, 42

Rosewald, Julius, 93

Royal Air Force (RAF), 21

Royal Navy, 21

Royal Swedish Academy of Sciences, 49

Sabel, Charles, 134, 157. *See also* Flexible production

Saint-Simon, Henri de, 16, 17

Satisficers, 135–36, 149–50. *See also* Job enrichment

Satisficing theory of choice, 53–54, 60–
61, 66–67, 213 (n. 23). *See also* Si-
mon, Herbert A.
Scanlon, Joseph, 133
Scanlon Plan, 133, 171, 174
Schein, Edgar, 170
Schmidt (worker), 73, 104, 129
Schumpeter, Joseph, 45, 81, 102
Scientific management. *See* Post-
Taylorism; Taylorism
Scott, William G., 129–30
Searle, John, 74–75
Sears, Roebuck Company, 93
Selznick, Philip, 142
Sensitivity training, 8, 98, 100, 171;
ideal of democratic leadership, 104,
109–11, 130–31; and corporatism,
104–5; and bureaucracy, 104–5,
120–21; origins of, 105–13; Jacob
Moreno's influence on, 108; Kurt
Lewin's influence on, 108–11, 112,
131; invention of, 112; early ideas of,
113–16; and stranger groups, 114,
116–17; and encounter movement,
117; family or workteam groups,
117–18, 119–20; and Chris Argyris,
118–19, 123–24, 130–31; and blue-
collar workers, 121; and white-collar
workers, 121–22; popularity of, 121–
22, 127; research methods of, 122–
24; psychological damage from, 124;
bureaucratic criticism of, 125–27;
radical right-wing criticism of, 127;
similarity to bureaucracy, 128–30; results of criticism, 130–31; and Japanese management, 131. *See also*
Corporatism; Lewin, Kurt; Post-
Mayoism
Servan-Schreiber, Jean-Jacques, 160
Servomechanisms, 64, 70. *See also* Cybernetics; Simon, Herbert A.
Shaw, Cliff, 65

Short-term thinking. *See* Risk aversion
Simon, Herbert A., 4, 8, 104, 105, 196,
201, 212 (nn. 14, 21); and post-
Taylorism, 49, 57–58, 62, 68; two
phases of work, 50; youth, 50; critique of neo-classical economics, 50–
52, 53, 60–61; and positivism, 51;
and logical positivism, 51, 63; critique of classical organization theory
and Taylorism, 51–52; and institutional economics, 52; and Chester I.
Barnard, 53, 55; satisficing theory,
53–54, 60–61, 66–67, 213 (n. 23);
epistemology vs. ethics, 54, 68; organization theory, 54–57; and Mayoism, 55; concept of authority, 55–56;
criticism by neo-classical economists,
58–61; criticism by political scientists, 61–62; as a Hobbesian thinker,
62; at Illinois Tech, 62–63; at University of Chicago, 63; and Carnegie
Tech (Carnegie-Mellon), 63, 65, 69,
71, 73; work in cybernetics and artificial intelligence, 63–71; and heuristics, 65, 66–67; and behaviorism,
67–68, 215 (n. 79); and sociobiology,
68; similarities to Taylorism, 68, 72,
77; honors of, 69; cybernetics and
management theory, 69–71; influence
on management theory, 71–73; influence on management education, 73–
74; criticism of Simon's cybernetic
theories, 74–76; defense of own cybernetic ideas, 76–77. *See also* Operations research and management
science; Post-Taylorism
Simonism, 71–74. *See also* Simon, Herbert A.
Sloan, Alfred P., 87
Smiddy, Harold, 88, 90
Smith, Adam, 154
Sociobiology, 68

Sociodrama, 108, 112. *See also* Sensitivity training
Sociotechnical systems theory, 140, 156. *See also* Job enrichment
Spann, Othmar, 79
Speedup, 151, 184
Stahl, Friedrich, 80, 102
Stakhanovism, 91
Statistical quality control, 172–73. *See also* Quality control circles
Stigler, George, 59
Stock market, 46, 47
Storing, Herbert J., 61, 62
Strauss, George, 142
Stromquist, H. Shelton, ix
Structural-functionalist sociology, 4
Sweden, 194
Syndicalism. *See* Anarchism; ESOP
Syntax, 65, 74–75
Systems theory, 25–27, 47, 208 (n. 11)

T-Group: origin of name, 114, types of, 114, 117, 119–20. *See also* Sensitivity training
Tönnies, Ferdinand, 170
Takagi, Haruo, 182
Takezawa, Shin-Ichi, 181
Tavistock Institute of Human Relations (London), 140, 156. *See also* Job enrichment
Taylor, Frederick W., 104, 201, 203; as organization theorist, 4, 51; influence of, 5, 9, 18; ideas of, 11–12; Peter F. Drucker's opinion of, 12, 158; parody of, 129; and hegemonic management, 147–48, 197; and engineering approach to management, 158–59. *See also* Corporatism; Post-Taylorism; Taylorism
Taylor, James, 156
Taylor, William, 2

Taylorism, 79, 85, 105; radical studies of, 5; prominence of, 5, 9; problems caused by, 7, 12; relationship to bureaucracy, 9; and Peter F. Drucker, 12, 86, 158; workers' responses to, 12–13; as source of corporatism, 18, 158, 185; and operations research and management science, 23, 24, 43, 47; Herbert A. Simon's criticisms of, 49, 51; similarity to Simonism, 72; and sensitivity training, 128–30; and job enrichment, 132, 134, 136–37; and technological determinism, 153–54, 156; and Japanizers, 167, 168, 169, 173. *See also* Corporatism, Post-Mayoism; Post-Taylorism; Taylor, Frederick W.
Teamwork. *See* Japanizers; Job enrichment; Quality control circles
Technocracy, 16–17
Technological determinism, 2–5, 201; and Taylorism, 153–54, 156. *See also* Chandler, Alfred D.
Terkel, Studs, 146
The Institute of Management Science (TIMS), 28
Theory X, 41, 95, 136, 138, 174. *See also* Post-Taylorism; Taylorism
Theory Y, 95, 130, 135, 138, 170–71, 174. *See also* Corporatism; Democratic management; Post-Mayoism
Theory Z, 170–71, 172, 181, 182. *See also* Japanizers
Thunhurst, Colin, 42
Time-and-motion study, 7, 20, 21, 25. *See also* Taylor, Frederick W.; Taylorism
Tosi, Henry L., 96–97
Totalitarianism, 81
Trist, Eric, 140
TRW, 175
Tucker, David, 233

U-boats, 21
Unions, 11–13, 85; and sensitivity training, 121; and job enrichment, 145–46, 151–52, 226 (n. 39); and quality control circles, 183–84. *See also* Job enrichment; Quality control circles
United Auto Workers (UAW), 152
Urwick, Lyndall, 51, 72

Veblen, Thorstein, 1, 45, 99, 195
Vega (car), 145–46
Versagi, Frank, 181
Vietnam War, 33–34, 143–44
Vogel, David, 209 (n. 2)
Vogel, Ezra, 167–68, 232 (n. 47)
Von Neumann, John, 63–64

Wagner Act, 106, 184
Waldo, Dwight, 61, 62, 63
Wall Street, 46
Walton, Richard, 146, 170
Wayne, John, 166
Weber, Max, 1, 4, 53, 92, 104, 110, 209 (n. 12)
Weinstein, James, 2
Weizenbaum, Joseph, 74, 75
Western Behavioral Science Institute, 117

White-collar workers: and sensitivity training, 121–22; and job enrichment, 155; and Japanizers, 172. *See also* Drucker, Peter F.; Knowledge workers; Management by Objectives
Whitehill, Arthur, 181
Whitsett, David, 158–59
Whyte, William F., 164
Whyte, William H., 116–17
Wiebe, Robert, 2
Wiener, Norbert, 63–64
Williams, William A., 2, 103
Wolf, Marvin, 184–85, 186
Wolin, Sheldon, 61, 62
Woolsey, Gene, 41
Workers' science of operations research, 21, 42–43. *See also* Operations research and management science
Work in America report, 132, 146. *See also* Job enrichment
Work simplification, 133
Works Progress Administration, 107
World War I, 106, 133, 178
World War II, 21–23, 78, 111, 178, 186
Wrapp, H. E., 99

Yorks, Lyle, 158